Law, History, and Justice

LAW, HISTORY, AND JUSTICE

Debating German State Crimes in the Long Twentieth Century

Annette Weinke

Translated by Nicholas Evangelos Levis

berghahn
NEW YORK · OXFORD
www.berghahnbooks.com

Published in 2019 by
Berghahn Books
www.berghahnbooks.com

English-language edition
© 2019, 2024 Berghahn Books
First paperback edition published in 2024

German-language edition
© Wallstein Verlag, Göttingen 2016

Originally published by Wallstein Verlag
Gewalt, Geschichte, Gerechtigkeit: Transnationale Debatten über deutsche Staatsverbrechen im 20. Jahrhundert in 2016

The translation of this work was funded by Geisteswissenschaften International – Translation Funding for Humanities and Social Sciences from Germany, a joint initiative of the Fritz Thyssen Foundation, the German Federal Foreign Office, the collecting society VG WORT, and the Börsenverein des Deutschen Buchhandels (German Publishers & Booksellers Association).

All rights reserved. Except for the quotation of short passages for the purposes of criticism and review, no part of this book may be reproduced in any form or by any means, electronic or mechanical, including photocopying, recording, or any information storage and retrieval system now known or to be invented, without written permission of the publisher.

Library of Congress Cataloging-in-Publication Data
Names: Weinke, Annette, 1963- author.
Title: Law, History, and Justice : Debating German State Crimes in the Long Twentieth Century / Annette Weinke ; translated by Nicholas Evangelos Levis.
Other titles: Gewalt, Geschichte, Gerechtigkeit. English.
Description: New York : Berghahn Books, 2019. | "Originally published in German as Gewalt, Geschichte, Gerechtigkeit: Transnationale Debatten uber deutsche Staatsverbrechen im 20. Jahrhundert." | Includes bibliographical references and index.
Identifiers: LCCN 2018026905 (print) | LCCN 2018027206 (ebook) | ISBN 9781789201062 (ebook) | ISBN 9781789201055 (hardback : alk. paper)
Subjects: LCSH: Social participation--Germany--20th century. | Political participation--Germany--20th century. | Debates and debating--Germany--20th century. | Germany--Politics and government--20th century.
Classification: LCC DD232 (ebook) | LCC DD232 .W4513 2019 (print) | DDC 943.087--dc23
LC record available at https://lccn.loc.gov/2018026905

British Library Cataloguing in Publication Data
A catalogue record for this book is available from the British Library

ISBN 978-1-78920-105-5 hardback
ISBN 978-1-80539-708-3 paperback
ISBN 978-1-78920-106-2 web pdf
ISBN 978-1-80539-902-5 epub

https://doi.org/10.3167/9781789201055

Contents

Acknowledgments	vii
Introduction	1
Approach	4
New Trends in Legal Historiography	10
Chapter 1. The Hague—Berlin—Versailles	17
International Criminal Law before World War I	18
History Management in Wartime, 1914–1919	27
Debating the Responsibility Clauses of the Peace Treaty	37
The Heidelberg Association and Max Weber's "War Guilt" Intervention	49
Conclusion	65
Chapter 2. Washington—Nuremberg—Bonn	69
International Law versus Human Rights?	70
Jurists as Lobbyists and Historians	74
The Frankfurt School Goes to War	85
Hermann Jahrreiß and the Nuremberg Defense Strategy	92
West Germany Joins the Genocide Convention	102
Conclusion	111
Chapter 3. Bonn—Ludwigsburg—Jerusalem	116
Allied Law and the German "Victims' Community"	117
West German Historians and the "Führer Order"	127
Eichmann, Arendt, and Justice	140
Conclusion	153
Chapter 4. Salzburg—Bonn and Berlin	157
"Transitology" and Samuel Huntington's "Third Wave"	159
The Politics of the Past after German Unification	175

"Mercy Before Justice"? The Amnesty Debate of 1994–1995   191
Conclusion   207

Final Reflections   210

List of Abbreviations   221

Select Chronology   225

Notes   229

Bibliography   289

Index   321

Acknowledgments

Other authors before me have observed the close yet uncanny correspondence between German history and the evolution of modern international humanitarian law. Although numerous studies have tackled this phenomenon, very few attempted to investigate it from a transnational and *longue durée* perspective. To a certain extent, the idea of using German history as a way to tell a discursive history of modern humanitarian law in the twentieth century followed logically from my prior work. During my past two decades at Friedrich Schiller University Jena and other institutions, my academic interest has focused on issues of transitional justice, humanitarian law, and human rights, mainly during the period after World War II. In particular, I have written about international attempts to respond to German state violence through new legal processes and systems, from the Nuremberg trials to the efforts to prosecute leaders of the former East German regime. Over time, through my monographs and my participation in team research projects—most recently on the history of the Federal Foreign Office under the Third Reich and in the Federal Republic of Germany—I gained access to a large body of new sources that comprise much of the foundation for the present book. My interest was also awakened in taking the story further back, not just to the charges and countercharges raised during World War I and the creation of the "Versailles system" in its aftermath, but also to the origins of humanitarian law in the late nineteenth century and the German reception of it at that time.

I thank Norbert Frei for having encouraged me to take on this adventure, alongside the everyday tasks of university teaching and administration. He has always stood by me with courage and good advice. As the evaluator and editor of the series "Beiträge zur Geschichte des 20. Jahrhunderts," he gave decisive support to the creation of the original German version of this book.

The English edition has been made possible by the generous support of the Börsenverein des Deutschen Buchhandels, which in 2017 chose the book for an award under its "Geisteswissenschaften International" program. The program's purpose is to fund translations of new, innovative works in the humanities and social sciences in order to make them accessible to an

English-speaking audience. Aside from the Börsenverein and its academic jury, many thanks go to Marion Berghahn, Chris Chappell, Amanda Horn, Caroline Kuhtz, and Kristyn Sanito from Berghahn Books for including the book in their program and for handling the many practical tasks of editing and publication. I will of course always be grateful to Nicholas Evangelos Levis, who is not only a dear friend but certainly the most competent and reliable translator I know. A trained historian himself, cooperation with him is always exciting and intellectually stimulating.

There are a great many others whom I must thank for their help and suggestions in creating the original project, starting with my fellow members of the research group on Human Rights in the Twentieth Century at the Fritz Thyssen Foundation, who convene semiannually for intensive discussions in Cologne. I am very grateful to Michael Stolleis, who also served as an external evaluator on the original project. Eckart Conze and Christoph J. M. Safferling invited me to the Research and Documentation Center for War Crimes Trials at Philipps University of Marburg, allowing me to present my findings and theses to the center's research colloquium. Arnd Bauerkämper also helped enrich my work by organizing a colloquium event at the Free University of Berlin.

Finally, my thanks are due to my colleagues in Jena, who helped me in more ways than they can know in completing this book. First among them I must mention Volkhard Knigge, who also evaluated my habilitation project and whose own writings were an important source of inspiration for the present work. I have enjoyed countless useful and often fascinating discussions with my current and past colleagues at Jena, including Kristina Mayer, Daniel Stahl, Jacob Eder, Tim Schanetzky and Dietmar Süß, as well as Jan Eckel, who for a time graced us with his presence at the Jena Center on the History of the Twentieth Century. This book also reflects a long series of discussions over recent years with the students who attended my seminars on the history of human rights and the international law of war. Especially heartfelt thanks go out to my colleague Tim Schanetzky for taking time away from the considerable burdens of his own work to read and correct an earlier and much more raw draft of the German manuscript. Any remaining mistakes or vagaries are of course my responsibility alone.

This book is dedicated to my life partner, Christian Kruse. His humor helped me get through the hard times when the original book project seemed endangered by the difficulties of combining university work, getting by as a long-range commuter on the ICE train, household management, and the usual turbulence of living under one roof with a teenager. For his support through all the years, mere words cannot suffice.

Berlin, September 2018

Introduction

This book is a history of international legal efforts to confront the phenomenon of state-organized violence in the twentieth century. This history can be told in several ways, and I shall begin by broadly summarizing three possible approaches or metanarratives. The first—and until now, the predominant version—describes a series of rises and declines in which new forms of warfare and other state violence repeatedly emerged, in each case prompting attempts to contain violence by means of international law. This macrohistorical spiral of action and reaction is thought to have driven the development of humanitarian international criminal law, as well as attempts to establish institutions in the fields of conflict management and war prevention.

The first version tends to be contextualized within the larger history of European nation-states and to adopt the top-down perspectives of classical political and diplomatic histories. The developments it describes are usually considered native to a European or transatlantic "modernity" or "high modernity," a period that runs roughly from the mid-nineteenth to the late twentieth century.[1] An earlier and overlapping "long nineteenth century," meaning a historical period that ends in 1914 rather than 1900, is usually portrayed in this narrative as an era of economic prosperity, bourgeois civility, and a relative absence of interstate violence in Europe.[2] All the same, new military technologies arose in the mid-to-late nineteenth century. Nationalist tensions intensified. A "culture of war" that transcended class differences emerged and unfolded its power to mobilize populations.[3] These factors transformed national military strategies and eventually led to a far-reaching dissolution of limits on state violence. This transformation had already become evident in the Franco-Prussian War of 1870–1871, again during the Balkan Wars and Ottoman breakup conflicts starting in 1912, and, most dramatically, in the Great War that broke out in 1914.[4] The response in the aftermath of World War I, according to the first narrative, was unprecedented in the history of European peace settlements. An international alliance formed that included great powers and smaller states in the effort to prevent war by using legal means—and in the attempt to enforce prosecutions against members of the defeated aggressor (the German Empire) under international criminal law. This undertaking failed, however, and the Allied politics of international criminal law fell apart.[5] And so the pattern of action and reaction, of states committing violence without limits and an international community of states responding with legal containment after the fact, was reenacted in the mid-twentieth century.[6] After the defeat of National Socialist Germany, the victorious Allied powers again engaged in an effort to institutionalize a humanitarian, international criminal law. This, too, was not established for a longer term. Only after the end of the Cold War, finally, did the vision of a world order based on human rights take a step closer to reality, as evidenced by the establishment of a permanent International Criminal Court (ICC).

A second way of telling the story focuses instead on the middle level of nongovernmental and quasi-state institutions that began to spring up across Europe and the United States during the mid-to-late nineteenth century. In recent years, this version has found more and more followers among historians of social movements, who have come to regard past legal and historical debates about forms of state-organized violence and mass violence as new and fertile research resources that may allow better understanding of how various social groups came to participate as actors in defining agendas and pursuing solutions for transnational problems.[7] This "transnational" perspective seeks to link the history of international relations to the social history of transnationally active groups and networks.[8] The specific subject of study is the formation of a political circle that was still oriented around the nation-state and its institutions, but that depended on the existence of a transnational space for its own effectiveness and legitimation.

The prehistory of these civil society groups is located mostly in early humanitarianism and antislavery movements. They put the problem of unlimited state violence on the political agenda for the first time in the 1860s, making it into the target of (trans)national public debates and campaigns.[9] Together with international law experts, they became essential carriers of liberal internationalism, which aimed to advance an evolution of international political and legal norms.[10] Above all, the increasing role of mass media in politics made it possible for civil society organizations to reach new kinds of audiences, to go beyond states and nationally delineated publics. Hoping to transcend the logics and the limits on expression imposed by national domestic situations, they intentionally adopted the prepolitical language of natural law and human rights. Although they continued to define themselves as members of specific nations, they asserted that warlike violence and its resolution should no longer be treated as the rightful business of current or former belligerents. They instead assumed that a kind of "international public" had arisen and that it could act as an authority in settling questions of legal and moral norms.[11] This orientation around an imagined "international society" or "humanity" (albeit one that did not include all humans) became an indispensable condition for transnational human rights activism and "moral politics."[12]

Finally, a third way to tell the story is conceivable and will be pursued herein. The discipline and practice of humanitarian law—while they can be traced back to particular conjunctures of international politics, academic discourses, and human rights activism—will be treated herein mainly as the means by which actors defined themselves and others in ways that altered reality and created new realities.[13] Adopting terms and methods that have been devised in recent years within the two research fields of transitional justice (TJ)[14] and the politics of the past (*Vergangenheitspolitik*)[15]—meaning the politics of history, memory, and juridical dispute over the past—this study will examine the twentieth-century transnational debates about German state violence with the intent of exploring what kinds of discursive strategies and social practices were employed, and in what contexts, by actors seeking to prove the illegality or legality of given acts of violence to an audience of international and national publics.

This approach is based on the supposition that the process of criminalizing state injustice was not limited to a simple codification of norms. Instead, agreement around particular norms was reached within a contested terrain of political, societal, and cultural negotiation. The rather unstable disciplinary status of international criminal law, as well as its specific modus operandi of using the historical contextualization of incriminating actions to buttress demands for sanctions and punishment, contributed to an often narrow intertwining of legal with historical legitimation strategies in jurisprudential writings. This was even truer in the nonjudicial realms of governments, ministries, civil society, and scholarship, which will be the main subjects of this study. Efforts at setting norms were never just that; they were always also about which historical interpretations would prevail and who could claim hegemony over historical interpretation.

The debates over German state violence, which ran through the entire twentieth century and transpired under a series of very different circumstances, allow us to see how humanitarian law emerged in tandem with an international realm of communications and conflict—within which actors attempted to justify their positions using a combination of legal, historical, and moral-political arguments. These discussions would contribute, on the one hand, to a fundamental change in the character of international criminal law over the course of the twentieth century; on the other, they also influenced public perceptions and appraisals of cases of state violence. One particularly sustained effect can be seen in the fact that state violence today is defined and judged more than ever in the binary categories of human rights.

Approach

The following study begins with the assumption that the transnational debate about German state violence in World War I would have been impossible without the earlier rise of liberal internationalism in the late nineteenth century. Liberal internationalism is understood here as a border-crossing politics and a set of academic disciplines capable of autonomous development. For our purposes, this phenomenon is important above all as a carrier of modern international law (including the law of war), for its functionally dependent interpretations of history (especially public history) and tendency to give these a juridical form, and for a moral approach to politics (and human rights).

Second, this study will argue that debates about German state violence involved competing concepts of internationalism and combined law, history and (moral) politics in sometimes incompatible ways, creating unpredicted frictions and dynamics that took on lives of their own. Actors strove to differentiate themselves from their antagonists but also engaged in mutual borrowing and opportunistic repurposing of concepts, rhetoric, and tropes. The basic thesis of this book is that a comprehensive view of all these factors is needed if we are to understand why debates about illegitimate manifestations of violence arose at different times and in differing historical contexts—and why these discussions followed particular paths and patterns in each case.[17]

With this approach, the following study also addresses several current research controversies concerning the historical origins of "the human rights turn" in international law (especially the law of war), the rise of a globally anchored "processing and memory imperative" regarding traumatic historical events, and the resulting tensions between the disciplines of law and history.[18] But the aim herein will be to go beyond the limits of these controversies. In the following, therefore, the main concern will not be to sound out and define the disciplinary and professional differences or commonalities of justice and history in their confrontations with modern state criminality.[19] The intent is also not to revisit the controversy that already overshadowed Hannah Arendt's book on Adolf Eichmann, when Arendt famously doubted the opinion of the

Israeli chief prosecutor at the Jerusalem trial that judicial strategies of evidence and narrative were fitting tools for the representation of genuine historical events.[20] Instead, this study approaches the problematic from a new perspective: international law and, in particular, humanitarian international law are understood as comprising an incipient space of transnational communication and dispute, within which various actors positioned themselves regarding the phenomenon of organized state violence, argued over the historical causes underlying this phenomenon, and debated the resulting consequences for politics and policy. The longitudinal framework allows us to explore what long-term consequences and dynamics arose out of these intensified interactions among the subsystems of law, scholarship, and politics.

During the past two decades, researchers have taken a greater interest in the relationship between moral politics and the disciplines of law and history, but this has been mainly because of developments outside the academic realm. Even as victims of state violence brought cases before national and international courts in the 1990s, hoping that they would gain official recognition of the injustices perpetrated against them and that the perpetrators would be punished, a parallel and intensive academic controversy arose over the causes and consequences of this "juridification of history."[21] As voices within the field of transitional justice especially have argued, humanitarian international criminal law by the late twentieth century had become a central medium for establishing the public memory of past experiences of violence and for allowing individuals to attain their own moral self-understandings.[22] This view attributes the human rights turn after World War II partly to the spontaneous formation of a global community of outrage, which was inspired by an informed recognition of National Socialism's criminal foundations. In this telling, the punishment of NS elites under international criminal law also helped to initiate processes of self-transformation among the German people, above all by affirming and strengthening legal norms. Credit is also given to the specific approach of the Nuremberg prosecutors, who presented indictments fortified with wide-ranging historical interpretations of the NS regime and its politics. All this created a historical model available for adoption by other states and societies undergoing the transition from dictatorship to democracy, so this interpretation goes, and the model was adopted in many cases starting in the 1970s at the latest.[23]

Much of the TJ literature represents the view that the successive breakthroughs of the human rights idea—and of a related, critical view of state power—came thanks to the emancipation of civil societies, which, after 1945, gradually overcame inhibitions and acquired the strength to prevail against overwhelming challenges. Other voices are more skeptical about this linear success story,[24] and a variety of objections have been raised: any decision to respond to past state violence with court trials or truth commissions necessarily involves multiple political actors and relationships enacted within particular constellations of power. In transitional societies, the indictment of state functionaries under international law has often served as an alternative to more far-reaching social and economic reforms. When justice ventures into the traditional territory of historical studies, the results are, at best, a shortened, functional form of history, one that may not actually be historically relevant. The juridifying trend has prompted defenses of the historical discipline against cooptation. The fashioning of criminal courts into authorities on historical justice raises the risk of overloading the state, of exuberant judicial interventionism, and of a creeping loss of scholarly autonomy.[25] Finally, the skeptics are also critical of viewing the twentieth century in the style of an optimistic, "Whiggish" history, one that construes a narrow causality between state human rights violations and their subsequent sanctioning under international law.

If we historicize these issues, it is striking how quickly the early efforts of humanitarian and military international law inspired controversial public debates about violence. Much like today, commentators in the early twentieth century warned that the law had been overstretched by morality and demanded a stricter separation of law and history. Heated debates unfolded about which among all the violent occurrences of the recent past demanded a legal intervention and which should be regarded simply as a subject for the historians. These debates, in other words, can partly be understood as expressions of complex reorientation processes, as means by which actors come to terms with collective experiences of extreme violence or with far-reaching political and historical ruptures—as a rule, both.

The reasons for the law's increasing importance as a means for dealing with crises and ruptures of varying intensity throughout the twentieth century merit a closer analysis. At first glance, it should be clear that this development was not linear and that it did not rest on a unified, quasi-timeless definition of "the law." Instead, we may suppose that the many vagaries and ambiguities of legal talk are precisely what make it so attractive as a vehicle for normative attributions and ideological suffusions. The indeterminate language of the law could be mined as a resource in political controversies and in the struggle for public opinion. Underlying the undeniable increased resort to legal language were processes of power politics at both the negotiated and explosive extremes. More than this, however, it was a means for addressing upheavals in the political and moral order following historical ruptures that felt irreversible. Yet the legal talk could simultaneously fulfill the opposite function: to invoke the law is to suggest continuity, to give a sense of an identity and a tradition worthy of protection.

These theses will be elaborated on throughout this study, based on evidence from the twentieth-century debates about German state violence.

Unlike "transitology" discourse, this study will not present a general discussion of the direction, effectiveness, and acceptance of international law interventions, or the role therein of the German case. While this field of research often takes a normative approach, the aim here is also not to show whether the universalist norms of humanitarian international law contributed to the development of a critical and self-reflexive understanding of history—based on a German recognition of domestic guilt and culpability—during the first fifty years of the Federal Republic.[26] The subjects here shall be neither the conceptual framework of international law nor of soft-power "law in action"[27] but rather the discourses that proceeded from these.[28] In the process, resort will of course be made to concepts and categories devised in the democracy research of the last few decades. In contrast to transitology, which generally enshrines "truth" and "historical justice" as immutable Enlightenment ideals, these are understood herein as discursive and contingent concepts that must be located within concrete historical connections. Proceeding from recent political history treatments of the "language of human rights," this study will ask why actors at given times in various contexts took up the binary language of international law; what notions, expectations, and interests they associated with it; and what consequences followed.[29]

This approach requires that existing material be structured according to particular temporal and thematic divisions, so the argument to follow is developed through a sequence of four chronological blocks covering the entire twentieth century. The periodization is oriented to the established caesuras of political and legal history, but with variations. Although each of these great ruptures provided compelling reasons to make an issue of state violence, many of the resulting debates developed their own, unexpected dynamics. Certain controversies became self-perpetuating over long periods precisely because juridically stamped history narratives and images engaged in moralistic excesses.

Given that this study is also about the cultural deep effects of the law, it follows that chapter 1 starts with an overview of the development of the modern international law of war. The late nineteenth-century lobbyism of academic experts and peace activists, international agreement on the Geneva and Hague norms, and the emergence of a transnational critical public each turned into key prerequisites for the outbreak of a far-ranging debate on German international law violations after the start of World War I. These discussions gave rise to the innovation—one as yet barely researched in the historical literature—of actionable history, or what historian Raphael Gross has described with the rather awkward term *Geschichtsbarkeit* ("historability"),[30] echoing the legal terms of "actionability" or "judiciability." How well a historical case could be functionalized became a determining factor. Various contemporary history institutes arose—some called forth by states, some by civil society initiatives—to take on the work of documenting the actions, sites, responsibilities, and victims of violence by belligerents. This activity was often connected with explicitly punitive policy goals. One might say that the formation of a punitive history culture and a "preemptive historiography" (Erich J. C. Hahn) during the war partly paved the way for the later developments at Versailles. The peace conference controversies over proposals to put German politicians and military officers on trial are approached from two angles. On the one side, it is shown how the victorious Allied powers, having aggressively made an issue of German norm violations during the war, faced pressure afterward to actually do something about it. They struggled to find an acceptable legal, moral, and political solution. On the other side, a study of the domestic controversy about German "war guilt," along with the emergence of a German historiographic field devoted specifically to "war guilt" studies, raises the question of whether and how the German intellectuals' understanding of Allied international law policy influenced the official German stance during the negotiations.

While German resistance largely derailed punitive international law approaches after World War I, the aftermath of World War II saw a large-scale application of these norms for the first time.[31] But this experiment in punitive policy also had a longer prehistory. As will be shown in chapter 2, the proceedings against representatives of the NS leadership required, first, a reconceptualization of the conventional international law of war but also, second, the development of a coherent historical narrative about the motivations of the Third Reich that could legitimate the planned revolution in international law with both the public and policy makers. Among those most involved in the project of developing this narrative were "Jewish think tanks" and a group of exiled German social scientists whom the Office of Strategic Services (OSS) in Washington invited to participate in planning for the Allied occupation of Germany.[32] In studying the cases of Raphael Lemkin, the Polish-Jewish international law expert, and Jacob Robinson, the New York jurist originally from Lithuania, one question that arises concerns the epistemological pitfalls. What happens when a self-appointed contemporary history research project simultaneously pursues the legal policy goal of making German occupation crimes sanctionable under international law? As for the academics who worked for the OSS, a study of their views on US human rights and international law policies during the war years leads to curious findings, at least in the case of Franz L. Neumann, the well-known author of *Behemoth*. During the war, he was outspoken in his rejection of judicial interventionism à la Robert Jackson, yet in the end he played a key role in preparing the International Military Tribunal (IMT) at Nuremberg. How can such astonishing intellectual transformations be explained?

The use of historical contextualizations in indictments predictably inspired counterreactions. Chapter 2 accordingly concludes with a study of the German side. What was the role of the German defense attorneys at the Nuremberg trials? The case of the Cologne law scholar Hermann Jahrreiß allows an evaluation of how lived experience affected how he conceived his role as a defense counsel at the IMT. How and in what ways did he and his associates attempt to rebut the historicizing approach of the Allied prosecution? Chapter 2 concludes with a study of the political maneuvers behind the scenes before West Germany's surprising early ratification of the Genocide Convention in 1953. The decision involved the paradox of resisting humanitarian law while appropriating it for political purposes.

Chapter 3 turns to a matter that has received little research attention until now, asking in what ways did the Allied punitive programs in the early Federal Republic of Germany actually set off complicated processes of appropriation and reevaluation. It begins with the observation that a rejection of Nuremberg law took hold early in the West German political realm, with the public, with academics, and in judicial sentencing praxis. The example of the "euthanasia" trials is examined in exploring whether this also brought about a change in the historical contextualization of the crimes being prosecuted. In addition, the question of how contemporary historians in West Germany positioned themselves regarding the proliferating historical interpretations of the Nuremberg trials is pursued. The "historians' controversy" around the "Führer order" will be examined in modeling how a mutual reinforcement of historiographic and juridical interpretations developed within an academic environment characterized by a more or less obviously articulated hostility to "Nuremberg historiography" (which was denigrated either as simplistic or as a sophisticated revival of "collective guilt" reproaches) and by a broad neglect of the NS murder of the Jews. Chapter 3 then turns to the rather different constellation that arose during Eichmann's trial in Jerusalem. This was a world-spanning event, one with far-ranging implications, also for the young field of Holocaust studies, because of the prosecution's unapologetic identity politics and human rights agenda. How did the West German jurists and contemporary historians react to this challenge?

Finally, Chapter 4 makes the big leap to the era after the Cold War. In one way, this complicates the study's perspective, since the concepts of transitional justice serve no longer as heuristics but as objects of scrutiny.[33] Samuel P. Huntington's programmatic text, *The Third Wave*, is presented as a case study in discussing how an emergent transitology conceptualized itself and its academic and research strategies. Among the constitutive ideas of the field was the aspiration to support postdictatorial states in their "transition" to democracy by providing social science expertise. The central postulate (that successor governments had a "duty to process" the past in cases of serious state violations of human rights) rested on a liberal and individualist understanding of human rights. Since transitology achieved the status of a global dispositive for a time in the 1990s, this section also considers the conception of "historical truth" on which the imperative to "process" and remember rests, and asks what effects it had, both on perceptions and on judicial treatments of systematic state violence.

Given that the discourses of transitology often treat reunified Germany as an exemplary case, the final sections treat the post-1989 German debates about injustices committed in the dissolved German Democratic Republic (GDR) by the ruling Socialist Unity Party of Germany (SED). The focus is on identifying the ruptures and continuities of the "transition." To what extent did the investigative "enquete" commissions called to life by the German Bundestag in 1992 and 1995 represent a new form of "processing," one with a stronger humanitarian sensibility and less readiness to accept state violence? What role was played by the ways in which East German actors viewed the German-German postwar history and the end of the GDR? How important was it that an official culture of "overcoming the past" (*Vergangenheitsbewältigung*) had been established in West Germany during the preceding decades—one that downplayed human rights and international law issues, and was otherwise defined by a strong effort to differentiate the FRG from Communist East Germany?

New Trends in Legal Historiography

In the 1970s, human rights became a central aspect of international political communications and were elevated into a "central ordering principle of Modernity."[34] The collapse of the bipolar world order starting in the late 1980s, the incipient crisis of modern statehood, and the advance of globalization all contributed to reinforcing this trend throughout the 1990s. With this backdrop, liberal humanitarianism—at least in the estimation of numerous historians, social scientists, and moral philosophers—at times achieved the status of a secular religion and a "surrogate for politics."[35] Parallel to the growing influence of nonstate actors in framing and raising awareness about human rights violations around the world, the nongovernmental organizations in the field began to network, scientize, and institutionalize. The most tangible expression of convergence between human rights activism and the discourses and self-concepts of academics was the meteoric rise of TJ itself.

Transitional justice is a typical "catch-all expression" (Frédéric Mégret), one that slips easily into many different cultural and linguistic realms. It describes a wealth of different phenomena. In its more narrow sense, the term covers the juridical and administrative processes undertaken after a completed change of political systems with the intent of punishing justiciable acts, providing reparations to victims, and restituting robbed properties. A broader definition includes political education, public commemoration, and academic treatments of historical injustice. In their cumulative effect, these are supposed to drive cultural change and more thorough democratization.[36] In the disciplinary terminology, "transition" normally refers to the shift from dictatorship to democracy, while "justice" conveys a kind of liberal-individualist understanding of the idea, as has become characteristic of recent international human rights activism on the whole.[37]

Originating in the context of political upheavals in Central and South America, the concept soon became a global medium of democratization in so-called transition societies.[38] Since the 1980s, the academic discussion on transitional justice has gone through several phases, giving rise to several distinctions and subfields. Although juridical and nonjuridical strategies to "process the past" are occasionally treated as mutually incompatible alternatives, transitology in essence was and remains a product of the human rights breakthrough of the 1970s and 1980s, and the rights talk that has proceeded ever since.[39] TJ scholarship often camouflages a teleological model of history in the definition of "system change" as a linear, legally supported break with the past, and strains to construct causal connections between the punishment of serious human rights violations and democratization. Both tendencies harken back to the discipline's moral-political developmental phase.[40]

Since the 1990s at the latest, transitology has worked with a self-reflexive concept of "processing" legitimated via legal strategies, above all in two ways. First, successful democratization is tied to the structural implementation of a state under rule of law; this goes together with treating the objective of punishing systematic acts of state violence as an imperative. Second, the penal procedures against former state functionaries are conceived as part of a societal confrontation with the past and with the "right to truth" about past state injustices.[41] In this function, criminal law partly enters into a productive if tense relationship with history writing and partly displaces the latter altogether.

As with the scholarship on human rights, the historicization of transitional justice is still in its early stages.[42] While legal scholarship and political science have long plowed this field, historians overcame their reluctance only a few years ago. One reason for the delay was that, for a long time, consciousness of the fact that norms and rights are subject to constant historical change was underdeveloped. The dominant understanding instead was essentialist, viewing "the law" as a kind of container for timeless values and principles. The historical approach prevailing in legal philosophy and jurisprudence, in which the present-day validity of given norms depends mainly on the context of their origination, further reinforced this idea. Only more recently has the literature begun to give more attention to the historicity of legal terms and discourses. Proceeding from the methods of the culturally turned "new political history," the assumption increasingly is that rights and juridical practices must be conceived as part of a "cultural history of the political" in the twentieth century, one that not only codetermines political actions and language but also structures them.[43]

In recent years, attempts have been made to write a history of human rights and liberal humanitarian international law as a "genealogy."[44] The intent, first, is to stress the contingencies and dynamics that underlie rights discourses. Second is a desire to draw the line against the teleological triumphalism of conventional "Western" human rights discourse.[45] Common points for discussion include the observation that the increased importance of rights talk in political communication is global and arose in several different historical contexts. Contrary to claims of universal validity and universalist rhetoric, rights talk is often deployed to unite diverse interests and generally (although not always) very particular motives. These discourses are subject to changing conjunctures. Changes tend not to emerge from the inherent logic of the law to quite the same degree that the legal scholarship commonly imagines. Instead, the controversies around the validity, construction, and reinterpretation of law far more often arise in the wake of decisive political events.

In his overview of the history of human rights before and after 1945, Stefan-Ludwig Hoffmann specified several reasons why the human rights discourse of the nineteenth and twentieth centuries suffered temporary disappearances and an unprecedented rise. First, it received its earliest impulse from the movement to abolish slavery—the success of which paradoxically came just when European colonialism increasingly sought legitimation in racist rather than religious rationales. Second, the rise of the European nation-states elevated forms of law and constitutionalism that foregrounded the rights of "citizens" rather than "people." Third, the "juridification" of wars, beginning with the emergence of humanitarian international law in the second half of the nineteenth century, served further to codify the unequal relations between the European powers and other territories of the world. Although some of the worst belligerent practices were delegitimized, a concurrent tendency reduced the rights of combatants, and this extended in part to civilians. As a fourth influencing factor, Hoffmann identifies the continuing power of the nation-state idea well beyond World War I and the associated politics regarding minorities—above all, Jews in Eastern Europe.

Hoffmann goes on to identify another four sets of conundrums in the post-1945 period. A paradox of the postwar order was that the human rights discourse of the war years, grounded in a common system- and bloc-overlapping front against NS Germany, was reshaped after the war into an instrument for battling Communism. Second, in the wake of decolonization and anticolonial liberation struggles, a competition arose between liberal-democratic, socialist, and postcolonial conceptions of human rights. The number of nation-states exploded, especially in the 1960s. Third, the 1970s saw the formation, primarily in the Western industrial nations, of a "new" humanitarianism that rejected state violations of human rights, as well as imperial exploitation, and resided mainly in nonstate actors and networks. Fourth, the fall of Communism strengthened the legitimacy of the Western human rights discourse but also brought new tensions and splits, since it was followed by the return of interventionism justified in humanitarian terms.[46]

This longer view sheds new light on several matters. First is the contrast between classical liberal narratives and those that portray human rights as the product of a "global history of violence and conflict." Second, debates about rights have come not only at the end but often also at the beginning of political crises and controversies. A historical overview gives only conditional confirmation of the supposed evolutionary convergence of democratization, liberal legal cultures, and a peaceful world order, although the claim is still happily postulated, down to this day. These connections do exist but tend to work more on the domestic level and have had almost no demonstrable impacts on foreign relations. Over and over, post-World War II developments have forced the conclusion that there is no autonomy of the law, at least not on the international level. Even as legal arguments have become more important to political communication, the corresponding legal institutions, treaties, and agreements have little influence and remain nonbinding.[47]

The last statement highlights a conceptual problem with the above narrative as a whole. If international law is so weak and ineffective, why have actors put so much stock in legal semantics and discourses? What have been the short-term and long-term consequences? And what about the contrary cases, in which the institutions and codifications of international law had undeniable consequences in the political realm, as with the fatal effects of the Versailles punitive provisions on the domestic politics of the Weimar Republic? Regardless of heuristic advantages, a strict transnational history of terminology and discourse evinces certain weaknesses and inherent limits. The characteristic developments of the twentieth century cannot be understood very well without discerning how a great many actors and institutions existed alongside the terms and discourses, and how these actors not only used the law as a vehicle for implementing their various interests but also pursued "international law politics" (Andreas Fischer-Lescano) in a highly active way.

There has been a recent boom in works of legal history—mostly affirmative pieces upholding the categories of Wilsonian "idealism"—that describe the outstanding contributions of American politicians, jurists, and activists in developing modern international law. Among the various critiques, one point of objection is that these works uncritically reproduce the universalist, missionary self-image of the "city on the hill."[48] Although these arguments are valid and justified, this should not mean downplaying the central influence of the United States. For one thing, US behavior in the twentieth century shows that an engagement for human rights and liberal international law most certainly can go together with imperialist and colonial policies. From the American perspective, the law often, but not always, serves as an instrument of geopolitical expansion and a legitimation of violence; the history of US colonial wars offers a wealth of illustrative materials.[49]

Moreover, the processes of rupture following 1989–1991 make it obvious that the American contribution to the juridification of international politics cannot be overestimated, even if human rights rhetoric and government action often diverge. The influence of liberal legalism and constitutionalism is not limited to the shaping of norms and institutions. That may not even be the most important place to look. This discourse has been far more effective along the cultural dimension, where the egalitarian and pluralistic elements of American legal thought are mixed with ethical-religious and social-psychological motifs.[50] These mirror the experiences of American constitutionalism and its confrontations with the dictators and totalitarian regimes of the twentieth century, especially those in Europe.

Opinions in the literature nonetheless differ on how far the human rights and international law developments of the twentieth century were shaped by Europe's history of dictatorship and violence. Its importance has been relativized with assertions in recent years that the breakthrough for human rights activism as a "politics of the unpolitical" was achieved only in the 1970s, after leftist protest movements were hit with "political disillusionment" following the struggles over the Vietnam War.[51] Around the same time, the political and regulatory influence of the United States received a new accent. As a victorious Allied power, according to this argument, the United States had played a leading role in the codification and institutionalization of humanitarian international law in the immediate wake of World War II, but the onset of the Cold War forced a retreat to the bare-knuckle rules of realpolitik. It was only when this was discredited by the US involvement in Vietnam that Jimmy Carter's presidential administration rediscovered human rights as the "moral grounds of legitimation for a new US political and economic hegemony in a time of global integration of markets and spaces."[52] Certainly, the two world wars, National Socialism, and Stalinism continue to be seen as important prerequisites that made possible the creation of various human rights institutions after World War II, including the United Nations, the Council of Europe, and the Organization of American States (OAS). However, the skeptics emphasize that because of the bipolar global conflict, the attraction of these institutions remained relatively limited. Their functions were of a primarily declaratory style. They were instrumentalized in efforts to delegitimize political and ideological adversaries. Meanwhile, the parallel creation of military security structures, primarily designed to avoid a new world war, contributed little toward solidifying the idea of a universal protection of human rights that transcends citizenship, although it had already been articulated at Nuremberg and has been developed further since.

Against this skeptical current, another strand in the literature instead sees the development of transitional justice as coming at the end of a long-term process that originated during World War I and achieved a first culmination with the Nuremberg trials.[53] In this reading, the appearance of new forms of violence and the military defeat of National Socialism played a decisive role in the "politicization" and "modernization" of international law. It was above all the decision to remove the status of the German Reich as a subject under international law that created a state of exception; in the immediate postwar years, this was used for a creative advancement of international law. In this reading, after a long phase of latency, a new global model of *transnational* justice formed in the late 1980s. It harkened back to the Nuremberg pattern, modifying and advancing it. While earlier international law had stood in competition with national law—insofar as the latter was supposed to be abrogated in times of serious human rights violations—international law meanwhile had access to an overarching cultural paradigm that enjoyed allegiance in many transition societies, as well as among a great many private persons and organizations. According to this reading, a process had begun in which the ideal values of humanitarianism could be successively integrated into national legal regimes. Thus, in a thoroughly pragmatic tradeoff, postdictatorial states were thought to have the options of punishment or amnesty, juridical establishment of truth or historical enlightenment, integration or political lustration, while private actors could use the transitional justice model to pursue their restitution demands or to initiate perpetrator-victim dialogues.[54] The common quality of these various historical "processing" strategies, however, lies in their public performance of the law, justice, and justice-like procedures aimed at establishing collective but, even more so, individual responsibilities for state injustice yet at the same time providing the means to achieve distance from such responsibilities.

Chapter 1

THE HAGUE—BERLIN—VERSAILLES

In the mid-to-late nineteenth century, European and American international law experts and networks of moderate pacifists began to advocate for the "juridification" and "humanization" of interstate wars. Their concerns were inspired by the increasing mechanization of warfare, the formation of mass armies, and the ideological and moral styling of militaries into "schools of the nation." At universities and in private civil associations, members of the educated, liberal middle classes engaged on behalf of banning certain war technologies, regulating the provision of medical care to the injured, and giving more protection to civilians. The humanitarian law of war became a prestige project of liberal-progressive internationalism,[1] at times acquiring impressive momentum compared with other areas of international law. This was related to structural changes in the international system and to the rise of a morally motivated, transnational public. It was attributable also to a combination of specific experiences of violence and their treatment in the media. The Swiss businessman Henry Dunant's descriptions of the battlefields at Magenta and Solferino, in June 1859 during the Second Italian War of Independence, set off a wave of public sympathy that was decisive in the emergence of the International Red Cross movement and the convening, in 1864, of the first Geneva Convention.

The following decades saw a series of important advances in the new humanitarian military law leading up to the signing of the Hague Convention in 1899, which can be described as its first international codification. While the two Hague Conventions of 1899 and 1907 would prove in practice rather limited in actually containing wartime violence, their most important political meaning was in creating a sphere of state and semi-state communication that facilitated discussions about war and peace as well as legitimate and illegitimate forms of state violence. Humanitarian law thus became a catalyst and a medium for a transatlantic discourse of self-understanding among experts and analysts, most of them dedicated to emancipatory goals. As a great many examples show, however, their work also consistently served to legitimate the imperialist power politics of individual states, fomenting among them a more instrumental interest in international law.[2]

This two-faced nature of humanitarian law was a key reason why its political importance remained high throughout World War I. The Great War's outbreak in 1914 immediately set into motion a set of inherent dynamics. Military and ideological confrontations fed a public discourse on state violence that appealed back to the norms and ideals of the Geneva and Hague conventions. Because of their ambivalent attitude to regulations under international law, the government of the Wilhelmine Reich and the elites of imperial Germany found themselves in the crossfire of this controversy from the start. Their acts were treated and judged by the Entente Powers (aka the Allies, or until 1917 the "Triple Entente" of Britain, France, and the Russian Empire) under the standards of international military law. Efforts to document German actions, both for historical purposes and in preparation for possible criminal judgments, started early. The creation of this "preemptive historiography"[3] continued to influence discussions after the war. Criminalization of the enemy followed almost as a necessary and logical consequence of the compilation and public presentation of evidence. Academics and writers published within an emerging field that established new relations among international law experts, parties with historical and political interests in the phenomena of state and military violence and victims of violence, and internationally networked communities of peace activists. From 1918 to 1919, these three strands would converge on the "punishment clauses" of the Treaty of Versailles.

The victorious Allies' international criminal law policy set off divided reactions within Germany itself. The military and political collapse of November 1918 started a lively controversy about German guilt both *for* and *in* the war. In part, this drama saw an interweaving of legal with historical categories; in part, it moves to play the fields of law and history against each other.

International Criminal Law before World War I

Beginning in the mid-nineteenth century, several impulses set into motion the rise of international criminal law, both as a modern academic discipline and as a medium for defusing international conflict. The most important factor was a change in perspective regarding interstate wars. The internationally publicized events of the Crimean War of 1853–1856, the American Civil War of 1861–1865, the Franco-Prussian War of 1870–1871, and the Russo-Ottoman War of 1877–1878 made it seem urgent to expand the ancient and medieval laws of war so as to deal with the realities of modern warfare. Leading the discussion was a small group of European and American jurists of national and international law who understood themselves individually as representatives of their own nations but collectively as the "legal conscience" of a kind of "civilized" way of life associated mainly with Europe and North America.[4]

Unlike most scholars of German national law, who were still under the spell of the Right Hegelian school of thought, the ranks of international law jurists were filled mostly with cosmopolitan liberals. Their work aimed to establish, on an international level, some of the same achievements that had been gained through national legalization processes—for example, to secure fundamental rights to life, liberty and property, or to implement collective and individual rights of self-determination.[5] Given that international law lacked a common sovereign and an effective executive, they vested their hopes in "society," or, more precisely, in an international "family" of emancipated and self-determining European citizens, as the source of legitimation for international law. In their aspirations, this "family" was open to all who possessed self-consciousness as carriers of an enlightened, liberal "sense of right and wrong." This was based in a common belief in the possibility of human self-improvement, and in the spirit of humanism and Christianity. The primary addressees of this discourse were the educated strata of European societies, although the concept originally also included the Muslim peoples of the Ottoman Empire.[6] Membership in this new form of community under the law was determined not by nationality but by one's agreement with a moral ideal.

In short, there is no fundamental case for the idea that the international law discipline only discovered human rights as the basis of its legitimation in the 1970s.[7] On the contrary, renowned jurists like Johann Caspar Bluntschli and Pasquale Fiore propagated a "right of world citizens" in the Kantian sense, one that should transcend the categories of nation, class, race, and—in increments—gender. This first generation of academically educated international law jurists sought to bridge the contradiction between human rights and citizen rights by replacing the criterion of nationality with vague ideas of Occidental cultivation, civility, and morality. Thus, despite its universalist claims, the liberal concept of an *esprit d'internationalité* in practice also had nationally exclusive qualities. To take Germany as an example, an exclusive and rather national "internationality" did not appear simply in the wake of the political upheavals of the 1880s, when the Bismarckian government engaged in a hostile confrontation with leftist notions of internationalism; rather, as in other countries, it also developed inherently from the conception of the new international law as a standard of "civilization."

Concepts of civilization among the educated classes, proceeding from Protestant progressive ideals of self-education and self-discipline, gave impulse to hierarchization of "communities under rule of law." This engendered a split in legal opinion regarding members of one's own cultural or civilizational milieu and the "barbarians." The European "civilizing missions" in the rest of the world, which rested on the "three pillars" of market economy, law, and religion,[8] were reflected in the construction of various legal and moral spaces to judge non-European societies according to the Europeans' notions of their will to perform, their usefulness, and their habitus.[9] This legal understanding not only had political and social effects on the treatment of such societies by the colonial masters and missionaries but also indirectly impacted academic debates in Europe. First, the classification of some peoples as "uncivilized" and "barbarian" regulated who was to be excluded from the protective functions of the law.[10] The British, for example, sought to justify their reprisals against Boer civilian populations during the 1899–1902 uprisings in the Orange Free State and Transvaal by arguing that the Boers could not be counted among civilized peoples[11] because of their acceptance of slavery. In the British self-image, the abolition of slavery had come to be regarded as a singularly British accomplishment.[12] In the opinion of a few jurists, the distinctions between center and periphery, between sovereign and nonsovereign formations, and between civilized and uncivilized societies were central to the conception and social practice of modern international law, insofar as the demarcation from "others" started what Antony Anghie has called a dynamic of legal "definition, identification and categorization."[13]

Thus, in the aspirations of the cosmopolitan international law jurists, the "legalization" and "humanization" of war was a matter of overarching social relevance. With this backdrop, efforts to open a public debate about the future of international law came early on.[14] It was soon obvious that the legalist utopianism of law scholars did not meet with the unanimous agreement of national elites. Especially strong resistance came from militaries, who correctly saw academics impinging upon and threatening the interpretative monopoly that they traditionally claimed over matters of war and peace. In Germany, given the Wilhelmine empire's nearly uncontested prioritization of the "primacy of the military" (Gottfried Niedhardt), it is no wonder that efforts to codify international law met with the greatest skepticism among members of the military's German General Staff.

Jurists at the Institut de Droit International (Institute for International Law) went far to accommodate military concerns in the writing of the *Oxford*

Manual, which laid down fundamental principles for the wartime treatment of civilians, prisoners of war, the wounded, spies, and parliamentary deputies. Passed in 1880, these regulations included a limiting passage acknowledging "necessities of war."[15] This did not prevent Helmuth Graf von Moltke, the German field marshal, from condemning the handbook. The triumphant hero of the Franco-Prussian War made little secret of his contempt for the Kantian peace treatise, which had become a sensation within the bourgeois peace movement.[16] Disparaging the international law jurists' proposals and addressing Bluntschli in particular, Moltke advised them to stop dreaming about "eternal peace" and instead recognize that war was an unavoidable part of the divine world order. Only military virtues like "courage and self-denial, loyalty to duty and willingness to sacrifice" could prevent society from sinking into "hollow materialism." Moltke was willing to admit that customs of warmaking had in fact softened to a degree, but he attributed this entirely to the introduction of general conscription and the "strict discipline already managed and experienced in times of peace." The recent victory over France was the perfect example of how wars should be run: above all, by the maxim that they are to be ended as quickly as possible. To this end, it was necessary to have "every not *abjectly condemnable* means available" and "to engage all sources of support for the enemy government . . . their finances, railways, food, even their prestige."[17] For this reason, he refused the rationale of the Saint Petersburg Declaration of 1868, according to which belligerents had the right only to "weaken enemy armed forces."[18] It should be noted that during World War I, Kaiser Wilhelm II and Chancellor Theobald von Bethmann-Hollweg would both use a similar line of argument in justifying the aerial bombardment of French and British civilians.[19]

In his recent accounts of twentieth-century human rights history, Samuel Moyn has pointed to the interdependency between the development of international law and the activism of various social movements.[20] But the question of how the public, political parties, and the slowly growing peace movement reacted to the emergence of the modern international law of war in the late nineteenth century has still not been adequately researched.[21] There are indications that legal attitudes and ways of thinking influenced public discussion far beyond the great international conferences—and be it simply so as to engender polarization between advocates and opponents of an international law regime. Not least among the reasons that international law jurists were able to achieve a relatively broad appeal, law talk provides important ideal and discursive resources that can be put to use in political controversies. As a relatively young discipline, international law also evoked a utopian potential that above all spoke to and mobilized the sentiments of progressive educated classes. A key factor in the relative success that international law jurists achieved with their efforts at codification was surely that a transnational public had already formed in the wave of abolitionism. Highly motivated in moral and political terms, this public represented the appellative authority for both the academic networks and the (partly identical) peace movement to address.[22]

The peace movement, which would also play an important role in the 1918–1919 debates about the international law provisions of the Treaty of Versailles, consisted of two main camps. Next to the socialist and radical pacifist branches, which saw the solution for the armaments problem and the growing danger of war above all in the realization of broad political and social rights and freedoms, a faction of moderate pacifists tended to support the normativization efforts of the liberal international law jurists. Just like the pacifist associations of notables, they were devoted to an elitist progressive optimism that understood the activity of peace politics as an expression of purposive rationality. Among them was a decisive resistance to pacifism on mere ethical-humanitarian or religious grounds, which were considered unscientific and ineffective. In Germany, this form of "organized pacifism" received its exemplary embodiment in the pre–World War I period through the Association for International Understanding (Verband für internationale Verständigung), founded in 1911. Its chair, Hans Wehberg, was one of a handful of pacifists among German international law jurists. He sought to advance Alfred Hermann Fried's theory of international law as a professionally neutral and "passive science."[23] Under Wehberg, the association propagated a faith in growing economic and cultural interdependence. It sought to brand the military buildups demanded by the emerging and numerous national-chauvinist mass organizations as hostile to progress.

Part of the bourgeois peace movement dissolved at the beginning of World War I, or even joined the pro-war camp. Another part came together as Bund Neues Vaterland (BNV), the "alliance for a new fatherland." During the war, BNV consistently supported nonannexationist positions and agitated for the idea of a future world peace order.[24] Anachronistic organizational structures and the lack of backing from either of the two big German churches meant that the organized peace movement of the German Reich was at no point able to mobilize the kind of mass movement that would have been necessary for its political cause to prevail. A further reason for its failure was in the early split between ethical-humanitarian and technocratic international law orientations. In addition to their neutrality on domestic questions, their refusal to adopt positions on social politics or democracy, their "reduction of the peace problem to a question of regulation under international law," and, finally, the distancing of organized pacifism from the ideas of the original Peace Society all caused a fundamental weakening of the German peace movement.[25]

Why, then, did international humanitarianism as well as legalism gain so much ground at the turn of the twentieth century? They were engaged in a mutual reinforcement process that rested on a complex web of causes. The mutual relationships of politics, power, and law did not develop along a linear axis. Progress in the codification of the still-young field of international law often went hand in hand with violations of international law. The formalization of state governance, the burgeoning of nationalism, and the supplanting of premodern "rob and plunder" colonialism by "classical" or "high" imperialism all combined to raise a "contradiction between national pathos and the functional pressure to set rules."[26] This paradox endures as an important structural characteristic of international relations.

In any case, the tensions between state foreign policies, which were increasingly laden with nationalism, and the simultaneous regulatory development of interstate relations would manifest above all in the realm of humanitarian law.[27] The first paths were cut in the early 1860s by Dunant, the Geneva businessman. His religiously motivated activism underlay the foundations of both the International Committee for Relief to the Wounded, which would eventually become the International Committee of the Red Cross (ICRC), and of the first Geneva Convention, "for the Amelioration of the Condition of the Wounded in Armies in the Field," in August 1864. Further steps in codification were similarly achieved on the relatively less contentious territory of *jus in bello*, law *in* war. In 1863, the Lieber Code for Union Forces in the American Civil War became the first national military handbook that regulated the treatment of prisoners of war, guerillas, slaves, and intellectual property.[28] The war of secession also led to a criminal trial still considered very important in the literature, because of its supposedly paradigmatic influence on the American course of action after 1945.[29] Following the Civil War, in the face of public pressure, Henry Wirz, the commandant of the notorious Confederate prisoner-of-war camp at Andersonville, Georgia, was indicted for murders and mistreatments committed against the fifteen thousand Union soldiers interned there. While Wirz was convicted and executed in November 1865 after a highly controversial trial, Washington more or less quietly buried concurrent plans to try the president of the Confederacy, Jefferson Davis, and its former secretary of defense, James A. Seddon, on charges of conspiracy to kill President Abraham Lincoln.[30] Decades later, during the US debate over possible criminal trials of the Imperial German leadership following World War I, domestic conservative opponents of President Woodrow Wilson raised the trial of Wirz, who had been of German origin, as a precedent for war crimes trials. During the Paris talks, however, the American delegation only brought up the Wirz case as a means of persuading the reluctant Europeans of the advantages of national military tribunals, as opposed to international courts.[31]

A year after the Franco-Prussian War, the jurist Gustave Moynier—a cofounder of the International Committee for the Relief of the Wounded who succeeded Dunant as its president—proposed an international tribunal or an investigative commission that would look into legal violations committed during that war.³² Taking up an idea first devised by his colleague Gustave Rolin-Jaequemyns, Moynier argued that mere moral condemnation would be insufficient in persuading belligerents to follow the Geneva Convention. He demanded that European governments also pass amendments to their national criminal law, to assure that violations of international law would in the future also be actionable in national courts. But Moynier's initiative failed to catch fire among the Red Cross societies and the leading international lawyers. A German criminal lawyer, Carl Lueder, called the idea unrealistic: no state would be prepared to provide its own citizens for prosecution before an international court. Other jurists argued that the time was not yet ripe, instead calling on academics to keep working stubbornly for the day when an international court could become a reality.

A multistate agreement on the international law of war thus did not come into being before World War I. Next to the well-known Geneva Conventions, we are left with the Hague peace conferences of 1899 and 1907 as the most important milestones of these early codification efforts.³³ The Hague Conventions were accepted more or less without objection by nearly all the signatory states. In the absence of a common regulatory framework, there was an agreement on the formula that was presented in the preamble to the 1907 Hague Convention (IV) Respecting the Laws and Customs of War on Land, wherein the signatory states obligated themselves to treat civilians and combatants according to the "rule of the principles of the law of nations, as they result from the usages established among civilized peoples, from the laws of humanity, and the dictates of the public conscience."³⁴ Additional clauses in regard to *ius in bello* (again, law regulating acts during a war) included the prohibition of certain kinds of weapons (dum-dum bullets, poison gas, sea mines) and requirements that combatants wear distinguishable uniforms and that spies, prisoners of war, the wounded, and neutral parties be treated humanely.

On the initiative of the German delegation to the 1907 Hague Convention, another provision was added to establish the duty of state "compensation" (*Wiedergutmachung*) in the case of serious violations of the rules.³⁵ As the rationale, the German side pointed to a basic principle of private law, according to which anyone who intentionally or by illegal conduct violates the rights of others must compensate for the damages: "We also believe that the responsibility for every unexpected action taken by members of the combatant forces in circumvention of the Agreement should accrue to the governments to which they belong."³⁶ In keeping with this proposal, the Hague land-war convention added a provision regarding state liability for individual violations of international law. The revised Article 3 of the Hague Convention IV therefore read: "A belligerent party which violates the provisions of the said Regulations shall, if the case demands, be liable to pay compensation. It shall be responsible for all acts committed by persons forming part of its armed forces."[37] Chancellor Bethmann-Hollweg would refer implicitly to Article 3 in his famous "Necessity Knows No Commandments" speech of 4 August 1914, when he announced to the governments of Belgium and Luxembourg that there would be "reparations" for the "wrongs" committed against their neutrality—after Germany's intended military goal had been achieved. This is how he put it to the deputies of the German Reichstag: "We are now in an emergency [*Notwehr*, literally meaning self-defense]; and necessity knows nothing of commandments! Our troops have occupied Luxembourg, perhaps also Belgian territory . . . in contravention of the commandments of international law."[38]

After the Armistice of 11 November 1918, however, when the Allies confronted the representatives of Imperial Germany with demands for reparations and compensations, they no longer recognized any such duty to compensate.[39] Notwithstanding that, within a few weeks of the 1914 invasion, the Reich military leadership had developed wide-ranging plans for annexations that would also include Luxembourg and Belgium, in 1919 the German negotiators expressed surprise and dismay only regarding the supposed illegality of the Versailles reparations and "war guilt" provisions.[40]

In 1907, together with the Russian delegation, the Germans also submitted an amendment to prohibit the forced recruitment of enemy combatants as laborers.[41] The issue of internationalized jurisdiction, however, was rejected at the Hague Conventions as impinging upon the sovereignty principle. A discussion on the concept of "war crimes," a term coined by the international law jurist Lassa Oppenheim in 1906, was also not allowed to proceed.[42] Instead, there was a general fundamental agreement that matters of jurisdiction should be left to national civil and military courts. The only supranational solution to pass was the establishment of a voluntary international court of arbitration on questions of war prevention. Although arms limitations were relegated to the margins, the parties agreed on a renewed avowal to protect the territorial integrity of neutral states. Thus, just a few years before the German assault on Belgium, the final text of the Hague declaration revived neutrality as a principle within the international community of states.

The Hague Convention of 1907 was ratified by twenty states within four years. Next to the United States, which had organized the second Hague "peace conference," the signatories included all European major powers and several Latin American states.[43] Imperial Germany provided its certificate of ratification by November 1909. By order of the Prussian War Ministry, the German field service regulations (*Felddienstordnung*) were amended in 1912 to add the full text of the 1907 Hague Convention. Three years, later the German General Staff issued a secret bulletin for officer-training purposes that included excerpts from the Hague regulations. In December 1911, furthermore, a full compilation of the Geneva and Hague conventions was issued, intended for distribution among troops in the event of a mobilization.[44]

Despite these various measures, the Germans were criticized internationally long before World War I for their supposed failure to implement international law agreements. This was first raised in 1902 after the General Staff issued a controversial memorandum titled *Kriegsbrauch im Landkriege* (Wartime Conduct in Landwar).[45] While exponents of the German legal and political academic establishments came to a mostly positive assessment of this text, their British and French colleagues found that the German military was ignoring the spirit and letter of the 1899 Hague Conventions through an absolutist rendering of the principle of "military necessity."[46] It was argued that the German military was exclusively oriented around experiences of the Franco-Prussian War, with a further tendency to recall only the French, and not the German, violations of the rules. One of the most vehement critics in Great Britain was James Molony Spaight, a military jurist and author of the handbook *War Rights on Land*. During World War II, he would be among the most assertive supporters of "moral bombing"—a circumstance that illustrates how thoroughly the legal condemnation of given war technologies depended on context and contemporary assessments of right and wrong.[47]

Given the differences between German and Franco-British understandings of the Hague provisions, it might seem that German international law violations during World War I in a sense expressed a long-standing rejection of law that German entry to the Hague Conventions had merely served to camouflage. The American military historian Isabel V. Hull, after an intensive examination of the conceptual patterns and mentalities of the Prussian military in the late nineteenth and early twentieth centuries, reduced this to the fundamental question of whether the German side was willing to observe contract under humanitarian law. Hull's comparative analysis shows a long series of important similarities but also dramatic differences between the German and the French and British attitudes. Skepticism about codified law was by no means an exclusive domain of the Wilhelmine elites. The British—and among them, especially, officers of the Royal Navy—spoke disparagingly of the supposed civilizational achievements of international law. For example, First Sea Lord Admiral John A. Fisher wrote that it was "the inevitable result of conferences and arbitrations . . . that we always give up something. It's like a rich man entering into a conference with a gang of burglars."[48]

Nevertheless, the British and the French took far greater effort than the Germans did to harmonize their national military handbooks with Geneva and Hague regulations. They assigned the task not to low-ranking officers but to renowned academics like the Austro-British expert Lassa Oppenheim. On the German side, by comparison, it was not long before conflicts developed between Foreign Office (AA) and military institutions, and the diplomats necessarily came out the losers. Despite the growing respect enjoyed by international law since the late nineteenth century among Imperial Germany's civilian elites, they were unable to implement demands for better harmonization of national with international law against the structurally more powerful military. However, contrary to the accusations of consistent German treaty violations raised by the Entente Powers after 1914, neither the Kaiser nor the civilian and military leadership had engaged in a long-planned and witting violation of existing regulations.[49]

History Management in Wartime, 1914–1919

After all attempts to negotiate a solution for the Austro-Serbian crisis of July 1914 had failed, the Great War that followed brought unprecedented tests for international law. The war exceeded all past military conflicts from the first day forward. This was true not only of the scale of the war effort on all sides. Enormous armies were recruited, transported, and maintained. Civilians were also mobilized on a massive scale, in the belief that they were necessary to keep arms industries and infrastructures running. Yet the cultural mobilization from day one was also entirely unprecedented in intensity and extent. It involved the intellectuals, writers, artists, and academics of all the participant nations.[50] To the extent that by the end of 1914 it had become obvious that a swift end was unlikely, the political importance of the propaganda kept growing. The grave effects of industrialized warmaking on populations were no minor factor, and motivated governments to pay special heed to moods on the "homefront." World War I came to be identified as a "total war" above all because of the immense deployment of both traditional and innovative propaganda weapons. The propaganda in this initially inter-European and eventually worldwide confrontation was not limited to dissemination of news, fomentation of moods, or defamation of the enemy. Rather, propaganda and military conduct itself soon became entangled in a "purposively rational complex."[51]

Nationalist suggestion and autosuggestion started a circle of violence and counterviolence that progressively diminished prospects for diplomatic efforts to mediate or negotiate. While the Germans styled their war effort into a struggle for national and cultural self-assertion, the Allies interpreted theirs as a moral crusade against "evil" and a degenerate civilization. The clash of arms was imbued with eschatological significance. Substantive differences between politics and propaganda were increasingly obscured. The essentialization of enemy images was accompanied by a tendency to self-mystification and moral hubris. Thus, all war parties came to see themselves as innocent victims of a hostile aggressor whom one could face only by the exertion of all social forces and with absolute interior unity. In the wake, traditional categories of politics, law, and morality fell increasingly into doubt. Only through pervasive all-encompassing indoctrination and ideologization was it possible for the British press to cast Wilhelm II—who, after all, was the grandson of Queen Victoria and cousin of King George V—as the "Berlin Butcher" (Horatio William Bottomley), while church leaders gave him the title of "Beast" and "Antichrist."[52] Inverting all values that had been earlier agreed at the Hague Conventions, German scientists, like the celebrated chemist Fritz Haber, lauded the use of poison gas as a "humane" weapon.[53]

Research on the roles in all this of the new international law discourses and their influence on the shift in mentalities remains only in the beginning stages. Fundamentally, it can be agreed with John Horne and Alan Kramer that the public, which had only ever taken a superficial interest in the debates around international law, surely retained that attitude during the war.[54] But the rationales and justifying contexts of a transformative international law had been planted in the consciousnesses of European elites long before 1914. It is clearly inadequate to see the common resort to legally based arguments during the war as expressing no more than a growing state of delusion and self-reinforcing political loss of touch.[55] As we have seen, since the Hague Conventions at the latest, international law was firmly established as a medium of international diplomacy and as a transnational sphere of communication. It follows logically that the belligerents now accused each other mutually of violations of international law agreements. But the conditions of the war contributed to numerous changes in the received discourse.

Arguably, the most important of these was about the principles of state sovereignty and immunity. Before 1914, these were seen as absolute quantities, as the indispensable foundations of interstate agreements. The war cast them increasingly in doubt. To the extent that ever-greater numbers of civilians were dragged into misery, and as it no longer seemed certain that their own governments could protect them, calls to punish those responsible for the war under international law came early and loud as a means for establishing deterrence. Therein was articulated the idea of a revolutionary renewal of politics and the law, one that in certain ways marked a renunciation of the evolutionary progressive ideas of the old cosmopolitan international law jurists and bourgeois peace movements. That such radical demands met with high support in politics, science, and the public was in the end largely due to the potential for coalition building. While liberals saw this as a first step toward building a world peace order by means of law, conservative circles understood the law above all as a suitable vehicle for mobilizing nationalist and chauvinist morale. In the final analysis, however, as James F. Willis showed in his profound study of the international debate on the punishment of war crimes, different reasons were decisive in each country's turn to ascribing increased importance to the law and in their shift of accentuation toward a more punitive international law policy.[56]

The debates over international law violations were also closely associated with the emergence of a justice discourse that mirrored changing ideas of law, history, and morality. These developments can also be traced back to the late nineteenth century. With the rise of a dynamic concept of history and the associated critique of historical objectivism, the discipline had turned more openly to adopting juridical forms of narrative and rationale. In distancing themselves from the objectivity ideal of classical historicism, prominent exponents of the Borussian school of historiography, such as Heinrich von Treitschke, propagated a moralizing view of history.[57] Parallel to the formation of a supranational public, demands were raised for an overarching moral authority before which national states would have to justify their conduct. That the Catholic Church was not considered for this function was above all due to its practiced policy of *imparzialità* (impartiality). In the end, the Vatican shrank from siding with either of the two big war alliances, given large Catholic populations in Germany and the Austro-Hungarian Empire and general reservations about French republicanism and British Protestantism.[58] Since there was no secular court, the "neutrals"—preferably meaning the United States—were cast in the role of an imagined "world court."

In the end, the conjuring of timeless standards of justice was connected to the emergence of a phenomenon that Horne and Kramer term the "community of truth." Above all, this describes the circumstance that all the groups in politics, science, and religion who traditionally understood themselves as values communities were subject to more powerful pressures of conformity in the wake of the cultural mobilization. It was often difficult for these groups to believe the propaganda myths of one side or the other, because behind these they saw a conscious manipulation of the "truth." But this did not in the end prevent the calling forth of a truth norm understood as absolute once their national partial identities were endangered.

One highly conspicuous example for this kind of behavior can be seen in the refusal of the German Social Democratic movement to take a stand on international law. Even as French and Belgian socialists raised demands for a debate on German war crimes in their own countries, the leadership of the Social Democratic Party of Germany (SPD) issued a short dismissal wrapped in Russophobic rhetoric. An army in which half the soldiers were Social Democrats could hardly be more barbaric than the "unculture and barbarism of Czarism," they averred.[59] The party's right wing, led by Adolph Koester and Gustav Noske, did not question Berlin's claims that the Belgian civilian guerillas, the *francs-tireur*, had provoked the German military into taking necessary and justified reprisals. On the contrary, they defended this assertion aggressively against accusations from abroad. The SPD executive committee did not dispute that this supposedly "impartial" position coincided with that of the imperial High Command of the Armed Forces. Instead, they defended the latter's violations of international law against their own socialist comrades from abroad. Even in the penultimate year of the war, SPD secretary Philipp Scheidemann rejected a proposal from Belgian labor leaders to appoint an international socialist commission to investigate German war atrocities in Belgium.[60]

With the increasing absorption of the so-called homefront in the war effort, the need grew to forensically document the serious effects of this on impacted civilian populations. Several countries appointed state commissions charged with investigating and documenting war crimes. Early in the war, these were mostly concerned with the conduct of the German troops who massacred civilians after illegally infringing on the borders of Belgium and Luxembourg only to discover that native resistance was unexpectedly broad. First the Belgian and then the French ministries of justice had already called forth such commissions in August 1914.[61] Their mission was to record eye-witness accounts of acts taken during the destruction of Belgian and French towns. The British government, which justified its entry into the war as a response to the German invasion of Belgium, appointed its own ministerial investigation in the fall of 1914.[62] Generally, these commissions were managed by senior civil servants and judges but with the participation of renowned historians and legal scholars. A few reports were completed and published, while others were made available to the public in excerpts.

To inform the international public of German violations of international law, the so-called Bryce Commission published a report of more than 350 pages in May 1915, a few days after the sinking of the British passenger ship *Lusitania*. To maximize its circulation, the report was sold for the symbolic price of one penny. The Bryce Commission conducted witness interviews in investigating incidents at thirty-eight Belgian sites and included estimates of civilian deaths.[63] Although it did not pass without methodological dispute, the Bryce *Report of the Committee on Alleged German Outrages* contributed to weakening the initial attitudes of rejection among liberals who had opposed British war entry.[64] Major attention was also drawn to publications by the English constitutional law scholar John Hartman Morgan and Joseph Bédier, a literature professor at the Collège de France who built on Morgan's work. The French war ministry allowed Morgan and Bédier access to the captured diaries of German officers. Bédier put particular emphasis on maintaining standards of source criticism in his brochure *Les Crimes Allemands d'après des*

Témoignages Allemands. To assure objectivity, he consciously avoided describing German atrocities through the statements of French, Belgian, or British soldiers, since he was unable to verify these. Morgan's and Bédier's source editions gave much impulse to the international debate over how to respond to German war crimes. After the German capitulation, these created a basis for raising accusations against German military leaders—for example, against Lieutenant-General Karl Stenger, who would play an outstanding role in the Weimar-era national trials of war crime defendants at Leipzig.[65]

These various commission reports shared a mixture of court-style evidentiary presentation and the use of suggestive language. A preference for horrifying details sometimes came at the cost of historical precision, however, since many witness statements were included in the documentations absent verification. Although the writers, most of whom were respected academics, had to deal with the criticism that their investigative methods and forms of publication went against recognized academic standards, the procedure was largely considered legitimate. James Bryce, a historian educated in part at Heidelberg, a jurist, and pedagogue, saw the German outrages in Belgium as the expression of a reckless militaristic mentality, a characteristic that he was convinced was deeply rooted within the culture of the Prussian military elite in particular and that he considered one of the primary causes of war.[66] Bryce hoped his documentation would appeal to the traditional values of "Englishmen" and help to constitute a global community of outrage. This kind of public relations mission of course might stand in the way of an impartial examination and evaluation of the facts. Many an exponent of this quasi-official form of historical research would become prisoners of their own mission before the war was out. In 1979, the Australian historian Trevor Wilson would describe the dilemmas of the Bryce Commission trenchantly:

> Bryce did not have the choice of telling the truth or telling falsehood. If he proved so scrupulous in his investigations that he might have to deem the tales of sadistic acts unproven, then—inadvertently but inescapably—he would be helping to propagate a much larger untruth: that the whole notion of deliberate and calculated atrocity by Germany upon Belgium was unfounded.[67]

In a certain sense, the reports represented an early form of oral history from the victims' perspective. The fact that the main impulse for the witness interviews came from the hope of eventual trials may have constituted their historical-cultural value but also entailed the methodological problems typical of this genre.

In a category rather different from the commission reports were the official and quasi-official "color books" (e.g., white book, blue book, etc.). Color books had a longer tradition in the history of European diplomacy, but in the course of World War I they developed into one of the most important propaganda instruments in the controversies over the question of "war guilt." Soon after the war started, almost all the European governments published selections of their diplomatic files, seeking to demonstrate their own efforts for peace and refute accusations of war guilt. Characteristic of the color books was that they were created to exploit opportunities and serve clearly defined political purposes. Because of their overwhelmingly instrumental function, criteria like scientific objectivity and correctness fell by the wayside. A selective publication praxis and systematic manipulation of the documents, which could go as far as distortion of meaning in the presentation or out-and-out fabrication, were typical of this genre. Also native to the color books was the trouble taken to reinforce the effect of authenticity in the edition technique, hoping to nip any accusations of falsification in the bud.[68]

Because of its conduct in the 1914 July Crisis and violations of Belgian and Luxembourgish neutrality, Berlin assuredly carried a heavy portion of responsibility for the outbreak and subsequent enlargement of the war. Nevertheless, German civil servants themselves initiated the so-called war guilt debate in the late summer of 1914. At the behest of the imperial leadership, the Reichstag had already been presented with a white book on the war's outbreak on 4 August 1914. The editor was Kurt Riezler, who had served as Chancellor Bethmann-Hollweg's most trusted adviser since 1909 and was a coauthor of the annexationist secret war plan that came to be known as the "September Program." By the end of August, State Secretary Gottlieb von Jagow had assigned his deputy secretary, Alfred Zimmermann, the job of bringing together documents from the Foreign Office archives for an expanded publication. In planning the archival edition, von Jagow's guiding motif was to demonstrate how the "Ring of the Entente" had closed itself ever more tightly around the German Reich.[69] The collection was issued as an official government publication not long after, under the title *Preliminary Memorandum on the Outbreak of War*.[70]

Although all other European war parties worked just as meticulously in creating these exorbitantly designed historical falsifications, German ministerial servants and academics displayed exceptional fervor when it came to protecting their own publications against charges of manipulation and to exposing the enemy's as falsifications. With a very high estimation of their own expertise in the area of philologically schooled source criticism, and seeing as how the color books served the German war effort, editing contemporary files was viewed as a "holy research mission."[71] The first German white book on causes of the war ignited such fiery debate that for the rest of the war its authors would try many measures to extinguish it. Within the war's first weeks, doubts were already raised about the then untouchable right of states to conduct war—the *ius ad bellum*. Soon after came the first demands that those responsible for starting the war should be punished; the German war guilt researchers started busying themselves with efforts to choke off this undesired discussion by every means, but without success.

Parallel to the debate on the causes of the war, a second controversy also broke out at an early stage, concerning the possible punishment of international law violations. This focused at first on the German treaty breach of invading Belgium. Considerable international dismay followed the chancellor's declaration to his parliament that the violation of neutrality was an act of "urgent self-defense." In the follow-up, various factors contributed to intensify the anti-German mood throughout western Europe, keeping German war conduct in the public eye. The unexpectedly massive resistance to the German invasion in western Belgium was met with collective shootings of civilians, taking of hostages, rapes, plunder, and destruction of entire towns. Abhorrence was roused especially by the ravaging of the medieval university city at Louvain (Leuven), where the priceless library was burned to the ground by German troops. Prime Minister Herbert Asquith told the British dailies that this was "the greatest crime against civilization and culture since the Thirty Years' War . . . a shameless holocaust . . . lit up by blind barbarian vengeance."[72]

The German response to accusations of lawbreaking—or more, specifically, of "war crimes"[73]—from Brussels, Paris, and London, as well as from several famous international law scholars, was to commission a new white book in September 1914. This one came from the Prussian War Ministry's office for investigating violations of military law.[74] Its was meant to prove that German war acts overall constituted legal reprisals, rendered necessary by the illegal *franc-tireur* guerilla war waged by Belgian and French civilians.[75] Its arguments harkened back to the German Reich's rationales for harsh measures against the civilian population of Paris after the Franco-Prussian War.[76] The new white book also espoused "war positivism," a doctrine that had already been aggressively represented by the German delegation during the Hague talks.[77] The highly one-sided compilation of witness statements was intended to shore up the barely credible claims of high-ranking German officers, who stated that what they had faced in Belgium was nothing less than an insurgency.[78] The volume failed to deliver the effects hoped for by the foreign and war ministries, however. On the contrary, its thorough omission of grievous attacks on civilians and its portrayal of German soldiers as the real victims were taken abroad as a tangible provocation. It served as unintended proof for the Allied thesis that the German High Command did not feel bound by the 1907 Hague Convention (IV) respecting the Laws and Customs of War on Land.

Spirits were unsettled further in October 1914 when a group of ninety-three German academics, artists, and writers issued an exhortation titled

An die Kulturwelt! (To the civilized world!), which refuted charges of legal violations in drastic terms. Once again, this statement did not deny fundamentally any of the accusations raised by the Allies. Following the same line as the government declarations, it reinterpreted the German military acts as legitimate measures of "urgent self-defense" and claimed just cause. These were a punishment of "treacherous murderers." The proclamation also denied the Western powers any right to speak as "defenders of the European civilization," given their alliance with "Russians and Serbs" and their incitements of "Mongols and Negroes against the white race."[79]

With Hans Wehberg among the very few exceptions—in November 1914, the international law scholar and pacifist resigned from the editorial board of the journal *Zeitschrift für Völkerrecht* in protest of its nationalistic stance[80]—most German national and international legal scholars supported their government's position of war positivism wholeheartedly.[81] Antonius Maria Romen, for example, citing studies by Carl Lueder, Johann Caspar Bluntschli, Philipp Zorn, and Franz von Liszt, wrote a defense of taking local Belgian dignitaries as hostages, terming it an acceptable reprisal. The renowned international law jurist Karl Strupp served the press department of the 18th Army Corps command. Among other duties, he was responsible for censoring writings that criticized the government written by his colleague Wehberg. In a commentary on the Hague land war convention, Strupp admitted there had been isolated cases of violations, but he portrayed German actions in Leuven as measures forced on the High Command by the Entente countries' own legal violations. The German community of international legal scholars also largely agreed with the Reich's fatal February 1915 decision to respond to the British sea blockade—itself questionable under international law—with the tactic of unrestricted submarine warfare.[82]

Violations of international law were far from a German monopoly. All belligerents in World War I committed more or less serious breaches of the Geneva and Hague conventions. In retrospect, the question arises of why the international community focused almost exclusively on the German Reich. Why was it primarily German acts and statements that catalyzed punitive international law initiatives in response? How is it to be explained that the plight of the Germans' victims stirred up solidarity worldwide, while German civilian victims of the British blockade, whose numbers presumably were many times greater, were for a long time lamented only at home?[83]

The sympathy gap is attributable to various causes. One important factor was that the circumstances and character of the best-known incidents were highly unusual by the standards of conduct usually applied within Europe itself. The attacks on Belgium and Luxembourg were only the first in a whole series of blatant international legal violations that seemed almost designed to attract public attention.[84] The first use of poison gas, the bombing of undefended cities from the air, the unlimited U-boat war, the sinking of the *Lusitania*, the judicial murders of the British nurse Edith Cavell and the merchant ship captain Charles Fryatt, the mass executions of Belgian civilians, and the forced deportations of Belgian civilians to labor deployments in Germany led the British writer Austin Harrison, for example, to a conclusion shared by many others: "Ruthlessness is the German war motto." The supposed high culture of Germany was in reality, as Harrison wrote, "the attitude of the bully."[85] The summary conviction and execution of Cavell within a few days' time, based on a dubious "war treason" charge, prompted Dutch Minister of Foreign Affairs John Loudon to remark that this had been no simple "crime" but a great "stupidity."[86] Overall, such incidents were laden with an exceptional potential for rousing public moral outrage. Often innovative and drastic measures of German war conduct at land and sea, coupled with aggressive justifications from the civilian and military leadership, repeatedly offered easy opportunities for enemy propaganda to brand the Wilhelmine Reich as a foreign body within the international community, a danger to "civilized" values.

The Kaiser was also a liability. In both the European and the American public, the German monarch was considered the primary aggressor, a megalomaniacal despot with a contrary relation to international law.[87] A full ten years before the war, he had repeatedly told diplomats from both Belgium and Denmark that he would not feel bound by neutrality agreements in the case of a war.[88] This history bolstered the supposition that Wilhelm II had personally ordered the German war fury on the Western front. It would provide an important point for the push to put him on trial after the war. In reality, recent research has shown that, on war questions, Wilhelm generally relied on his military advisers. At times, he even criticized their more radical proposals: he initially objected to plans for bombing civilian targets in Great Britain and for expanding the U-boat war to unarmed enemy commercial ships. He did so out of tactical or moral reservations, however, and not out of regard for international treaties and agreements.[89]

The academic establishment also behaved in ways that incited accusations against German war conduct. Like Chancellor Bethmann-Hollweg's famous speech to justify the war, texts from the ministries on questions of war guilt and military acts in Belgium were received abroad as unmitigated provocations. The "Manifesto of the Ninety-Three," whose ranks included renowned legal scholars, and the ambivalent attitude of the German international law establishment about the Geneva and Hague conventions all served to stir up powerful doubts among their French, British, and American colleagues about the scholarly integrity of the German discipline. Leading American jurists responded by warning of a complete collapse of the international legal order. In the words of the international law jurist, Nobel Peace Prize laureate, and former Secretary of State Elihu Root, "International laws violated with impunity must soon cease to exist and every state has a direct interest in preventing those violations which if permitted to continue would destroy the law."[90] John Westlake, a major contributor to the land war convention as a cofounder of the Institut de Droit International, accused the German side of putting their military "success" before the law.[91]

In his epoch-spanning 2010 history of modern law of the armed forces, Daniel Segesser argues that the German and Allied legal communities' positions during World War I were incommensurable simply because jurists, like other intellectuals, had willingly allowed themselves to be integrated in the war efforts of their respective countries, accordingly functionalizing their scholarly arguments.[92] While there is a core of truth there, the focus on national perspectives does not do justice to the complexity of the debates among the legal scholars. Certain changes in the development of international law had already begun before the war, and the military conflict served to accelerate and multiply these. In part, this involved an unfolding of ideas that had been devised earlier in connection with violent events on the European periphery. In the case of Bryce, his earlier work on attacks against national and religious minorities in the Balkan wars caused him to intensify his legal position regarding the German atrocities in Belgium.[93]

Hull takes a different approach in her 2014 comparative study of how German, British, and French experts understood the law. Based on her earlier intensive work on a turn-of-the-century military culture that she identifies specifically as German, the US historian also discerns a German exceptionalism in matters of international law, seeing its roots in the Franco-Prussian War. She argues that German theories of military law were incompatible with British and French understandings, above all regarding the question of international law's origins and in the relation between positively framed law and allowable exceptions. Starting around the turn of the century, it became rather self-evident among British and French jurists that international law should be interpreted as an expression of the universalist values of a "civilized" community of nations and as a public (world) conscience. After the Hague conventions, German jurists by contrast began to understand law as proceeding from a personalistically conceived state interest. They operated with terms out of individual national criminal law, such as the "state of urgency" and "self-defense."[94] Although they could have identified with the ideas of Geneva and The Hague, they instead agreed with their military leaders that international military law, before all else, must reflect the dynamics of the international world of states with its supposedly natural clash of interests between "strong" and "weak" powers.[95]

This may have been why the elastic concept of "military necessity" was so popular among German jurists. *Clausula rebus sic stantibus* (the doctrine of exemption from prior agreements due to changed circumstances) came in reaction to the German Empire's objectively real yet inconfessable weakness. By the end of 1914, it had become clear that the rapid military victory envisioned by the German High Command before the war had failed to materialize. Originally conceived in 1905 by Count Alfred von Schlieffen, the plan to crush the French army in short, decisive strikes proved unrealistic. Germany also failed to win support in neutral countries (other than in Sweden) for its declared ambition to be recognized as the new international keeper of the peace. The German legal community's response was to coalesce almost fully (with very few exceptions) around the argument of "war positivism." This put the jurists on an increasingly slippery slope. A series of international law violations—the first use of poison gas with intent to kill, the illegal keeping of prisoners of war within the exclusion zone of thirty kilometers from the front—were variably defended as appropriate reactions to a supposed "state of emergency," as tactical gambits in a fluid war situation, or as logical consequences of technological superiority in armaments.

Critics like Moyn and the US military historian John Koogan have reproached Hull for a comparative approach that, in effect, accepts the dichotomies of the Versailles system and its outdated "guilt" discourse. They consider it ahistorical to attribute a one-sided and conscious breach of international law to the Germans at a time when the Geneva and Hague legal orders were still in an altogether fluid state.[96] This argument fails to recognize that Hull is concerned not with reviving the war guilt debate but with revealing the contradictions and blind spots in the interpretations and applications of international law circulating at the time. Although all participants in World War I transgressed against positive law and customary law in more or less serious ways, German discourses and practices were distinct from those of the British and French insofar as even the most blatant violations of the Geneva and Hague rules were not only aggressively defended but also hypostasized into the basics of a "new international law" under German aegis.[97] The high visibility of the war crimes emanating from Germany coupled with a theoretical discourse that—in defense against a simultaneously formed transnational critique with a strong moral tinge—explicitly declared these crimes as preemptive defense acts by a German state surrounded by enemies are qualities that indeed rendered the German case an exception within the common shelter of the international law of war and made it into a threat to its foundational ideas.

Debating the Responsibility Clauses of the Peace Treaty

In the first years of the war, demands that German politicians and military commanders be subject to punishment were discussed above all in the international daily press. In the world of legal experts, they arose only occasionally and with relative restraint.[98] At times, the discussion even fell silent as the war dragged on and a victory over the German Reich seemed ever more remote.[99] Demands for war crimes trials always reverberated most strongly in Great Britain. The UK Foreign and Commonwealth Office was the most active in repeatedly suggesting war crimes trials as a possible sanction for the mistreatment of Allied prisoners of war. This was usually met with rejection from the British War Office and Army Council, however.[100] The UK Foreign Office made much ministerial hay in the spring of 1918 out of the news that the German Reich leadership had temporarily planned to topple the king of Romania and put members of his army before military tribunals.[101] After that, as calls for a criminal reckoning with the Germans gained traction with the American public, the British took the lead in pressing the idea during the war's final phase. In January 1918, still many months before Germany's definitive defeat, Asquith's successor, David Lloyd George, again called for trials in a speech before the New York Bar Association, rousing the disapproval of the American president. In October 1918, the French government reiterated its interest in financial reparations and criminal proceedings. After the Armistice of 11 November, the British cabinet unanimously backed the prime minister's proposal of 28 November to put Wilhelm II before an international court on charges of leading a war of aggression and commission of various war crimes.

Although no one in the British cabinet harbored sympathies for the German monarch, there was some skepticism among them about the plan. One concern was that the legal basis for a trial was weak. There was also fear of "creat[ing] a Hohenzollern legend like the Napoleonic legend."[102] Many of the diplomats were worried that demands for punishment would overburden the coming peace negotiations. In the end, however, an ambitious trial program was backed by the Conservative partners in Lloyd George's coalition and, as proved to be decisive, by the media czar Albert C. Harmsworth (Lord Northcliffe), publisher of the *Times* and the *Daily Mail*, along with leading opinion makers like the writers Arthur Conan Doyle, Frederic Harrison, Lord Middleton, and Baron Wrenbury. It seemed that hardly any of the politicians in charge had considered the sensitive matter of whether the German state would be ready to extradite its own citizens or whether the Dutch were willing to surrender Wilhelm II after his flight to Holland.[103] This lent a measure of irreality as Lloyd George led his coalition to victory in the "khaki" elections of December 1918 on the slogan "Hang the Kaiser."[104]

In January 1919, as Allied politicians began to work out terms for the first preliminary peace talks, it became clear that the issue of war crimes trials would cause serious disagreement between the Europeans and the Americans. Even as Lloyd George advocated that an advisory committee of legal experts be appointed to stipulate the statutes governing an international court, Woodrow Wilson sought out nonjudicial solutions, at the very least for the case of the emperor. It remained unclear what concrete measures against Wilhelm II he would be willing to back, but it was apparent that he considered the debate on war responsibility misguided.[105] Wilson rejected on principle the idea of a tribunal against the Kaiser as imagined by Lloyd George and by French Prime Minister Georges Clemenceau. The US president feared that the Germans would interpret an undertaking of this kind, if falsely managed, as a one-sided demonstration of power, as a revenge measure. It would place his own ambitious project of a multilateral peace order on the wrong track from the start. At the same time, Wilson also shared worries that general impunity might give further sustenance to the militarist currents in Germany. But this was trumped by his concern that a politics aimed at retribution and revenge would drive the majority of Germans into the waiting arms of the Bolsheviks.

In the time that followed, Wilson warned repeatedly against making a martyr of Wilhelm II. Fully in the vein of the evolutionary approach advocated by the old cosmopolitan international law scholars, he attempted to persuade the other leaders that the democratization of Germany and the creation of the League of Nations as an alliance for international order and of effective arbitration mechanisms would provide solid preconditions for the further development of international law.[106] The British prime minister was not impressed with these arguments. Almost prophetically, he argued to Wilson that the main issue was not revenge for past injustices but the credibility of the new order to be built. Guaranteeing that required robust means and mechanisms, he wrote: "If the League of Nations is to have some chance of success, it must not appear as just a word on a scrap of paper. It must have the power from this moment to punish crimes against international law. The violation of treaties is precisely the sort of crime to be of direct concern to the League of Nations."[107]

It was because of these irreconcilable differences that the consultations on an inter-Allied prosecution program came to an unsatisfying compromise. At the initiative of George and Clemenceau, planning for the peace conference in Paris was given over to a "Commission des responsabilités des auteurs de la guerre et sanctions" (here referred to as the "first commission," created on 18 January 1919 and responsible for investigating war guilt and war crimes) and a "Commission des réparations de dommages" (the "second commission," created on 25 January 1919 and charged with determining reparations for damages). The two commissions were populated with international legal experts.[108]

The first commission was organized in three subcommittees. After several months of often-heated discussions, they presented a series of recommendations for civil and criminal court proceedings against the German Reich. These would partly provide the basis for the punitive clauses of the Treaty of Versailles (Articles 227–230) and the clause on German responsibility for initiating the war (Article 231). On the thorniest question of all, that of German war guilt, the first subcommittee used the published German color books to arrive at a conclusion that was historically questionable because it rested entirely on situational factors. It determined that the Wilhelmine empire had rejected all mediation efforts by the Entente in July 1914 precisely because it had sought a pretext for military confrontation. Because they had oriented their actions so as to make war unavoidable, Germany and Austria-Hungary had started the war: "La guerre a été préméditée par les Puissances centrales." (The war was premeditated by the Central Powers.)

In their later defense against the punitive clauses of the Treaty of Versailles and its supposed attribution of exclusive German guilt for the war, German foreign policy officials and international law jurists asserted that Article 231 had wholly adopted the findings of the first subcommittee. This was not the case, however. Although the wording of the treaty's infamous "war guilt paragraph" indeed creates the impression of criminal accountability, it relates solely to procedures for reparations.[109] As Walter Schwengler determined in his analysis of the complicated process of coordinating a common Allied position, the phrasing of Article 231 reflected a compromise induced by the Americans and designed to bridge the US-European divide on the liability question. The Allies agreed on a vague formulation that attributed the losses and damages suffered by the Allies and associated governments to the "aggression of Germany and its Allies." In Schwengler's words, only "a short mental step sufficed to go from the original idea that Germany was responsible for war damages to its moral condemnation as the aggressor."[110] Article 231 thus linked the "war guilt" question to reparations.

The first commission's second subcommittee, meanwhile, following a proposal by the French legal scholars Ferdinand Larnaude and Albert de Lapradelle, investigated whether the German leadership had made itself guilty of an international crime by invading Belgium. After thorough consideration, this subcommittee found that unleashing a war of aggression was an outrage to the "conscience" of the world (*conscience publique*) and would be condemned by history. Existing international law did not foresee culpability for aggressive war, however, so a prosecution of state organs or individuals was impossible. Conceding to the view that neutrality violations should constitute especially serious breaches of international law, however, the subcommittee recommended that provisions be established for the future punishment of aggressive war, and proposed that a body be created for the prosecution of such crimes. The Allies responded to these recommendations with Article 227 of the peace treaty, which announced the appointment of an international body to determine whether the Kaiser was responsible for neutrality violations. Given the lack of culpability under international law, however, this body was supposed to deliver a political and moral answer to the question, not a judicial verdict.[111]

The third subcommittee, finally, issued an extensive catalog of penal provisions concerning the law of war, meant to serve as the basis of future war crimes trials.[112] US Secretary of State Robert Lansing, who chaired the commission, and his colleague James Brown Scott sought until the end to move the Europeans away from the question of an *haut tribunal* (high tribunal). Hoping to avoid any form of tribunal against the deposed German monarch, their minority opinion proposed an international commission of historians and archivists who would explore the questions of "guilt for the war" and "guilt in war" using German archival documents. The Americans imagined that the report could be concluded and published by the end of 1919 so as to provide the international public with a thorough basis for judgment.[113]

Given this very tight timeframe, we may question the motivations behind Lansing's proposal. Was the whole thing meant as a maneuver to distract and delay, or was it in fact intended to continue dealing with the problem of international law violations *after* the peace treaty had been signed? On the one hand, it can be confirmed that Wilson wanted to avoid any appearance of a courtlike procedure against the Kaiser and gave directions to that effect to the US delegation in Paris. There are indications that the US secretary of state shared Wilson's view that punitive measures would be harmful to building a stable peaceful order in the long term. The decisive factor in Lansing's negotiating line, however, was surely that he considered the humanitarian aims of modern international military law misguided in the first place. Some years earlier, Lansing had confessed his fundamental opposition to war crimes trials to the columnist Walter Lippmann. In a private memorandum written a few weeks after the sinking of the *Lusitania*, Lansing wrote accordingly, "The practical standard of conduct [in the war] is not moral or humane ideas but the necessity of the act in protecting national existence or in bringing the war to successful conclusion."[114]

In the estimate of one leading American official, the secretary of state's legal opinion was that practically any atrocity was acceptable as long as it served the interests of national security.[115] Even as Lansing assumed the pose of an uncompromising positivist at Paris and in later inter-Allied meetings, he concealed the reality of a stalwart realist and power politician who refused to allow Europeans to criminalize wars by creating the international precedent of trials against the carriers of German sovereignty.[116] In contrast to Wilson's hopes that international law could be consensual rather than confrontational, or Wilson's belief that the Europeans' punitive policy plans were excessive, Lansing simply rejected any international agreement that would limit sovereignty.[117] In the final analysis, however, none of the victorious powers taking part in the negotiations saw their own ideas prevail. The result was a watered-down compromise that could be interpreted freely as either, victors' justice or a legal farce. The punitive clauses of the Treaty of Versailles lent only highly conditional support to the cause of international law, although several important advances were made.[118]

From the beginning, the inter-Allied discussions were followed closely in Germany. Long before the victorious powers agreed on demands for reparations, German diplomats feared that threats to the Reich could arise from the compensation clauses of the Hague Conventions. As we saw earlier, Article 3 of the Hague land war convention had been inserted because of strong pressure from the German delegation at the time. It foresaw that states would pay for the damages and losses that they themselves had caused. Legal experts at the German foreign ministry were aware of this material connection between the war guilt question and the resulting legal consequences, and sought to react with preventive countermeasures.[119] With the imperial system on the brink of collapse on 7 November 1918, Wilhelm Solf, a state secretary in the foreign ministry under the government of Prince Maximilian von Baden (the last imperial chancellor), directed his agency's intelligence division to gather material to help refute the anticipated Allied accusations. Solf wrote:

> In the imminent peace negotiations, the question of war guilt and the atrocity question will play a special role; we will be forced not only to defend ourselves, but to meet the adversary's attacks with counterattacks. I therefore request that all apposite material . . . be made ready . . . (This may also include material on the lying propaganda of the Entente and its methods.)[120]

Solf's in-house order marks the moment of birth for the field of "war innocence research," as Klaus Grosse Kracht ironically termed it. Under the aegis of the German bureaucracy, this was to be cultivated into a kind of post-1919 "syndrome," or at least into a "serious historical neurosis" that would plague the political culture of the Weimar Republic to the bitter end.[121] Also in November 1918, the first German government after the Armistice and revolution decreed that "Department M" of the AA's intelligence division should create a "commission on violations of international law and war customs by members of the Entente armies." This was called the "War Guilt Department," or "Special Office von Bülow" after its first director, State Secretary Bernhard Wilhelm von Bülow. It was expected to gather incriminating material against the Entente, as well as "material exonerating the German army members accused of the same crimes by the Entente."[122] Before it was even known what reparations the victorious powers would demand from the

German Reich, or what charges might be used to justify reparations, the first German civilian postwar government sought to intercept the anticipated war guilt accusation with an organized counter-campaign that, in its substance, would employ the well-known international legal principle of *tu quoque* (you, too).[123]

A similar aim lay behind a note addressed by the new German government to the main victor powers on 28 November 1918. This clever piece of diplomacy adopted the proposal of the American delegation at Paris: to appoint a neutral commission that would investigate war guilt. The note further called on all former belligerents to declare they were prepared to open their archives and allow interrogations of decision makers. The Germans thus hoped to keep the war guilt question out of the peace conference altogether and to counter impressions that the German Reich bore some kind of particular responsibility for the war's outbreak. But the Allies rejected the initiative, much as they had the former imperial leadership's October 1918 proposal for an independent commission to investigate international law violations by all parties in the war.[124]

Contemporary historians long ago concluded that early Weimar governments were not really forced to pursue such an inflexible course. For a very long time, however, West German historians of the Cold War era generally believed that the post-World War I governmental politics of the past enjoyed substantial and unconditional support among the German people. In the meantime, this has been largely refuted.[125] In fact, during the early post-World War I years with their many upheavals, a variety of political spheres saw highly self-critical discussions about the pre-1914 era and the war itself. A kind of flourish was delivered in the 1918 Bavarian Documents (*Bayerischen Dokumente*) inspired by the pacifist Wilhelm Foerster and published by Kurt Eisner, a leader of the postwar Independent Social Democratic Party of Germany (USPD). Eisner served as the first premier of the Free State of Bavaria, from November 1918 until his murder in February 1919. Foerster was one of the very few among the ninety-three signatories of *An die Kulturwelt!* who later distanced himself from its nationalist message. Around the end of the war, he came into secret contact with an agent of the US Department of State. He hoped it might be possible to soften the harsh armistice conditions with "steps toward a full and open admission of the guilt and misdeeds of the German government at the beginning of the war, and the atrocities of its war conduct."[126] For his part, Eisner was deeply convinced of the Wilhelmine government's responsibility for the outbreak of the war and sought to force the firing of compromised officials like Wilhelm Solf and Matthias Erzberger.

As the provisional-era premier of Bavaria, Eisner had access to confidential reports from July and August 1914 originally filed by Bavarian state delegates to the central government in Berlin. On 23 November 1918, Eisner began to publish excerpts from these.[127] In design, these releases were similar to the instant history produced by the imperial government agencies during the war. As with the color books, Eisner's was a decontextualized form of historical presentation. In the style of court exhibits, the selections chosen for the *Bayerischen Dokumente* cast the worst possible light on the Wilhelmine government, especially on the conduct of Chancellor Bethmann-Hollweg during the July Crisis.[128]

Eisner and Foerster's initiative was not the only effort to expose the war's history. Even before the Kaiser's flight to Holland, in mid-October 1918, the Bavarian Social Democrats demanded the appointment of a state court that would investigate responsibility for the failure of "earlier peace actions."[129] While this model was based on the concept of state courts as defined in the unusual constitutions of the southern German states, the newly self-declared "Central Council" of the mutinous Imperial German Navy apparently imagined it as a revolutionary tribunal. On 9 November, even as the imperial government was collapsing and the German revolution had begun, the Naval High Council demanded a "people's court for the investigation and conviction of the persons responsible for the war." In the revolutionary council's imagining, this court would pursue criminal trials of exponents of the imperial system for having circumvented efforts to prevent the war. There were also proposals to indict those responsible for wartime "terror verdicts" by military and special war courts.[130] By mid-December 1918, a column in *Die Rote Fahne*, the organ of the Communist Spartacus League, demanded that the ongoing revolution be secured through a special tribunal, "before which the main perpetrators of the war and its expansion shall be condemned." It named the prospective defendants as "the two Hohenzollerns, Ludendorff, Hindenburg, Tirpitz, and their co-perpetrators, as well as all counterrevolutionary conspirators."[131]

The Communist Party of Germany (KPD), founded at the turn of the year from 1918 to 1919, included the idea of a tribunal in its party program. As Ulrich Heinemann correctly commented in 1983, however, the KPD's proposal suffered from contradictions that were unlikely to be overcome. In the party's simple Marxist conception, the Wilhelmine government and the functionaries of state, justice, and military had led Germany into war but in doing so merely executed the interests of the imperialist bourgeoisie. There seemed to be little sense in having them condemned by a revolutionary people's court. Most German socialists also saw little promise from advances in international law. Along with pacifism, it was considered a typically bourgeois maneuver of distraction, aimed at maintaining class power. Given this backdrop, we may plausibly suppose that the KPD was less interested in uncovering culprits than in raising its own profile. First, these proposals differentiated them from the Majority Social Democratic Party of Germany (MSPD), which led the newly-formed revolutionary government in Berlin. In fact, the MSPD leaders, Friedrich Ebert and Philipp Scheidemann, were among those mentioned as potential defendants because of their own conduct during the war. Second, the hope was to boost the party's reputation internationally. The morally battered German workers' movement could again become a vanguard in the "exposure of those responsible for the war of world capitalism and its main apologists, Clemenceau, Lloyd George, and Poincaré."[132] Finally, it had already become apparent during the war that even leftist German politicians found it hard to classify the brutal conduct of the German army against unarmed civilians as a breach of international law.[133] This surely also influenced the KPD's attitude on the question of punishment.

But the ideas of the left were not the determining factors for how Germany would respond to the responsibility clauses of the Treaty of Versailles. The Council of People's Deputies, the executive body of the revolutionary government in Berlin from November 1918 to February 1919, ceded the preparations for peace negotiations almost entirely to the old imperial ministries. In other words, the task was monopolized by civil servants who had survived the transition from the old foreign ministry.[134] Their interest was to banish discussion about possible German international law violations altogether from the realms of parties, parliaments, and publics. The early years of the Weimar Republic would see the formation of a confusing fabric of official, half-official, and private organizations that sought to instrumentalize the issue for their own academic, professional, propagandistic, journalistic, and political causes. Not unlike modern think tanks, a whole series of new institutions arose during the political upheavals. Operating outside the universities and traditional academic research institutes, they devoted years of intensive work to knowledge production, political consultancy, science policy, and academic lobby work.

Until now, the historical literature has referred to this conspicuous sector within the Weimar-era academic landscape mainly by the term already in use at the time, as "war guilt research."[135] For various reasons, it seems advisable here to resort to the broader terms of "juridical history writing" or "history management." [136] As Horne and Kramer have already shown in their major study on the *franc-tireur* topos, the "war guilt research" was not at all limited to rebutting war guilt charges, but aimed at a general exoneration from all accusations against Germany, including those of crimes against civilians and prisoners of war. "History management" furthermore describes the academic politics and sociological dimensions of the field, which the literature until now has largely ignored. Several profound consequences for German academic culture arose from the circumstance so that in 1918 and 1919, for the first time, the country was forced, from without, to confront the conceptual categories and moral concepts of modern humanitarian law. Historians of the Weimar era nowadays recognize that this would lead to devastating political effects, even if we also allow the long-standing acknowledgment that the Weimar-era scholars of "history management" often displayed prodigious innovation and productivity.[137] It is furthermore undisputed that the discipline of international law, barely developed in Germany until that time, received an immense and epistemic impulse through the events of 1918–1919.[138]

In detail, this development meant that the German debates on "Versailles" created a wealth of new networks, social spaces, and fields. Historians, theologians, sociologists, and legal scholars exchanged views on the problem of overcoming the consequences of the war with politicians, ministerial bureaucrats, and high-ranking justice functionaries.[139] These discourses involved classical academic institutions like scientific societies, associations, research institutes, and newspapers, but also included new state-appointed expert commissions, investigative committees, and even court procedures. The structures and actors of these new organizations therefore merit a closer look.

Transcending epochs, a form of étatism has always been characteristic of the German academic landscape. This follows in the long tradition of state support for the sciences under both the Kingdom of Prussia and the post-1871 unified German Reich. Without a doubt, a common feature shared among the new organizations founded after World War I was that they remained close to the state. Of course, the political and military collapse of the old order was a central factor in the emergence of most of these organizations. Yet this meant, decisively, that these groups were able to form close relationships with the new state institutions at an early stage, regardless of their relatively broad range of political affinities. The traditional fixation on the state acquired several new sets of meanings under the specific conditions of an early Weimar Republic marked by defeat in war, by a peace treaty perceived as a humiliation, and by the resulting revisionist aspirations. First, the crisis-driven shock to the traditional étatist system involved humanities scholars in new areas of research and new issues and methods. This was often motivated by a desire to provide justifications and defenses against the outside world.[140] Some of the best-known examples of this are to be found in the 1920s booms in the fields of "Geopolitics" and "Ethnic History."[141] Second, the new research fields were strongly oriented to meeting growing demands for official research and political consultancy. Starting in the early 1920s, a great many German academics took part in researching the causes and the course of military events in World War I under the catchphrases of "nonpartisanship" and "truth research."

Again, the spectrum of the so-called war guilt research went far beyond the narrow bounds implied by the name. It covered issues of politics, military history, and legal history. During the entire interwar period, it remained a domain of the Reich foreign and interior ministries, as well as the Reichswehr (defense) ministry, which was established in October 1919 out of the merger of the Prussian War Ministry with the Imperial Naval Office. Their relations with the ministries had wide-ranging effects on the self-understanding and research interests of the participating academics. As an important early factor, most of their new institutions had been founded under great time pressure and without clear political guidelines. This generated a degree of separation between the new institutions and the traditional disciplines. It also encouraged a kind of aimlessness regarding program and academic ethics. An exemplary case is that of the Reichsarchiv, essentially an academic think tank absorbed into the Ministry of the Interior. Intended as a historical and national archival research institute—a "novel, institutional hybrid"—the Reichsarchiv was created almost overnight by ministerial decree, without prior consultation with the ministry's own advisory committee of established archivists and professional historians.[142]

Just as influential were the webs of personal connections forged under the pressures of upheaval with associated loss of perspective. The historical literature has often noted that old and new elites, conservatives, liberals, and Majority Social Democrats all shared a consensus in refuting the imputed Allied claims that Germany bore "sole guilt" for the war and in effecting revisions to the Treaty of Versailles. Despite this basic unanimity, the personal level was rife with habitual contradictions, differences in mentality, and more or less deep-seated tensions in worldview and ideology. This was tangible in relations between the academics, whose ranks were filled overwhelmingly from the national Protestant upper classes, and the Social Democrats in government. Although most MSPD politicians had stuck to the policy of "interparty peace" in wartime and avowed their patriotism during the war, they were always suspected of lacking national feeling and an inclination to pacifism or, at any rate, dilettantism in matters of power politics and foreign policy. The old elitist-étatist self-conceptions and the resulting mistrust of the new political elites showed themselves especially in attitudes toward Jewish German parliamentarians. Max Weber, who had accompanied the German peace delegation to Versailles in the spring of 1919 as a member of the Heidelberg Association (see the last section of this chapter), wrote in a later memorandum that politicians of Jewish heritage should not be allowed to question military leaders' testimonies to the Reichstag, as he suspected them of antimilitarist resentments.[143]

Animosities and tensions were also rife within the new organizations. The new interior minister, Erich Koch, appointed the liberal Berlin historian

Hans Delbrück to chair the Reicharchiv's newly established historical commission. Open grumbling about this broke out among the Reichsarchiv personnel, most of whom had worked as civil servants under now-demoted officers of the military's General Staff. Koch was a member of the liberal German Democratic Party (DDP), the junior coalition partner in the government of the MSPD.[144] Delbrück was considered a critic of the wartime High Command's policy of "peace through victory." He had drawn attention to himself as a candidate for the job in November 1918, when he, Friedrich Naumann, and Carl Legien wrote a call demanding that the revolutionary provisional government appoint a nonpartisan commission to investigate accusations of German atrocities during the war.[145] A few months later, Delbrück changed his mind. Writing as the editor of the highly prestigious annual journal *Preussische Jahrbücher*, he accused the foreign ministry of showing too much reluctance to release documents that would help refute the "war guilt lie."[146] In May 1919, he appeared along with Max Weber, Max Graf von Montgelas and Albrecht Mendelssohn Bartholdy as a signatory to "Professors' Memorandum," which the AA used in the hope of influencing the Allies during the Versailles talks (the story of which is covered in the last section of this chapter). While Delbrück had made a name for himself before the war mainly through his studies of Bismarck, he would advance his career throughout the 1920s as a leading figure of the semiofficial war guilt research.[147]

These early divisions between established academics, up-and-comers, and "lateral entrants" from other fields cannot be underestimated as factors shaping the development of these networks, for all the rhetorical avowals of common goals. Although the established and recognized professors primarily set the tone for public debates and international conferences, the practical research and edition work fell mainly to the newcomers and the busy autodidacts. In the early 1920s, it was symptomatic when Foreign Minister Walter Simon, an independent, was unable to convince his favored candidate, the ambitious historian Peter Rassow, to take the job of director at the new Central Office for the Study of War Causes. This organization was entirely financed by the AA yet presented to the world as an independent front.[148] Established professionals were not generally attracted by the prospect of serving years under ministerial aegis, where they would be forced to pursue predefined research missions.

Recruitment problems were also encountered in the making of the documentary edition *Die Große Politik der Europäischen Kabinette* (The great politics of the European cabinets). This was commissioned by the conservative bureaucracy in the wake of a controversial documentary release by Karl Kautsky, a USPD politician who had served as an AA undersecretary. The project was able to attract Albrecht Mendelssohn Bartholdy, the legal scholar teaching in Hamburg, to serve as one of the authors, lending credibility on international law issues. In the absence of other willing alternatives, two coauthors were found in the Orientalist Johannes Lepsius and the librarian Friedrich Thimme. They proceeded to fight each other over the quality standards required by such a historically and politically weighty edition. Since all three authors fundamentally agreed that the publication would be vitally important in advancing the German argument against war guilt, they were willing to tolerate politically motivated interventions from the ministry's War Guilt Department as an unpleasant but in the end necessary evil.[149] It is important, therefore, to stress that scientific qualifications, academic rank, and status within the scientific community had little to do in determining which individuals fit best, or to what extent, within a government-run system of historical engineering, or how far they were willing to accept regimes of censorship and self-censorship.[150] Mendelssohn Bartholdy, who can be counted among the founders of Weimar-era international law studies, would profit enormously from his contractual engagements with the AA. Thanks to payments from the War Guilt Department for his work on *Die Große Politik der Europäischen Kabinette* and other projects, he was able to return to Hamburg and start his own institute, finance a journal, and put out a four-volume short edition of *Europäischen Kabinette*.[151]

The Heidelberg Association and Max Weber's "War Guilt" Intervention

With but a few exceptions, the leadership of the governing MSPD in the early months of 1919 regarded the continuing demands for historical investigation of prewar and wartime events with a peculiar indifference, one that extended to foreign policy dimensions. Despite the MSPD's overwhelming victory in the 19 January 1919 elections to the first National Assembly, it delegated the history issue to its junior coalition partner, the DDP. On the operative level, however, the job was actually left almost entirely to the archconservative civil servants at the old Reich foreign ministry. It was true enough that the prospect of putting incriminated representatives of the old regime before a state court to face possible fines, loss of office, or loss of their right to vote held appeal for the MSPD party base, given its domestic political orientation. But the MSPD conspicuously avoided more thoroughgoing reforms, major purges of the old civil service, or public discussions of the imperial elites' share in war guilt. As an explanation for this reluctance, some historians have argued that the party could not have been interested either in embarrassing its bourgeois coalition partner or in discrediting the traditional forces of order. Furthermore, the party leadership was supposedly thinking nationally. They did not want to retrospectively cast a poor light on their own policy of "interparty unity" during the war.[152] Other researchers go further, however, stressing that the postwar MSPD remained trapped in the same cost-benefit thinking that had made it possible for the Social Democrats to vote for the war budget of August 1914 in the first place—the very same fateful circumstance that led to the eventual split of the original SPD into a "Majority" and an "Independent" party, also giving rise to the KPD by 1919. The same story was being repeated after the war. In keeping with the party's history, the MSPD was once again displaying a tactically justified deference to the old forces of order.[153]

The most decisive factor in what Heinrich August Winkler has called the "overcontinuity" of the German revolution, however, was that a large part of the MSPD leadership simply could not fathom why both the Allies and even members of their own party considered the German conduct of the war to have constituted a violation of international law. Given that the party's right wing still adhered to the imperial thesis that a "war of encirclement" had been waged against the German Reich, and given that they continued to deny most of their country's war crimes, the Versailles responsibility clauses must have indeed seemed to them like the Allies' "manifestation of an unbroken hostility continuing from the war."[154] Thus, the MSPD gave little priority to the political aim of achieving either a social or a moral break with the old regime.

Returning to the weeks immediately after the revolution of early November 1918, the provisional government, the Council of People's Deputies—which was initially shared equally between the MSPD and the USPD—had also done its best to delay discussions about how to deal with the war's consequences until after the January 1919 elections of a National Assembly. But well before 1918 was out, several events raised the matter of what to do with the fallen monarchy's government archives, starting with the Bavarian premier Kurt Eisner's publication of reports written during the July 1914 crisis. The AA claimed that this publication entailed "devastating consequences" in that it compromised diplomatic secrets. Matthias Erzberger, a politician with the German Centre Party and chair of the provisional government's armistice delegation, warned of adverse effects on the coming peace talks. In reality, the MSPD had every reason to be grateful for the nudge from the USPD politician Eisner.[155] The response to Eisner's move in both the bourgeois and the leftist press abroad was positive. The MSPD met with an astonishingly gentle reception at the 1919 International Socialist Conference, held in Berne, Switzerland, mainly because of a misconception among the majority of the non-German delegates, who mistakenly believed the MSPD leadership shared the same self-critical positions on the war guilt question as did Eisner and his fellow USPD comrade Karl Kautsky.[156]

Within days after Eisner began publishing the Bavarian papers on 28 November 1918, the Council of People's Deputies appointed Kautsky, along with Max Quarck of the MSPD, to review the government's files on the 1914 July Crisis, and to prepare these for publication.[157] If Berlin itself would open the archives, it could possibly improve its position in the peace talks. This would also push back against the radical left's proposals for a popular tribunal. Quarck, an official in the Reich Ministry of the Interior, soon left his job and the project behind. Kautsky continued the work on curating the documents for a published edition.

Kautsky's mission took aim at the sore point of German "war guilt." We may safely presume he was aware of the explosive potential. The Council of People's Deputies had assigned him the task explicitly—unlike with Eisner—of first acquiring an overview of the existing stores of files. As soon as the material had been viewed in full, it was to be brought before the Berlin cabinet for a decision on publication. Although this timeframe did not allow for a proper scholarly edition, it was the political leadership's first attempt to act on the pressing question of German war guilt and regain some leeway for action.

Everyone seemed to have forgotten, however, that the old ministerial bureaucrats regarded the issue as their own, exclusive domain. They had already begun to take action. Recall that even before the Armistice of 11 November, Wilhelm Solf, a career civil servant on colonial matters, had ordered his staff to compile a color book that would prove the true guilt for the war lay with the Entente Powers, and that war crimes had been committed by Germany's enemies. It need hardly be added that there was little or no enthusiasm at the AA for Kautsky's project of a documentary edition with the opposite aim: of revealing the German government's actions during the 1914 July Crisis. Solf resigned from the AA in December 1918, but the work continued. Solf's order of 7 November 1918 had also created the War Guilt Department (aka Special Office von Bülow) to coordinate "war guilt" defense. Given the advanced Allied investigations on German rights violations in the war, it was doubtful that yet another German color book would have had any effects on the public.

Before the Paris talks began in January 1919, German academics and intellectuals generally held back from public expressions concerning war crimes or the causes of the war.[158] There were two notable exceptions. The first was the aforementioned call for an archival investigation published in *Berliner Tageblatt* by Hans Delbrück, Carl Legien, and Friedrich Naumann. The second was a protest petition to the regional government of Baden, signed by seventy-eight Heidelberg secondary schoolteachers, opposing the opening of German government files.[159] In February, a second, far more exclusive group statement would announce the founding of a "Heidelberg Association,"[160] the goals and function of which will be addressed below.

On January 17, one day before the Paris Peace Conference convened and two days before the National Assembly elections, a leading "Heidelberger" spoke out on his own. This was none other than Max Weber. The world-famous economist, jurist, and sociologist took on the imminent peace talks in a column published in *Frankfurter Zeitung*, which he had favored as his platform for publicity during the final years of the war.[161] Weber blasted the unauthorized publication of the Bavarian papers by Eisner, unconditionally laid the blame for it with the provisional government in Berlin, and declared his own, distinctive position on German war guilt.

That German domestic politics was dealing at all with a question as absurd as "war guilt," Weber wrote, was to be blamed above all on the circumstance that "literati" now ruled the land. "Weak natures, not capable of looking reality in the face," were seeking to win the world's ear and "gratify their souls, ecstatic by birth, by rummaging through the feeling of a 'war guilt.'" Because they did not want to acknowledge that this war, like any other, had been decided by military power alone, they perceived the defeat as a "Judgment Day court" and thus some kind of "guilt" in whatever form must be construed. Victory in war, however, says nothing about which party has "the law" on its side. In this latest war, as with all other wars, the words of Friedrich the Great applied: "the God of Battles" sides with the larger battalions. Now this dilettantish regime had come along, Weber continued, looking to awaken the impression that there was any agreement between itself and some kind of "silent Germany." Thus, the time had come to call out to the world and declare: "It is not true. This literary folk is not Germany. Their conduct does not correspond to the true inner position of the Germans regarding their fate in war."[162]

Weber also rejected the plans for Kautsky's publication on the July 1914 crisis, which was still in preparation. Of this, he wrote that certain forces were seeking to solve the question of guilt for the past, especially for wars, by publishing files—a one-sided publication at that—on the direct pretexts of the war's outbreak. But what really demanded exposure, Weber wrote, was the "childishness of such an endeavor."[163] Anyone presenting the New Year's speech by Napoleon III, the Ems Dispatch of 1870, or the Austrian ultimatum to Serbia in 1914 as actual "reasons" for the outbreak of war in each of these cases could only be described as a "halfwit." In the final analysis, only one power had unconditionally wanted the war, and that was Russia—or, rather, the "system of Czarism."[164]

Weber's essay was almost as harsh as the pronouncements coming out of the nationalist camp, and it typified a view found widely among conservatives and national liberals alike. To Weber, the controversial issue of "war guilt" represented a historiographic question that was almost impossible to answer: Which of the European Great Powers bore the main responsibility for the outbreak of the war? But Weber's interpretation of "war guilt" loaded the term with a high historical and ideological charge and overstretched its semantics. Obviously, his view diverged completely from that of the history activists at the USPD. But he was equally hard on the MSPD government's more limited plan to examine the files from the weeks just before the war. Their hope was to gain insight into the 1914 government's internal processes of decision and opinion formation, perhaps to outline the horizons, expectations, perspectives, and aims of the decision makers. In its own way, Weber's perspective was even more limited. His focus on war causes largely omitted the simultaneous international debate about humanitarian law—especially the rather specific and multiply documented accusations concerning German crimes in Belgium.

Weber counterposed his negative outline of the war guilt phenomenon with his own understanding of interstate war, which drew on the traditional categories of Wilhelmine great power doctrine and "world politics." Since he regarded the military defeat of the German Reich as the consequence of a failed "selection of leaders,"[165] the German task now, in his view, lay above all in bearing this harsh but well-earned fate "manfully." His thoughts were with the future, he averred. Any reasoning about a "guilt" that lay in the past seemed to him nothing more than the moralizing of an "old maid." In building a postwar order, such thinking was dangerous and destabilizing.[166] For this same reason, he thought the transitional government's disclosure policy was so misguided. What Weber missed, however, was that the Council of People's Deputies was hoping to publish papers from the 1914 July Crisis as a means for enacting a rupture with the tradition of the imperial government's color books—precisely because this legacy was threatening to damage the credibility of German foreign and domestic policy for many years yet to come. Let us recall that the AA at this same time was still vesting hopes in color book propaganda as a means to counter Allied claims. It should be clear that while Weber did not fully agree with the ministerial bureaucracy on this point, his interests and theirs were largely convergent.

At the least thanks to his excellent connections with the liberal international law jurist and moderate pacifist Walther Schücking, Weber should have been more aware that the issue of German international violations had become far more important now that the war was lost. It was not radicals but the DDP politician and finance minister Erzberger who had demanded a commission to investigate the treatment of prisoners of war in Germany. Schücking was appointed to chair it. Intended to preempt Allied calls for punishment by presenting a German investigation first, the commission instead found itself under fire from the AA. Schücking's experience was symptomatic for the dilemma of the liberal legal scholar who took on a government assignment. After his commission investigated the execution of

Charles Fryatt, he officially declared it legal. Internally, however, he called it a "wretched judicial murder."[167]

In the final analysis, the role of the AA and other Reich agencies in the war crimes question posed a clear case of an old civil service exceeding its jurisdiction at great cost to new policymaking. This was the bill for the new government's failure to renew personnel at the agencies and was also because of the MSPD's own insecurities. The problem of Weber's intervention lay mainly in the way he made himself the speaker—wittingly or not—of the authoritarian administrative state, in that he strongly impugned the transitional government's legitimacy on a central political question. He fostered the ongoing polarization in the public debate, attacking the government's politicians personally as "weak natures" and accusing them of betraying the national interest.[168] Despite his strong critique of imperial Germany's conservative officialdom—he held them largely responsible for the country's defeat because, despite their ostensibly nonpartisan ethos, they had often intervened "combatively in the political argument"[169]—Weber had taken the side of the traditional elites, quickly and unconditionally, on one of the most important issues of German foreign and domestic policy. His polemical foray into "war guilt" used the exaggerated semantics of the ministerial bureaucrats, supported their apologia for Germany, and bolstered their resistance to the Weimar government's groping attempts at national self-criticism.[170]

"War guilt" became a major public drama for the first time in the spring of 1919. It began with a 13 February speech by new Prime Minister Philipp Scheidemann (MSPD). Introducing his government, he also called the former supreme military commander of the imperial armed forces during the war, General Erich Ludendorff, a grandiose and reckless gambler. Ludendorff immediately demanded the appointment of a state court to investigate the accusations against him. The nationalist (*deutschnationale* and *alldeutsch*) press went into overdrive against the government and its "submissive peace."[171] On 14 February, Ulrich Graf von Brockdorff-Rantzau, an independent in the cabinet who had received the AA portfolio, held his first speech before the new National Assembly. On the question of German infringements upon international law, Brockdorff-Rantzau admitted the Wilhelmine Reich had brought a historic guilt on itself. But he was not talking about the world war. He was referring to the mistaken German attitude toward international law at the Hague peace conferences of 1899 and 1907. He refused to concede a specific German responsibility for the outbreak of the war or for unrestricted war conduct. Since Germans had more reason to complain about the "war plans" and "atrocities" of their enemies, they were now ready to agree to a commission of "nonpartisan men" who would examine guilt for the war and guilt in the war, Brockdorff-Rantzau said. But he insisted that every attempt by the former enemies to set themselves up as sole judges would have to be rejected. Not without pathos and references to the historical philosophy credo of the German idealist enlightenment, Brockdorff-Rantzau closed his speech with the famous line from Friedrich Schiller: "World history is the world court."[172]

Many have said that Brockdorff-Rantzau's strategy for the Paris Peace Conference relied on skewed priorities and mistaken perceptions that led to a fatal narrowing of the German negotiating line.[173] Invoking Wilson's Fourteen Points to the victorious powers and hoping to put through the German "legal standpoint" centered on a withdrawal of the war guilt charge, he provoked exactly the opposite of what he might have achieved. His inflexible negotiating style sparked the Allies to drastically reinforce the war guilt thesis, as seen in their note of rebuke to the German side of 16 June 1919, which included the first known use of the term "crimes against humanity." Guided by the firm conviction that international law was on his side, Brockdorff-Rantzau, an elite diplomat of the old school, bet everything on one card and thus maneuvered the young republic into its first great crisis.

Less attention has been paid to the presence of interest and pressure groups in the larger milieu of the AA, and to the efforts of these groups to influence the German negotiating position at the Paris talks. How can we assess their contribution to the legal position that Germany presented officially? Starting in the war's penultimate year, the Reich foreign ministry began to convene various expert committees modeled on the US policy advisory group led by Walter Lippmann and known as The Inquiry.[174] Its German analogues were assigned to prepare for peace talks and outline political plans for the postwar period.[175] The ministry continued calling forth semiofficial organizations of this type after the war. Perhaps the most important would prove to be the Heidelberg Committee for Legal Policy, known more simply as the Heidelberg Association.[176] Meeting for the first time at the house of Max Weber in February 1919, this gathering of heavyweights would largely be devoted to political consultancy and public relations work. Most of its members were bourgeois liberals who had backed nonannexationist aims during the war or had stepped up as critics of the invasion of Belgium. After the war, many of them joined the newly founded DDP or were close to it. Prince Maximilian von Baden, who in October 1918 had been installed as the last chancellor of imperial Germany and asked to sue Wilson for peace, was the official initiator of the committee and acted as its chair. He was joined by a who's who from politics, the military, and the diplomatic corps: Gottfried Prince of Hohenlohe-Langenburg; former General Max Graf von Montgelas; Konrad Haußmann; Ludwig Haas; Constantin Fehrenbach; and the diplomat, Konrad-Gisbert Freiherr von Rombach. A single industrialist was present among them: the Baden-based entrepreneur Robert Bosch put up most of the group's funding.

The group's relations with the AA ran mainly through Kurt Hahn, himself a former ministry employee and the former right-hand adviser to "Prince Max." Hahn had persuaded Maximilian of the need to support Germany's troubled foreign policy by creating the association as a private group. The group's public side would feature a wealth of high-carat scholars and writers, impressive names of the time like Hans Delbrück, Walther Schücking, Hans Wehberg, Alfred Weber, Hermann Oncken, Lujo Brentano, Friedrich Curtius, Friedrich Meinecke, Johannes Lepsius, Albrecht Mendelssohn Bartholdy, and Ernst Troeltsch. The "Heidelbergers" took pains to be identified as an independent institution, but it is unlikely that many observers saw it that way. Anyone with experience of the German foreign policy establishment would have known that Hahn had maintained his association with von Brockdorff-Rantzau. It was also general knowledge that Max Weber was close to Walter Simons, the director of the AA's legal department.[177]

Signed by twenty-two members, the group's founding statement was clear about its core mission. The tone was moderate, the style decisive. It demanded a "legal policy" (*Rechtspolitik*) in which the German Reich would be treated as a state among equals. Underlining that the group's members had condemned the "injustice to Belgium" during the war, they still identified a "common guilt among all the belligerent Great Powers of Europe" and confidently refuted any and all one-sided condemnations of imperial Germany. The "enemy politicians" who had been responsible for the "planned incitement of peoples," and who now claimed the authority to "judge and punish," were only continuing the pursuit of "imperialist war aims." The statement, titled "For a Legal Politics,"[178] went on to the now well-worn demand to appoint a neutral and nonpartisan investigative commission that would have free access to the archives of all belligerent nations. Otherwise, the signatories expressed their confidence that the German-American exchange of notes in October 1918 constituted a binding preliminary contract (*pactum de contrahendo*) that the victor powers would also have to honor.[179]

Unlike the Delbrück-Naumann-Legien declaration of November 1918, in which the issue of determining war responsibilities was still linked to a change in elites, the Heidelbergers' manifesto saw it strictly as a foreign policy matter. They not only emphasized their intent to lead in this area but also signaled agreement with the AA that the issue should be kept out of parliamentary debates. There were reasons to fear such debates would arise anyway, however, at the latest once the Kautsky papers were published. As a result, the Heidelbergers soon put the USPD politician's project in their crosshairs.

The task of launching a publicity campaign against Kautsky's work once again fell to the grandiloquent Max Weber. He sent a new column to the editors of *Frankfurter Zeitung*, this time with a request for accelerated and "conspicuous" publication. It was published within two days, on 22 March

1919.[180] The AA had been informed of Weber's column in advance.[181] Weber had heard the news that the Allies had again rejected the appointment of a neutral commission. In his view, this justified fast action, lest the initiative on war guilt pass to the USPD. The Heidelbergers hoped to avoid partisan parliamentary investigations, preferring a body of politically uncommitted persons that, as Weber added, should naturally also include pacifist circles.[182]

In his column on "The Investigation of the Guilt Question," Weber proposed a new process for documentary disclosure projects. Warning against any "one-sided" German disclosures and noting that the color books had lost their power to persuade the public, Weber suggested the creation of a new body dedicated solely to archival work. This would not be a court, however, since guilt in a legal sense was not at issue. Rather, the new body should be empowered both to evaluate the documents and to conduct hearings of the former decision makers:

> These personages are still living, for the most part, and it should be an urgent matter to assure that explaining the motives behind their actions should not be abandoned to the memoirists of future decades but that they all should be brought in contraposition to each other and induced, on the basis of the files, to give exhaustive statements, when possible under cross-examination, to an authority that is in every way unprejudiced. This body would divide its work into three basic areas: 1. explaining disputed facts and connections; 2. exhaustively determining the picture of the world situation visible to the German statesmen, based on the information available to them; 3. explaining their conduct and its motives in the face of this emerging picture of the situation.[183]

In a lecture delivered a short while later to students in Munich, Weber went beyond his article in warning against one-sided admissions of guilt and premature disclosures of files. He compared the conduct of the victorious powers to that of a scorned lover. He described the efforts of the German politician-investigators as undignified and unmanly:

> Instead of acting like old ladies looking for the "guilty party" after a war—when in fact it was the structure of society that generated the war—now every masculine and austere posture must tell the enemy: "We lost the war, you have won it. That is now finished. Now let us talk about what consequences to draw, in keeping with the material interests that were at stake, and—the main thing—considering the responsibility to the future, which above all is the burden of the victor." Anything else would lack dignity, it would backfire. A nation forgives injury to its interests but not injury to its honor, least of all an injury that comes of such sanctimonious dogmatism. Every new document that comes to light after decades brings back to life the undignified hue and cry, the hatred and the outrage, instead of allowing the war at its end to be given a proper burial.

A war can only end through objectivity and gallantry, Weber argued, and above all through "dignity." This aim could not be reached through a stance of "ethics," for in reality that would mean a "lack of dignity on both sides":

> Instead of worrying about what the politicians' proper concern should be, the future and their responsibility to it, they occupy themselves with politically sterile, unresolvable questions of guilt in the past. Doing that is a true political guilt, if any there ever was. And this is how we overlook the undeniable falsification of the whole problem through mean material interests: the interests of the winner in achieving the highest possible moral and material profit, in gaining advantage through [our] admissions of guilt. If anything is vulgar, then that is it. That is the consequence of exploiting "ethics" as a means of appearing to be in the right.[184]

As a theoretical underpinning for his argument, Weber introduced "absolute ethics," which he identified as the greatest threat to a peace deal. This "sentimental-ethical" approach, which he distinguished from that of the proper politician's "responsibility ethics," demands the publication of all documents that incriminate one's own land and an unconditional admission of guilt: "The politician will find that a success in this effort does not advance truth but obscures it through abuse and the unleashing of passions; only a planned ascertainment of all sides by nonpartisan people can bear fruit; every other way can have consequences for the nation that pursues it that will not be repaired even decades later." But "absolute ethics" fails to consider these consequences, according to Weber's in the end pessimistic conclusion.[185]

Weber's interventions on the war guilt question were an expression of his self-concept as a political publicist certain of his own objectivity and orientation to scientific values. He saw no contradiction in calling for an independent investigation to clarify the war guilt question while simultaneously announcing to the public that the central responsibility of the Russian Empire was already incontrovertibly established.[186] Given that he constantly pointed out real historiographic problems, like access to documents and source interpretation, his scholarly policy and the methodological premises of his engagement are fair game for closer analysis: Weber's conceptions, only vaguely indicated, prefigured several elements that would persist in the field of "German guilt" research. The kind of history written in this genre after 1919 was marked by a fixation on international, military, and diplomatic history and by a strongly "propagandistic basic impulse."[187] Always guided by the desire to refute the ostensible Allied accusation of war guilt, the German history discipline projected the conflict situation of 1914 sometimes back to the early nineteenth century and sometimes as far back as the Peace of Westphalia of 1648.[188] Not to be overlooked is Weber's historicist bent, which was quite distinct from both the "history of mentalities" being developed in France at the same time and from the social history discussions of the pre-World War I period.

Several statements by Weber make it clear that while he mistrusted disclosures of official documents, he did not fundamentally doubt the necessity of disclosure. His proposal to institutionalize war causes research can be seen as an attempt to stave off the undesired social consequences of uncontrolled disclosure.[189] He found it expedient to keep the framework of AA control, to include the historic German decision makers in the work of interpretation, and to use hermeneutic technique in assessing archival documents. All this was meant to prevent the gaze into the arcanum of power from distorting historical truth or producing a false understanding of the history. Weber counterposed the advantages of historiographic proximity to the state and the employment of philological historical methods against the disadvantages of opening the archives to the victorious powers or of allowing access to certain undesirable sectors of the German polity and public. Essentially, this approach meant that the initial historicization and intellectual monologue would be conducted by elites. It also played history against the law, and vice versa. All this still managed to ignore, however, that German academic history had already thoroughly compromised itself via its far-ranging identification with German war aims; outside Germany, the discipline was seen mainly as the ideological handmaiden of Prussian militarism.[190] For that reason alone, Weber's idea must have seemed intolerable to Germany's former war opponents.

Weber had his reasons for submitting his latest article to the *Frankfurter Zeitung* with a request that the editorial board accelerate publication. On the day the article appeared, 22 March 1919, the Scheidemann cabinet was due to deliberate on Kautsky's documentary collection, which was almost ready to publish. At the sitting, Friedrich Ebert (MSPD), the first president of the new republic, freshly elected by the National Assembly, spoke decisively in favor of publication. His opinion was that Germany must take a stand in the coming peace negotiations and admit its historical responsibility. The "sins of the old government should be condemned utterly" and the attitude of the new government set down in an official statement. Ebert added that a state court should be appointed to determine the guilt of key actors in the war.[191] The new finance minister, Eugen Schiffer (DDP), objected that an admission of guilt would take the "last measure of self-respect" away from the people and allow the adversary to triumph. Minister Eduard David (MSPD) answered that anything incriminating in the German documents was already known to all: "If we join Schiffer in admitting to a preventive war, we are admitting everything that the Entente is raising against us."[192]

David kept up the push for publication at the next cabinet meeting. Because the Kautsky documents highlighted that Germany was the central mover of the July Crisis, David believed disclosure would tend to exonerate. It would not justify German actions but could explain them. However, David was unable to persuade enough members of his own party. Scheidemann's opinion was looking to be decisive. At the end of the meeting, his recommendation was to avoid publication "for the time being."[193] It may be supposed that the prime minister was still assuming that the government would appoint a state court, that this would investigate the accusations against imperial politicians and military officers, and that it would also handle his recent dispute with Ludendorff.[194] Minister of the Interior Hugo Preuß later submitted an amended bill to empower a state court, but—quite apart from the lack of an international dimension—neither the DDP nor the German National People's Party (DNVP) could be moved to abandon their opposition to the idea in any form. A compromise was finally found. Parliamentary committee hearings on the guilt question would be convened in August 1919. This ended up giving the deposed military men a platform for their own accusations that Germany had been "stabbed in the back" (the *Dolchstoss* myth).[195]

As the parliament was just beginning to debate the institutional form of this process in March 1919, the German delegation to Paris was preparing for its appearance at the peace conference. As Ulrich Heinemann would determine in his 1983 work on Germany's "repressed defeat," the officials at the Reich foreign ministry who were responsible for the talks pursued a dual strategy. They hoped, first, to decouple the war guilt problem from all other topics of negotiation. Second, they prepared intensively for a counteroffensive of accusations against the Allies, hoping to put them under pressure by presenting documentary evidence of Entente misdeeds.[196] This suggests that the Heidelbergers were already included in the ministry's plan. They had promised nothing less than to expose "enemy atrocities" during the war, violations of German private property, Allied "Armistice atrocities" since the war's end, and the ultimate war guilt of the Russian Empire.[197] And, of course, the AA and the Heidelbergers were consonant on these and other habitual questions, given their shared notions of national "honor" and "dignity."

After the cabinet shelved the Kautsky project, its management was transferred to two Heidelbergers, Montgelas and Schücking. Against his will, Kautsky was gradually neutralized. First, he was deprived of the "technical editorship" of the files. Then he was asked to surrender any secret documents in his possession. Soon after, he was refused entry to the ministry archives on Wilhelmstrasse in Berlin.[198] Having taken the matter out of the USPD politician's suspect hands, the AA was satisfied that no controversial revelations would hit the public eye before the Paris talks. However, they also got wind that a potentially critical edition of documents from the July Crisis was being prepared in Austria. Shortly before receiving the draft of the peace treaty from French President Georges Clemenceau, the German delegation received word that documents possibly incriminating the German imperial government had been located in Vienna.[199]

The further course of the Kautsky project is well known. The AA soon ceased to consider it advisable to suppress the documents. Montgelas and Schücking would issue a mildly defused version in December 1919 under the title *Die deutschen Dokumente zum Kriegsausbruch* (The German documents on the outbreak of war).[200] Kautsky countered with his own edition soon after, justifying his intervention with the comment that he had always approached the work in the Rankean tradition of telling history ("as it really happened," in Ranke's famous motto) and not as a "prosecutor."[201]

After the AA's War Guilt Department had succeeded in placing Montgelas and Schücking in charge of the official edition, the idea arose to recruit yet another body of experts, historians, and jurists to act as a support team for the German delegation at the Paris conference. Weber, Montgelas, Delbrück, and Mendelssohn Bartholdy were all called upon. Again, all four were active Heidelbergers. Mendelssohn Bartholdy was also working on the aforementioned *European Cabinets* project commissioned by the AA. All four academics agreed to the plan, although they were surely aware that accepting this mission meant venturing out on thin ice. In early March, the government had issued "Guidelines for German Peace Negotiators" that strictly prohibited invoking the war guilt question in the course of a diplomatic counteroffensive.[202] But for men who had publicly styled war guilt into a question of national honor, it was presumably a matter of patriotic duty to heed their own call. It should not be ruled out that more than one of the four Heidelbergers on their way to Paris had accepted the AA offer on condition that they would be allowed to treat the guilt question offensively, without regard for the cabinet's guidelines.[203]

Arriving in Paris, the four Heidelbergers soon discovered that the German negotiators had already drafted an official statement for them to sign. In violation of his orders from Berlin, Brockdorff-Rantzau wanted to use this in a counterattack against the report from the Allied war guilt commission. The statement had been prepared by the AA's War Guilt Department. An appendix featured documents from its archives, including papers out of the color book then in preparation. Nothing was expected of the professors, other than that they should add the weight of their signatures to the prepared official statement.

Complications arose. First, von Brockdorff-Rantzau sent back the first draft for being "too polemical."[204] Several drafts were yet to come, but the "Professors' Memorandum" with its appendices was finally circulated to the other nations' negotiating teams on 28 May 1919.[205] The AA's real aims in enlisting the academics had been clearly stated by Bernhard Wilhelm von Bülow, the director of the War Guilt Department. In a message a few days earlier to an AA undersecretary, Freiherr Langwerth von Simmern, von Bülow had written:

> Our intent is to appoint a professors' commission to evaluate the adversary's report. Their verdict will neither bind nor obligate the government. It will be able to effortlessly refute the adversary's main points of accusation and will then present material from the prehistory of the war showing that the Entente, above all Russia, had been toying with war for years. The material is thoroughly persuasive. It is meant to give our friends in neutral and enemy countries an opportunity to step up for our rights. Until now they have been silenced with the argument that we alone, as the sole guilty party, have earned a punishment.[206]

If the Professors' Memorandum was made in Wilhelmstrasse, what share in it belongs to the signatory academics? What responsibility do they bear for a paper that, in the opinion of several historians, was intended to advance the ministry's "policy of disaster"—to provoke an invasion and a European-wide revolutionary crisis?[207] The editors of the complete works of Max Weber, who have been the most thorough in analyzing the origins of the memorandum, have pointed out that serious differences of opinion arose among the four academics. The arguments centered on Delbrück's assertion that the violation of Belgian neutrality was itself justified as an act of power politics. The mood grew so tense that more than one of the four men threatened to go home.[208] An agreement among them was managed only at the last minute. Even as the government sent a new dispatch underlining its prohibition on the use of the guilt question, on the evening before the memorandum was to be submitted to the Allies, all four men finally put their signatures to it. It was submitted.

The last part of the memorandum especially shows the unmistakable influence of Max Weber.[209] This section completely ignores any aspects of international law, and displays particular harshness in its tone and wording. It asks whether certain governments may have been interested in seeing a war for political and economic reasons and argues that the answer is evident in the conditions offered for the peace. As with Weber's contributions to *Frankfurter Zeitung*, Russia is once again identified as the most culpable power, as the only power that planned and successfully brought about a war. Of imperial Germany, the memorandum admits only that serious mistakes were committed out of nervousness. These are attributed to a "small group of chauvinist literati," the same group still negatively influencing international opinion to this day.[210]

Given these correlations between Weber's press columns, the public declarations of the Heidelbergers, and the revised version of the memorandum, the thesis that the AA put the four professors in Paris under "no negligible measure of political pressure" is only conditionally plausible.[211] The memorandum includes a series of points that the Heidelberg Association had aggressively upheld at its meetings and in public statements. Yet there are also unmistakable signs that the academics felt awkward about their role. Each one displayed obstinacy at times during their joint revision of the text.[212] The point, nevertheless, is that they took part consciously and actively in circumventing an official guideline from the cabinet in Berlin. This was rooted in the manner in which they attempted to adapt their concept of academic independence to the new political conditions. In a situation in which the victorious powers were determining the future of the German people, and in which apparently inexperienced outsiders had hijacked the country's fate, the four Heidelbergers saw that their ethical obligation was to intervene in the controversies of political opinion using the tools of a "fighting science" so as to support German foreign policy with their academic expertise. Thus, the argument that the four-man commission in Paris had surrendered its "independence" needs to be put to rest or heavily revised.

Among the Allies, this manner of engagement prompted negative memories of the German agitprop during the war. The thesis that imperial Germany had simply waged a defensive war against czarism was not considered credible. The demand that Germany be put on an equal footing in the investigation of the war's causes was taken as an unmitigated provocation.[213] There was also disappointment that the German experts—whose ranks included a renowned international law scholar in Mendelssohn Bartholdy—had apparently accepted the AA's version of the history without objection.[214] Although Mendelssohn Bartholdy was well acquainted with the complicated provisions of reparations law, he apparently did not trouble himself to explain these to the ministerial officials or to point out the serious consequences of escalating the talks. In the end, it was a loss in credibility for those liberal German jurists who relied on internationalism and understanding among peoples that one of their leading exponents had allowed himself on this most sensitive of points to follow rudderless in the AA's wake. Mendelssohn Bartholdy carried the counterpolitics of the officialdom, hoping to influence the building of the League of Nations but at the same time still working for a revision of the responsibility clauses.[215]

Although their mission in Versailles provided the four Heidelbergers with a drastic demonstration of the limits to their claims on political influence, this did not keep them from further involvement in the politics of war crimes. Their engagement on the war guilt question had caused the Allies not to withdraw but to reinforce the punitive clauses of the peace treaty. Now the Heidelbergers tried to make up for lost terrain by turning to the equally sensitive matter of the Allies' demands for extraditions of German officials and military officers suspected of war crimes.[216] Max Weber continued to be the one among them who seemed most inspired by the thought that his actions might influence the political developments. In mid-May, a few days before his journey to France, he had written a personal letter to Erich Ludendorff. Not long after, he informed the foreign minister that he had done this. Weber's letter to the ex-general, who by then was sought as a war criminal, asked him to set an example together with other high-ranking military figures. They should surrender themselves willingly for detention by the Allies as prisoners of war, Weber urged. He wrote to Ludendorff that this would have "undoubted effects on the country." In any case, Germany was "powerless to constantly protect anyone against violent measures." As is evident in the notes of his contemporary, the legal scholar Richard Thoma, Weber believed that Ludendorff's surrender would be an indispensable move toward rescuing the "honor of the nation."[217] Over the longer term, Weber was perhaps hoping for a reconstitution of the German General Staff, which he continued to see as the future lynchpin of a regenerated German power state.[218]

Ludendorff, who had returned to Germany from Swedish exile just a few weeks earlier, was not thinking even for a moment of complying with the Allied extradition orders by offering himself up for prosecution voluntarily. He could rely on officials at the foreign and military ministries to back him up. The government, meanwhile, was predictably split on the question. The victorious powers' repeated requests in 1919 for extraditions of leading German military officers and politicians had gone without results. The two ministries had founded a joint department to defend against such efforts. A secret organization was built to set up eight thousand potential hideouts for the fugitives in every corner of Germany.[219] Given the high emotional and symbolic meaning assigned to the extraditions issue by the German side, the British finally expressed a readiness for major concessions. In early 1920, Gustav Noske—minister of the Reichswehr, as the reorganized German military forces were known—threatened that he would resign his portfolio and leave "Germany to the chaos" if the victorious powers insisted on extradition. Lloyd George finally agreed to allow the Germans to pursue prosecutions under national law.[220]

The first German war crimes trials were finally called in 1921. The prosecutor for the cases, Ludwig Ebermayer, had published a call in many German newspapers inviting all persons named on Allied extradition lists to present themselves to him on a voluntary basis. The further course of the proceedings reflected a strong unwillingness to comply with Allied demands for prosecution. By the end of the year, several public trials had been held against seventeen defendants, with guilty verdicts pronounced only in four cases. By 1927, the court of jurisdiction had dismissed another 1,700 cases through rulings of blanket exoneration.[221] The verdicts caused split reactions among German international law scholars. Several accused the government of having bent to pressure from abroad. Others opined that the Leipzig trials at least represented a first step toward prosecution of such crimes in the future. Most, however, shared in the prevailing public opinion. The Allied accusations had been nothing more than a propaganda spectacle, and the meager number of convictions proved it.

Conclusion

In the second half of the nineteenth century a problem consciousness and an increased sensitivity for certain phenomena of political mass violence formed among parts of the European public. In educated, liberal, bourgeois circles, among those who saw themselves as the carriers of the new discourses, excessive political violence came to be seen as an undesired accompaniment of interstate military conflict. In the age of border-crossing commercial and scientific relations, wars between nation-states were viewed as counterproductive and increasingly as regressive. Major wars like the Crimean War and the Franco-Prussian War posed obstacles to the wider dissemination of European civilization. In this spirit, a relatively broad civil society movement of international lawyers, "organized" pacifists, and other exponents of a politically conscious, liberal internationalism formed starting in the 1860s, advocating for the "humanization" of war and for legal restrictions on the conduct of war. One characteristic of this early species of transnational activism was that it was not concerned with the abolition of war as such or with political representation. Whether grounded in political, religious, or academic terms, the interest above all was to attenuate the humanitarian catastrophes caused by the mechanized warfare. This movement therefore focused mainly on the wounded combatants of national armies, but also aimed to protect other vulnerable groups: civilians, prisoners of war, religious and national minorities, and freedom fighters.

Goals that were more ambitious were pursued by those exponents of the flourishing study of international law who began to describe themselves as the "Men of 1873," referring to the Institut de Droit International, which was founded in Ghent in 1873. Their concern was to advance the institutionalization and codification of the international law of war and to achieve the illegalization of certain military practices and types of weapons. They were only relatively successful. Although the international law lobbyists never got close to winning over all governments and social groups to their cause (the Wilhelmine government, the Prussian military, and even German international law scholars remained largely immune), and although their progress in the setting of norms was often disappointing, they did largely succeed in influencing public perceptions and communications on the issue of political violence. On the eve of World War I, the older metaphysical idea of war had already retreated before a more ambivalent attitude. While wars between "civilized" states were acceptable only if they could be kept within a framework of regulated norms and standards, all measures appropriate to securing the major colonial powers' claims to dominion over stateless societies in Africa and Asia were, in principle, considered acceptable.

Although the 1904–1905 Russo-Japanese War had already exposed the limits of liberal international law doctrine, World War I would prove to be the actual trial. It posed an extreme endurance test, not only for the idea of a purposively rational, transnational academic culture but also for the new Geneva and Hague conventions. Despite its failure to achieve moderation of the national war machines or increased protection of noncombatants, the reformers' legalist paradigm did set off an intensive discussion about Germany's infringements of international law. This debate was partly steered by governmental propaganda machines but also attributable to the increased tendency of the academic communities in the various countries to engage in cultural self-mobilization.

It was above all the German invasion of Belgium and Luxembourg in violation of international law, as well as the attacks on French and Belgian civilians in the summer months of 1914, that caused prominent scholars on the Allied side, including legal experts and historians, to begin documenting and conducting legal assessments of such occurrences. This activity had two primary aims: first, to preserve the sources and testimonies of German war atrocities for history and for posterity; second, even as the war continued, to gather evidence for later indictments and reparation demands against the imperial German government. National history cultures were soon also sucked into this wave of legal "processing" of history. The growing significance of juridical categories was linked to a fundamental change in perspective for historical writing. The compilers of the many commission reports focused strongly on people affected by the violence of war, and for the first time, they included civilian victims in large numbers.

In the spring of 1918, as the collapse of German forces on the Western front signaled a coming end to the military conflict, the British, Belgian, and French governments raised calls to make the issue of German international law violations the main subject of the peace negotiations. Although there was an absence of previously applied international law norms for this (the concept of "war crimes" had been introduced, for example, but was not yet in wide usage), the consensus among the governments and leading international lawyers in the United States and Europe was that courts should judge not only the countless German violations during the war but also Germany's responsibility for the war. But the US delegation in Paris raised reservations against punitive international law and succeeded in greatly weakening the Europeans' prosecution project. While the catalog of sanctions for war damages was quite precise, the planned tribunal against the deposed German monarch finally turned into a nonbinding recommendation. It is telling about the American attitude that they preferred a multinational historians' commission as an alternative to an *haut tribunal*. In their view, the international public and not a criminal court should judge who was guilty of the war and who was guilty in the war.

After the announcement of the Versailles "guilt clauses," an animated controversy broke out in Germany over whether the deposed imperial civilian and military leadership was responsible for the outbreak of the war after all. The representatives of the USPD and of "organized" pacifism at first advocated strongly for investigating the role of the imperial German government in the 1914 July Crisis that preceded the start of the Great Warthe war. A one-sided publication of secret government files from the weeks before the war was also intended to send a signal to the international public. It was meant to demonstrate that Germany's new democratic leadership was undertaking a political and moral break with the past and willing to investigate the warmongering politics of the former imperial elites. While the MSPD leadership regarded such initiatives with mixed feelings, at times they were put under considerable pressure to comply by their own party base. Reacting to the exposés of the USPD Bavarian premier Kurt Eisner, in December 1918 the new government in Berlin assigned to the USPD deputy Karl Kautsky and the MSPD man Max Quarck the task of reviewing the imperial government files from the 1914 July Crisis and preparing these for publication.

At the AA, meanwhile, the expectation during the revolutionary months of 1918 and 1919 was already that the Allies would pose exorbitant demands for reparations. A dual strategy was devised in reaction to the ongoing debate: first, with an eye to the coming German-Allied peace talks, a special department was created to compile yet another color book containing documentary materials that supposedly incriminated the Entente Powers. Second, the ministry commissioned the renowned jurist Albrecht Mendelssohn Bartholdy to curate its own edition of foreign policy files. This project was meant to refute the anticipated war guilt accusation. At the same time, the bureaucrats still hoped to stop the edition planned by Kautsky and Quarck, which was seen as undesired competition and as a threat to the German negotiating position at the Paris talks. The enlistment of Mendelssohn Bartholdy, a highly eminent scholar in questions of international law, was apparently also intended as a way of building a bridge to the academic networks.

With a view to advising the government on the coming peace negotiations, about two dozen politicians, diplomats, and academics came together in a committee on legal policy in early 1919. This was called the Heidelberg

Association. The twenty-two founding members were overwhelmingly liberals and moderate conservatives who had supported nonannexationist aims during the war. For this reason, they condemned the "injustice against Belgium" while also asserting a "common guilt of the belligerent Great Powers of Europe." The Heidelberg Association categorically rejected every form of international criminal law consequences for the German Reich. They instead called for a neutral investigative commission that would have free access to all government archives. Max Weber, one of the intellectual leaders of the group, fronted these positions in press articles and public lectures. He condemned leftist ideas of convening court or parliamentary hearings on German war crimes as dangerous outgrowths of an absolutizing "sentimental ethics." His counterproposal was to set up a circle of experts who would work together with the political decision makers of the former imperial cabinet to evaluate the prewar archives. His conviction was that a question as wide ranging as that of Germany's responsibility for the war must be kept away from daily political debates.

The flip side of the Heidelbergers' attitude, however, was a nearly unlimited support for the unrealistic and confrontational policy of the German foreign ministry. The ministry intentionally undermined the Berlin government's guidelines on these matters. This became especially conspicuous at the spring 1919 talks in Paris, where Weber and three other leading members of the Heidelberg Association lent their academic reputations to the ministry's War Guilt Department and thus reinforced Brockdorff-Rantzau, the leader of the German delegation, in his uncompromising course. Mendelssohn Bartholdy, as an internationally respected liberal representative of his discipline, also fell in line behind the AA and its orchestration of what came to be known as the new field of "war guilt research." While most practitioners of history at universities—with the exception of Hans Delbrück—stayed away from this controversial field, the young German discipline of international law studies cooperated with the semiofficial campaign work and was infected early with what historian Michael Salewski has called the "Weimar revision syndrome."

Chapter 2

WASHINGTON—NUREMBERG—BONN

Among historiographers of the National Socialist era it has become a common refrain to highlight how the work of pioneers who were not professional academics contributed greatly to the research field's emergence.[1] Now, this is not to downplay the role of the German and Austrian social scientists who laid down some of the most influential guidelines for subsequent understandings of National Socialism and the Third Reich in the 1930s. As one example, Ernst Fraenkel's concept of the "dual state," as his 1941 book was titled,[2] has proved fairly durable to this day. But the observation is true of two groups who, during World War II, grappled with the ideological foundations, system of rule, and politics of the NS regime. The first are the European and American exponents of the international law community and the international peace movement who advocated for the criminalization of aggressive war and a judicial treatment of crimes considered categorically National Socialist. The second were the members of Jewish "legal think tanks" formed in Great Britain, the United States, and elsewhere. Many of the latter group had suffered racialist persecution together with their families and communities. Their organizations took on the mission of compiling and preserving for posterity all the widespread and often-scattered reports on NS acts of violence that could be secured. Often, they did so in the anticipation that NS leaders would one day be subject to criminal prosecution and that victims of persecution would raise demands for restitutions and compensations from Germany.[3] Granting differences in focus, these two groups shared several connections and goals. In the war's aftermath, they converged in a period of institutional partnership, above all around the series of war crimes trials held at Nuremberg by the International Military Tribunal (IMT) and later by the US military occupation authorities. The two groups shared the primary concern of finding adequate legal, historical, and moral responses to crimes that, in their execution and magnitude, exceeded what had until then been thinkable.

The charges raised at Nuremberg often relied on innovative legal constructs and on specific historical interpretations of the NS regime. In response, the lawyers representing the German defendants pursued a strategy of partial cooptation, adopting some of the same concepts used by the Allied prosecutors but giving these different meanings and applying them to other contexts. By the time the Federal Republic of Germany (FRG) was founded in 1949, this had helped give rise to a fixed canon of historical narratives and national apologias that served to style (West) Germans into victims of a "victor's justice," one that was repugnant to a true understanding of human rights. This "anti-Nuremberg" discourse was often highly effective, but a concurrent and contrary German discourse also arose in the precincts of the new state and establishment. Rather than focusing on the supposed injustices of "Nuremberg," this aimed instead to profile the FRG positively as a supporter of liberal human rights thinking on the international stage.

International Law versus Human Rights?

National Socialist expansion policy and the crimes of the German occupation regimes, above all in Eastern Europe, gave rise to wartime discussions closely tied to a specifically "Western" human rights discourse. It reflected both past experiences with the League of Nations and current political constellations. A curious difference from the war crimes debate during World War I was that, at least during the first two years of World War II, almost no voices among German war opponents called attention publicly to the international law violations of the NS leadership or demanded punishment for German war crimes. In a paradoxical reversal of fronts, the issue was seized mainly by pro-regime German legal scholars, such as Karl Lasch, Axel Freiherr von Freytagh-Loringhoven, Carl Schmitt, and Friedrich Berber, who accused the Western powers of having started a "criminal war of aggression against the German people."[4] Not until after the German attack on the Soviet Union did the London-based exile governments of German-occupied countries issue the "St. James Declaration" of January 1942, which called on the Western powers to take a position on the legal question. The same moment saw the first published legal literature concerning the question of whether German war leadership was criminally culpable.

More recent historical research works often portray an evolutionary process of mutual reinforcement between the human rights politics of the western Allied powers and concurrent discussions on potential criminal prosecution of German occupation crimes, leading as a whole to greater consciousness for the importance of human rights.[5] In reality, the two discourses evolved separately from one another, notwithstanding several connections, and did not develop in a particularly linear way. While the human rights rhetoric under the leadership of President Franklin D. Roosevelt was soon enough expanded into a central medium of a liberal, neo-Wilsonian discourse by which the Allies defined themselves, before the latter part of 1943 the discussions on possible legal reactions to German mass crimes barely proceeded beyond a limited realm of human rights specialist bodies and organizations formed by NS persecutees. Caution about this on the political level was because of various differences of opinion among the Allies, recollections of the failures after the end of World War I, and the inherent difficulties of a legal approach to the matter.[6]

While the great powers of Great Britain and the United States had long refrained from public condemnations of NS race and extermination policies, Roosevelt's Four Freedoms speech of 6 January 1941 marked the beginning of a series of pronouncements in which the US government avowed commitment to democracy and security—understood as economic stability and safety from belligerent threats—as well as to individual civil and human rights.[7] These statements were aimed, first, at adopting some distance from what were seen as the failures of the League of Nations system and its legal regime of collective minority rights.[8] Second, they showed an intention to present a universalist concept against the NS vision of a consistently particularist international law. Since traditional terms like "civilization" and the "self-determination of peoples" were seen as more or less discredited by the interwar period, the human rights idea seemed to pose a persuasive alternative to the old League of Nations order.

A few historians, most recently Elizabeth Borgwardt, have been right to point out the substantial gap between the Allies' human rights rhetoric during the war and their actual policies in practice. This was true not only on the international level, where German atrocities in Eastern Europe were played down or went unacknowledged, but also in regard to the western powers' own domestic and colonial policies. For example, the detention of 130,000 US citizens of Japanese descent, in violation of their human rights, was met with Roosevelt's full approval.[9] Nevertheless, the Western-liberal human rights discourse did develop greater attraction before the end of the war. Various reasons for this can be adduced. Presumably, the president had a clearly anti-Nazi rather than a general antitotalitarian approach in mind,[10] but the publics of the Western countries perceived his Four Freedoms speech and the US-UK Atlantic Charter of August 1941 as an Anglo-American antithesis to totalitarianism, one aimed against Stalin as much as Hitler.[11]

Thus, first, long before the onset of the Cold War, the emerging Western human rights concept dovetailed with an interpretation of National Socialism and Communism predominant in the West—one in the mode of totalitarianism theory, which saw the primary conflict lying between the individual and the supposedly omnipotent state.[12] Second, American internationalists and neo-Wilsonians could identify well with a concept that accessed Wilson's universalist project without resorting to his rhetoric. Third, this ambiguity offered a way to conceal the serious differences of opinion between the United States and the United Kingdom, which had arisen especially in the realm of colonial policy.[13] Fourth, and possibly decisively, as the Reich's policy of radical Germanization in occupied German-minority areas unfolded, even the Allies came to see the postwar complete expulsion of ethnic Germans from Eastern Europe as inevitable. This made a revival of interwar minority rights inopportune.[14] As diverse expectations and interpretations accumulated around the human rights talk of the American New Dealers, much speaks for the hypothesis that its thorough success relied above all on its far-reaching conceptual ambiguities. The historian Samuel Moyn has spoken, rather disparagingly, of an "empty vessel" suitable for a series of entirely different needs.[15]

Does this backdrop suffice to posit linear connections between Roosevelt's state-interventionist New Deal, the Western human rights rhetoric, and the later Allied prosecution program, as so many have argued, teleologically, but generally without empirical confirmation? What differences, commonalities, and overlaps can actually be seen? Punishing NS perpetrators was undoubtedly a theme during the war, one discussed in a variety of societal connections, and it has received mention in the literature, if not yet thorough exploration. Long before grand politics took the first steps toward internationalizing and institutionalizing the prosecution of "Axis criminals," which would lead to the establishment of the IMT, international lawyers, peace activists, and NS persecutees were having their own early thoughts about this issue.

The catalyst for the international criminal law debate came with the German invasion of the Soviet Union in June 1941 and the crimes of the SS-led Einsatzgruppen, the units that moved into territories under German occupation and conducted massacres of local populations on a massive scale. On 13 January 1942, the exile governments accredited in London convened at St. James's Palace to issue a statement emphasizing the exceptional brutality of German war conduct and their own determination to conduct eventual criminal prosecutions of the perpetrators.[16] As the continuing radicalization of the Germanization project in Eastern Europe became ever more evident, and as several Western politicians reacted with threats of reprisals that prompted associations with past bloody suppressions of colonial uprisings,[17] many legal scholars' associations began to form in Europe to consider the problem of German war crimes. Leading the way were the International Commission for Penal Reconstruction and Development (aka the Cambridge Commission) and the London International Assembly.[18] They drew members mainly from the ranks of established international lawyers in Europe and the United States, among them many Jews who had emigrated or fled from continental Europe.[19] At the same time, legal journals began to feature articles that reflected this greater interest in prosecuting German occupation crimes.

For the jurists, it was logical to pick up from the concepts and semantics that had formed during the debate about German war crimes after 1914. A big difference, however, was that the ratification of the Kellogg-Briand Pact of 1928 had meanwhile awakened an additional interest among the international law scholars in whether aggressive war was punishable as such. The particularities of the German occupations in Eastern Europe raised a series of additional legal questions for which the formalized international law of war had no ready answers. One line of discussion revolved around the complex of collaborators, another around the role of criminal organizations and the importance of command structures.

The exact dynamics of interactions between scholarship and policy in this area of human rights for now remains unclear, but a look at the wartime debates among international legal scholars shows that there were connections. This was concealed by the fact that the legal scholarship for various reasons often avoided the term "human rights."[20] Human rights thinking was nevertheless evident in thematic treatments of German war crimes that expanded or transcended categories like national affiliation and state sovereignty, neither of which had been subject to question during the interwar period. Following Daniel Segesser's comprehensive evaluation of the international literature, a great many wartime publications showed a preference for the rapid creation of an international criminal court. Such a measure would serve to avoid the kind of stalemate that followed World War I but also assure that it would be possible to prosecute crimes against Jews and stateless persons and crimes occurring at multiple sites in different countries.[21] More implicitly than explicitly, this suggested that there should be no absolute obstacle to future prosecutions of crimes against people who were citizens of the perpetrator state itself.[22]

A few commentators viewed it as a compelling interest to expand international law into an authority for public education and moral self-definition that could counteract doctrines of values relativism. The Jewish Czechoslovakian publicist Viktor Fischl drew a contrast between the public attention raised by the case of the British nurse Edith Cavell during World War I and the widespread apathy about the fate of the European Jews.[23] In addition, it was thought that the conditions of rule in totalitarian states practically compelled prosecution. Because the NS regime had drawn large strata of people into its policies of plunder and extermination, criminal prosecutions would serve to undermine the sense of solidarity and community among them.[24]

Unlike the discussions after 1918, when the Americans above all objected to prosecuting carriers of state sovereignty, this issue was barely contested any more among the jurists. The London International Assembly found "that rank and positions, however exalted, confer no immunity upon the accused in respect of war crimes, and that those in high places who ordered them should be held responsible as well as the actual perpetrators."[25] But there remained much political and historical debate about what exactly constituted a war crime and to what extent one could reinterpret the constitutive criteria for it. Sheldon Glueck, a Harvard criminologist originally from Warsaw, was of the opinion that many German crimes were not directly connected to the war but nevertheless could be prosecuted as war crimes. He agreed with the proposal of several Soviet authors that industrialists and bankers should also be put in the dock after the war, since they had participated at least indirectly in NS crimes.[26]

Most international lawyers engaged in scholarly debates on German war crimes avoided using terms common in the human rights discourse.[27] Perhaps they wished to avoid repeating the mistakes of World War I, when scholars' engagement in rhetorical offensives had awakened exaggerated public expectations. But even as human rights terms were avoided, human rights concepts played a central role in the programmatic planning for a later legal treatment of German occupation crimes. The demand that individuals be recognized alongside states as subjects under international law was not a mere theoretical point but came with concrete proposals on how to practically implement it. The proposal to create an international court for the prosecution of NS perpetrators bespoke utopian thinking insofar as it posited the existence of a universal morality, seeing NS terror as the concern of an imagined international community that must defend common values of humanity and morality. A few jurists additionally pleaded that the criteria for war crimes be expanded to include the persecution of minorities during peacetime. Finally, the search for means to criminalize wars of aggression can be seen as both a reinforcement and a weakening of the principle of state sovereignty. Overall, it is clear that important parameters for the Allied prosecution of the NS leadership were formulated long before the end of the war.

Jurists as Lobbyists and Historians

If the demand to punish German functionaries after World War I was mainly grounded in the argument that the Wilhelmine Reich had violated international treaties in its form of war conduct, then the discussion about the NS regime's crimes included another dimension. Based on often-extensive historical documentation and analysis, many jurists justified reviving metapositive natural law and human rights with the opinion that National Socialism constituted a new kind of ruling system with partly new forms of ruling techniques. Punishing the leading strata of the Third Reich was considered necessary so as to reconstitute the norms that had been damaged. Others, however, considered it even more significant that the NS regime had established a form of statehood that threatened to undermine the international state system from within.[28] The latter thesis was upheld most decisively by the Jewish Polish jurist Raphael Lemkin.

Although Lemkin and his work have received much attention in recent years,[29] it remains almost unremarked that he had begun to advocate for an evolution of humanitarian international law in the 1930s. He was openly alarmed at how the mass crimes against Assyrian Christians in Iraq and against Armenians in Turkey had gone unpunished despite contemporary attempts at legal treatments.[30] Still a young scholar and as an employee of the Codification Commission of the Republic of Poland, he worked both on standardizing Polish law and on reinforcing the international laws protecting minority rights that, for the first time, had received a fragile institutional foundation via the League of Nations system.[31] In Lemkin's view it was a serious problem that the League of Nations foregrounded protection of state integrity while neglecting other legal goods that seemed just as existential in the maintenance of societal order. He proposed that destruction of cultural goods and use of state violence against domestic groups be included under the international legal categories of "vandalism" and "barbarism." In this, he was proposing to unite universalist human rights with particularist group rights, both of which he saw as threatened by the homogenizing tendencies of modern nation-states.[32]

During the war, Lemkin discerned grave theoretical and political dilemmas posed by the realities of German occupation rule in Poland, which he had experienced firsthand as a member of the Polish underground and then continued to follow as a jurist advising the Board of Economic Warfare in the United States. We may assume that his intensive occupation with NS ideology and practice gradually made it clear to him that the ethnic-racist Germanization program in Eastern Europe embodied a new vision for political order that went well beyond conservative European power politics or modern high imperialism. On the contrary, he saw in it a system in which instruments of state power were used solely to implement a biologistic population policy of displacement and destruction. The Third Reich thus undermined the foundations of modern statehood and threatened the rational principles of existing international law. While he had become a persistent if reform-oriented critic of the modern international legal system in the interwar period, he now saw himself forced into the role of defending it against the intentional hostility of a European great power.

In 1944, Lemkin published his magnum opus under the rather bulky title *Axis Rule in Occupied Europe: Laws of Occupation, Analysis of Government, Proposals for Redress.* It is uncertain to what degree this work, begun in 1943, was influenced by earlier models. Certain similarities with the juridical history writing following World War I are easy to recognize. Out of the book's seven-hundred-plus pages, more than half feature reprinted legal texts, regulations, and court rulings that Lemkin had collected over his years in the underground and in exile. The first part covers the "German Techniques of Occupation." Lemkin employs minute detail in describing the roles of Reich administration, police, law, courts, and state financial agencies—not, however, of private business enterprises—as they exercised rule over the occupied territories. A following section devotes just sixteen pages to proposing a new criminal charge under international law that he coined by combining the Greek *genos* (race or tribe) with the Latin *cidere* (to kill): genocide. In Lemkin's definition, this signified "a coordinated plan of different actions aiming at the destruction of essential foundations of the life of national groups, with the aim of annihilating the groups themselves."[33]

By comparison, a section on "The Occupied Countries" comprises about a fifth of the book's length comprises and describes the various occupation regimes imposed by the German Reich and its European allies on a case-by-case basis. Lemkin systematically reviews NS practices, mechanisms of political and administrative suppression, economic exploitation, and cultural destruction in each country. A disproportionately short section, just four pages, covers "The Legal Status of the Jews." This has given rise to much speculation about how much Lemkin, who would lose almost his entire family in the Holocaust, actually knew about the NS destruction of the European Jews at the time of writing.[34] Judging this is difficult because his book shows numerous contradictions in retrospect. The short length of this chapter contrasts with its far-reaching conclusions, which imply that the murder of the Jews is unprecedented in international law:

> The treatment of the Jews in the occupied countries is one of the most flagrant violations of international law, not only of specific regulations of the Hague Regulations, but also of the principles of law of nations as they have emerged from established usage among civilized nations, from the laws of humanity, and from the dictates of public conscience—principles which the occupant is bound to respect.[35]

While there are indications that Lemkin was fully aware of the fate of the Polish Jews—he speaks of factorylike killings by gas, electrocution, and quicklime, as well as ghetto liquidations[36]—how much he knew about treatment of the rest of the European Jewish population is unclear. Revealingly, he observes that all Jews brought to Poland from the rest of Europe received the same treatment as the Jewish Poles.[37] That the fate of the Jews is given only a short treatment in *Axis Rule*, and that Lemkin does not mention the radical anti-Semitism of the National Socialists at all, does not automatically suggest an unconscious denial. He may have known that the leaders of the European exile governments in London had advised Jewish organizations to avoid emphasizing the singularly anti-Jewish dimension of the German occupation crimes, as this might have given a public platform to NS racial theory.[38] More fundamentally, Lemkin adopted a position on the special fate of the Jews that distinguished him greatly from other Jewish émigrés. While scholars and scientists who were driven out of Europe no longer believed in the protections of international law, and therefore advocated for a Jewish state, Lemkin pleaded for drawing the lesson from the Jewish catastrophe that international law had to be strengthened.[39]

"*Axis Rule* was pathbreaking, immensely well informed, but also a curious book," the historian Anson Rabinbach has written.[40] The book's confusing effects, evident today in the far-ranging discourse on Lemkin's concept of genocide, arise above all from the contradictions typical of a "juridical history writing" that aims, on the one hand, to educate about a given historical phenomenon but, on the other hand, sticks mainly to the normative and strategic arguments typical of legal writing. Aspects like the book's positivist, documentary style are understood more easily when one sees it for what it actually was: an expert and public contribution to the then-ongoing international discussion on potential punishments for German occupation crimes.

More recent debates on the origins of "genocide" as a term, however, have largely overlooked its context. *Axis Rule* was Lemkin's intervention in a controversy that had achieved a world-political dimension by November 1943,[41] after the Big Three signed the Moscow Declaration on atrocities calling for trials of all war crimes perpetrators to be held in the countries where crimes were committed but also, in the final sentence, of all "German criminals whose offenses have no particular geographical localization and who will be punished by joint decision of the government of the Allies." This enshrined the punishment of war crimes as a central aim of the war and acknowledged the intent to achieve this within a transnational framework.[42] Meanwhile, the United Nations Commission for the Investigation of War Crimes (UNWCC), founded a year earlier, had begun compiling lists of suspects and collecting evidence. Given that the Moscow Declaration had explicitly referred to "atrocities" by "German officers and men and members of the Nazi party," it is conspicuous that Lemkin's book instead speaks of the Axis, meaning not only Germany and Italy but also the various allied states and collaborating forces in occupied territories. Another special feature of

Axis Rule was that it did not make use of concepts and terms from established international law, instead placing the German occupation regimes within an interpretative framework that until then had been reserved for describing European imperialism and high imperialism.

The picture that Lemkin drew of German occupation practice in eastern and central Europe largely correlated with the asymmetrical model of rule used by the European great powers in their overseas colonial territories.[43] Lemkin's emphasis on the role of state bureaucracies and their wide-ranging executive authorities especially recalled the type of administrative and racial hegemony that the colonial powers had gradually imposed around the world in the nineteenth century. On the other side, Lemkin's description also implicitly included his opinion that the NS system went beyond the techniques of rule deployed in imperialism and colonialism. The most important difference for Lemkin was that NS occupation policy was not primarily aimed at utilitarian goals like the conquest, subordination, and economic exploitation and recruitment of native peoples as labor power. For example, in its relocations of large population groups, traditional colonial policy aimed to allow new settlement or the reeducation of colonized populations in religious or cultural patterns. Such impulses were only partly followed by the National Socialists. They instead pursued a comprehensive and radical new order through a population policy guided by ethnic-racial criteria that held regard neither for state borders nor for economic or cultural infrastructures.[44]

Lemkin otherwise assumed that the Jews would only be the first of the victim groups in this policy of a blood-based renewal and that sooner or later all other groups defined as unrelated to Germans by blood would be displaced or killed.[45] He considered the racial ideology to be so important that it was not even fully congruent with achieving the military victory of the German Reich. Even if the Germans and their allies were to lose the war, their practice of starvation policy and other measures of extermination would put them at a numerical, physical, and economic advantage for many years to come. Lemkin therefore found the idea of "Germanization" to be mistaken, because the National Socialists were not aiming at a renationalization or denationalization but at a demographic "engineering" that would assure a biologically justified dominance.[46]

In this fulminating analysis, which differed from his contemporaries' in its consistent refusal of a theoretical framework or historical contextualization, Lemkin classified German occupation rule as a colonial order of a new type that would eventually destroy the old European nation-state model and its multiethnic realities. His comparison of the various regions of Europe under occupation showed how the insane idea of an Aryan master race was being transformed into an inhuman social reality above all with laws and regulations. Well before the war's end, Lemkin thus developed an unconventional and heuristically stimulating perspective on the Third Reich that history scholarship would first assume about seventy years later.[47] Hannah Arendt would also conclude that National Socialism rested on a new way of combining racism and bureaucratism, although both had long been among the principles of rule used by imperialist administrative officials until then—but Arendt presumably never read Lemkin's study.[48]

Given that Lemkin wanted his text to be received as "Proposals for Redress," what legal conclusions did he draw from his own findings? In Lemkin's opinion, the German conduct of war aimed to reverse certain developments in modern international law since the nineteenth century. By waging war against populations, they undermined the doctrine, originally going back to Jean-Jacques Rousseau, that war is waged between states and their armies, not against populations, and that soldiers are therefore to be viewed as representatives of their respective states of origin.[49] Unlike many other international lawyers, Lemkin did not see the German measures in eastern Europe as merely arising from a radical military doctrine. Rather, he thought that the policies of disenfranchisement, expropriation, and mass destruction of entire population groups were aimed at establishing a permanent civil order with late-colonial characteristics. For this reason, the provisions of the Hague Conventions, already in terms of their approach, were inadequate for dealing with the violent potential of German occupation crimes. He therefore regarded establishing the legal stipulations of genocide as a necessary addition, and as an alternative to the Geneva and Hague laws of war, since genocide was "a problem not only of war but also of peace."[50]

Lemkin's thesis that NS occupation policy aimed at a comprehensive new order via population policy and the establishment of racially structured *Lebensraum* also determined his proposals for how criminal law should respond. *Axis Rule* repeatedly points to the outstanding responsibility of Hitler and the National Socialist German Workers' Party (NSDAP) for German occupation policy in eastern Europe, but when describing the specifics of its practices, Lemkin more often writes of "the Germans" and "the German techniques of rule." The operative carriers, in his view, were the civil administrations and the organs of police and justice in the occupied territories, while military and industry took on a peripheral role. He devoted much attention to the Gestapo and the SS, ascribing to them a leading role in the implementation of population policy. Without fully clarifying where exactly he wanted to draw the line for criminal culpability, the structure of the book resulted in a relatively broad concept of guilt. Given his presumption that the crimes were not simply effects of war conduct or "sporadic incidents of ill-will" but rather consequences of a program of destruction planned and prepared well before the war, he demanded that simple membership in these groups be made punishable.⁵¹ Concretely he proposed using the Anglo-Saxon stipulations for the crime of conspiracy or its continental analogue, "criminal association." Given that entry to the Gestapo and SS was voluntary, he wanted to foreclose the argument of "action following orders."⁵²

Next to the 1944 plan associated with US Secretary of the Treasury Henry Morgenthau Jr., *Axis Rule* was perhaps the most systematic and radical attempt to proceed from an analysis of NS practices of rule toward conclusions supporting a criminal treatment of state-led mass violence. In no small part thanks to his thorough knowledge of the various European legal systems, Lemkin was well positioned to distinguish the specifics of the predominant German occupation type from those of other occupation regimes. In contrast to the German emigrant Ernst Fraenkel, who in his 1941 work *The Dual State* had distinguished between a "normative state"—indispensable for the functioning of the private economy if by no means lawful—and a "measures state,"⁵³ Lemkin posited a legalist practice of persecution with all administrative branches more or less equally connected in its division of labor. But his most important contribution to the debate among international jurists was that he opened the way to a reinterpretation and modification of Geneva and Hague law by focusing on the extraordinarily destructive dimensions of NS population policy.

His idea that the systematic disenfranchisement, plunder, and murder of entire population groups should be understood as the result of a "conspiracy" that included Germany's old and new elites would find an open reception in Washington, where the problem of "Axis criminality" became a primary concern by the end of 1944. Despite his radical approach to criminal law and the ambiguities of the genocide concept as he presented it (which overall was counterproductive in judicial practice), it provided one of the most important conceptual foundations for the indictments at Nuremberg. It is difficult for us to tell whether it was also a factor that Lemkin's creation rested on an analysis of National Socialism that was deeply conservative and Eurocentric, with an implicit orientation to a Victorian "standard of civilization" and its inscribed "hierarchy of civilizations."⁵⁴ For all the invocations of its supposedly modern character, he basically saw the NS state as an atavistic regression to an earlier "barbarism." The dichotomous contrast of "barbarism" and "civilization" relied on an idealizing projection of the European nation-state model, in which the practice of (late) colonialism outside Europe and the problems of decolonization were still largely concealed.⁵⁵

Even as the war still raged, Lemkin was not the only Jewish European intellectual and legal scholar to advocate for a robust, expansive, and inclusive understanding of international law. The jurist Jacob Robinson, who had fled to the United States from Latvia, presented another such vision in July 1943. Long before such ideas were current at the US Department of War, Robinson proposed that the persecution of German, Austrian, and Czechoslovakian Jews and stateless persons in the period *before* the war's start in September 1939 could also be categorized as criminal acts and charged under international law. Regardless of whether these acts were illegal under national laws in force at the time of commission, he believed Allied prosecutors could classify them as actions taken in preparation for war, which would be in violation of the Kellogg-Briand Pact's ban on aggressive war.[56]

Robinson's biography as an international lawyer, an amateur historian, and a lobbyist in some ways paralleled that of Lemkin.[57] Born in 1889 in the Lithuanian town of Seirijai (Serej), he completed his law doctorate in Warsaw. He was taken as a prisoner of war by Germany in World War I. After his release, he directed a Jewish gymnasium for several years before his election to the Second Seimas (Parliament) of Lithuania in 1923 as one of seven deputies representing the Jewish minority group. As the member of several international legal bodies in the 1920s and 1930s, including the European Congress of Nationalities, Robinson devoted himself intensively to League of Nations minority law and helped initiate the famous Bernheim Petition to the League of Nations of May 1933. This successfully blocked implementation of NS policy over the Jewish minority in Upper Silesia until 1937. In 1940, Robinson and his family successfully fled to the United States, where he started teaching law at Columbia University. A few weeks after his arrival, in February 1941, he founded the Institute of Jewish Affairs (IJA) with support from the American Jewish Committee (AJC) and the World Jewish Congress (WJC). Robinson directed the IJA until 1947. Conceived as a Jewish legal think tank, the institute today remains devoted to studying the modern history of European Jewry and the creation of expert briefs for use in proceedings on reparations and international law.[58]

Recent years have seen intensive debate over whether the strategies of the American prosecutors in the postwar trials contributed to a later minimization or even distortion of the Holocaust.[59] This argument decontextualizes how the murder of the Jews was perceived at the time, but it also conceals the fact that the Holocaust only became a distinct issue at Nuremberg in the first place because of the engagement of Jewish groups and personalities. The example of Jacob Robinson allows insight into the various underlying motives, how these changed over time, and how scholarly and legal policy goals repeatedly came into conflict. After the European exile governments spoke only vaguely in the January 1942 St. James Declaration about German "acts of violence thus perpetrated against civilian populations,"[60] the IJA's work at first focused mainly on raising consciousness within the Allied and associated countries about the exceptional character of German's anti-Jewish persecution measures.[61] One step, for example, was to advocate that the UNWCC receive a Jewish representative. The IJA also began to collect documentary evidence and commission historical research on Germany's Jewish policy before September 1939.

The Riegner Telegram of August 1942, sent to the WJC offices in New York and London from its General Secretary Gerhart Riegner in Geneva and based on information from highly placed German informants, helped to crystallize the already-forming awareness among Jewish organizations that the NS leadership's intentions regarding European Jews under their occupation regimes were nothing less than exterminationist. Efforts were redoubled to find a suitable frame of analysis that could combine historical and legal arguments. Robinson was well aware that scientific objectivity claims could not so easily be brought under a single umbrella with politically effective legal lobbying. Early in 1942, he had clashed with the British section of the WJC because he did not fully share its view that the war crimes against eastern European Jews could be attributed to a developed, centrally steered plan for their destruction. Robinson thought this concept was both exculpatory and historically dubious. He preferred instead to foreground what German Jews had already experienced starting in 1933. Robinson believed that from the perspective of the National Socialists, Jewish Germans were seen as being like socialists, exponents of political Catholicism, and Protestant followers of the Confessing Church who refused NS doctrine. They posed an obstacle to the preparation of military expansionism. That was why these groups first had be cleared out of the way by administrative and pseudojudicial measures, before the attack on Poland could follow. Persecution of the Jews was the dynamite in the hands of the conspiring group, with which they followed the aim "to explode democratic societies."[62] In a thoroughly contradictory way, Robinson used elements of the NS "people's community" (*Volksgemeinschaft*) propaganda to support his argument that the anti-Semitic persecution measures since the 1933 seizure of power were meant above all to serve the preparation of a German war of conquest.[63]

At the latest, with the end of the war in sight at the turn of 1945, the expected criminal trials became the IJA's foremost priority, as Mark A. Lewis showed in his work on the WJC and IJA at Nuremberg. Concretely, they worked toward the goal of a "Jewish count," to be achieved through the submission of an amicus curiae brief to the court.[64] This was modeled on the legal institution under Anglo-Saxon case law, similar to the *Nebenklage* (accessory prosecution) under German criminal law, which allows a partisan assessor to represent the interests of an involved group. While the IJA's historical and political writings until then had mostly taken an educational approach, legal aspects now came to the fore. Thus, the first part of the IJA's *Book on War Crimes*, created in 1944, presented the persecution of the Jews as a linear process that had unfolded through individual stages since the 1920s according to an original plan. The second part developed this thesis of a "criminal conspiracy against the Jewish people" and was written in the style of an indictment and supported by witness reports, press clippings, legal texts, and excerpts from the speeches of the NS leadership. Given his intensified contacts to the Office of Strategic Services (OSS), Robinson gave marching orders to his coworkers: "Now we are not only historians; we are primarily attorney generals. . . . Here we must have sources for every statement—facts, names, dates."[65]

When the American chief prosecutor at Nuremberg, Robert H. Jackson, received Robinson for the first time in the summer of 1945, the latter presented remarkably precise statistical material about Jewish fatalities and reiterated his thesis of conspiracy: "The Jewish people," he declared at the time, "are the greatest sufferer of this war, if not in absolute number of its casualties, certainly in relative numbers." They therefore had

> a case of [their] own against the master Nazi criminals and their accomplices. The Jewish casualties are not a pure incident of the war or its preparatory stage, but the result of a well-conceived, deliberately plotted and meticulously carried out conspiracy. Hitler is the arch criminal, and Alfred Rosenberg is his philosopher. A 'science' was created to equip the 'gang' with rational justification for their infamous deeds.[66]

Although Jackson had met before with representatives from the WJC and the IJA and politely but firmly rejected the idea of a Jewish representative to the court, Robinson argued that their common goals should predominate. He pointed out that the US government had also adopted the idea of a conspiracy trial early on, after the British proposal to summarily execute NS functionaries and military officers and Morgenthau's plan for a "tough peace" had both fallen apart. The Israeli political scientist Shlomo Aronson attributes the government's turn to lobbying efforts by the New York lawyer Murray C. Bernays, whom the US Department of War had commissioned to devise a legal framework for war crimes trials. Bernays's proposal for overcoming the restrictions of Hague law was to conceive of crimes before the war as "conspiracy," a view Aronson asserts that Bernays picked up above all through his close contact with the Jewish organizations.[67] Even if empirical backing for Aronson's claim is on the thin side, there are indications that Bernays was inspired by IJA activists' intentionalist interpretations of NS policy. Soon after the meeting between Robinson and Jackson, in fact, the "Jewish Desk" at the OSS opened an institutional channel to the IJA.

IJA efforts and US pressure were among the reasons why the issue of the murder of the Jews entered into the Nuremberg indictments, as evidenced in the phrasing of a "common plan or conspiracy" in the first point of indictment and of "crimes against humanity" in the fourth point. These usages were conspicuous if not central to the charges.[68] Out of all the powers at the

International Military Tribunal, only the American agencies had built close contacts to Jewish nongovernmental organizations. At the IMT session of 11 December 1945, the US prosecutor William F. Walsh drew an oppressive panorama of persecution actions in the German-occupied territories of Europe, using documentary and filmed evidence gathered by the IJA over the several preceding years.[69]

Although their interests were not fully congruent, both sides in this partnership hoped for far-ranging strategic advantages. The IJA hoped that the worldwide shockwave of the Jewish catastrophe would provide an opportunity to modernize received international law through the addition of human rights criteria. They also hoped that detailing the history of persecution in court would bring progress toward the legal, symbolic, and political recognition of the special fate of the Jews. The American prosecutors were mainly interested in serving the aim of war prevention by enforcing the criminalization of aggressive war. By connecting two different if simultaneous historical processes—the legal and economic discrimination against German-Jewish citizens before the war, and the German politics of revisionism since 1933—their hope was also to decouple crimes against humanity from simple war events and to buttress the case historically that German elites had been involved in preparing the war. Since it was predictable that the accused German functionaries would mount every possible defense against intervention in state-sovereign immunity as unprecedented, and above all attempt to dismiss the charges as ex post facto, the American approach was to use the example of the German Jews in proving that the NS legal system had always been unlawful at its core.

The historian Donald Bloxham has argued that the American war crimes program resorted to using the Jewish NGOs' expertise and evidence only for instrumental reasons. This allowed the Americans to elevate the moral and educational claims of their ambitious project and to gloss over the evidentiary problems of a conspiracy accusation.[70] Playing on *Tyranny on Trial* (the title of the Nuremberg prosecutor Whitney H. Harris's memoir), Bloxham writes that the criteria for charging conspiracy worked like the "tyranny of a construct."[71] Bloxham's claim that the destruction of the Jews had a different significance for the US prosecutors than it did for Robinson and IJA employees can hardly be dismissed out of hand. Largely ignorant of the sociopolitical contexts, the prosecutors presented the repressive measures against German Jews as symptoms of a militarized society, and reduced anti-Jewish policy in occupied territories to an effect of excessive war conduct.

With hindsight, the compelling conclusion is nevertheless that the Americans' moral and political approaches were doubly justified. On the one hand, the experience of World War I had shown that the intended revolution in international law could be achieved only through a creative reinterpretation of the familiar legal tropes. On the other, the holistic if at times clueless court treatment of the murder of the Jews still made a fundamental effort to reckon with its "break with civilization" (Dan Diner) and its historical significance. The strategy may have stood on weak conceptual or empirical supports. The narrative of "conspiracy" may have lacked a measure of historical plausibility. Neither Jackson's team nor the OSS nor even the IJA placed much emphasis on racial anti-Semitism. The conservative judges at Nuremberg may have been unimpressed by the innovative turn to actionable history (what Raphael Gross termed *Geschichtsbarkeit*, or "historability"). But it is a stretch to hold any of this against the named actors.

The Frankfurt School Goes to War

When Franz Leopold Neumann's *Behemoth: The Structure and Practice of National Socialism* was published in 1942 by Victor Gollancz in London, the international debate on how to treat German war and occupation crimes had reached a dead point.[72] Although the study quickly became "a kind of bible" in the circles of American experts on Germany,[73] several passages in which the author expressed doubts about criminal trials went almost unnoticed. The book's title, indicating a high degree of self-confidence, conveyed Neumann's central thesis in one word. The former trade-union lawyer saw the Third Reich neither as a form of absolutism under the Führer nor as an authoritarian state. Instead, four competing power blocs—party, military, state bureaucracy, and monopoly economy—had taken on aspects of state power. In NS Germany, this process of usurpation and mutual radicalization had largely dissolved the ruling principles of the modern state. Terror and anarchy and a "totalitarianism" reliant on "monopoly economy" took over the former functions of rights and legal rationality.[74] The Third Reich could thus be described as an "un-state," a "behemoth." The term was clearly meant as a play on the title of the well-known seventeenth-century treatise by Thomas Hobbes, *Leviathan*, which described how an absolutist state power arose to create order and peace and push back the "behemoth" of unlimited violence in civil war.[75]

Coming from a Left Hegelian perspective and as a critique of Carl Schmitt's decisionist reading of Hobbesian state theory,[76] Neumann's analysis of the NS system also flowed into his observations on international law. Like many other non-fascist authors of his time, he came to the hardly surprising conclusion that the interwar period's League of Nations system had failed. Some of the reasons he gave for this, however, were surprising. On the one hand, he posited that the National Socialists had succeeded, with help from international lawyers in the German national-conservative camp, in destroying the unity of universalist international law by creating a new particularist international law, even if this made partial use of old terms. This "denial of the state and of state sovereignty," according to Neumann, was reflected especially in the abandonment of minority rights protections for the NS "law of 'folk groups.'"[77]

But Neumann saw the international law order also under threat from the liberal side. As an example, he cited a speech delivered to the International Bar Association in 1941 by none other than US Supreme Court Justice Robert H. Jackson, the future chief prosecutor at the Nuremberg IMT. In the speech, delivered soon after enactment of the US Lend-Lease policy to assist Great Britain militarily, Jackson condemned Axis violations of the Kellogg-Briand Pact of 1928 and responded with a plea to revive the theory of just war.[78] Neumann regarded this demand as a dangerous admixture of law with ethics, wherein the intrusion of natural law categories would hollow out the core of modern international law. The example of the Third Reich showed that dispensing with the "mask of the state" served to make the actual center of political power invisible. For this reason, it was all more worrying when liberal international lawyers weakened state sovereignty by elevating citizens of a state to subjects under international law, thus creating "divided loyalties" between one's country of origin and the international community.[79]

With a view on the creation of an international postwar order, Neumann furthermore declared:

> We need not dwell on the methodological difficulties arising from the theory of dual sovereignty. We can readily admit that any future international order set up after the destruction of fascism must have a proper psychological basis as well as the material means of maintaining an international community. That is not the present problem, however. However passionately we may desire the elimination of fascism, we cannot close our eyes to the possibility that it may not be wiped out. It is therefore of the utmost importance to lay bare the propagandist character of National Socialist conceptions of international law and the dangers inherent in the doctrine of dual loyalty. The following pages might well be entitled: *In Defense of State Sovereignty*.[80]

Long before the Roosevelt administration would settle on pursuing a judicial solution for NS leadership crimes, Neumann struck a clear position on this crucial question for Allied postwar planning. Both the idealistic international law philosophy of the New Dealers and the parallel debate on punishing German carriers of sovereignty were on the wrong track, Neumann believed, since they undermined the legal unity of the state and thus its function as the guarantor of the international legal order.

Neumann's monumental overall analysis was the decisive reason why he and a series of other social scientists were enticed away from the New

York-based Institute for Social Research in 1942 and enlisted in the building of the country's wartime spy agency, the Office of Strategic Services.[81] This became the start of several years' collaboration between the Washington war bureaucracy and a group of high-carat German academics. It was a paradoxical constellation. Most of the participating scholars were emigrants and thus classified as "enemy aliens." They continued to view themselves as Marxists or exponents of democratic socialism. Neumann's writings had been quite critical of liberalism in the twentieth century and of the New Deal. Also recruited into the OSS, his colleague Otto Kirchheimer had traced back the rise of fascism to, among other factors, the structural deficits of the ostensibly neutral and apolitical liberal state under rule of law.[82] Writing of his own experiences with this experiment in war-related contract research, John H. Herz, another emigrant who was employed at the OSS Research and Analysis Branch (R&A), commented: "It was as if the Left Hegelian world spirit had taken up residence in the Central European Division of the OSS."[83]

The driving force behind this unusual alliance was William J. Donovan, a successful Wall Street lawyer, member of the Republican Party, and personal friend of President Roosevelt. The "conservative interventionist" made it his mission to place spy work on a new footing by way of systematic scientization. His vision of enlisting the expertise of social scientists, economists, jurists, and psychologists for the war effort were in a sense consonant with the holistic theories of the German leftist intellectuals. Stimulated by the relatively open American academic system, the schooled Marxists had found it easy to synthesize their various analyses of politics, economy, and society into a big picture.[84] Otherwise, they all shared Neumann's conviction, expressed in the foreword to the first edition of *Behemoth*, that psychological warfare was a form of "politics" that had to be used to effect a separation between the NS leadership and the "great mass of the people."[85] It was thanks in no small part to a system of scholarly control and self-control, guided by a strict imperative of "objectivity," that the German policy reports from the R&A Central European desk under the direction of Eugene M. Anderson enjoyed such an excellent reputation among US government agencies.[86] The eighty-volume series of *Civil Affairs Guides* and the *Civil Affairs Handbook Germany* produced in 1944 under orders from the US Department of War, which would serve as the blueprints for administering liberated European territories, were put through a rigorous prepublication "purgatory of seven circles" (the R&A desk itself, the Foreign Economic Administration, the Department of State, the US Army and Marines, Interagency Editorial Committee, and the Pentagon's Civil Affairs Division).[88]

Research activity at R&A more or less followed the turns in American policy on Germany generally. The first phase was mainly concerned with classical espionage missions of gathering and evaluating information. Other issues gradually came to the fore. By the summer of 1943, the group worked from the premise that the military defeat of the German Reich had become inevitable and so gave increased emphasis to "questions of (negative) occupation and disciplinary processes and (positive) reconstruction processes."[89] According to Tim B. Müller's 2010 history of these "warriors and scholars," the more that Herbert Marcuse and Neumann learned about the true extent of the murder of the Jews, the more their earlier functionalist explanations for anti-Jewish policy—such as Neumann's thesis of anti-Semitism as a useful "spearhead of terror"—began to fade from their reports and memoranda.[90] Still they persisted in using sophisticated historical analysis to counter metaphysical constructs such as Winston Churchill's invocations of a supposed "Prussian militarism" or a "Teutonic urge for domination."[91]

The R&A reports on Germany, however, encouraged a sobriety that did not lack for passion, despite the spatial distance. Until shortly before the war ended, hope remained that the military invasion of Germany might be avoided by a self-liberation from within. Like the leadership of the Social Democratic Party's exile organization in the United States, the Association of Free Germans, the reports vehemently criticized the Allied war aim of "unconditional surrender."[92] The scholars' original ambivalence about the project of an Allied occupation is obvious in a December 1943 memorandum written by Neumann, Marcuse, and Felix Gilbert. They prophesied that if they had to invade Germany, the Allies would face an insurmountable dilemma: "In order to make sure of their victory and to remove the German danger, they will have to march into Germany and occupy her, but in doing so, they will probably prevent the anti-Nazi reaction of the progressive forces then coming to its fulfillment, and thereby will prevent a solution of the German problem which would give a better guarantee for future peace than any peace treaty could provide."[93]

Although the role of the R&A team in preparing the Nuremberg trials still generates controversies today, the literature is mostly in agreement that the conceptual, theoretical, and empirical foundations of the Allied war crimes program more or less continued with the approaches developed before 1945. In other words, it is believed that the wartime planning had foreseen the combination of a retroactive punishment of serious human rights violations with a forward-looking reconstruction of Germany as pillars of the postwar international order.[94] Neumann's papers make it clear, however, that the participation of the émigré scholars in this project was not at all without its frictions. Even in the second edition of *Behemoth*, published in 1944, Neumann emphatically reiterated criticisms of plans to judicialize the war and engage in judicial interventionism on humanitarian grounds. It was perhaps inevitable that differences of opinion with OSS management would eventually arise. Neumann's involvement at Nuremberg would necessarily have been preceded by a rethinking process and major intellectual effort on his part. Since Neumann did not write about his motives, however, in hindsight we can only speculate about whether he revised his own thinking about the regime, underwent a late reconciliation with judicial activism, or simply felt the pressure to conform as a professional.[95]

Donovan's tireless alacrity assured that the German experts from R&A were brought into the preparations for the IMT soon after Jackson's appointment as the American chief prosecutor. In the fall of 1944, the OSS director began to flood the Department of War with memoranda and position papers on the war crimes question. This led to an institutional cooperation with the military Judge Advocate General's Corps starting in December.[96] After Jackson's nomination in May 1945, the OSS officially received the mission of advising the American prosecutors in compiling the list of defendants, securing the relevant evidentiary material, and laying down legal-theoretical foundations for the coming trials. It is difficult to assess the degree to which the R&A experts were initiated into the running discussions about a judicial treatment of "Axis criminality" or maintained contacts with other official and civil-society organizations also involved in this complex.

Some insight can be gained from an internal paper that Neumann submitted to his division chief on 4 May 1945, two days after Jackson's appointment to head the IMT. While Neumann had once accused the Supreme Court justice of trying to reverse the civilizational achievement of separating law from morality, he now asserted that Jackson had spoken out against trials and for the summary execution of the NS leadership. There was a danger, Neumann claimed, that "influential circles" in Great Britain would support this option, since the British were afraid that their appeasement policy might be brought up in a trial. Moreover, Neumann predicted the coming trial would run into problems if a way could not be found to investigate the crimes of Germans against Germans. Finally, he pleaded that for political reasons German courts should participate in announcing convictions for the crimes. Given that Allied and international courts could not take on more than an "insignificant number" of cases—Neumann threw out a number of five thousand—it was all the more important to give German courts a meaningful role in the processes as a whole.[97]

That Neumann possessed only inexact notions of the international law policy goals of the American war crimes program at the beginning of the four-power occupation can be read into his notion that German justice agencies would play an important role in the judicial investigation of NS crimes. This view would prove to be accurate at a much later stage, but in the spring of 1945, it would have seemed altogether utopian. However, the comments also show that his earlier fundamental opposition to internationalist legalism as conceived by Jackson had already given way to a more pragmatic attitude.

Confronted with the historic challenge of helping to solve the legal problems in the preparation of the "trial of the century" (Bradley F. Smith), the R&A scholars apparently made the effort to catch up on lost terrain and to influence the American prosecution concept as much as they could. The difficulty in this task lay in combining a coherent narrative out of their own analyses of the NS system of rule—which, as we have seen, was of a structuralist bent—with the individualist scheme of a prosecutorial indictment.

The idea that National Socialism relied on an antagonism between "ruling" and "ruled" classes was fundamental to the theory of "psychological warfare" as it had been developed above all by Neumann. As Barry Katz found in his lucid 1989 study on the war research by R&A, this entailed specific concepts of identifiable guilt and responsibility that could be used in the charges.[98] Since the view still prevailed that every form of German statehood had fallen with the Nazis' seizure of power, a substitute political order had to be modeled from which one could derive decision-making processes and structures of command, and above all culpable responsibilities. Neumann and Kirchheimer pleaded for taking literally the "leader principle" developed in the works of prominent NS legal theoreticians and politicians—like Ernst Rudolf Huber, Werner Best, Otto Koellreuter, and Hans Frank—and turning it against the NS leadership.

In their study on *Leadership Principle and Criminal Responsibility*, the R&A scholars argued that every institution and organization of the Third Reich was constructed along a tight, hierarchically ordered lines, with persons authorized by Hitler at the summit of each. The Führer also formulated the political-administrative guidelines and commands guiding all the subordinate organs. But this was done not by a rigid delegation of tasks from above but by an expansion of the authorities of the "subleaders," who were given the autonomy to interpret and apply the guidelines in the sense intended by the regime as a whole. With this theory of domination, which in the opinion of many scholars served to retroactively "legalize" the arbitrary rule of the National Socialists,[99] the OSS scholars sought preventively to undermine the expected defenses of a "command emergency" and collective responsibility. They accomplished this by understanding the ideological claims and the actual practice of rule as a unity and making it into the basis for evidentiary presentation in court: "In reversing these standards [those of NS ideology] and in making the Nazi leaders responsible for what we consider as war crimes, they would indeed have to answer for what actually has been done in accordance with their own standards and policies."[100]

Next to the question of how a punishment for crimes against German citizens before 1939 could be grounded in lawful standards without reproach, in early 1945 the jurists in the Department of War were most concerned that the NS regime presented them with an exorbitant number of suspects.

Colonel Bernays, encouraged by legal scholars like Lemkin and Robinson, hoped to manage this by introducing the new criminal criteria of conspiracy and organized crime,[101] while the R&A scholars were more vague and partly contradictory on this point.[102] Most of their treatments, relying on Neumann's theory of elites, tended to stress the responsibilities of Hitler, his closest associates, and the leading groups of the party, business, bureaucracy, and military. The "socialization of violence" (Michael Geyer), meaning a widespread readiness to commit violence among broad strata of the population, was treated as a consequence of "terrorist technocracy" in a highly industrialized society that allowed a dissolution of individual responsibility.[103] This echoed the view that the seizure of power had occurred against the will of a large part of the German people, most of whom had stood behind the Weimar democracy.[104]

Although we are still mostly in the dark about the reasons, it must be stressed that the R&A team's analyses contradicted some of the administration's ideas. While administration jurists used the regime's anti-Jewish laws as evidence to show that NS law was in reality a non-law, Kirchheimer argued that a core of lawful norms and legal principles had remained unaltered. Norms like the law against murder were never revocable, "even though they were never enforced when politically inconvenient."[105] This thesis of partial legal continuity after 1933, which can hardly be reconciled with *Behemoth*, would later become an important formula for the German defense at Nuremberg.

By contrast, interpretations of the anti-Jewish policy remained more or less in harmony, even if the various attempts at explanation differed in nuance. A basic unanimity prevailed regarding the opinion that the genocide of the European Jews proceeded from a long-term, centrally steered plan handed down by the NS leadership. This was closely bound with the concept that persecution measures against German state nationals and aggressive suppression of foreign societies were fundamentally two sides of the same coin. Although Marcuse had gradually distanced himself during the war from Neumann's functionalist "spearhead" theory of NS anti-Semitism,[106] his works for the R&A still interpreted anti-Jewish policy as a safety valve instituted by the NS leadership to give vent to suppressed class-based tensions. A memorandum in June 1945 expressed almost a textbook version of a Marxist tendency to trivialize racialized, radical anti-Semitism:

> 1. The Jew was the weakest enemy of Nazism; the attack on him therefore was the most promising and the least risky one. 2. The Jew was the one enemy against whom the Nazis could hope to unite otherwise divergent masses of supporters. 3. The elimination of the Jew, as a competitor, would be most profitable to the petty-bourgeoisie which furnished the largest mass support

for the Nazi movement. 4. The Jew was found in all countries; Nazi anti-Semitism was therefore a convenient means for mobilizing potential Nazi allies in foreign countries. . . . 5. The ubiquity of the Jews as arch-enemy provided the Nazis with a justification for carrying the struggle for power beyond the frontiers of the Reich.[107]

To recapitulate, the concept papers created by the R&A team in preparation for the US war crimes program relied on a selective reception of the international debate and displayed a rather ambivalent attitude to New Deal legalism. Not least because of Donovan's orders, they strove to help the administration solve the international law challenges posed by the IMT program; but overall the expatriate social theorists remained skeptical of criminal law as a means for solving the German problem. Their disagreement with the policy direction in fact increased after the immediate postwar period,[108] which has been characterized as a "Nuremberg interregnum" (Jeffrey Herf). In 1949, Neumann introduced his retrospective on the trials with the highly sobering remark that the Nuremberg and Tokyo tribunals had created as many problems as they had solved.[109]

Despite the social scientists' serious reservations about the central concepts deployed in the American indictment—including conspiracy, war of aggression, and individual culpability under international law—points of contact remained. At the same time, the civil servants at the war department consistently used analytical frameworks borrowed from the Neumannesque sociology of power, assuming an antagonism in Germany between the ruling NS power blocs and the ruled masses. They also shared Neumann's opinion that the regime had been a structure without form, based on a non-legal order. At the London conference to ratify the IMT statute, Jackson stated clearly that he intended to criminalize domestic incidents only if these could be connected to the planning of aggressive war.[110] Thanks to a few points of agreement, as well as a dose of pretending, the R&A scholars were able at least partly to identify with the Nuremberg project. Although they were still convinced that the aim of democratic reeducation could only be achieved through a politically based disempowerment of the ruling strata, they nevertheless put their expertise at the service of the planned trials.[111]

Hermann Jahrreiß and the Nuremberg Defense Strategy

In recent years, the remark by the US deputy prosecutor at the IMT, Robert M. W. Kempner, that Nuremberg had become "the greatest politilogical and historical research site of all time,"[112] has turned almost into the slogan of a booming Nuremberg mythology. This catchy but trivializing formulation conceals too easily that the "Nuremberg laboratory" was not so much a site of objective and distanced historical research as a battleground. The court proceedings offered a forum where disparate and often conflicting interpretations of NS-era history were produced and publicly negotiated.[113] For the German participants, the point often enough was to create a "purified memory" of the past that could serve the function of a new beginning.[114]

Alongside the defendants themselves, their defense attorneys took on a leading function in constituting common historical images and basic narratives.[115] It is often overlooked that most of the lawyers did not simply act to execute their roles as defenders, but displayed a high degree of personal initiative and agency.[116] The twenty-seven defense attorneys and fifty-four assistants who appeared before the IMT from October 1945 to October 1946[117] comprised a fairly socially homogenous group.[118] Besides the legal scholar Franz Exner and the international lawyers Hermann Jahrreiß, Herbert Kraus, and Ernst Wolgast, two other academic legal scholars were present. The rest were practicing lawyers and former official jurists who had been dismissed from the justice agencies.[119] In 1937, Kraus had been forced to vacate his professorial chair in Göttingen because of differences with the regime. Otto Kranzbühler, a naval judge advocate, had been employed as a law of war researcher by the Kaiser Wilhelm Institute for International Law since 1934.[120] None of the other Nuremberg defense attorneys possessed experience in the disciplinary specialties of IL. The general scarcity of personnel who were both qualified and not incriminated is indicated by the fact that at least one-quarter of all licensed lawyers before 1945 had been members of the NSDAP, SA, or SS.[121] Georg Fröschmann, an assistant defense counsel for Joachim von Ribbentrop (the German foreign minister since 1938), had belonged to both the NSDAP and the SA. Alfred Seidl (defense counsel of Hans Frank and Rudolf Hess), Fritz Sauter (defending Walther Funk and Baldur von Schirach), and Hans Laternser (defending members of the General Staff and military services commands) were also party members until 1945. Hans Gawlik, who defended the SS itself as an accused criminal organization, was formerly a "party comrade" and a prosecutor employed by the "General Gouvernement," the occupation regime imposed on the rump territories of Poland not annexed by the Reich or by the Soviet Union in 1939. There is no evidence that any of the German defense attorneys were politically or racially persecuted under the NS regime. The only exception was Exner, who would have qualified as a "level 2 Jewish crossbreed" under the race laws.[122] Despite his genealogy, the criminal attorney continued to teach law in Munich until 1944 and was able to establish himself as one of the Third Reich's leading experts in "criminal biology." His publications had hailed the typical criminal-policy measures of the regime, including the sterilization of delinquents.[123]

While it can be presumed the professional defense lawyers at Nuremberg accepted their mandates out of a mixture of material and idealist interests,[124] the motives of the participating academics appear far more complex. The case of the international law scholar Hermann Jahrreiß indicates academic predilections that not only oriented the content of his published work but also gave rise to a particular style of defense. Jahrreiß spent the last year of the war away from his home university in Cologne, teaching instead at the Tyrol state university in Innsbruck, Austria. This was likely why Exner, a former colleague from their days at the University of Leipzig, took an interest in Jahrreiß in the summer of 1945. Exner invited him to help in the defense of Alfred Jodl, whom the Allies intended to indict at Nuremberg. Jodl had served the German armed forces, the Wehrmacht, as chief of the General Staff. He and Exner had shared a long-running friendship. Exner's offer to Jahrreiß was well timed, as the latter had been fired by his old university soon after the war. An examining body under the legal scholar Hans Carl Nipperdey,[125] appointed by the British occupation authority, had recommended that the University of Cologne let go of two out of the nine tenured professors in its law department: Hermann Krawinkel, a former NSDAP member, and Jahrreiß, who had never joined the party.[126] Jahrreiß was cited instead for his anti-English publications, of which he had in fact produced a long series during the war.[127]

Jahrreiß, born in 1894, had followed a path similar to that of many other German international law scholars after World War I. They had benefited from the boom in demand for political consulting and the associated professionalization and institutionalization of their discipline (see chapter 3).[128] Jahrreiß chose an international law thesis for his doctorate in 1921 at the suggestion of his teacher and mentor Richard Schmidt. A lecturer at both the Leipzig Faculty of Law and the German Academy for Politics (DHfP),[129] Schmidt was a passionate exponent of the then fashionable new discipline of "geopolitics." With Schmidt again as his adviser, Jahrreiß presented his habilitation manuscript (the qualifying work for tenure) just two years later to the Department of Public Law, International Law, and Legal and State Philosophy at Leipzig.[130] Jahrreiß's habilitation subject, which would become akin to a life's pursuit and determine his research activity over the next three decades, posed questions typical of the era: To what extent was the 1919 Treaty of Versailles binding? What consequences could be derived for the German Reich and the international state order?[131] After several years as a lecturer in Leipzig and Greifswald, Jahrreiß was hired in 1937 by the University of Cologne, where he enjoyed his most productive period of work. He issued monographs and longer commissioned works at an almost annual pace, all while remaining busy as an editor and as an adviser to clients. Although he apparently refused an offer to join the Faculty of Law in

Kiel, he did develop increasingly intensive contacts to a professor there, Paul Rittersbusch. A former assistant to Schmidt, Rittersbusch was a shooting star of the now highly "ethnic" German doctrine of international law, and active as a coordinator within the rising field of foreign studies.[132]

Despite his close connections to the networks of the "geopoliticians" and his work on the international law commission of the Academy for German Law (DASR), Jahrreiß treated his discipline as a practical science. Until the start of the war, he remained loyal to IL's universalist fundaments and its idea of a uniform terminology. This changed after 1939 as he was increasingly influenced by Carl Schmitt's "grand area" (*Grossraum*) theory. Following his dispute with the international lawyer and SD member Reinhard Höhn in 1937, Schmitt had shown more of an interest in IL issues. At Rittersbusch's invitation, Schmitt delivered a 1939 lecture at the University of Kiel to present his idea of a continental European "grand area order" that was irreconcilable with the "international law order" of the "Anglo-Saxon great powers."[133] Starting in 1940, Jahrreiß joined the "Humanities War Mission," an academics' initiative led by Rittersbusch and financed by the German Research Foundation (DFG). Jahrreiß was named leader of its international law group. In preparing the initiative's launch, Rittersbusch chaired an April 1940 conference in Kiel, where Jahrreiß helped to develop an interdisciplinary profile for the group. The war mission aimed to "elucidate in a scientific and incontestable way the idea of a new European order, which in the final analysis is the point of this fight [the war], and to manifest the truth and reality of the life of the European peoples."[134] Under Jahrreiß's aegis the participating legal scholars produced five brochures by 1944, all published by Hanseatischen Verlagsanstalt in a series called Transformation of the World Order.[135]

In his writings for the Humanities War Mission, Jahrreiß reached for the heights as a propagandist for a Germanocentric understanding of Europe. Borrowing from Schmitt's grand area theory, he posited the existence of four "political continents" or "grand areas" that found themselves in constant antagonism. Unlike classical international law, where all the talk about "humanity and freedom" in reality merely expressed the power interests of the "Anglo-Saxon imperium,"[136] the new European continental order under German-Italian leadership was based on the principle of "political self-determination." For the moment, the outer geographic borders of this continental formation in the making were not simple administrative but actually defensive lines. They should not yet be considered final. If the Soviet Union should still exist after the war, these borders would run along the Ural Mountains. In the vertical direction, the future continent would stretch over a zone between the North and South poles. "Eurafrica" would become a "reserve region."[137]

In September 1941, even as Jahrreiß was delivering his vision of a continental European grand area order under German-Italian leadership, political and military events had already overtaken him in several ways. On the Soviet battlegrounds the Wehrmacht, the SS, and the occupation policing authorities were occupied with trampling the laws of war underfoot, extinguishing entire population groups, and allowing millions of prisoners of war to starve. In the occupied territories of Poland, the SS and the German civilian administration had established a regime of terror aimed at both economic exploitation and forced Germanization. The radical racism of the National Socialists, relying on the concept of unchanging natural laws and the vision of an eternal fight for life and death, did not mesh well with the premises among moderate German international lawyers that their country's "final victory" would be followed by something like a hierarchically stratified "defense and economic community" of European peoples. Categories of geopolitical spheres of influence and binational relations were, in the end, irreconcilable with the biologistic utopianism of the NS worldview. Like many other national-conservative legal scholars, Jahrreiß was unable and quite possibly unwilling to comprehend the murderous consequences of the racial ideology until it had reached its bitter end. It cannot be ruled out altogether that he clung to the illusion that the leadership would uphold certain legal rules. This does not change the most important facts about him. As a key node within the public intellectual network of grand area researchers, and through his voluntary work for the Humanities War Mission, Jahrreiß helped provide the terms and tropes on which more explicitly committed theoreticians of destruction like Werner Best and Reinhard Höhns could build.[138]

As we have seen, from 1945 to 1946 Jahrreiß found himself in what he surely regarded as a deplorable personal situation. Exner's offer to have him hired as an assistant defense counsel at the IMT trial would have at least provided temporary employment. Next to the daily canteen food, cigarettes, and state lawyer stipends—the Allies were paying a monthly wage of 9,500 Reichsmark for mandatees[139]—there was also the prospect that one might influence the legal opinions and historical interpretations of the Allied victors, perhaps even refute these on certain points. The thought seems not to have occurred to Jahrreiß that there might be anything dubious in his participation in the trial, given that it was based on the very same humanitarian law and laws of war that he had done so much to roll back and demolish in the preceding years. All this notwithstanding, there are indications that during the early years of his career, he had shown an interest in the Leipzig war crimes trials after World War I, making for a possible additional motive for his participation at the IMT. This, however, cannot be confirmed.

The indictment of Jodl and twenty-three other "major war criminals" was based on stipulations in the Nuremberg Charter, which was ratified in London in the summer of 1945 by the four victorious Allies—the United States, the Soviet Union, Great Britain, and France—that had taken over zones of military occupation within German territory. In keeping with the vision of US Chief Prosecutor Jackson, the criminal trial of the former Nazi leadership was intended to revive movement toward a lawfully supported world peace order, which had stalled during the interwar period. The indictments therefore tended to highlight charges of "Crimes against Peace" (or conspiracy to commit war as stipulated under Article 6a of the Nuremberg Charter), with additional charges for "War Crimes" (Art. 6b) and "Crimes against Humanity" (Art. 6c). While the American and British prosecutorial teams were tasked with proving that the defendants had participated in a "common plan or conspiracy" to "plan, prepare, and wage a war of aggression," the French and Soviets were mainly responsible for proving the charges of war crimes and crimes against humanity perpetrated in the course of the war. Colonel General Alfred Jodl, one of Hitler's closest military advisers before 1945, was charged under all these counts. He was accused of having played an important role in German war preparations and of having coauthored countless orders in violation of international law, including the infamous Commissar Order of June 1941, which ordered the summary execution of any and all Soviet political commissars identified among captured troops.[140]

In addition to serving as an assistant counsel in Jodl's defense, Jahrreiß was tasked with presenting an expert brief on whether "peacetime crimes" were punishable under international law. The latter was the more important job, since he would be speaking on behalf of all the defendants. His opinion would address three legal questions: Did the allegations involve punishable offenses, and if so, were these offenses punishable at the time they were committed? Was the state itself punishable for the alleged acts, and was it possible to hold state functionaries individually culpable for allegations against the state? And was the court at Nuremberg in particular empowered to punish the criminal acts? In his brief, delivered before the court on 4 July 1946, Jahrreiß's answers were all in the negative. At the time when they began their campaigns of conquest, he argued, the German politicians and military officials now in the dock would not have been capable of recognizing the illegality of their actions. The League of Nations charter, the Kellogg-Briand Pact, and the two mutual nonaggression treaties that the German Reich had signed with the Soviet Union and with Poland were not applicable. On the contrary, the international security system of which these treaties were part had already been rendered obsolete before the start of the war, and recognizably so. None of the participating states felt bound by such arrangements. Regarding the charge of aggressive war, Jahrreiß ruled out any culpability, either for states or for individuals. By the force of their sovereignty, states were empowered to decide freely on the "ultimately existential questions" of war and peace.

Functionaries had also not incriminated themselves, Jahrreiß argued, since they had acted not as "Herr Müller or Schmidt," that is, as random individuals, but as representatives of the state: an entity that the common European understanding held to be above personhood.[141] If the indictment "in the name of the world legal community" intended to "legally condemn individual men for their decisions on war and peace," it would engage in a "privatization" of the state—indeed in its "demolition." The trial was, in fact, retroactively demolishing the former German state for actions taken during a period in which its sovereignty had still stood "in full force."[142] In supporting this legal opinion, Jahrreiß cited the well-known Austrian American jurist Hans Kelsen, who had been in US exile since 1940. In a 1943 law review article on responsibility for war crimes, Kelsen had argued that the violation of international treaties justified collective punishment of the responsible states, but that individual culpability among state leaders was possible only if a state had agreed explicitly to allow the criminal prosecution of such individuals in a prior international treaty.[143]

The German defense teams at Nuremberg made a habit whenever possible of backing their arguments with citations from exiled Jewish legal scholars.[144] But in this case, the device was also likely inspired by Jahrreiß's own past. Kelsen had been driven out of his professorship at the University of Cologne in 1933, after the Nazis came to power, and Jahrreiß benefited directly from his well-regarded colleague's departure when he was chosen to replace Kelsen as coeditor of the prestigious law journal *Zeitschrift für öffentliches Recht*. Beyond the attempt to paper over the international isolation of German legal studies, Jahrreiß's rhetorical invocation of Kelsen before the IMT may have also been intended to cast a harmonious light on the harsh reality of personal relations under the Third Reich. In hindsight, the irony of this cooptation was that Jahrreiß presented Kelsen as though he were an absolute opponent of ex-post-facto law. Yet, of all national and international lawyers, Kelsen had been among the most tireless in his advocacy of institutionalizing culpability under international criminal law.[145] This proved significant in the future evolution of the West German anti-Nuremberg discourse, insofar as the argument of *nulla poena sine lege* (no penalty without a law), which would become the leitmotif against Allied prosecutions, was attributed to Kelsen, who could be presented as doubly above suspicion—as a democrat and as a Jew.[146]

Jahrreiß used the first part of his testimony to sing the praises of state sovereignty. He blamed the Western powers and the Soviet Union for the alleged nullification of the international security system—but not Germany. In the second half of his lecture, he turned to the internal conditions of the NS state. This part was not republished in the later printed versions, but its effects were lasting. For it was here that Jahrreiß outlined the elements of a collective "command emergency," which would become a key construct in justifying acts under the regime. Using elaborate prose, he argued that the "will of the Führer" had become the "organizational guiding principle" for the entirety of public life in Germany starting in 1933, with every individual directed by it.[147] Under this "Führer Principle," officials and civil servants had willingly subordinated themselves to Hitler's commands, seeing these simply as a form of bureaucratic governance. That they did not question the obligatory nature of his orders could be attributed above all to the behavior of the international community, who had recognized Hitler as the legal German head of state. In the final analysis, it was foreign recognition that caused most Germans to see little point in resisting the tyranny themselves.

Jahrreiß's presentation to the Allied judges drew a picture of the relations of power in the Third Reich that perpetuated the propaganda and political morality of the NS "people's community" (*Volksgemeinschaft*) while reflecting little of the complex and contradictory realities of the Third Reich. Although it is unclear how much Jahrreiß knew about the analyses of the Neumann group in detail, his analysis was conspicuously similar to the latter's sociological power model of the totalitarian leader principle. Of course, the social scientists of the OSS had stressed the responsibility of the four power blocs of party, business, military, and bureaucracy and had attributed practical autonomy to the many "subleaders." Jahrreiß paved over such distinctions to create a schematic dichotomy of Führer and Volk. Connecting to the earlier public campaigns against the "dishonor of Versailles," he furthermore presented Germany's development since World War I as a matter of a destiny that perforce would culminate in the lust for military revanchism and aggression. Leeway in making decisions and personal autonomy were peripheral factors in this deterministic interpretation. If these even existed, they were to be found exclusively on the side of the western powers. The German people as a whole were the well-intentioned and cruelly seduced victims of the despot to whom they had been abandoned by the rest of the world (*das Ausland*).[148]

Given this backdrop, it is no surprise that Jahrreiß saw only a functional meaning in the "new" humanitarian international law and treated it as more or less analogous to the punishment clauses of the Treaty of Versailles. Many German commentators noted his abbreviated and deeply pessimistic view on the future of international law and the human rights ideal. "Notwithstanding that the acts of the defendants would have been considered criminal in most civilized countries," a correspondent of the *Berliner Tagesspiegel* wrote, the defense argument seemed to lack "any hint of understanding that this is an unprecedented case of historical justice in progress." The judge in this trial was "history" itself. It was to history that the tribunal was responsible. Those who adopted the position that the state, and not individuals, should be held answerable for crimes against international law merely demonstrated their own inability to draw forward-looking lessons from the experience of the past twelve years, the commentary concluded. Most of the German lawyers at the IMT apparently lacked awareness that they stood before the court not only as "representatives of the accused but as representatives of the German people."[149]

Was it really the case, however, that the German defense lacked a deeper understanding of the trial's historic dimensions? The French historian Annette Wieviorka has argued that the IMT was "historic" in a double sense: first, because the prosecution wanted to convey a particular historical narrative, and second, because it wanted to write history by criminalizing war itself.[150] This set up a kind of dialectical interaction. The German defenders took up the prosecutors' claims of historicity and generalized these in a way that went far beyond the narrower interests of their clients. Generally, they attempted not to prove the innocence of the accused but to relieve the entire German population from supposed accusations of "collective guilt."[151] For this purpose, they put the legend out into the world that the legal consciousness of the Germans had been so befogged by the many contradictions, solecisms, and injustices of the universalist international law of Versailles and Geneva that, by 1933, the people were no longer capable of mounting an effective defense against National Socialism. The defenders furthermore engendered the impression that crimes against German nationals and foreigners alike could be traced back to diverse and unspecified "Führer orders." These were so obligatory by nature that no German could have possibly questioned them.

Hermann Jahrreiß's brief to the IMT rejected the new "legalist paradigm" (Michael Walzer) of the four victor powers and the United Nations—which henceforth would hold not only states but also individuals accountable as subjects under international law—as a violation of the ex-post-facto principle. His argument focused mainly on the charge of crimes against peace, the penalization of which was indeed highly controversial. It was also clear, if implicit, that Jahrreiß hoped to stretch his rejection of retroactive justice into grounds for dismissing the other charges, of war crimes and crimes against humanity. The definitions of the latter two, however, were far less controversial.[152] Jahrreiß's opinion on these would become relevant in 1947, when he testified on the importance of the Führer system as an expert witness for the defense in the case of *United States vs. Josef Altstoetter et al.*, "Case 3" in the US military's Nuremberg follow-up trials, also known as the Justice Case.[153] The retroactivity defense was invoked in the trial of sixteen high-ranking NS jurists, insofar as the indictment relied not only on the IMT statute but also on the occupation authorities' Control Council Law No. 10 (CCL 10) of 20 December 1945.[154] Unlike the IMT statute, which closely linked crimes against humanity with crimes against peace, CCL 10 expressly allowed charges for crimes against humanity independently of an aggressive war or war planning context. Concretely, this allowed the judges at United States Military Court III to deliver convictions against defendants for actions taken against German citizens *before* 1939. The *Altstoetter* indictment concerned categorically NS injustice laws, such as the "genetic health law" (*Erbgesundheitsgesetz*) of 1934 and the "racial defilement law" (*Rassenschandegesetz*) of 1935.

Jahrreiß's strategy distinguished him from Carl Schmitt. After 1945, the latter stuck with his blanket condemnation of humanitarian international law.[155] Jahrreiß did not attack the premise that criminal norms under international law were binding, however. With regard to the punishability of the jurists under indictment in *Altstoetter*, he instead claimed that none of the defendants could have developed awareness of committing an injustice under the circumstances of the time. German jurisprudence during the Weimar period was such that it fostered an unconditional fealty to the letter of the law among jurists, according to Jahrreiß. It was especially democratic legal scholars, like Gerhard Anschütz and Gustav Radbruch, who had elevated procedural legality into the most inviolable standard. After the Nazi seizure of power in 1933, this meant that most jurists recognized Führer orders as law of the land, although their status as a source in jurisprudence was dubious. Questioned on this claim by the chief judge in the case, Jahrreiß declared that Hitler's orders were also treated as obligatory even if these openly violated international law.[156] The US military court did not reject this thesis of "positivist corruption" but merely regarded it as immaterial to the case. Unlike Jahrreiß, they saw no retroactivity problem insofar as the behavior of NS jurists was judged against norms and standards that *were* known at the time of the act yet were ignored anyway. The judges used the opportunity to point out that Jahrreiß had at least implicitly admitted the existence of a core reserve of internationally recognized norms that were still operable under the NS regime.

Despite this, Jahrreiß' argument in *Altstoetter* proved pathbreaking in the treatment of NS judicial injustice, both in the Western occupation zones and in the Federal Republic after 1949. He had in effect handed the entire justice community a justification with which they could counter both criminal and historical/political accusations. It comes as no surprise that this thesis of jurists as "victims of legal positivism" soon came to play a central role in the politics of the past as debated in the young FRG.[157] It was soon put to use by Hermann Weinkauff, the first presiding judge of the West German Federal Court of Justice (BGH) and would be revived through numerous variations right up until the 1980s. What is more surprising is that Jahrreiß, who did not invent the thesis but was perhaps its most important popularizer, did not ever again claim it as his achievement.

Jahrreiß came from the post-World War I generation of German international law scholars who turned the work of "national rebuilding" and the revisionist fight against "Versailles" into integral elements of their professional ethos. Up until the outbreak of war in 1939, they continued to profess the traditional concepts of international law with its respect for state sovereignty and for obligations entailed by interstate agreements. Both geopolitics and the increasingly popular grand area research were among the ideologies bridging the moderate jurists with those who attempted to erect a new, radically particularist, ethnic-racial "international law" on the ruins of the old League of Nations system. The example of Jahrreiß shows how this nationalist shaping of scientific understanding continued to have effects after the epochal transition of 1945. Abandoning the Anglophobic and anti-Semitic polemics of the Nazi era, his expert briefs and court pleadings nevertheless connected the Nuremberg trials to the old and familiar image of an international legal system designed *against* the German Reich, as though it were all self-evident. He saw the Allied occupation government after 1945 setting up the same constellation as the League of Nations regime after 1918. Like the other prominent German legal scholars who put their expertise in the service of the Nuremberg defendants, Jahrreiß made an important contribution toward assuring that West Germans would perceive the Allied court convictions in a highly selective way as "victor's justice," all the way until the 1980s.

West Germany Joins the Genocide Convention

Several signals in the late 1940s made it increasingly obvious that international legalism in the American mode had passed its peak. One came out of Nuremberg in April 1949, when verdicts were handed down in the proceeding usually known as the Ministries Trial or the Wilhelmstrasse Trial (after the Berlin street on which many ministries were located). Following the IMT, military courts in the American zone of occupation held a series of twelve trials in which defendants were drawn from German elite groups. This was the last of the "Nuremberg follow-up trials" to reach a verdict. The defendants in the Ministries Trial had included career diplomats, top economic planners, industrialists at state-owned enterprises, a finance minister, a Gestapo chief, occupation officials, and bankers. Most of them came away with conspicuously lenient sentences, which were shortened further after a review process. The convictions came exclusively on charges of war crimes and crimes against humanity. The IMT's ambitious original plan, of achieving the criminalization of aggressive war, was now seen more or less as having ended in failure.[158]

On 9 December 1948, after a long debate, the United Nations General Assembly voted to approve the Convention on the Prevention and Punishment of the Crime of Genocide. The conflicts during the negotiations provided an additional sign that the mobilizing power of the human rights discourse was on the wane. Despite this latest official confirmation of the Nuremberg principles, individual states harbored serious reservations. The memories of the war remained fresh, but no majority could be mustered for the creation of a permanent international criminal court, leaving enforcement of the Genocide Convention within the territorial jurisdiction of states. This was a serious setback for the push to institutionalize international criminal law.[159]

Advocates of a more robust humanitarian law could still dismiss these problems of codifying and implementing the new criminal charges as the product of interstate skirmishes. But the idealism of its American pioneers was truly shaken by developments in Germany. Just as the Nuremberg project had reached its end, and even as two major hurdles had been cleared on the international level with the passage of the Genocide Convention and the Universal Declaration of Human Rights, the Western occupation zones seemed to be gripped with a widespread rejection of anything even remotely associated with "Nuremberg." It was no coincidence that Franz Neumann, who by 1949 was teaching at both the Free University in West Berlin and Columbia University, felt compelled to call on the Western occupation governments to preserve the historically valuable Nuremberg trial files for future researchers. The legal track seemed to have run into a roadblock. Always the skeptic, Neumann did not believe that the Nuremberg effort had achieved any educational successes in post-Nazi Germany. Of course, many Germans considered the trials to have been fair and just. But these supporters were clearly in the minority and had no political influence worth the name. The country's pace-setting elites had turned almost unanimously against "Nuremberg." "The powerful groups in Germany tend to use the trials as political instruments either to attack the West or to offer themselves as Allies against the East, or to attack all victorious powers," Neumann wrote. He was prepared to entertain an analogy to the interwar period: "It is conceivable (and even likely) that the trials will play a similar role to the famous 'War Guilt Lie' after 1918."[160]

Neumann was particularly sensitive to developments in the Western occupation zones, for understandable reasons. Campaigns were underway to gain clemency and amnesty for the Nuremberg prisoners. Neumann was convinced that these were being steered by the deposed German elites in the hope of reaping benefit from the mobilizing and integrative effects. He did not doubt that this represented a concentrated attempt to turn the sociology of power—once an impetus of the Nuremberg project—against the occupation powers. He thought it had met with alarming success after only a very short time. This was evident in demoscopic surveys ordered by the US High Commissioner on the advice of Neumann and other Germany experts. A first survey of selected samplings of the German population, conducted in the weeks before the IMT verdicts were announced in October 1946, had found that most Germans thought the trials were political but considered them overall to be "fair." Four years later, the proportion holding that opinion had fallen to 40 percent.[161]

These and other similar findings caused the Americans to conclude, as is well known, that they needed to show more flexibility in carrying out the Nuremberg verdicts. In bilateral negotiation rounds with German authorities, the Americans tried to convey the impression that they were prepared to understand German sensitivities about the "war criminal problem." The Americans' internal papers reveal cluelessness about why a defiant attitude was prevailing in German society. Writing in 1953, one employee of the US Department of State frankly admitted failure and conceded that the Germans' underlying motives were a puzzle to him: "From the political point of view, the crux of the war criminal problem in Germany is the refusal of a large number of Germans to accept the principles underlying the trials or the findings of the trials. . . . In spite of all the Western powers have said the contrary, the trials are generally portrayed as acts of political retribution without firm legal basis."[162]

For many years, the research discourse on the politics of the past in the early FRG has tended to portray the German engagement on behalf of the Nuremberg prisoners as bespeaking a high degree of irrationality and a deep-seated aversion to Western values. The lack of acceptance for the Nuremberg verdicts is treated as evidence that the early FRG had chosen to place itself outside the Western human rights discourse. The phenomenon of mass identification with a relatively small number of convicted NS perpetrators is read as a sign of the persistence of the "people's community" ethos, characterized by exaggerated nationalism and a strong desire for a "normality" purified of the past.[163]

A more nuanced view has been advanced in recent work, like Lora Wildenthal's 2010 biographical study of the Social Democratic international law expert Rudolf Laun. Wildenthal emphasizes that the early FRG was home to two parallel and distinct human rights discourses. The interpretation inspired by the Allies foregrounded the human rights violations under Nazi rule so as to raise West Germans' political culture and consciousness of the past. Meanwhile, especially on the political right wing, discussion focused mainly on allegations of human rights violations against the German people by the victorious powers. This national-apologetic discourse even saw Germans as the actual inventors of the human rights ideal, attributing the achievement variably to Luther, the Hutterites of the sixteenth and seventeenth centuries, or the Weimar constitution.[164] It portrayed Germans as a major victim of human rights violations in the twentieth century. Whether the blame was put on the Treaty of Versailles, the NS regime, the expulsions of ethnic German populations from the Soviet-bloc countries, or the Allied occupation governments, this perpetual victim identity allowed its exponents to demand equal say and treatment on the international stage with an urgency that often bordered on the frivolous.

The self-image popular among West Germans, that they were the victims of the violent regimes of National Socialism and Communism, went along with a desire to profile the FRG in the area of international human rights policy. These were among the reasons that, soon after the founding of the FRG in 1949, a debate broke out about whether West Germany should join the UN Genocide Convention. It was set off by the efforts of Raphael Lemkin, whose tireless years of lobbying after the war had moved the United Nations to recognize his definition of genocide as a singular crime under international law. Transforming the General Assembly's 1948 declaration into binding law required at least twenty out of the then sixty UN member states to ratify the Genocide Convention. Lemkin's efforts contributed to a further resolution in December 1949, sponsored by the ambassadors of Australia, Cuba, and the Philippines, that empowered General Secretary Trygve Lie to invite a dozen non-UN states to join the Genocide Convention: Korea, Italy, Laos, Cambodia, Vietnam, Ceylon, Jordan, Monaco, Bulgaria, Romania, Hungary, and the Federal Republic of Germany.[165]

As it turned out, twenty-four UN member states joined the Genocide Convention by October 1950. This meant that it would take force on 12 January 1951, if only on a de jure basis. Its de facto effect remained rather symbolic, since no agreement had been reached on enforcement mechanisms. In December 1950, Lie did in fact invite the FRG to join the Genocide Convention.[166] The West German foreign and justice ministries called on their government to join as quickly as possible. Also in favor was Erich Kaufmann, adviser on international law to the first West German chancellor, Konrad Adenauer. The Federal Foreign Office stated that accepting the Genocide Convention without conditions was desirable insofar as "the conduct of the National Socialist government" was in fact the reason that it existed in the first place. But it was considered at least equally important that "crimes of these kinds were committed and are still committed in the Soviet-ruled countries and so the FRG as a party to the treaty will have the possibility of intervening there should its interests at some point make this appear desirable."[167]

The almost unanimous position in favor of the Genocide Convention among the ministerial legal experts was rather surprising. The Soviet Union and a series of Eastern Bloc states were among the first signatories to the Genocide Convention, whereas the FRG's two most important Western allies, the United States and Great Britain, still kept their distance because of domestic politics. In addition, the now-despised Nuremberg indictment had peripherally included charges of genocide, although the IMT verdict would omit the term (much to Lemkin's consternation). For these and other reasons, the ministerial advisers in Bonn might have found it easy, in 1950, to view the Genocide Convention as a relic and revival of the very same "Nuremberg law" that West German policy and courts had been working to extinguish ever since the FRG had achieved its status as a semisovereign state in 1949.

In its dealings with the Allies, the first West German government had rejected even an implicit recognition of the Nuremberg verdicts. All the parties elected to the first Bundestag supported a series of clemency and amnesty laws that largely benefited persons who were culpable for NS-era criminal acts, even if this was often concealed by the legal language. A group of former Nuremberg defense lawyers and leading West German jurists came together in the spring of 1949 as a network to lobby for clemency and amnesty. Showing an acute sense for the symbolism of the politics of the past, they borrowed a name from their forerunners at Versailles and called themselves the Heidelberg Circle. In effect, they ethnicized the principle of *nulla poena sine lege* by declaring it an inalienable principle of German law. The FRG would ratify the European Convention on Human Rights (ECHR) in 1952, but only once it was granted the caveat that West Germany did not need to recognize the ECHR's citation of the Nuremberg principles, and although the ECHR from the beginning had been intended by its framers more as a tool for reconstituting a bourgeois, Christian-conservative Europe than for distancing Europe from National Socialism.[168]

Despite the initially positive reaction in Bonn, the planned West German entry to the Genocide Convention was soon bogged down in delays. The project was revived again only in the summer of 1953, a few months before the country's second parliamentary election. By then, the international frontlines around the issue had become even murkier as the East-West conflict had escalated and unstable coalitions prevailed within UN bodies. The United States had suspended any attempt at ratification even before the inauguration of the new Republican president, Dwight D. Eisenhower.[170] The Soviet Union continued to brandish the convention as a weapon of agitation against the United States and the old colonial powers, but at the same time hesitated to complete its own ratification process.

Despite his failing health, Lemkin continued to pursue the hope of implementation with great élan, even as its prospects diminished. In the face of the political stalemate, he developed an inclination to extreme anti-Communism.

He grew mistrustful of a group of liberal and left-liberal human rights activists around Eleanor Roosevelt and of the American and European international law experts who had participated in the planning and implementation of the Nuremberg trials. He became convinced that the latter group had conspired to incite the Chinese government to submit a text to the International Law Commission (ILC) for the Code of International Offenses against the Peace and Security of Mankind with the intent of dissolving the legal stipulations defining genocide back into those for the main Nuremberg offenses of aggressive war, war crimes, and crimes against humanity.[171] Seeing only friends or enemies wherever he looked, Lemkin began to identify all the actual and presumed enemies of the Genocide Convention as "Nuremberg jurists" and a "fifth column" of the Soviet Union.[172]

In the early 1950s, Lemkin began to intensify his contacts with US-based diasporic associations such as the Ukrainian Congress Committee of America, the Hungarian National Council, and the Americans of German Origin. It was in a sense only a matter of time before he would seek allies in West Germany. He found a mediator in the Vienna-born journalist Julius Epstein, who had worked for several years during the war for the US Office of War Information. Epstein found work in the 1950s as a correspondent for the Dusseldorf business paper *Industriekurier*, among other periodicals. In July 1953, Lemkin sat with Epstein for a long, exclusive interview that would be reprinted in several West German papers, including *Der Tagesspiegel* in West Berlin. Epstein used his own connections to make sure that Chancellor Adenauer would read about what the ethnic German associations in the United States were hoping to gain out of a rapid West German entry to the Genocide Convention.[173] Asked about the FRG's response to the invitation from the UN general secretary, Lemkin answered that delays did not serve the country's interests because it was missing the opportunity to bring before the United Nations the matter of Communist crimes against Germans. He pointed out that the Sudeten German expellee associations had published a "white book" in 1951 that accused the Czechoslovakian government of having pursued genocide against the ethnic German population.[174]

Although Lemkin made explicit his wish that Adenauer would take the opportunity, the chancellor kept his cards hidden until after the Bundestag elections. It is conceivable that Adenauer preferred not to be seen giving in to the West German war criminal lobby's demand that he negotiate with the Allies on clemency for "Nurembergers" while simultaneously pursuing a victims' status for the German minorities in Eastern Europe at the United Nations.[175] After his victory in the September 1953 elections, the expellee associations raised the pressure on his government in tandem with the Bundestag group of the Deutsche Partei (DP). The national-conservative DP had entered as a junior partner in the multiparty coalition supporting a parliamentary majority for Adenauer's Christian Democratic Union and its Bavarian sister party, the Christian Social Union (CDU-CSU). The first query from the DP camp in the new parliament called on the government to explain why the FRG had still not joined the Genocide Convention despite repeated demands that it do so.[176] Within the expellee community, which numbered more than ten million, the Sudeten German press especially began to bang the drums.[177] The government's expert report favoring entry to the Genocide Convention, which had been prepared long before, was taken off the shelf and dusted off, theoretically allowing action before the end of the year.[178]

But another nine months passed before the ratification law went into effect.[179] Over the course of 1954, Lemkin himself intervened in the West German legislative process to influence the wording of the proposed new genocide paragraph (§220) in the German federal legal code. Via unknown channels, he learned in May 1954 that the government's legislative draft was phrased to completely distort the stipulations defining the crime of genocide—at least, this was the view of the term's inventor. The stipulations for genocide in the convention's original English text define it as actions to bring about the "destruction" of national, ethnic, racial, or religious groups. Without realizing the possible international consequences, the ministerial advisers writing the FRG version rendered this in German as *Ausrottung*, meaning "extermination." The more extreme term, "extermination," had been employed at various points in the Nuremberg statutes and files, as well as in the IMT verdicts, which repeatedly referred to the murder of Jewish populations as a process of "extermination." The implied change from "destruction" to "extermination" (*Ausrottung*) at least indirectly allowed the conclusion that the NS genocide of the European Jews (or at least the way in which it was idiomatically described in the IMT verdict) would pose the standard for determining whether genocide was committed in other cases. *Ausrottung* would be amended to *Vernichtung*, a more literal translation of "destruction," in the German ratification bill.

This sign of terminological decay drew a very angry reaction from Lemkin. By that time, it had come to be considered good etiquette in the everyday political business of the young FRG to flatten all language indicating a difference between NS destruction policy during the war and the expulsion of German minorities from central and eastern Europe after the war. Lemkin was convinced that the translated deviation was not a mistake but an intentional act of sabotage, behind which one must presume lay the hands of leftist human rights activists. He turned for help to a series of West German politicians who his sources assured him shared his aversion to Nuremberg law.[180] Lemkin wrote letters to Franz Seidl, the CSU deputy who headed the Bundestag legal committee, as well as to the former justice minister

Thomas Dehler of the economically liberal Free Democratic Party (FDP), the professor Eduard Wahl of the Heidelberg Circle, and a functionary of the Sudeten German expellee association named Globig. Lemkin used the visit of a Bundestag delegation in New York to further speak on the matter with Bundestag President Eugen Gerstenmaier (CDU), SPD Vice President Carlo Schmid, the FDP politician Erich Mende, and an SPD deputy, Jakob Altmaier. To each of his interlocutors, Lemkin repeated like a mantra that the new genocide paragraph would be rendered "useless" in regard to a criminal treatment of the expulsion of ethnic Germans unless the West German legislation could be purified of all terms that came from the IMT statute or the Nuremberg verdicts.[181] He also insisted that the criterion of "serious emotional damage" be added, since only this would be appropriate for the "suffering of eleven million expelled Germans."[182]

As though his mission was to free the Genocide Convention once and for all from the reputation that it represented a moral and legal reaction to the Jewish catastrophe, Lemkin was asking the West German amnesty supporters to accept a timeless concept of genocide. To Professor Wahl of the Heidelberg Circle, Lemkin wrote in German:

> As the writer of the Genocide Convention I can assure you, my dear Herr Professor, that I introduced the term "destruction" (without an adjective) especially for the purpose of emphasizing an encroachment on the sociological fabric of the group *as such*. In light of history and sociology, the destruction of a national, religious, racial and ethnic group is possible without the disappearance of the members of the group. By contrast, the terms of "Nuremberg law" are of an exclusively physical nature, operating as they do with extermination and annihilation.[183]

In his correspondence with West German politicians, Lemkin, who had himself suffered horribly from the Holocaust, used three main arguments for a revision of the legislative draft. First, it could not employ any terms that recalled "Nuremberg law" or that had been adopted at the Nuremberg trials. Second, the stipulations defining genocide had to be phrased so that they could potentially be used for a criminal investigation of persecutions committed during the expulsions of German minorities from central and eastern Europe. Third, the impression had to be averted that the definition of genocide was connected in any necessary way to the Nazis' anti-Jewish policy. Instead, Lemkin was consistent in foregrounding Stalinist crimes.

However, this subjective interpretation of the Genocide Convention would meet with only a limited echo among Lemkin's West German interlocutors. Their agreement with Lemkin was limited to a single point: a common front against everything that might in however vague or nebulous way be interpretable as the expression of the punitive "Nuremberg" legal culture. In Bonn, there was much skepticism about the practical applicability of the genocide legislation for use against the "expulsion crimes." The legal experts at the Foreign Office, for example, had realized without doubt at an early point that—contrary to Lemkin's claim—the FRG would never be able to make the expulsions into the subject of an international criminal law complaint against the Communist peoples' democracies. Such an action would shatter all the dams against the Nuremberg principles and retroactive punishment of NS-era crimes that the West Germans had raised with such care during the preceding years.[184]

West German entry to the Genocide Convention did, however, seem attractive as a political option because its creator was a Jew who had fled from Poland, as well as a US citizen who had devoted himself to the goal of reconciliation among peoples. The early awarding to Lemkin of the Federal Cross of Merit (*Bundesverdienstkreuz*) was thus bound up with the political purpose of creating a symbolic connection to the person of Lemkin himself. With care taken not to offend the sensibilities of the voters, the official German valedictories for Lemkin referred to his Jewish identity only in encoded form. At a ceremony to mark the German entry to the Genocide Convention, one employee of the Foreign Office referred to it quasi-religiously as an act of expiation following the murder of forty-nine members of his family. Lemkin himself was described as a cosmopolitan idealist:

> Probably only few people have realized as Professor Lemkin did from his earliest youth the necessity of good will among people. Born in a country where Lithuanians, Germans, Poles, Russians, and other nationalities lived together, he felt in early life how important mutual understanding and friendship are for the welfare of all people. His striving for equality and justice led him later to the study of law. After receiving his law degree at the University of Lwow, he set himself with the eagerness of the youth to promote better understanding. But he soon realized that the protection of people is not only the concern of an individual but also the concern of the community. In the early thirties 600 Christian Assyrians were murdered in Iraq. This event led him to dedicate his life to the protection of people of different nations, religions, and races.[185]

In hindsight it may today seem like a paradox that the FRG entered the Genocide Convention just when most international experts had declared the project dead and the United Nations had suspended work on an international criminal code.[186] Looking beyond the demands of the ethnic German expellee associations, this conjuncture may have been precisely what made ratification attractive to the Adenauer government. Compared with the ECHR, which the FRG had been among the first to join in the early 1950s without fully comprehending its wide-ranging effects,[187] the new West German genocide paragraph reaped important gains on the international trading floor with little fear that there would ever be any associated liability. In other words, the true value of the Genocide Convention for the young FRG came in the symbolic and political dimensions, while its practical meaning tended to zero.

Conclusion

While, during World War I, it was primarily the legal scholars of the Entente states who introduced the issue of German international law violations to the political agenda at an early stage, the frontlines in World War II at first ran in an opposite direction. Soon after the German invasion of Poland, prominent international lawyers on the German side took the stage in a rather absurd inversion to accuse the British government of having started a "criminal war of aggression" against the German Reich. Despite the horrific violence in the conquered territories of Poland, it would take almost two years for the international debate on German war conduct to slowly start getting into gear. A first impulse came in Roosevelt's State of the Union address of January 1941, in which he first posed his concept of human rights, "the Four Freedoms," as a counter to Hitler's "New Order."

Even then, it still took another year before the issue gained steam. The German invasion of the Soviet Union and the rapid dissemination of news about the Einsatzgruppen massacres in Eastern Europe finally led to the January 1942 St. James Declaration in London by the accredited exile governments and the French national committee, demanding a legal investigation of German crimes. German occupation rule also became an object of discourse among international law experts. Next to the discipline's leading Anglo-American exponents, it was above all exiled scholars from Germany, Austria, and Eastern Europe who pushed the discussion forward. In fits and starts, they began to debate the question of whether the NS techniques of hegemony represented a new historical phenomenon that demanded an expansion of the traditional international law. Although no uniform position was to be reached as yet, many of the jurists could agree by then that the extent and character of the German violence against civilians and above all against Jews would compel a corresponding criminal law response after the war.

As the war went on, it fell especially to the Jewish jurists who had been driven from Europe to confront the problem of Nazi mass violence. In hindsight, the influence of certain scholars and organizations can hardly be overestimated. Their work during the war was highly influential in the emergence and shaping of a legalist discourse on NS injustice. Because of their legal education and professional tendencies, they attempted to understand these new forms of unlimited state violence mainly in legal categories and terms.

Their descriptions of NS persecution and annihilation practices were often normatively overelaborate, overemphasizing the state machinery of persecution and downplaying ideological and mental factors. Another characteristic of the scientific style of the exiled jurists was a strong orientation to praxis. In part they adopted elements from the interwar period experiences with the various bodies of the League of Nations, and in part they turned to entirely new methods.

The legal think tanks that arose during the war sought to combine research work, human rights policy lobbying, and judicial activism. These organizations tended to be informal and displayed a fluid self-understanding of their profession that corresponded to the exceptional character of their self-appointed mission. From the perspective of the leading protagonists, the exceptional forms of NS regimes of violence and the resulting humanitarian catastrophes compelled them as far as possible to ignore the existing disciplinary boundaries. Depending on the interlocutors and the context, at different times the same people might act as experts in law, archivists, researchers, or historians. This oscillating profile was bound up with two far-reaching ambitions. They wanted to document for posterity and historiographically locate the special fate of the Jews in World War II, and they wanted this activity to initiate a human rights reformation in international law.

The production of scientific case studies and expert reports was a key specialty of the Jewish NGOs and judicial activists during the war. Although these works generally arose with a view to later criminal prosecution or restitution processes, they generally involved far more than the collection of evidence, taking of eyewitness testimonies, or identification of perpetrators. Works like Lemkin's *Axis Rule* instead aimed at comprehending what was essentially new about the German occupation system in eastern Europe on the broadest possible empirical foundation. Historical and political analyses and comprehensive documentary appendices sufficed only as a background panorama, against which the author delivered his wide-ranging legal and political demands to the public. Works like *Axis Rule* and the diverse studies by the IJA connected to older models from World War I, but also embodied a new kind of juridical history writing. This proceeded from three more or less clearly defined sets of motives. First, the public and future generations had to be educated about the wide-ranging persecution and annihilation plans of the Third Reich. Second, the authors engaged in a form of forensic investigation that could serve as a basis for criminal indictments and restitution schemes. Third, all this effort was meant to influence the ongoing international law discussion on German mass crimes to take a human rights turn.

It was not a coincidence that European scholars like Raphael Lemkin and Jacob Robinson found especially good working conditions in the United States. Before the United States entered the war, a large part of the academic public had already gathered in the camp of liberal interventionism. This intellectual grouping was interested in every form of scientific expertise that could be fielded to counter the country's political and military neutrality. Afterward, starting in 1943, a heated controversy broke out within the US government bureaucracy over the future conditions of peace for the German Reich. For those who advocated a tough peace, thorough knowledge of German occupation crimes was always also a form of political argument. Unlike in the other combatant countries, the United States offered a living in academic infrastructures and a readily receptive intellectual community that made it possible not only to engage the issues on a scientific level but also to become effective on the public and political level.

Despite this advantageous starting point, the recruitment of left-wing German social theorists by the OSS was still a bold experiment in scientific politics. A thorough political vetting by the Federal Bureau of Investigation was necessary before a group of high-carat scientists were hired out of the New York Institute for Social Research in 1942 to set up shop in Washington as the newly founded Central Europe Division of the clandestine services. While the group's main task initially was to evaluate the content provided by intelligence sources in Germany, after 1943 they were increasingly involved as advisers to American postwar planning, providing economic analysis and other needed expertise. And then, when the OSS chief William J. Donovan sent orders in the fall of 1944 that the division should begin working out legal-theory concepts for a planned tribunal proceeding against the NS leadership, this necessarily prompted initial rejection from several of the German R&A scholars. First, they were surely in agreement with the tone-setting leaders of the Social Democratic exile community that a punitive policy toward Germany could lead to a dangerous solidarity between the ruling elites and the broad mass, who would inevitably turn against the occupation powers. Second, Franz Neumann, the leading mind of the group, had long ago adopted a position against a human rights expansion of international law and liberal interventionism à la Jackson. In his greatest work, *Behemoth*, he had been unambiguous in declaring that after fascism was shattered, the principle of state sovereignty would have to be reinforced rather than hollowed out even further via the "doctrine of dual loyalty."

But by the start of 1945, the group's earlier opposition to the internationalist legalism of the American New Dealers had given way to a skeptical pragmatism. The most important contribution of the Neumann group to the preparation of the American indictment at Nuremberg was to develop an analytical concept that could justify the plan to place leading elites in criminal detention. As we have seen, this was accomplished through a model of the regime's political and social order that took the NS legal theorists' faith in the "leader principle" literally and turned it against the NS elites themselves. The idea was to preempt the defense from claiming that the exceptional conditions of states under totalitarian rule left no room for individual decision-making or responsibility. But, ironically, it gave the counsels for the defendants at Nuremberg an argument in turn, which they used to build their thesis of a blanket "command emergency."

For a national-conservative legal scholar like Hermann Jahrreiß, who had played an outstanding role in the Third Reich in building international law doctrines that promoted the regime theoretically and practically, taking on a role with the defense at the Nuremberg trial of the main war crimes perpetrators provided the opportunity for professional rehabilitation in two ways. First, the presence at the proceedings of many legal experts from abroad could be exploited to help the German legal studies discipline break out of the peripheral status and international isolation into which it had maneuvered itself during the preceding twelve years. Second, Jahrreiß saw a chance to gloss over the fact that he had at least temporarily become an unacceptable political burden for his home university in Cologne.

Jahrreiß played a pivotal role in the proceedings thanks to his dual role as an assistant counsel for the defense of the former chief of the German General Staff, Alfred Jodl, and as an expert witness on the legal stipulations of crimes against peace. He made himself into the mouthpiece for the "German legal standpoint" and created the impression among the Allied judges and the German public that German legal scholarship had already crystallized uniform positions on controversial issues of international law. His reports and spoken testimonies constantly hammered on the point that the Allied prosecution was in violation of the ex-post-facto principle. While he denied that German carriers of sovereignty were culpable for the aggressive war, arguing that they had been incapable of developing an awareness of right or wrong because of the inconsistencies of the Versailles system, he also postulated an ubiquitous "command emergency" as the reigning domestic condition of the Third Reich. After the IMT, this line of argument would greatly influence subsequent prosecutions of NS crime, insofar as most defendants were able to argue that that a retroactive criminal prosecution ignored the legal reality of the NS dictatorship and was therefore illegal.

The German rejection of the Allied legal model was combined with an interpretation of the history that seemed to adopt a legitimate disciplinary approach. Jahrreiß drew an image of the relations of power under the Third Reich that mimicked the sociology of power developed by the OSS scholars. He categorically rejected their premise, however, that the participation of leading social strata in the war preparations and occupation crimes could be attributed to both their interests as a class and their own self-determined action. Jahrreiß countered the structural history approach of the American researchers with a perspective "from within," one built on the foundation of the lifeworld, primary experiences, and value horizons of a supposedly homogenous "people's community" (*Volksgemeinschaft*). He thus expressed the view that in the final analysis, the history of the Third Reich was accessible only to the "ethnic comrades" (*Volksgenossen*) themselves, although he kept this more implicit than explicit. This raised a wall against both ex-post-facto international law prosecution *and* any historical judgments "from the outside."

Jahrreiß and other German international law experts of the time were nearly unanimous in rejecting the legalist paradigm advanced by the victorious Allied powers. But if they hoped to gain a hearing on the international stage, they could not avoid using the language of humanitarian law and human rights. Despite the common front against the punitive program of "Nuremberg," an alternate, "ethnicizing" human rights discourse also formed early on among West German international lawyers, who strove to portray Germans as victims of the West's own fissured concept of human rights. In this discourse, the Germans emerged not only as the true inventors of the human rights ideal but also as the people who had suffered the most from the persecution measures imposed on them by foreign states and their own state, by the Parisian peace order, by the NS political order, by Allied occupation policy, by the mass expulsions of ethnic Germans from central and eastern Europe, and by prolonged imprisonment as POWs. As soon as the foundation of the West German partial state made it possible for them to organize, the ethnic German expellee associations took up all these tropes. In this way, they became one of the first groups in the young FRG to engage in systematic lobbying on behalf of human rights.

This constellation was among the leading reasons that the Federal Republic, although not yet a member of the United Nations, developed an interest in entering the Genocide Convention at a time when American-style internationalist legalism was already in decline. Although the United States and Great Britain had withdrawn from the project, following the 1953 Bundestag elections the Adenauer government quickly joined the Genocide Convention, giving in to pressure from the Sudeten ethnic German expellees and from the CDU-CSU's junior partner in parliament, the Deutsche Partei. A key role was played therein by Raphael Lemkin, who attempted to influence the legislative process through his contacts to representatives of the Heidelberg Circle. This unusual alliance made it possible to present the new genocide paragraphs of the German legal code as a reconciliatory measure to the liberal camp while selling it to the political right wing as a symbol of anti-Communism, a fight of human rights against Communist rule.

Chapter 3

BONN—LUDWIGSBURG—JERUSALEM

❧•☙

In the 1950s and 1960s, the fledgling Federal Republic of Germany sought for its own ways of handling the National Socialist past. In the early phase of this activity, West Germany attempted to modify relations with its Western allies: the United States, Great Britain, and France. Allied political leaders were prepared to make concessions on German demands that Allied trial sentences not be executed in full. But this course of consensual reconciliation was always subject to limits because of the periodic flare-ups of Western public indignation over the continuity of elites between the Bonn Republic and its NS predecessor regime. A second limiting factor lay in how the Allied punitive program had started a dynamic of "processing the past" (*Vergangenheitsbearbeitung*) and of explanation and education (*Aufklärung*). This had laid down certain structural paths. Soon these were also trod, at times unwittingly and unwillingly, by the same German actors who saw the sociopolitical experiment of top-down democratization that used the tools of international law as fundamentally flawed. The practice behind the normative West German neologism of "overcoming the past" (*Vergangenheitsbewältigung*)[1] soon turned into both an intentional counterproject to "Nuremberg" and an unconscious mirror image thereof.

Once the "anti-fascist" critics of the young FRG had largely been silenced by the emergent anti-Communist consensus of the early 1950s, the task of advancing West German society's confrontation with the past fell mostly to two specific groups of experts. Populating this cutting edge were jurists and historians—a remarkable circumstance, because both professions had to be considered more or less "heavily compromised" by the roles they had played under National Socialism.[2] The continuing efforts at criminal prosecution of NS cases—and the many kinds of legal disputes over various forms of remediation and reparations for damages and injury caused during the war— meant that scholars in the two disciplines were often called on to engage with historical case material. For the most part, this involved a curiously tight institutional collaboration between the two professions. Historians and jurists would jointly develop a specific professional mode for classifying NS mass violence.

Allied Law and the German "Victims' Community"

Insofar as the Allies withdrew from the fields of criminal prosecution and juridical history management by the late 1940s, these same areas were gradually taken over by intellectuals of the FRG and integrated officially into what we would today call its politics of the past (*Vergangenheitspolitik*). Most of the FRG's political leaders saw the foundation of a semisovereign West German partial state as signaling a clean break with the epoch of occupation rule. They made this belief especially evident in the series of amnesties and acts granting immunity from prosecution that were whipped through the first West German parliament as soon it was convened.[3] The newly elected governing coalition was led by the Christian Democratic Union-Christian Social Union (CDU-CSU) as the ruling party under Chancellor Konrad Adenauer, with the economically more liberal Free Democratic Party (FDP) and the national-conservative Deutsche Partei (DP) as its junior partners.

Alongside the amnesty laws, a second measure that would prove at least as consequential to the future of West German "processing of the past" avoided the sovereign parliament and was pursued in relative quiet. In April 1951, the government requested that the Allies suspend the requirement that German courts apply the occupation authorities' Control Council Law No. 10 (CCL 10).[4] The initiative came from the FDP-led Federal Ministry of Justice, the representatives of several German states, and the first president of the supreme court, the Federal Court of Justice (Bundesgerichtshof), Hermann Weinkauff. It may be presumed that Weinkauff used legal research provided by the Heidelberg Circle. At internal consultations, he pleaded for a suspension of CCL 10, arguing that the Allied statute was impossible to reconcile with German legal thinking and, in any case, posed an inadmissible interference in the country's sovereignty. Formerly a high judge of the NS-era Reichsgericht, Weinkauff now termed it "unbearable" that West German courts could still deliver the death penalty under CCL No. 10, since the FRG had abolished capital punishment two years earlier in Article 102 of its constitution, the Basic Law (Grundgesetz).[5]

It would have been prudent of Weinkauff not to belabor the background of the country's abolition of capital punishment. A rather surprising swing in opinion in favor of abolition had occurred among Christian Democrats in 1949, just before the first Bundestag elections, at a time when the CDU-CSU faced a potential loss of right-wing votes to the DP. The DP had opportunistically adopted abolition as a platform plank. While movements against capital punishment had arisen in nearly all the postwar states of Western Europe—generally as classic projects for left liberals and social democrats—the nationalist right in the FRG had managed to make the issue its trademark. It need hardly be added that the postwar German nationalists did not argue against capital punishment, because the National Socialists had retroactively introduced it as a sentence for arson in the law of 29 March 1933 (following the Reichstag fire). They also took no pains to condemn the NS state's massive use of the death penalty as a means of terror and as the legal flank for NS racial and extermination politics during the war.[6] Rather, politicians of the DP argued (and nearly all West German parliamentarians would have agreed) that a putatively excessive use of the death penalty by the Allies would rob Germans of their opportunity for an "inner catharsis."[7] Ironically, the first beneficiaries from the resulting end of Germany's seventy-eight-year tradition of capital punishment (dating back to the activation of the original German imperial legal code in 1871) were NS prisoners whom the Allies had condemned to death.

The FRG government's initiative for a repeal of CCL 10 came just as the campaign to grant clemency to the Landsberg death row inmates was reaching a high point.[8] It was only a few months earlier that two Bundestag deputies, Richard Jäger (CSU) and Gebhard Seelos of the Bavarian Party (BP), had led a relatively obscure rally for clemency in the small Upper Bavarian town of Landsberg, the location of the Allies' War Criminal Prison No. 1 for convicts and defendants drawn from the upper echelons of the NS system and society. A crowd of about one thousand people gathered near the prison gates to demand forgiveness for the "red jackets," as the condemned were called. Many of them had been commanders of SS Einsatzgruppen or of concentration camps in the SS-administered system of labor and death camps, the KZs. Beyond this immediate goal, the clemency demand was part of a movement against Allied "foreign law" in general. It drew from an apologetic discourse that reached back several years to the Nuremberg trials and the first wave of criminal prosecutions. West German courts were also involved.

There were several reasons why CCL 10 had become an outstanding political symbol in the controversy over national self-determination with regard to treatment of the past. One decisive factor was that the American-led

Nuremberg follow-up trials against members of the NS-era elites were carried out on the basis of CCL 10, rather than on the original statute for the International Military Tribunal.[9] In most of the Nuremberg follow-up trials, this made no difference. The major exception was Case 3, the trial of NS-era judges and lawyers. Understood metaphorically as a trial of "the law itself," as Lawrence Douglas called it,[10] the course of this proceeding was determined by historical preconceptions and inconsistencies embodied in the Allied legal framework. Simply put, the American prosecution strategy was based on mutually contradictory legal premises. The chief prosecutor, Telford Taylor, argued that his charges against exponents of the NS justice system, who were German citizens, were possible only through the ex-post-facto application of crimes against humanity under international law. At the same time, however, Taylor used analyses by the German-born OSS legal expert Otto Kirchheimer, who argued that the German legal tradition had not been suspended under the NS regime and therefore could be applied to NS-era judicial injustice. As we saw in chapter 2, the German defenders recognized the contradiction inherent in deploying both these arguments in tandem. They exploited it to support a defense strategy that concluded in the exculpation from any liability of the entire German legal profession.

The occupation authorities in the British and French zones, meanwhile, had established a mandatory application of CCL 10 in German courts for all cases in which the victims had included German citizens or stateless persons. This gave rise to further resistance among the West Germans. High-ranking West German jurists contested the use of CCL 10 as an intervention in the autonomy of the legal sector. Among the critics were several figures who were considered politically clean, including the chief judge of the regional appeals court in Celle, Hodo von Hodenberg.[11] He asserted that the ex-post-facto application of international law provisions constituted a violation similar to the National Socialists' own treatment of political opponents and "foreign elements." Hodenberg wrote:

> A truly objective justice, as we know, can never be achieved. . . . If an act cannot be judged according to the standards of objective law obtaining at the time it was committed, but only by those that we subsequently consider to be "higher justice" or "material justice," then this can only mean that the judge's own emergent "healthy sense of the law" is supposed to overrule the criminal law applicable at the time of the act. If, however, it is argued instead that the demand to apply a "higher justice" is a general demand—meaning a demand of the people's community [*Volksgemeinschaft*]—then the law guiding the judge is replaced, exactly as in the Nazi era, by the "healthy legal sense of the people's community." The result, however, is that the legal sense of the people's community is set against the formal law's guarantee of protection to the individual, and this means also the implementation of the principle

first established by the Nazis themselves in 1935, that "the protection of the people's community shall demand unconditional priority over the concerns of the individual."[12]

Hodenberg, a CDU politician who was also active with the new "Heidelbergers," argued further that the Allied occupation authorities had prohibited retroactive punishment as a condition for the reactivation of an autonomous West German justice system.[13] His brief evaded the actual problem of how justice could be achieved for the victims of the Nazi-era justice system, given that it had become a component in the regime of persecution. In a conscious misapprehension of reality, he instead cast the NS-era justice system in the role of a passive victim. Starting in 1933, it had been pushed aside by the forces of the street. From this, Hodenberg derived the conclusion that West German judges would have to be all the more vigilant in fighting against the unreasonable demands of the Allied occupation, for they would otherwise fall victim to extralegal influences for a second time.

The controversy over CCL 10 would have long-term effects on how West German legal professionals defined themselves. Most importantly, it provided an effective basic narrative for promoting group identity and consensus. The critique of Allied law reinforced the historical interpretation, already common among jurists, that the "foundations" of the German state and legal systems as protectors of social values had weathered the NS era fundamentally intact.[14] Following de-Nazification, the country's system of criminal law was therefore seen as continuing a mostly unblemished and uninterrupted German legal tradition. Most German jurists were presumed to have resisted the totalitarian terror and to have preserved minimum standards of rule of law, so they retained sufficient legitimacy to prosecute NS-era injustices. Prosecution efforts would necessarily proceed based on the prior German criminal code, however. A retroactive prosecution of NS-era crimes under international law was not only superfluous but actually illegal.

The equation of the NS perversion of jurisprudence with the alleged injustice of the Allied occupation revived the self-exoneration of German jurists as "victims of legal positivism," to quote the SPD legal policy spokesperson Gustav Radbruch.[15] This idea gained mobilizing potential from the promise that an entire professional class could be liberated from the "burdens of the past." National-conservative jurists in the vein of Hodenberg espoused that, by taking a principled and strong stand against the presumptions of Allied "victors' justice," it was possible to compensate for the "weakness" that many German jurists had shown when they applied Nazi laws formally. The accompanying presumption was that they had done so against their inner convictions, even if they had stated no objections.

Overall, this discourse mirrored a collective perception in which the deep-seated prejudices against humanitarian law, which had been expressed already in the German objections to the Treaty of Versailles, now merged seamlessly with the defense against the Allies' reform efforts. Much of the same legal philosophy and methodological arguments that had been used after 1918–1919 to block a more thorough confrontation with German war crimes in World War I were now redeployed. The example of doings in the Eastern Bloc proved useful in reinforcing this stance. Many West German jurists pointed out that the Soviets also required East German courts to uphold CCL 10.[16] West German jurists argued that these authoritarian interventions in the independence of Eastern Bloc courts confirmed the historical image of international law as an instrument of hegemony directed against Germans in particular.

The collective self-definition expressed in the juridical controversies over CCL 10 coupled a concern for professional reputation with negligence regarding the actual victims of Nazi crimes. Given these strong, widespread attitudes and patterns of thought, it seems all the more remarkable that the long-term result was not an even greater radicalization, as predicted by Franz Neumann, but rather a general adoption and acceptance of the liberal constitutional state. One of the unexpected effects of the CCL 10 debate was that the critique of the basis for Allied law encouraged the gradual transformation of the critics themselves. As Devin Pendas has argued, "The embrace of legalism by postwar German jurists as a weapon against unwanted Nazi trials had the important unintended consequence of disrupting a legal culture, that had, since at least the end of World War I, embraced a dangerous form of legal instrumentalism and a perverse rhetoric of nationalist substantive justice."[17] In the FRG, the demands for legal standards and for the realization of abstract principles went together with an internalization of forms, concepts, and values that greatly differed from the prior traditions of the German authoritarian state. The results differed greatly from the illiberal developments following World War I.[18]

For most West German jurists implicated in the NS system, the CCL 10 debate thus allowed a paradoxical form of self-exoneration. It rested on the reassuring (and false) historical narrative that the systematic abolition of constitutional principles after 1933 had taken place against the united resistance of their profession rather than with their active collaboration, as was actually the case. The jurists were able to create a kind of historical and political *cordon sanitaire*, one that they believed protected them against identification with the lawless Nazi state. In addition, many jurists who had not in any way actually advanced their careers during the Third Reich, or adapted themselves to its conditions, also spoke out against CCL 10 and Allied jurisprudence. Adolf Arndt, for example, one of the few German jurists who had been persecuted under the NS system, was among those whose objections to CCL 10 cannot be dismissed as his own personal, covert apologia.

Arndt took an early interest in the issue through his involvement with the prosecution of one of the first major "euthanasia" cases in the German state of Hesse. ("Euthanasia" was the euphemism for the regime's medical killing of hundreds of thousands of people at institutions for the mentally ill starting in August 1939.) The Hessian state justice minister and later Hessian premier, Georg August Zinn (SPD), had sought comprehensive investigations of former staff from the extermination facilities and intermediary detention centers at Hadamar, Eichberg, and Kalmenhof.[19] The legal basis was the May 1946 Hesse state law that governed the prosecution of NS crimes.[20] Prosecution of the "euthanasia" crimes was one of the few priorities pursued by West German jurisdictions in the immediate postwar years. This was thanks in part to CCL 10, by which the Allies had for the first time allowed German investigative and magistratical bodies to pursue NS-era cases on their own.[21] West German courts were reluctant to apply a form of international law created in London and Nuremberg, however. It was symptomatic that courts at first invoked both CCL 10 and the old imperial German code but later began to issue most of their judgments solely based on relevant provisions in national law, that is, those for murder, abetment of murder, and manslaughter. The consequence of this self-limiting turn to traditional German legalities was that the connection between the mass murder of the sick and mentally ill and the later genocide of the European Jews, the Romany and Sinti, "foreign peoples," and those "foreign to the community" was peremptorily suppressed from entering German case law.

Despite such ambivalences and legal uncertainties, the German authorities at first displayed diligence and consistency in the prosecution of the "euthanasia" complex. Initially, there were no reservations about working with the Allied institutions. The Hesse trials were all held in the Fourth Criminal Chamber of the State Court in Frankfurt and saw a close cooperation with the American prosecutorial body—the Office of the Chief Counsel for War Crimes (OCCWC)—and the legal department of the US military government for Hesse. The state government in Wiesbaden assigned a high political, legal, and psychological meaning to this trial. This was evident in the decision to use for the first time the new US zone regulation that allowed a state to appoint the in-court prosecutor from its own justice ministry. Zinn chose his close associate, Arndt, a lawyer whose persecution on racial charges by the NS regime seemed to make him an ideal candidate for the job.

Well before Arndt took over the Hadamar case in 1946, Allied justice had delivered the first legal precedent on the "euthanasia" complex in October 1945. The former Hadamar administrative director, Alfons Klein; the facility's former chief of medicine, Adolf Wahlmann; and five other defendants had been indicted for the murder of 476 Polish and Soviet forced laborers at the facility. They were tried by an American military tribunal set up by the US Army as a parallel structure to the Nuremberg process, convicted, and sentenced to death or long prison terms.[22] At the time, the US military court had exempted itself from jurisdiction over the crimes committed against the far greater number of German nationals killed at Hadamar. Thus, the Hessian authorities initiated the new proceeding on nearly fifteen thousand counts of murder committed against the patients at Hadamar. The Wiesbaden government welcomed the case as an opportunity to make a strong statement regarding the politics of the past. At the same time, they came under political pressure from the Evangelische (German Lutheran) church to provide a justification. The Evangelische bishop of Hesse, Theophil Wurm, had delivered a withering critique of the first German de-Nazification law, which Arndt himself had helped to write.[23] The state intended to demonstrate its ability to "process" the crimes of "euthanasia" not only to these domestic critics but also to the occupation powers themselves.

Arndt provided a programmatic description of this "Hessian way" and its special challenges in a June 1947 lecture at a West German-Allied judicial conference in Konstanz. His talk began with a blanket rejection of all efforts to overcome the problem of an ex-post-facto prosecution through the application of natural law principles. In this, he took aim at the theses of the renowned Heidelberg legal philosopher and former Weimar justice minister Gustav Radbruch (SPD). In the face of the Nazi regime's massive legal violations, Radbruch had called for a stronger religious foundation for law and thus for a "renaissance of the idea of natural law" in West German jurisprudence. Arndt, a Protestant, repudiated Radbruch's propagation of "a law superior to the law" as a "fashionable mistake."[24] He was equally vehement, however, in opposing the then incipient tendency of German courts to invoke the thesis of a "normative force of the factual," which basically would have recognized all the legal actions taken under Hitler. Arndt held that this positivist approach negated the right to resistance retroactively; the doctrine would also retroactively legitimize, as though it were a reasonable and recognized legal order, a system that in its own time was perceived by most contemporaries as an "order of injustice" or a "legal disorder."[25]

Thus, Arndt argued, the treatment of Nazi crimes under the West German justice system was in a state of fundamental "legal confusion." Arndt hoped to have provided the remedy with his own prosecutorial strategy in the Hadamar trial and the other "euthanasia" cases pending in Frankfurt. As a solution that would strike the needed balance between justice and legal security, and that would provide a necessary educational moment, Arndt proposed "autochthonous" self-purification: in other words, the replacement of Allied criminal trials and the retroactive Allied penal codes by an exclusively

West German pursuit of prosecutions. Only that, Arndt believed, could secure the German people's trust in the new legal order and reawaken their lost sense of the purpose of punishment. "Verdicts of the occupation courts," he was convinced,

> can find little resonance among the people as long as they cannot avert the feeling of lawlessness. If punishment is meant as revenge, or if it serves only to deter, then it may not matter which power delivers it. But if punishment is in some metaphysical sense an expiation, not only of the individual perpetrators but also of the entire people over whom the smoke of burned human flesh rose from Hadamar, then the prosecuting court must also rise from the people's own law.[26]

The audacity of Arndt's demand, that NS cases should henceforth pass entirely into German hands, lay in its delivery directly to Allied leaders—among those in his audience at Konstanz was the American prosecutor Charles M. La Follette—and in his timing. This was a full six weeks before the announcement of verdicts in the "Doctors' Trial" (Case 1 in the Nuremberg follow-up trials), which the Americans hoped would achieve a fundamental reckoning with the various forms of medical crimes committed under National Socialism.[27]

Arndt's plea for a restoration of German legal autonomy marked an important moment in the West German–Allied debate over democratization. At the same time, he avoided taking a clear position on the criminal prosecution of the "euthanasia" complex. His lecture did not address how much importance he wished to assign to the murder of patients as a historical event or how he intended to anchor it in the consciousness of German postwar society. His position on this, in contrast to the American prosecutors in Case 1, was surely influenced by his interpretation of "euthanasia" as a crime that above all had been committed against Germans themselves.[28] This allowed the same patriotically colored reading of Nazi repression that during the war had also been upheld by prominent members of the Social Democratic exile community.[29] Arndt refused to recognize that any regime measures had been taken primarily on behalf of the war economy and its interests, as was the usual view of the US prosecutorial class. In formulating indictments on conspiracy charges, they had portrayed the mass murder programs as being driven by utilitarian motives.[30]

As a target of racial persecution himself, Arndt had experienced the exclusion mechanisms of the ethnicized "people's community" firsthand. Despite this, his views were typical of majoritarian self-interpretations during the postwar era, insofar as he did not conceive of the preparation and execution of the "euthanasia" crimes as a complex of actions with a longer prehistory and internal rationality.[31] Instead, he sorted these crimes within an ideal typology of Nazi terror, the single components of which arose from a societal void, without positing connections between them. The ultimate source of the crimes, according to this postwar topology, lay in a terrorist party and state leadership—or, simply, in "Hitler's will." Another widespread tendency of the time was to posit a hermetically sealed covert zone wherein given crimes were carried out by a few responsible parties, with all other population groups completely excluded from knowledge of what had happened. Even those who had been responsible for the administration of the enterprise as a whole supposedly knew nothing about the specific plans for murder. This was in gaping contradiction to the simultaneous assumption that most of the population at large had rejected the murder of the disabled, which of course would have required that they possessed at least partial knowledge of the processes and methods of the killing program in the first place.

In this way, the line between regime perpetrators and victim groups became increasingly blurred by Germans' perceptions of themselves as victims—of the Nazi regime, of the Allied "victors' justice," and of the Communist expulsion of German populations from eastern European territories. A parallel change occurred among West German opinion leaders as they redefined the meaning of the Allied reeducation project despite their rejection of the Allied verdicts that had been intended to drive it. The result was to de-concretize the crimes while reconfiguring the purpose of prosecuting them. In a dialectic of differentiation from the democratization goals of the American occupation authorities, the brief years of the "autochthonous processing" wave saw an ethnicized formation of legal understanding—one in which the victims were once again excluded from the new collective, even as the majority was no longer defined ethnically as a "people's community" (*Volksgemeinschaft*). The exclusion strategy prevailed along two tracks. First, most West Germans were ready to acknowledge Nazi-era crimes only on the precondition that the model of a *particular* victim identity (such as was advanced in a contradictory but recognizable way in the Nuremberg trials) would be replaced by that of a *universalized* victim identity.[32] Second, the perspective of the real victims, insofar as it was present at the early West German trials at all, served as an anchor for the historical self-reassurance of the perpetrators and those complicit with them.[33]

This tendency to revictimize the victims found some form of expression in nearly all the early West German trials, but it hit especially hard with the surviving kin of the murdered sick, mentally ill, and physically handicapped patients, who never had the support of a strong lobby. Almost no statements from this group are available, leaving little chance to reconstruct their view of the first "autochthonous processing" wave. They may have felt some sense of satisfaction from the way in which most of the early cases concluded, with relatively clear attributions of guilt and very stiff sentences.[34] This phase ended by 1948, however. Despite a few outliers, most cases after that saw acquittals or light sentences of one to four years.

Once the West German constitution came into force, courts developed inhibitions about denying the exonerating arguments presented by the defendants. As Karl Teppe showed in the case of the Westphalian "euthanasia" trial of former staff from several clinics and sanatoriums, rulings passed down by the German Supreme Court for the British Zone (OGHBZ) and the later Federal Court of Justice (BGH, founded in 1950) sent important signals.[35] Both courts developed a series of exculpatory legal constructs that—although explicitly presented as exceptions—would find ubiquitous use in the lower courts, always on behalf of the defendants. One BGH ruling in November 1952 especially had the effect, in Teppe's words, of a "caesura," "changing tracks in the process, so that courts at all levels would still describe the illegality of acts by the accused in meticulous and strict ways, but were always ready to admit mitigating factors, to make allowances for the defendants' manner of behavior or personal motives, to open paths to exoneration."[36]

The shift in the image of the defendant went together with a shift in that of the crime. West German investigators had always proceeded from the mostly unspoken premise that only Hitler and his closest collaborators had known the true purpose of the "selections" and "transfers" that were carried out during the implementation of Nazi extermination policies. At the same time, a far greater circle of knowledgeable parties was implied by numerous common defense tropes, like the "collision of duties" allegedly suffered by defendants, or the "mistake of prohibition" (i.e., the belief they were forbidden from taking action to prevent illegal acts).[37] In the euthanasia cases, courts were also ready to accept an even more dubious argument that was advanced by psychiatric expert witnesses among others: that the separation of the "incurably sick" from the rest of the institutionalized population actually served to "rescue" the majority of still curable patients. Well before 1933, many doctors had demanded they be allowed to make prognoses about the "therapability" of patients. After the war, this attitude was no longer questioned and in fact was reinforced through many of the case verdicts. The concept of a "merciful death" similarly underwent a revival. The census and "removal" of supposedly incurably sick people was viewed no longer as the expression of NS population policy but rather as a supposed act of resistance, of *saving* the lives of others who were could still be cured.

All this serves to explain why West German medical professionals did not reflect on their own part in the crime and why no major shift in public opinion followed the trials. A survey in the late 1960s found that 40 percent of West Germans still thought that it was ethically justified to kill "barely aware" mentally ill patients.[38] The "paradigm of a selective-preventive social medicine," as Falk Pingel put it, survived despite the dramatic first wave of "euthanasia" trials. But this was the case only as long as the measures could be categorized not as typically National Socialist but as part of another, older tradition of exclusion.[39]

This juridical version of the history and accompanying criminological discourse also affected contemporary historical scholarship. Starting in 1951, Hans Buchheim of the Munich-based Institute of Contemporary History (Institut für Zeitgeschichte, IfZ) began to produce expert reports in restitution cases. He characterized the "euthanasia" complex as a process that was set into motion by a few people and undertaken at a remove from German society. He wrote that both the "killing of the mentally ill" and the "gassing of Jews" were "completely illegal measures" that the NS leadership "had sought to keep secret from the German people and the world public by every possible means." Over time, Buchheim found, the population at large had acquired knowledge about the killings, given the bureaucratic and judicial difficulties that arose from the constant falsification of causes of death. Nevertheless, no one was privy to the details of the "euthanasia" actions other than the leadership of the Reich, the "mainly responsible" doctor Karl Brandt, and a few "selection doctors." In particular, the managers of the facilities had been deceived about the true purpose of the "transfers."[40]

The claims that the mass killings of mentally ill and physically disabled persons had taken place in secret and solely based on a central command were relatively easy to refute through critical source reading, even in Buchheim's time. But the drawing of parallels between the murder of the sick and the murder of the Jews highlights that a mutually reinforcing convergence between the historical and juridical patterns of argument was already underway. History writing should have been aiming for the broadest possible contextualization as a professional requirement, but a court brief, even as written by a historian, narrowed events down to a set of related facts as required for deciding a case.[41] In part, these were based on hypotheses derived from consideration of the Allied military verdicts; in part, the latter were openly rejected. Although Buchheim's brief in the given example was submitted in a restitutions case, his argument was clearly influenced by questions of lawfulness and culpability. For this reason, his text also included thoughts on the legality of the "euthanasia" measures, although these did not fall within the range of competence usually assigned to a historical assessor.[42]

West German Historians and the "Führer Order"

An always embattled field lay between the postwar juridical policy of "overcoming the past" (*Vergangenheitsbewältigung*) and the concurrent reflections of public history. Some areas of it today remain controversial and obscured.

Among these are the way in which the West German professional historians who were studying the Nazi era contributed to creating the legend of the ominous *Führerbefehl* (Führer order).[43] The idea that the Final Solution was initiated in the spring of 1941 by means of a sudden, secret, and direct order from the Reich leadership to commit mass executions of civilian populations itself originated in the Nuremberg trials, further complicating the matter. Otto Ohlendorf, an SS commander who was called as a witness before the International Military Tribunal and was later charged as a primary defendant in the so-called Einsatzgruppen Trial (Case 9 in the Nuremberg follow-up proceedings), had sought to defend himself and his codefendants by claiming that Hitler, shortly before the planned attack on the Soviet Union, had personally issued an order that all Soviet Jews should be shot to death summarily without regard for their age or sex.[44] Ohlendorf claimed that he had received the murder order personally from the mouth of Bruno Streckenbach, chief of personnel at the Reich Main Security Office (Reichssicherheitshauptamt, RSHA), the central administration for the SS and Gestapo.[45] At the time of Ohlendorf's testimony, Streckenbach was considered missing, his whereabouts unknown. Ohlendorf could not have guessed that he would one day turn up and provide a contrary version of events (to which we shall return later). The judges of US Military Court IX believed Ohlendorf's story of what came to be known as the Führer order, and adopted it as fact in their verdict. They were of course far from willing to tolerate the legal logic by which Ohlendorf's defense sought to derive his exoneration. The judges did not agree with the defense attorney, Rudolf Aschenauer, a right-wing extremist based in Munich, who portrayed the attack on the Soviet Union as an act of "self-defense" against "Jewish Bolshevism." Nor did they accept Aschenauer's preposterous thesis that the commanders of the SS Einsatzgruppen, who had conducted massacres of hundreds of thousands of Jewish civilians who had been rounded up in occupied Soviet territories, had committed their acts under pressure from a "putative state of emergency."[46]

Although the claim of a secret order issued in advance of the main part of the genocide was based on Ohlendorf's unconfirmed hearsay, it found easy entry into early international Holocaust research. Among the first to accept it almost without reservation was the British historian Gerald Reitlinger. In his 1953 study, one of the few early comprehensive portrayals of the murder of the Jews,[47] Reitlinger stressed that Ohlendorf had made his statements in the dock as a defendant who was facing capital charges. Reitlinger also speculated that Ohlendorf might have been motivated by resentment when he accused the entire Wehrmacht High Command (OKW) of connivance in the Holocaust. Despite these observations, Reitlinger did not in any way cast doubt on the truth of Ohlendorf's testimony.[48] Rather, he considered it fully plausible that at least one "extermination order," and probably two, had been issued in 1941 and communicated orally among the responsible parties.[49]

Alongside several other early studies of the Holocaust, Reitlinger's work founded a historiographic tradition that more or less openly professed to be following in the footsteps of "Nuremberg." These authors made intensive use of the Nuremberg trial transcripts and exhibits as source material, and their studies generally adopted the perspectives and assumptions of the US prosecutorial agency, the OCCWC. In fact, more than a few of these authors had worked at Nuremberg and gathered their first experiences with the archives there, while others studied under scholars who had previously worked at the Research and Analysis Branch of the OSS.[50] The works do of course vary greatly in style and method but as a set were fundamentally shaped by the genuine perspective of the American prosecutors at the IMT and in the Nuremberg follow-up trials, and by their main thesis that the murder of the European Jews was undertaken as a common project by elements of Germany's Nazi and pre-Nazi elites. Now this idea was being presented for the first time on a broad, scholarly, and historical foundation.

Consistently argued from the perspective of the perpetrators, the narrative was that the Final Solution came as the result of innumerable, purposeful, intermeshing particular efforts and initiatives at the higher and middle levels, all of which went back to an original central order. While the "intentionalist" or "Hitler-centric" interpretation[51] that had connected all Nuremberg indictments was generally adopted without caveats in the first publications on the history of the genocide, these narratives tended to place it within a different horizon than had the prosecutors. US Chief Prosecutor Robert H. Jackson and his staff saw the genocide above all as the outgrowth of a hyperaggressive German militarism and imperialism. The first generation of Holocaust historians, most of them Jewish, tended to see it as the essential product of the Nazi regime in particular, one that could be explained with Hitler's radical anti-Semitism and personal hatred of the Jews.[52]

During the early postwar period, scholars in the emerging field of West German contemporary history tended to view these first comprehensive portrayals of the destruction of the Jews with relative skepticism and from a distance, for reasons that were both explicit and implicit. Nicolas Berg recently became the first historian to more deeply explore their motives.[53] Researching the history of National Socialism was considered one of the most important tasks facing modern historians, but there were many uncertainties among the West Germans about how best to go about it. The obvious obstacle during the early years was that of asymmetric access to the central German documentary archives.[54] This inevitably affected research perspective, but the obvious methodological problem served to obscure a more political dimension. Study of the recent past was also supposed to contribute to the democratization of

German society. At the same time, the West Germans widely believed that the "mistaken interpretations" of the Nuremberg trials required a corrective.[55] Furthermore it was generally—and falsely—thought that the Allied criminal prosecutions had thoroughly illuminated the history of NS extermination policy; this raised suspicions, at least within the broader public, that the early historical studies on the murder of the Jews were intended to continue accusing Germans of a "collective guilt."

Special challenges faced the first generation of mostly younger researchers who were employed starting in 1950 at the newly founded German Institute for the History of the National Socialist Era, which in May 1952 was renamed and remains known today as the Institut für Zeitgeschichte.[56] As their common vision, the founders of the institute believed it should build the new foundation on which Germans would recover their own history in the long term. During the early planning (in 1945), there was talk of an "advisory office for German matters" that would work with Western occupation authorities to help avert "rigidities and ill humors" in the de-Nazification process.[57] A shift in emphasis was to follow, however. Three years later, the plan was still for the institute to pursue the main mission of "enlightenment and democratic education of the German people."[58] New motives came into play, however, once the Americans wrapped up the Nuremberg follow-up trials; the last, the Wilhelmstrasse trial, in April 1949, ended with the conviction of a former state secretary at the Foreign Office Ernst von Weizsäcker and a group of other high ministerial servants. The institute was reconceived as a center to concentrate the scattered documents of the NS era, in an effort to regain for German historians the interpretative sovereignty that had been lost to the prosecutorial efforts of the Allies, as well as to the by-then booming field of historical journalism.

It was no coincidence that a discussion on how to name the institute broke out immediately after the Weizsäcker verdict. The apparent motivation was to help extinguish every memory of the effort at juridical "processing," given that the initiative came from the national-conservative historian Gerhard Ritter, who was based in Freiburg and had been appointed to the scientific advisory board of the institute when it was called forth in February 1949. It was Ritter who suggested the center be renamed the Institut für Zeitgeschichte. He called the original name "cumbersome" and said it evoked the impression "of a political enterprise to establish new atrocity histories."[59] Although Ritter's suggestion found much support within the committee, it would take three years before the new name was adopted. For the moment, the decisive opinion was that of his fellow board member and FRG President Theodor Heuss. He argued strongly for keeping the term "National Socialism" in the name to clarify the social relevance of the institute's research agenda. Heuss saw the institute's mission as legitimately including "a political purpose, even if of course solid scholarship is a prerequisite. It will depend on the works themselves to assure they do not produce the effect of polemical tracts." Experience showed, Heuss further argued, "that keeping the term National Socialism will make it easier to access material that is held privately than would be the case with a general name that only speaks to the scholars themselves."[60]

To the extent that the institute's profile as an "evidentiary center" for documents related to the NS era could be made apparent to all,[61] the legacies left by the Nuremberg prosecution would gain in importance. As interest in a broader popularization of the many trial proceedings and documents had largely declined among the American occupation authorities by the late 1940s, the West German thinkers were convinced that the time had come to secure access to these archives for West German researchers. The argument that they should use the court documents as a platform for their own research plans was therefore aimed intentionally at gaining Washington's political support for the planned institute. The designated future chair of the institute, Gerhard Kroll, a politician with the Bavarian CSU, made sure to tell the outgoing US military governor that the Americans would be well advised if they drew lessons from the failure of the earlier documentary edition project. It was evident, Kroll said, that

> publications of this kind are received with mistrust by the great mass of the German people and regarded as propaganda instruments of the occupation powers. Revelations from behind the scenes of the National Socialist time will be effective only once they are being received from a German office, one staffed with German men of recognized names and scientific reputations. The creation of a German research office is therefore an urgent political imperative that bespeaks the German interest as well as that of the occupation powers.[62]

The institute's self-determined political mission and privileged access to the court and defense files initially posed both a challenge and a dilemma. The staff in Munich wanted to contribute to the critical study of the NS period and thus expose the criminal essence of the system. At the same time, they did not want to lose their individual power or social influence by subordinating their scholarly interests to the dictates of a research program called forth from outside the academic realm; or have their work be predetermined by overdependence on a specific body of sources. Reservations against the supposed "black-and-white vision" of Nuremberg—as the institute's first general secretary, Hermann Mau, put it in a notable 1950 lecture[63]—not only became evident in the West German-Allied negotiations over the return of confiscated German documents, but also influenced the professional self-image and the programmatic approaches of the young discipline.

The result was the formation of a specific professional ethos among the first generation of West German contemporary historians, one defined in contradistinction to the ways in which especially the US prosecutorial agency was seen to have presented the German archives to the public exploitatively, partly for judicial, partly for political ends. This was evident in their invocations of a duty for them to show more "sobriety," "objectivity," and "factuality" in scholarly approaches to the most recent German history.[64] They expressed the desire to set new methodological standards for evaluating sources and determining their provenance. Their resistance to the accusatory gesture in the portrayal of historical circumstances (whether or not this tendency had been exaggerated before) tended to promote a stronger focus on structures and techniques of control, while individual behavior and motives tended to remain obscure. The expansion of contemporary history research into social and structural issues was a means of overcoming the crisis of traditional historical methods, given the recent great upheavals, but it also opened the way to skepticism regarding modernity and an "escape" from the German national history that had fallen into such discredit.[65]

The West German discipline of Contemporary History (*Zeitgeschichte*) thus began by assuming a double opposition: against the convention of personalizing explanations and against a "Nuremberg historiography"[66] imported from abroad. Given both these tendencies, however, the early, widespread, and relatively unsophisticated adoption of the idea that there had been a comprehensive secret order to murder the Jews becomes all the more puzzling. This was an assertion with enormous explosive potential; as a scholarly matter, it bore the stigma of originating with a courtroom cross-examination. In untangling this riddle, we begin by returning to Mau's post-doctoral qualification lecture (a career-defining German academic procedure known as the "habilitation") that he delivered in December 1950, just before assuming his post at the new institute.

Before taking a deputy professorship at Jena in 1944, Mau had spent three years as an assistant to Hermann Heimpel at the Imperial University of Strasbourg,[67] where he presumably first met the jurist Hellmut Becker, his coeval. Mau's next stop was the Eastern Front. After he escaped from the Soviet occupation zone, in 1948, Becker became an assistant for the influential professor Ernst Rudolf Huber. Mau, now a thirty-five-year-old scholar of medieval history, settled in Munich. He worked first for the Bayerische Rundfunk radio network and then as an adjunct lecturer at the University of Munich. Becker and Heimpel, Mau's academic mentor, advocated vehemently for his candidacy in the "often ferocious, ad hominem exchanges" among the institute's board members. These culminated with Mau's appointment as the institute's general secretary.[68]

Becker had served as the defense attorney to Weizsäcker in the Wilhelmstrasse trial of major ministerial figures. He and Mau enjoyed a chummy exchange of favors. Becker would allow Mau to have a look into his historically valuable defense files, while Mau used his good contacts among politicians and academics to serve as a covert spin doctor to the Heidelberg Circle and the clemency lobby.[69] Mau's late entry to the professional association of university lecturers on NS-era history meant that he did not meet the announced requirements for the institute job. Becker, who had been appointed to the IfZ's scientific advisory committee in 1951, saw this differently. He argued that Mau was a "modern kind of person," one who had personally maintained an "absolute distance from National Socialism" but nevertheless kept a keen eye for "what had happened during this time to people and to minds, the good as well as the bad."[70]

It may be safely assumed that Mau wrote his December 1950 habilitation lecture with the general secretary's job in mind, for the text reads like a program for the new institute.[71] In the first of two parts, about three-quarters of the whole, Mau expounded at length on the value of the Nuremberg trial documents to historical researchers. Proceeding from the observation that these sources would remain for some time the most important material basis for understanding the Third Reich, Mau gradually went into particulars. Regarding the value of the sources, he noted that the selection and curation of the files had been conducted with prosecutorial and not historical criteria in mind. More than any other example, however, the IMT showed how often law and history can hardly be separated from each other. One cause for this was that the defendants were high-ranking functionaries in the NS state and party. Furthermore, in this "procedure unfolding literally before the eyes of the world, almost every word [was] delivered in the face of history."[72] The initiators of the trial had never lost sight of their own historic role, and they proceeded from a "highly particular image of history" that influenced both the charges and the verdict.

To Mau it was clear that out of the published records of the trial, the transcripts of the oral witness testimonies constituted the sources of first resort for contemporary history research. Their greater value than the documentary evidence and written affidavits arose from "their human immediacy" and that, "at nearly every meaningful point, the defense took the opportunity of cross-examination, testing the credibility of the witnesses, providing important indicators for a critical overall evaluation" of testimonies.[73] Mau thus foresaw the IfZ's later credo of the "co-experiencing" and "co-suffering" witnesses. After clarifying with concrete examples, and thus building a kind of hermeneutic bridge to the Nuremberg printed material despite its problematic reputation within his set, he abruptly turned in the final quarter of his lecture to questions of NS techniques of control, the murder of the Jews, and complicity. The Nuremberg documents may have been dense for historians to penetrate, but they did succeed in providing the service that the prosecution had desired: "To present evidence, also before history, of war crimes and crimes against humanity on a scale and of a terribleness beyond all imagining." Anyone working with the documents, Mau held, must also never lose sight of this background of "apocalyptic horror," even if this meant casting "the brightest light on what is [only] a part of the whole picture."[74]

It was at this point that Mau added the critical observation that no one among the Nuremberg prosecutors had truly understood the "technique of totalitarian power." Because they had never lived in a totalitarian system—aside from the Russians, "who would have hardly wanted to give their Allied colleagues lessons on this subject"—their concern at Nuremberg had been to reconstruct personal responsibilities. What this overlooked, Mau held, was that totalitarian praxis so thoroughly distorted the constitutional designs of state and party that in the end, de jure and de facto circumstances had fully diverged. Only the wild growth of the various NS agencies and a perfect system of keeping secrets had made the destruction of the Jews—the "most horrific fact of National Socialist history"—possible in the first place. What the Nuremberg sources revealed about all this therefore required "recapitulation and supplementation." All possible care had to be devoted to determine "how many people truly knew about the extermination actions *by virtue of their office*."[75] This was necessary not to provide a "moral alibi" but to recognize the particular techniques of power that the regime had employed.

Anticipating the results yet to be discovered, Mau himself assumed that the circle of the "truly knowledgeable" was most likely limited to Heinrich Himmler, Adolf Eichmann, and Rudolf Höss. To support this thesis, he ended his lecture by pointing at the IMT trial and the Nuremberg files. These had "determined with certainty" that "in July 1941 [*sic*]," Hitler had issued a "Final Solution order" to Himmler. The exact instructions were then passed from Himmler, "avoiding several intermediate authorities, to the "Jewish Expert" at the advisory level of the RSHA, the SS commander Eichmann." Eichmann then charged the commandants of Auschwitz with the technical execution of the order. "The interplay of just three people," Mau concluded, had sufficed to set the "monstrous death machinery" in motion.[76]

Because the lecture went unpublished and Mau died soon after in a car crash, before he had a chance to reproduce these thoughts in a more thorough, written form, it may no longer be possible to reconstruct his arguments' origins and influences. It is also no longer possible to determine which documents and testimonies Mau employed in writing the text. While the gist suggests that he was aware of Ohlendorf's statements in Case 9, Mau deviated strongly from Ohlendorf's story, which was that the "liquidation order" was communicated orally starting on 31 July 1941 by Hermann Göring to the RSHA chief, Reinhard Heydrich.[77]

Read against the grain, however, such inconsistencies cast a light on the patterns of meaning creation and the authentication strategies of the early West German researchers. Mau's text displays an idiosyncratic fixation on the different, nonscientific system of referents employed by "Nuremberg," apparently with the aim of deconstructing its logics and rules, but also effectively reproducing these. In this way, Mau's lecture stands as a document typical of its time. The oscillation between two extremes—between an intensified actor perspective and a nearly opposite attempt to explain the murder of the Jews as the product of anonymous systemic circumstances—cannot be dismissed merely as an apologetic stance.[78] It may be a more important factor that the Allied prosecution program had created both a political-cultural environment and a semantic map for navigating it, within which the emerging German discipline of contemporary history would necessarily have to position itself in some fashion. In reality, this often meant that the discipline's relatively strong rhetorical demarcation from "Nuremberg" carried with it an indirect form of appropriation. In the case of the NS Jewish policy, the consequence was that a significant number of West German historians committed themselves early to the frame of a Final Solution order, without subjecting the problematic origins of this thesis to scrutiny or proofing its plausibility through a consideration of all available relevant sources.

It should be noted that during the 1950s, the Holocaust would play only a secondary role for West German historians. Despite this, the end of the decade saw further reinforcement of the interpretation that Mau had propounded. This was preceded by two developments that would have been unforeseeable in the early years of the FRG and that thoroughly changed the working conditions for contemporary historians. The first was the increasing presence and visibility of highly compromised NS perpetrators at the highest levels of West German society. This group eventually attracted scrutiny from state-level prosecutors and administrative supervisors.[79] Second, reparations case law became increasingly important and stimulated a demand for expert briefings. This would become the institutional specialty of the IfZ in Munich. This activity generally involved younger researchers and played a dual function in stimulating their careers. First, it opened new fields within NS-era history for them to plough. Second, working at the intersection of scholarship, justice, and political education had a productive effect on their own research.[80]

Nevertheless, not until the spring of 1958 did a West German contemporary historian provide expert testimony in a Holocaust trial brought before a West German court. The state attorney in Ulm prepared charges against ten former members of the NS State Police (Staatspolizei, or Stapo) in the town of Tilsit. The Stapo men had joined an SS Einsatzkommando auxiliary unit called the Tilsit Special Commando (Tilsiter Sonderkommando) in June 1941. In preparing for their trial, the chief investigator in the case against them, Erwin Schüle, commissioned a historical briefing on the process of the "Jewish extermination policy" during the first weeks and months of the German invasion of the Soviet Union. The briefing and expert testimony was provided by Helmut Krausnick, who had been employed at the IfZ as a researcher since 1951 and would later become the institute's director for many years.[81]

The charges in the Ulm case related to "extermination" actions undertaken in a strip of territory, twenty-five kilometers wide, along the border of East Prussia and Lithuania.[82] While planning the invasion and occupation of the Soviet Union in March 1941, the SS and the Wehrmacht (the German armed forces) agreed to terms under which any and all persons identified as "Jewish-Bolshevik intelligentsia" were to be executed on sight. After the Wehrmacht launched the invasion in June 1941, the Tilsit Stapo group entered the border area, along with special commandos from other locations, improvised police battalions, and Lithuanian auxiliary troops, and began to round up and massacre all Jewish men of military age. Starting in mid-August, special commandos in Lithuania and elsewhere also started killing all the Jewish women and children they could capture. In carrying out these missions, the unit commanders, who were drawn from SD and Security Police, generally used all means at their disposal. Within Lithuania, about 130,000 persons were killed by the end of 1941, representing most of the country's Jewish population, which was estimated at about 200,000 people. Out of this number, the ten defendants tried at Ulm were charged with more than 5,500 counts of murder.

Even given the new context of the late 1950s—when West German prosecutors had become far more active in pursuing NS cases—the curious influence of intentionalist interpretations of the Holocaust was still very strong. The old trope of the "extermination order" would play an outstanding role in the Ulm Einsatzkommando trial. Its revival was partly thanks to the unexpected reappearance of Bruno Streckenbach—the RSHA official whom Otto Ohlendorf had identified as the man who communicated the Führer order to him in 1941. His whereabouts unknown to the Western authorities for more than ten years, Streckenbach, former chief of the RSHA personnel department, was suddenly released from Soviet imprisonment in October 1955. He was detained at the West German returnee camp at Friedland, where investigators questioned him about the Führer order. Streckenbach at first remained silent, apparently honoring pleas from priests at the camp and the defense attorneys and relatives of imprisoned Einsatzgruppen commanders who feared that ongoing clemency proceedings might fail if Streckenbach talked. But when prosecutors threatened to charge him with having communicated the murderous order himself, he took the advice of his own lawyer and denied any responsibility. If any such order had indeed been communicated, Streckenbach claimed, then it could have only been done by the director of the RSHA agency for "fighting the enemy," Heinrich Müller, and in no case by Streckenbach himself.[83]

The Ulm Einsatzkommando trial ended with a bitter defeat for the prosecutors. They had presented a series of witnesses who testified that the first mass shootings, in the area of Garsden, had been committed with cover from the Wehrmacht, which had ordered reprisals against "Jews and Communists." The state built a case showing that the four primary defendants had shown a high degree of personal initiative in carrying out these orders. But in the end, the court convicted all ten defendants only on the lesser charges of aiding and abetting murder. As a mitigating circumstance, the verdict specified that the killings were carried out on an order originating from "Hitler, Himmler and Heydrich" and commanding that "all Jews would be physically destroyed without regard for age and sex." In arriving at this conclusion, the jury relied mainly on the opinion of the historical expert, Helmut Krausnick.[84]

In his testimony to the court, Krausnick had drawn an enormous arc that led from Hitler's speech to the Reichstag in January 1939 directly to the killing trenches along the border between East Prussia and Lithuania. Based on an assessment of documents from the Nuremberg Einsatzgruppen trial of Ohlendorf and other commanders, Krausnick concluded that Hitler and his closest collaborators had already made the decision to exterminate the Jews irreversibly in the spring of 1941, but also that they had at first kept this order secret from the military high command. Although Ohlendorf's credibility had been impeached by the contrary statements from the "crown witness," Streckenbach, and although a series of former commanders of the special units had retracted their earlier statements implicating Streckenbach as the messenger of the Führer order, Krausnick nevertheless held on to their claims that there had been something like a total "liquidation order" to kill all Jewish civilians without distinction and that it had been communicated orally to the Einsatzgruppen commanders before the start of the June 1941 invasion. It should be noted, however, that unlike Ohlendorf's defense attorney, Aschenauer—who was also present at Ulm as counsel to the primary defendant and former SD unit commander Werner Hersmann—Krausnick in no way suggested that the existence of an extermination order would therefore allow the conclusion that the defendants had been in a state of "command emergency."[85]

The Ulm verdict in a sense "canonized the fixation" on the Führer order that "seemed to confirm itself perpetually anew through the spiral of historians' court briefings and the verdicts resting on them."[86] This influenced the further course of both historiographic debate and criminal verdicts in NS cases. The assumption of a Final Solution order possessed a strong self-explicatory effect that greatly distorted any effort to consider the room for maneuver that was available to commanders and those under their command, let alone to examine their ideological backgrounds, socializations, or personal motives. Thus did an epistemological fog descend for many years over questions of contingent interactions between center and periphery, of situational factors affecting specific killing actions, or of personal initiative among the perpetrators on the scene.

In the claim of a Final Solution order, many West German courts came to see the additional mitigating factors that defendants simply had not understood the racist genocidal intent behind the order or had falsely assumed that refusing orders would automatically endanger their own lives. The supposed proof from the jurists and historians that the killings were the product of a previously agreed order also affected the images of the Holocaust in public history. The idea that the murder of the Jews had been decided well in advance and then put into motion according to plan after the invasion of the Soviet Union tended to reinforce the already-widespread tendency to view the mass murder as a "secret event in the closed special zones of 'the East,'" in places no witness could access.[87]

In the decades that followed, Krausnick stuck to his original theses,[88] and most courts continued to follow the version of an early comprehensive murder,[89] but new investigations against a series of Einsatzgruppen officers starting in the early 1960s provided a wealth of countervailing evidence. In the related interrogations of former SS and SD members, many suggested that Ohlendorf's original statement was actually an "official story" concocted with his defense attorney, Aschenauer. Eventually, this piqued the interest of Alfred Streim, the deputy director of the West German Central Office of the State Justice Administrations for the Investigation of National Socialist Crimes at Ludwigsburg (known as the Zentrale Stelle Ludwigsburg, ZSL). The Ludwigsburg agency was established in the late 1950s to coordinate investigations of NS crimes among the states of the FRG. Among his other activities at the Ludwigsburg agency, Streim had led investigations into the German treatment of Soviet prisoners of war. In the early 1980s, he set about conducting a thorough comparative analysis of numerous interrogation transcripts and documentary exhibits collected in West German court proceedings over a period of decades.[90]

Streim's first discovery was remarkable. Almost all the Einsatzgruppen and "Special Commando" officers who had claimed there was a secret Führer order but were questioned about it a second time, after the end of the Nuremberg trial sequence, had either retracted or strongly revised their prior claims that such an order had been given. (The only exception was a former officer in

Special Commando 7, Waldemar Klingelhöfer.) Second, Streim determined that the killings of civilians during the early months of the invasion of the Soviet Union had been undertaken in two phases. In the first, which lasted for several weeks, the killers had almost exclusively targeted Jewish men. Only in the second phase were women and children massacred, after they had at first been confined to ghettos and camps. For all the painstaking searches for evidence of an advance order to kill, none had been found. Most witnesses who were willing to talk about it did not have clear memories of it. From all this, Streim concluded that a Führer order in the sense of a "self-contained instruction" had apparently never been given. It seemed instead that what came to be called a Führer order was in fact a multitude of "single instructions" that gradually were construed as an order to carry out the complete murder of all Jewish civilians.[91] With a few modifications, this view, since the opening of the Eastern European archives, has come to prevail as the near-consensus explanation for the transition, in the second half of 1941, from a mass murder that was at first limited to Jewish men to the systematic destruction of all Jews in the occupied Soviet territories.[92]

The West German historian Eberhard Jäckel invited Streim to present his theses to an international audience of historians at the Stuttgart Holocaust research conference in May 1984.[93] For the first time, this brought wide academic as well as a good deal of journalistic attention to the dispute between Streim and Krausnick, which until then had been carried out largely in the shadows. So far, no extensive study has been devoted specifically to the Stuttgart conference and its importance to Holocaust research,[94] but it seems to have set off a turn regarding the issues, potentials, and limits of the knowledge transfer between Justice and History. The Ludwigsburg prosecutor's appeal—that the researchers should pay more attention to the files from West German criminal investigations—met with rather reserved reactions from the historians. At that point, the clash of schools between "intentionalists" and "functionalists" had reached a point of exhaustion, and Streim's reception made it obvious that neither side as a whole was aiming at a more intensive treatment of specific crimes and perpetrators.[95] One symptom of this was that, with the exception of the Israeli researcher Yehuda Bauer, none of the "intentionalists" present at the Stuttgart conference engaged in the dispute.

The frontlines of this debate did not really run between intentionalists and functionalists, however, or between historians and jurists. The real epistemological conflict was among perspectives on the murderous events themselves and, connected to this, the readiness to use the archives generated by all the court trials since the war as a decisive body of sources.[96] Streim's intervention at first found little echo within the research community.[97] Over a longer term, however, awareness of the historiographic value of investigatory documents has clearly grown since that time.[98] There has been a far stronger interest, especially since the fall of the Soviet Bloc, in the specifics of the NS occupation and population policies, which had largely been ignored.[99] The question underlying the Streim-Krausnick controversy, the one most relevant to the history of both disciplines, remains: To what extent have the historians and jurists changed in their self-understanding and in their ways of working-through their common occupation with the mass criminal activity of the NS era? It was only to become a subject for researchers beginning in the 1990s,[100] most dramatically in the wake of the Goldhagen controversy.[101]

Eichmann, Arendt, and Justice

On 23 May 1960, Israeli Prime Minister David Ben-Gurion announced in Jerusalem that his government had captured Adolf Eichmann—the former chief expert for the "Jewish question" at RSHA. The next day, the West German Bundestag was to meet a fateful decision. With the proceedings that would become known as the Frankfurt Auschwitz trials still in preparation, the opposition Social Democratic Party proposed an extension on the statute of limitations for manslaughter committed under the NS regime. This was rejected by the governing coalition of CDU-CSU and its junior partner, the FDP.[102] The majority argument used the opinion of Erwin Schüle, formerly the chief prosecutor in the Ulm case. The senior state attorney had been appointed in December 1958 as the first director of the new ZSL. A few weeks before the parliamentary debate on the statute of limitations, Schüle had stated on the record that "all major mass extermination actions of the war period have been covered systematically and investigated extensively."[103] From that moment, NS and regime perpetrators who were not accused of murder or abetment to murder—meaning most of them, thanks to the restrictive legal interpretations of rulings from the highest West German courts—had almost nothing left to fear from the German criminal justice system. A group trial against the higher echelons of the RSHA would be planned starting in 1963, but would be abandoned some years later because of a change in the law that in principle should have had little effect on crimes categorized as NSG (the official designation for "National Socialist Crimes of Violence").[104]

These structural parameters indicated that the Eichmann trial was unlikely to cause a late reorientation in West German investigations, but its effects on the West German politics of the past were immediate. Even before the trial itself could begin in a local Jerusalem court, Bonn formed an interministerial committee to coordinate the public relations response domestically and internationally.[105] The group was headed by Hans Gawlik, the foreign ministry's highest-ranking legal counsel. Their mission, as he told his team, was to demonstrate to the world that Eichmann had been one of a small circle of criminals who carried out their crimes in closed rooms, unbeknown to the mass of the German people. Meanwhile the Federal Press Office (Bundespresseamt, BPA) commissioned the NS researcher Hans Buchheim to answer the question, "What did the German people know about the persecution and extermination of the Jews?" The BPA published his answer as an expert report in May 1961. By far, most Germans, according to Buchheim, had possessed "no hostility against Jews," and they either knew nothing about the crimes or had been too afraid to take action.[106]

Even as the international media flocked to cover the Eichmann case, Holocaust research was still at an early stage. Raul Hilberg's magnum opus, *The Destruction of the European Jews*, is an instructive case. After delays of several years, the original edition came out in English and only in a highly abridged form from a small US publisher in 1961. It found hardly any reviewers in the FRG.[107] Although the print runs were high for Gerhard Schoenberner's *The Yellow Star* and Wolfgang Scheffler's *The Persecution of the Jews in the Third Reich*, both published in 1960, these works were by academic outsiders and newcomers.[108] Next to Gerald Reitlinger's *Die Endlösung* (1956),[109] the "big exception" was Léon Poliakov and Joseph Wulf's *Das Dritte Reich und die Juden* (1955).[110] But its reception served to confirm the rule, as the book was met with "more attention in the media than among the academics."[111]

Research about the NS police and terror apparatus in particular was full of gaps. There were no biographical studies of the leading Gestapo and SS officials, nor did any works examine in detail how the institutions functioned or how their political significance was viewed from within. In a formalist balance that was hard to justify in rational terms, West German scholars of contemporary history showed a surprising willingness to trust the word of the former perpetrators. Works like those on the history of the SS and SD by Shlomo Aronson and Heinz Höhne unmistakably displayed the fingerprints of Werner Best, a former deputy to Heydrich who began making court appearances as an eyewitness and expert on the perpetrators starting in the mid-1950s and who otherwise sought to influence the historiography.[112] Best worked to identify gaps in the historians' knowledge and learn about new findings, which he would then disseminate within his network of fellow Nazi veterans.

Given the incomplete knowledge of the causes, process, and consequences of the murder of the Jews, the initial West German reservations about the Israeli trial are not surprising. The public debates about the trial and the subsequent book by Hannah Arendt were intense, but the "German" attitude (insofar as there was enough expression of it to permit generalization) consisted of skepticism, nervousness, and defensiveness, combined with an initial feeling of inchoate superiority to the Israelis. Many statements on the trial convey a subtext that, ideally, the mass murderer Adolf Eichmann should have been reincorporated in the "continued people's community."[113]

Long before the Jerusalem trial reached the evidentiary phase and confronted historical facts, a West German discourse had developed that differed obviously from that of the 1950s. Until then, the public had been fixated on the stereotypes of the fanatical true believer and the pathological sadist. Now a new type was imagined: the "perpetrator alienated from his acts,"[114] someone like an executive at a big company who embodied the rationality and efficiency of a modern bureaucracy but also demonstrated the supposed subordination of the individual to the "totalitarian" system. In the first West German news reports after Eichmann's arrest, the former RSHA official for the Jewish question was already presented as a meticulous administrative specialist, someone who even as late as 1937 had shown no signs that he would "ever achieve any prominence, for good or evil," according to a leading newspaper columnist.[115] (Eichmann had joined both the NSDAP and the SS in 1932.) Years before Arendt's theses on Eichmann would reach a broad German public, the public discussion about him served as an empty vessel for meaning, allowing a reevaluation of the society's relationship to memory and history.

The West German debates on the Israeli court trial characteristically borrowed from the Critical Theory of the 1940s. In their analyses of fascism written during the war, social scientists like Franz Neumann, Herbert Marcuse, and Felix Gilbert used the semantics and narratives of "Fordism" to describe the sociopsychological effects of the NS regime. In their works, German society and in particular its working classes appear as the overwhelmed objects of a superindustrialized, mechanized system. Thoroughly rationalized labor processes had robbed the individual practically overnight of any sense of autonomy or moral conscience.[116] West German perpetrator discourse adopted the antimodernist thrust of this argument—shorn, however, of its "class specific" character. Even the factor of intensely racialized anti-Semitism—the significance of which as a motive was self-evident to Eichmann's Israeli prosecutors—was turned by the universalist interpretation into a kind of "barbarism inherent in the principles of civilization."[117]

The image of Eichmann as the "protagonist of a quasi-automatic mass murder" was not limited to the mainstream mass media[118] but soon also became a guiding maxim for West German justice. The surprise capture of Eichmann did in fact pose a serious test for the country's government and criminal justice system. Should Bonn send an official observer to the Jerusalem trial? What consequences should be drawn from this event? While the FRG had attempted to "process" the past exclusively by the means of national law, the Israelis were returning to the retroactive criminal statutes of Nuremberg and international criminal law.[119] The Israeli approach also cast a harsh light on the blind spots in the German "overcoming of the past" and its failure to take the problem of "deskbound perpetrators" seriously enough.[120]

No one was more aware of the difficulties of prosecuting this group using the conventional means of criminal law than the first director of the Ludwigsburg agency, Erwin Schüle. He pleaded with his superiors to use the coming trial as a means to revive long-delayed investigations. Although he knew that officials in both the foreign and justice ministries had recently reiterated opposition to making formal requests for Israeli help,[121] Schüle argued all the more passionately that a West German prosecutor should question Eichmann to acquire evidence for use in German proceedings. Prosecutions of "the upper echelons of RSHA, the personal staff of the Reichsführer-SS [Himmler], the Reich criminal agency, and other offices of the Reich" had often failed, Schüle said, because

> these groups of personnel rarely appeared to the outside world (as deskbound perpetrators). It is usually impossible to produce witness testimony against such perpetrators. People who could still testify about the decisions of the higher functionaries are themselves in danger of being subject to prosecution. This is why as a rule they dispute that they knew anything about the participation of their former superiors and colleagues in the preparation and execution of mass extermination measures. Documents that could be revealing about the involvement of such former higher functionaries are rare, following the destruction of the "Agency IV" documents at RSHA before the end of the war. Against the few remnants of documents, such as the "Wannsee Protocol," the participants object that they had taken part in talks only routinely, as representatives of their offices, and were therefore unaware of the reach of the decisions being made.

Schüle also argued that the Jerusalem trial might do serious damage to the FRG. One had to expect that compromised persons who were still serving in leading positions would be named. An interrogation could help prepare against the danger of such exposures.[122]

Although well intentioned, the initiative by which Schüle hoped to liberate the Ludwigsburg agency (even at the cost of disrupting the existing division of labor among jurisdictions)[123] would instead end with a bitter disgrace for him. A few weeks later, when the Frankfurt chief investigator, Fritz Bauer, was finally sent to the Israeli ambassador Felix Shinnar to sound out the idea that Schüle himself might be allowed to interrogate Eichmann, Shinnar replied that Schüle was unwelcome in Israel during the Eichmann trial because he had been a member of the NSDAP.[124] Ironically enough, one of Schüle's motives in the effort had been to avert potential controversies around Hans Globke, Adenauer's chief of staff at the German Chancellery. As a civil servant and legal adviser to the NS regime, Globke had authored the official state commentary on the Nuremberg race laws of 1935. But instead of Globke, West Germany's leading investigator of NS crimes became the diplomatic problem. After the Israeli rejection, and after major Jewish American organizations also warned about the possible image problem, Bauer proposed his own employee, Dietrich Zeug, as a worthy substitute.

Zeug, a Frankfurt investigator who had been assigned to Ludwigsburg in 1959, had acquired a strong command of the *Aktion Reinhard* material,[125] and the Hessian Ministry of Justice considered him the "best expert in the Eichmann complex."[126] The federal justice ministry and the legal team at the foreign ministry also thought Zeug was the right candidate. He was said to have the best grasp of ongoing cases, had worked in Ludwigsburg for long enough, and was, as a good start, "himself a Jew." Just then, however, the vetting agency in Bonn, the Zentrale Rechtsschutzstelle (ZRS), stepped in with a categorical refusal to give Zeug's trip an official cover, stating, "First of all, the same demand could be raised by the 'SBZ.'" (The statement used the abbreviation for the Soviet Occupation Zone rather than specifying the German Democratic Republic by name.) In addition, the ZRS argued, the FRG had to avoid the impression that it had any "special reason" to send its own observer to Jerusalem.[127]

In Bonn, it was of course obvious that the foreign ministry had especially good reasons to send a representative to the trial. Soon after Eichmann's capture, the ministry's legal counsel Gawlik, who had served as an attorney for SS and SD defendants at the Nuremberg trials, complained that the foreign ministry was about to face some difficult times. He was aware that back in the 1950s the Allies had provided copies of all files from the notorious NS-era "Inland II" department to the Israeli Holocaust memorial center, Yad Vashem. He therefore feared "attacks of the worst kind against the former Foreign Office."[128] Sending an observer from the West German justice authorities to Jerusalem was therefore a defensive priority for the top bureaucrats in Bonn and Stuttgart. However, they did not share the West German justice agencies' hope of communicating with the Israelis about the strengths and weaknesses of West German prosecution efforts or of possibly acquiring new documentary or testimonial evidence.[129] Their dominant motive, rather, was to prepare responses to any unexpected revelations from the defendant and to insure themselves against the unpredictable trial tactics of the Israelis. Bonn saw both these as serious risks.

It is debatable that the Eichmann trial would have been better received in the FRG if the West German representatives on the scene had possessed a more refined sense of its political and historical significance. The West German reception was more influenced by the fact that those who were sent as official observers to Jerusalem had mostly negative opinions about the proceedings. Zeug's main point of criticism, for example, was that, in his view, the Israeli prosecutors were insufficiently versed in the literature and the documentation and thus exaggerated Eichmann's role in the structure of the NS state's Jewish policy. In his reports back to the Frankfurt state attorneys, Zeug complained that the Israeli prosecution did not adequately research the "intricate division of responsibilities among the many offices involved in the 'final solution.'"[130] Instead of considering the complicated command relationships and the problems of a "command emergency," the Israeli state attorney Gideon Hausner concentrated on "describing more or less horrible details."[131] But the cardinal sin of the trial, in Zeug's view, was the utter failure in its attempt to "outline a historical picture of the persecution of the Jews from 1933 to 1945."[132]

Because the Israelis managed to locate little in the way of new documentary evidence, Zeug was highly pessimistic in his conclusion that the trial "is very unfertile ground for historians and prosecuting jurists, and will remain so."[133] This basic attitude was not affected by his boss Bauer's contrary observation that the trial strategy seemed less concerned with gathering concrete evidence than in stabilizing the fragile German-Israeli relationship. In late May 1961, Bauer had to implore his frustrated employee Zeug not to make a premature return to Germany:

> I believe that you should remain in Jerusalem. I will also convey this opinion to the Hessian minister of justice. I have never expected that you would learn anything substantively new from the Jerusalem trial. Many Israeli officials have told me repeatedly, however, that you have succeeded in winning a lot of sympathy in Israel. The state of Hesse is extraordinarily grateful to you for this service. For this reason your stay is valuable. Therefore, you should persevere.[134]

To the extent that the Eichmann trial was perceived as a fundamental challenge to West Germany's own national strategy of "processing the past," a negative stereotype took hold in the FRG. The Jerusalem process did not prompt a new orientation in the treatment of "ideological perpetrators" but instead cemented the already prevalent functionalist view of the perpetrators. Typical of this were Schüle's comments at a late 1961 Catholic Academy conference, where he rejected the Israeli objectives as follows:

> In my knowledge of things, Eichmann was not in reality the "Grand Inquisitor of the Final Solution" before whom even "Himmler trembled," as the prosecuting agency saw him. His position is more comparable to that of a coolly calculating managing engineer at a big business, who built and runs the business and its subsidiaries according to plans laid down by his superiors and who tirelessly assured that the machinery of destruction would run at full speed and would always receive new victims.[135]

This instrumental interpretation of the "deskbound perpetrator" fits with the idea that neither Eichmann nor his accomplices were seen as having recognizable individual motives of their own. The German agencies proceeded from a broad-brush assumption—in contrast to the hyperintentionalist perpetrator image presented by the Israeli prosecutors—that the leading elites of the terror apparatus had acted because of a "Hitler order" and not out of their own political or ideological convictions.

This largely structuralist understanding of crime and perpetrators was well established in journalistic as well as judicial and administrative "processing" long before the trial. This species of structuralism did not posit an institutional chaos, like the later "polycratic state" discourse did, but saw only an extremely hierarchical, rigidly organized form of state and regime.[136] Even before Jerusalem had entered the discovery phase, the image had taken root among the West Germans of Eichmann as an administrative specialist: a dedicated bureaucrat who coordinated and managed the factorylike murder of the Jews. Hannah Arendt's report on the Eichmann trial would intrude into this echo chamber. A German translation of Arendt's text was first published in August 1963 by the journal *Merkur*. The monograph came out with Piper Verlag a bit more than a year later.[137] As Arendt wrote in her foreword to the German edition, for an understanding of NS Jewish policy her report had relied above all on the historical scholarship of Gerhard Reitlinger, Raul Hilberg, and Joachim C. Fest.[138]

Arendt also harkened back to her own ideas as developed in the early 1950s for what was surely her best-known work, *The Origins of Totalitarianism*.[139] Therein she had explored the connections between the practice of colonial rule in the nineteenth century and the later forms of totalitarian regimes. As the *Elements of Shame*—the book's original working title—she had identified the nearly simultaneous rise of anti-Semitism, imperialism, and racism in the second half of the nineteenth century. In the emergence and subsequent symbiosis of these three ideologies, she saw a dangerous "racial-imperialist mixture" that fundamentally threatened the mature European national states.[140] In a central chapter, Arendt further advanced the thesis that both racism and modern bureaucracy should be viewed as new principles of sovereignty and organization that were first tested by the European colonial powers in Africa during the era of high imperialism. These experiences of colonial, strictly segregated racist societies—Arendt used the Boer Republic in South Africa as the leading example—created the conditions under which the "Judeo-Christian" idea of a "common origin for all mankind" lost its persuasive power and was supplanted by the "wish for the systemic extermination" of whole races.[141] Although it was a British civil servant who in the 1920s had half-ironically coined the phrase "administrative mass murder" as a proposed solution for the "Indian question," at the time the "extraordinary potentials to accumulate power and destructiveness" inherent in the combination of these two principles of sovereignty were not yet foreseen. It remained for the National Socialists, with their exceptional racial fanaticism, to achieve practical implementation of "administrative mass murder" as a solution for "all of the still outstanding demographic problems of the world."[142]

The interpretation of the genocide of the Jews in *Origins of Totalitarianism* was remarkable, first, for breaking clearly with contemporary views that either minimized the NS murder of the Jews or, on the contrary, explained it as a consequence of specific German traditions or a German "special path" (the *Sonderweg* thesis).[143] Arendt instead located the origins of the genocide in a European-wide history of violence related to the decline of the classical nation-state and the creation of "colonial parallel worlds" in Africa.[144] Second, Arendt's theses were "unusual" because, while still seeing anti-Semitism as a "precondition of National Socialism," in her development of the "boomerang thesis" she raised the question of the *degree* to which colonial racism had driven the transformation of the traditional, religious, and sociocultural anti-Semitism of Europe into its modern, biologistic variants.[145]

Arendt's perspective in *Eichmann in Jerusalem* was similarly universalizing, an exploration of the general conditionalities of mass murder in the modern era. Eichmann struck her as a mediocre, bourgeois conformist, whose "inability to speak was closely connected with an inability *to think*."[146] This characterization later set off several misunderstandings but was not intended to say that Eichmann was insignificant or lacked influence—an occasional claim from the defendant that his defense attorney, Robert Servatius, repeated ad infinitum. Rather, Arendt saw in Eichmann a "new type of criminal" who exploded the norms of law and morals.[147] She thought that a term like "genocide" was inadequate to explain the unprecedented and innovative nature of "what happened in Auschwitz." This is why she borrowed the term "administrative mass murder" from the history of English imperialism. She took the idea much further than she had in her study on totalitarianism, however, now stressing the supposed arbitrariness of the NS mass murder, which targeted not only a "foreign people" or a "different race" but also the "incurably diseased." This observation led her to the deeply pessimistic conclusion that any other group could, in the future, meet a similar form of persecution.[148]

Arendt's interpretation of the murder of the Jews comes even closer to a general critique of civilization in her foreword to the German edition of *Eichmann in Jerusalem*. Therein she took aim against the identity politics and goals of the Israeli prosecutors, who narrated a historical metaphysics of the Jewish "history of suffering," but she also reinterpreted the historical concepts that she had sounded out in *Origins of Totalitarianism*. *Eichmann in Jerusalem* did not adopt a simple functionalist paradigm (a barely developed view at the time)[149] or propagate a one-dimensional perpetrator image.[150] These interpretations of her work are too simplistic. Arendt herself did not see her protagonist as simply a representative figure within the Nazi terror apparatus.[151]

Her text includes many passages on the difficulties of understanding complicity in the Holocaust in its entire breadth and complexity. Closely borrowing from Hilberg's powerful analysis of the "destruction" as a highly complex, bureaucratic process made possible by the "comprehensive readiness" of many professional groups and specialists, Arendt's book described the oppressive panorama of a society that had identified almost completely with a task regarded as a necessity.[152] In this context, she argued that the consequences of the Eichmann trial were "nowhere as obvious" as in Germany.[153] She furthermore criticized the Israeli political leadership for their opportunistic refusal to use the trial as a means of exposing the "complicity of the entire civil service at the state ministries, the Wehrmacht and the general staff, the judiciary, industry and business" in the "final solution."[154]

Among the blind spots in the still underresearched history of the Eichmann trial's impact on postwar Germany, many texts continue to presume that the trial *must have* had an outstanding effect on the West German treatment of the Nazi past, generally without providing much empirical confirmation.[155] As we have seen here, the West German adaptations and reinterpretations of "perpetrator images" occurred over a much longer period, without following a mechanistic pattern. At least in the judicial realm, it is clear that neither the Eichmann trial nor Arendt's report of it alone served to prompt a "new" perpetrator image. At most, they would have merely reinforced the already-available stereotype—one very convenient for the selective investigative strategies of the West German criminal justice agencies.[156] The "Eichmann" reception did contribute to an emergent redivision of labor between criminal justice and research history. To put it simply, the criminal investigators continued to concentrate on the seemingly limited problem of perpetrators who had yet to be caught, while the professional scholarship turned to examining the consequences for contemporary German society.

While Arendt herself claimed that the Eichmann trial had a catalytic effect on West German prosecutions, this was in reality very limited. Recall that this chapter began with the Bundestag's failure to extend the statute of limitations for manslaughter in 1960, which came just one day after the announcement of Eichmann's capture. More fundamental were the differences between West German and Israeli strategies for "processing" the past. The representative of West German justice in Jerusalem, Zeug, would eventually cite Arendt herself as an authoritative witness of the supposedly deficient understanding of history among the Israeli prosecutors.[157] In November 1961, Ludwigsburg Director Schüle was already declaring with an undertone of triumph that the FRG would not need to initiate "a single new case" as a result of the Eichmann trial.[158] Given these reactions, we hardly need add that Arendt's thoughts on developing international criminal law and creating an international court for serious human rights violations went practically unnoticed in the FRG.[159] Only her former academic mentor, Karl Jaspers, would approvingly adopt that proposal.[160] No one in magistratical studies or legal philosophy seemed to have heard of it, with the exception of a young Hamburg criminologist named Herbert Jäger.[161]

Perhaps more surprising than the attitude of the jurists is how West German contemporary history scholars reacted, or did not react, to the trial. With the exception of Wolfgang Scheffler—who was appointed to the official West German observation team on the strength of his 1960 study of Jewish policy under National Socialism—it is remarkable that almost no historians showed interest in the progress of the Jerusalem trial. This changed after *The New Yorker* published Arendt's reports in 1961, and the Piper publishing house of Munich began to prepare a German edition of her work. The editor assigned to Arendt, Hans Rössner, first checked with his boss Klaus Piper before retaining a Stuttgart legal firm to explore whether the text of *Eichmann in Jerusalem* might infringe on anyone's individual rights. Rössner was thinking in particular of Arendt's mention of Theodor Saevecke—by that time a high-ranking police officer in Bonn with the BKA (the West German counterpart to the FBI or Scotland Yard) but previously the commander of an SS Einsatzkommando in Tunisia—or of Hans Krüger, the FRG minister for postwar expellees from former Reich or ethnic German territories. When the lawyers concluded that they could not recommend the manuscript be published in its present form, Rössner turned for advice to both the IfZ in Munich and the ZSL in Ludwigsburg, providing a single copy of Arendt's work to each. Thanks to research by Michael Wildt, we now know that without Arendt's knowledge, *Eichmann in Jerusalem* (as well as prior works by Arendt) had in Rössner been assigned to an editor who was himself not only a scholar of German history but also a former SS commander in "Agency III" of the RSHA (SD-Domestic): in other words, a man who under the NS regime had specialized in the defense against its ideological "enemies" in the arts and culture.[162]

The situation in the scholarly realm was not significantly better. Nymphenburger Verlag in Munich managed to preempt the publication of Arendt's German edition with an anthology of mostly negative commentaries on her work,[163] although it also included sympathetic articles by Bruno Bettelheim, Al Alvarez, and Rolf Schroers.[164] The volume included an essay by Golo Mann, a student of Karl Jaspers, who described Arendt's critical comments about the German resistance to the Nazis as "the most appalling defamations" that had "ever been leveled at this movement."[165] Meanwhile, the quarterly journal of the IfZ, *Vierteljahrshefte für Zeitgeschichte*—by far the most important publication in the West German field of contemporary history—published its single review of *Eichmann in Jerusalem* in April 1965.[166] At the time, the journal's editorial troika consisted of Hans Rothfels, Theodor Eschenburg,[167] and the institute's managing editor and director, Helmut Krausnick. Perhaps they decided not to award the review to anyone in house because the institute had evaluated Arendt's manuscript for Piper Verlag before publication. However, this does not explain why they chose not a historian or legal scholar for the assignment, but a Germanist. Their choice fell on the well-known literary scholar and journalist Hans Egon Holthusen, who had served the FRG foreign ministry as director of the Goethe-Institut New York from 1961 to 1964 while also heading the literature department at the West Berlin Academy of Arts.

Thanks to the success of his 1951 essay collection, *Der unbehauste Mensch*, Holthusen was also one of Piper Verlag's star writers,[168] which should raise suspicions that either the publisher or Arendt's editor, Holthusen's fellow Germanist Rössner, may have had an indirect role in the IfZ's choice of reviewer. It is more than a sideswipe at Arendt that she was given a reviewer who, at least within the scholarly community, had been known since 1960 to be a former member of both the NSDAP and the SS. That same year, the author Mascha Kaléko, a Galician Jew who had found a new home in the United States, had set off controversy with her public rejection of the prestigious Fontane Prize from the Academy of Arts, pointing to its director Holthusen's past with the SS.[169] The next year, Holthusen's appointment to simultaneous directorship of the Goethe-Institut New York met with criticism among Jewish German emigrant circles. Hannah Arendt was among those who defended him.[170]

Holthusen began his 1965 review of Arendt's book with the suggestion that the subject matter was "monstrous" but still lacked "objective" exploration as a "historical fact." Avoiding a discussion of the connection between law and history as treated in the book, however, his next paragraph turned to a frontal assault on the person of Arendt. He accused her of taking "the trial in her own hands" and setting herself up

> as the judge ... not only of the Germans of that time, including those who lost their lives in the struggle against Hitler, but also the Germans of today, who in her opinion only differ slightly from the Germans of that time; and not only of the European peoples, who—with the honorable exception of the Danes—are responsible for the crimes against the Jews to varying degrees, but also of the Jewish people themselves and of their behavior in the catastrophe. She also judges the judges of the Jerusalem trial (whom she more or less absolves), the prosecutor Hausner (whom she portrays as an overblown rhetorician and melodramatician), the defenders, the witnesses, and the ver-

dict finally delivered, to which she counterposes her own verdict text at the end of her book.[171]

Holthusen granted that Arendt was an intellectual with "a passionate love of the truth," but there was "also something fatal" in her "self-confidence" and her "boldness," adding that the "Jewish" author Jacob Robinson had recently found no fewer than "six hundred 'distortions of fact'" in the *Eichmann* book. The inescapable impression therefore was that "Arendt's love of the truth" maintained "only the most tenuous relation with the idea of truth as understood by history writers."[172] The book tried to combine three different issues, Holthusen argued: the problem of a "complicity" between executioners and their victims; the analysis of the Eichmann figure itself; and the criticism of "the Germans" as "the main guilty parties in the murder of one-third of the Jewish people." The first was what caused the "greatest controversy among the American and Israeli publics." For her claim that Jewish functionaries had "almost without exception collaborated with the Nazis in one way or another and for one reason or another," the author had relied on Eichmann's testimony and the book by Hilberg. But this was far from a new claim. Authors like Eugen Kogon, Arthur Koestler, George Orwell, and even Arendt herself had already made it obvious how "totalitarian systems" worked in general. Using mainly terroristic methods, these succeeded in bringing the dominated into a "frictionless" cooperation with the dominators and, in the phase of Final Solution, made the victim into the accomplice of the executioner.[173]

Holthusen was more critical of Arendt's image of the perpetrator as "any old contemporary of bland normality"[174] and asked if it was ever possible to understand someone like Eichmann. Holthusen suggested that his behavior in the autumn of 1944—apparently referring to the "Hungary action" to round up and deport all Hungarian Jews soon after the former ally was occupied by the German military—showed that Eichmann was not a man "of unconditional obedience to cadre." Holthusen preferred to reflect on whether "this scoundrel, this mixture of fool and monster" was not something far worse, meaning "a perfect Nazi: follower of a 'worldview' thrown together without a plan by wretched nobodies, out of hate, madness, and stupidity, and therefore an ideal niche for the Great Disruptor, the 'Diabolos,' in plain German: for the Devil." But the "evil" in this case should not be called "banal," for it met the criteria of "radical evil" as defined by Kant.[175] Holthusen thus baselessly invoked a category from moral philosophy that Arendt herself had employed in the early 1950s but explicitly renounced because of her experience with the Eichmann trial.[176]

In the final and by far longest section of his text, Holthusen finally turned to Arendt's judgment of the Germans and the FRG. It was no wonder to him that her critique of "the Germans" was no less "merciless" and "quite possibly even more severe" than her critique of the Jews. Adopting an ethnic first-person plural, Holthusen wrote of the Germans that "we . . . also welcome every lesson, even the harshest," but only if these consist in valid arguments and "generally known facts." Arendt, by contrast, was raising the claim that "eighty million Germans" had insulated themselves from reality because self-deception had become the moral basis for their survival. But if it was true that literally all of them had practiced this deception, Holthusen countered, then there would have been no need of forty thousand Gestapo employees, no "terror camps," and no "people's courts." Anyone reading such "reckless generalizations" in English might well "shrug it off as the common stereotypes one finds in those countries. But written in German and addressed to German readers, they sound more like a capitulation to systemic pressures than an expression of historical understanding."[177] In her critique of the conspirators behind the attempted assassination of Hitler and coup d'état in 1944, Arendt accused the "men of 20 July" of not being clear enough in their condemnation of the Hitlerian "Jewish policy." Yet no conspirator to high treason, Holthusen countered, would be obligated to record his thoughts "for the edification of posterity in secret dossiers and letters sent to vacillating field marshalls."[178]

While German intellectuals had shown "brilliance" in refuting Arendt's accusations, her American and Jewish critics had not devoted a single word to this "internal German" matter. Holthusen bewailed that many contributions to the debate in fact showed that non-Germans simply accepted Arendt's words about the Germans. In summary, he concluded that Arendt had provided neither an "airtight history" nor a "persuasive essay." "Through its solidarity-diminishing moralism towards the Jews . . . its unjust generalizations, its all-too shrill ironies, its provocative exaggerations with regard to both Germans *and* Jews," the book stood in contradiction to its own aim of appealing to the individual to reflect on the "uniqueness of his experiences."[179]

While the writer clearly drew on the "uniqueness of his experiences" as a former NS university lecturer and member of the SS, his fiercely negative review fit with the flood of polemics that hit the intellectual journals of the FRG in the wake of Arendt's book. Her critique of the national-conservative resistance to the Nazis provoked the strongest reactions, some displaying a "cultivated escapism,"[180] others an incorrigible moral relativism. The defensive, nationalist stances either saw Germans and Jews as having been equally victimized, or, following Holthusen's lead, styled postwar Germans into the victims of the emigrated Jewish German intellectual, Arendt. Also typical was the rhetoric of "objectivity"[181] if ironically coupled with a pronounced lack of interest in empirical facticity. The critics did not cover the historical background to the trial, which Arendt had so trenchantly described for a general public in her book, nor was much attention paid, in 1960s West Germany, to the research literature on the perpetrators, although these works were used repeatedly in the Jerusalem court.

Holthusen's review at least serves to confirm that Hilberg's monumental work was by then already being received with great interest among scholars. Given the reactions to Arendt's work on Eichmann, however, we may doubt whether the planned German translation of Hilberg's book was in fact stopped simply because of fears that his theses on "Jewish collaboration" would meet with protests.[182] The review is also illuminating for contradicting the claims made since, that really it was because of Arendt's one-dimensional portrait of Eichmann that West German contemporary historians became desensitized to the epistemological challenges of the perpetrator issue. The preponderance of the evidence suggests instead that this was more of a legend for the self-reassurance of the "guild" in the decades that followed. In a more general sense, this reading of Arendt's book allowed the debate to be reduced to an interior one among Jews. Despite this heavy shove from abroad, West German contemporary historians continued to tread along their accustomed paths.[183]

Conclusion

Until well into the 1960s, the West German confrontation with the mass crimes of the NS era was shaped largely by the historical concerns and criteria of evaluation inherited from the early postwar criminal justice proceedings. In retrospect, the complex and often contradictory interpretations established during the Nuremberg trials have proved robust. A specific interpretation of the Third Reich that was inspired in equal measure by the sociological theories of German wartime leftists in exile as by the hyperintentionalist views of US government officials took a detour through the American prosecutorial agency in the late 1940s on the way to its subsequent reimportation into West Germany. This bird's eye view, describing various crimes as consequences of state policy and long-term planning, influenced practically all early interpretative approaches to the Third Reich, even at a time when West German elites increasingly strove to gain distance from the educational impulse behind the US prosecutions.

In the late 1940s and 1950s, at least in West Germany, dealing with the many manifestations of NS injustice became above all a job for the reactivated magistratical class, just as the Allies had willed it. While the other functional elites preferred to withdraw from the task, many in the justice system saw it as an opportunity. A few realized at an early stage that pursuing rather than avoiding a professional occupation with the fields of prosecution, restitutions, and compensations would allow them to influence collective memory, to achieve the moral reconsolidation of their own professional class, and possibly even to break the Allies' interpretative hegemony. Even during the first wave of investigations by West German courts and prosecutors, while these were still governed under the provisions of CCL 10, there was an evident hope of revising the historical images that the IMT and the Nuremberg follow-up trials had left in the minds of many Germans.

One aim in the early euthanasia trials, for example, was to demonstrate that a prosecution of the mass murder of the disabled and sick was entirely possible based on traditional German criminal codes. This in turn would serve to render demands for the use of retroactive Allied law superfluous. This position was not just a question of law. Implicitly, it transported a self-image, popular with jurists, of a legitimate continuity in the German legal community, one that the NS experience had not damaged "at its core." These trials also aimed to create a stronger identification of the majority with the murdered patients, specifically by stressing their ethnic background as "Germans." This too was a conscious departure from the interpretation that the Americans had employed, for example, in the Nuremberg Doctors' trial. The same view was partly reflected in the historiography. The increasing entanglement between juridical and historical discourses was evident in many of the historical expert reports that the IfZ presented in civil restitution cases, which routinely fixated on legal rather than historical categories. Fundamentally, it was also an expression of the effort to refute the supposed "accusation of collective guilt" attributed to the Nuremberg prosecutors.

With the FRG's gradual recovery of sovereignty, the drive to revise the interpretations of the Western allies tended to decline. This was true of the new subdiscipline of Contemporary History, which was called to life jointly by the Germans and the Americans to pursue a critical understanding of the history and prehistory of the Third Reich using source-based research and, in so doing, to contribute to cultural democratization. Since the first generation of historians at the Institute of Contemporary History used the Nuremberg trial documents above all, it was predictable that this same group might be early in conceiving source-critical thoughts about this archival legacy. This was also true in a way of the wave of amateur historians who preferred to work with this material. The latter, mostly Jewish researchers had already started documenting German crimes during the war and continued their work after it. Their works focused on the mass murder of the European Jews, which was explored and explained from an intentionalist perspective.

Like most other West German historians, the ones at the IfZ at first falsely assumed that the history of the destruction of the Jews had already been thoroughly and conclusively explored during the early postwar trials. This partly explains why research interest in the issue was at first rather limited. Numerous outside impulses in the second half of the 1950s, however, prompted a much stronger interest in the Holocaust. The resumption of criminal cases in West Germany fostered a closer cooperation between prosecutors and historians in the field. Practically speaking, this usually meant that prosecutors and courts commissioned the expertise of historians to gain insight into the processes of decision-making and coordination that had culminated, starting in the second half of 1941, with the systematic murder of the Jewish populations of Eastern Europe. While IfZ researchers otherwise had a strong preference for structural history, in the matter of the Holocaust they tended instead to adopt a personalistic approach, which Hermann Mau, the IfZ's first general secretary, had already outlined at its founding.

Helmut Krausnick, one of the most reputable NS researchers in Germany, followed this same line in the expert witness reports that he submitted at various NS trials starting in the late 1950s. Most researchers in the field subsequently took up his thesis, that the murder of the Jews was initiated by a direct secret order from Hitler, although it lacked for empirical evidence. A reductionist form of this interpretation made its way into verdicts at all levels of the West German court system and became an important basis for the common finding that defendants were complicit but not guilty as perpetrators. Until the 1980s, the perception of the Holocaust was shaped by a dynamic in which history and criminal justice mutually reinforced a shared and narrow view of the murderous events.

Curiously, not even an event as profound as the Eichmann trial changed anything fundamental about this constellation. Even as the international attention for the trial set off fears among the highest circles in Bonn that they might once again be brought into association with the mass crimes of National Socialism, West German justice agencies leaned to a skeptical, wait-and-see attitude. This was evident in the style of the reports filed by the German observing prosecutor at the Jerusalem trial, Dietrich Zeug. Just as interesting, perhaps, was that the Ludwigsburg agency had by then created a profile of the "high-ranking ideological perpetrator" that was diametrically opposite to the one used by the Israelis in the Eichmann trial.

West German historians also showed surprisingly little interest in the trial, which cannot be explained simply as a byproduct of the controversy raging among them at the time over Fritz Fischer's book, *Griff nach der Weltmacht* (*Germany's Aims in the First World War*). The reactions of the academic guild are worthy of future study. Overall, they preferred to continue ceding the subject of Holocaust perpetrators to their counterparts in criminal justice. The biggest eruptions among them were only set off by Arendt's book when it appeared in German translation three years after the trial's end.

Symptomatically, these concerns centered mostly on the peripheral matter of how Arendt treated the attempted coup d'état against Hitler on 20 July 1944, with few impulses arising for West German Holocaust research until much later.

Chapter 4

SALZBURG—BONN AND BERLIN

‧

The collapse of real socialism as the hegemonic system of East Germany in 1989 was followed by the dissolution of the German Democratic Republic as a state in October 1990. These events coincided with a time of increased public interest, not limited to Germany or Western Europe, in the National Socialist era and World War II. Starting in the 1970s at the latest, the failure to recognize the lasting historic legacies of fascist regimes, anti-Semitic atrocities, and widespread collaboration in fascist crimes became increasingly important as subjects of discourse in the United States, Israel, and many Latin American countries. The traditional, heroically inflected narratives of the war gave way to a new, negatively focused memory culture that aimed to make an issue of the "suffering inflicted on others" in addition to (self-) "experienced" suffering.[1]

The ideas of "Holocaust remembrance" and the memory practices associated with it would not prevail worldwide until the 1990s.[2] Long before then, however, media events like the 1980s American television series *Holocaust* had refocused attention on the collective fate of the persecuted and murdered European Jews. This singular great crime came to represent a changed view of the past as a whole. During the early post-World War II era, interpretative patterns had been located within national historical frames or were defined by the friend/enemy attributions of the "totalitarianism" paradigm.[3] With the Cold War at its end, the understanding of World War II was increasingly defined by the experience of massively racist, religious, or politically motivated persecutions. This intensified, victim-centered view echoed among numerous commentators who came to see genocides as a constitutive property of twentieth-century history.[4]

These cultural shifts had arisen gradually in many Western countries over a period of decades. Now they also became relevant in the countries of the former Soviet Bloc, at the latest in the "miraculous year" of 1989.[5] With the end of the East-West conflict, most states previously under Communist rule came under the influence of a model of democracy and historical processing that considered "critical self-reflection" on a negative past to be a cornerstone in a new concept of identity, one that was part national, part transnational.[6] The effects were especially strong in the former GDR. The situation there was complicated by the fact that the West German model of "overcoming the past" (*Vergangenheitsbewältigung*) had long before acquired a kind of exemplary status among East Germans. Soon after the first freely elected GDR Chamber of Deputies convened, the body voted (on 12 April 1990) to recognize a shared responsibility for the history of persecution of the Jews, and issued a statement of apology to the state of Israel for the hostile foreign policy of the defunct SED dictatorship.[7]

But the "politics of regret," as the American sociologists Jeffrey K. Olick and Brenda Coughlin trenchantly named such phenomena, were not limited to rhetorical admissions.[8] As a long series of southern European and South American military dictatorships collapsed in the 1970s and 1980s following failed wars or economic crises, many of the successor states turned to juridical and historical methods in investigating the human rights violations of the deposed regimes. Starting in the mid-1980s, Argentina became one of the first states in the world to embark on the unpredictable experiment of a national "Nuremberg" process. Within the span of a few years, the country carried out criminal trials against leaders of the military juntas that had ruled from 1976 to 1982 and appointed an official commission charged with documenting the fates of the many "disappeared"—people who had been kidnapped and brutally murdered by henchmen of the regimes.[9] As the American political scientist Kathryn Sikkink convincingly argues, a legal innovation like the first trial against the former ruling general Jorge Videla would have been nearly impossible if international human rights organizations like the Inter-American Commission on Human Rights (IACHR) had not started the project of reforming international law along humanitarian lines several years earlier.[10]

These developments meant that in the early 1990s, the populations of the defunct Eastern European people's democracies were faced with two cultural innovations that were largely unknown to them, as they had not experienced their origins and development. The first, the remembrance of the history of the Jewish catastrophe, had by that time become transnational, with a universalization of its meaning. Despite the end of the East-West conflict, the Holocaust continued to be presented mainly using representational forms borrowed from American popular culture.[11] The second was a fundamental change in international discourses on human rights and international law. As late as the 1980s, international law had remained mainly a medium for regulating interstate conflicts. The new age of globalization saw a breathtaking "intensification of the international order,"[12] accompanied by an "intensification of transnational networks."[13]

Ever more actors from more and more countries now intervened in reminding states of their treaty obligations and urging them to respect human rights. The political activities of border-crossing NGOs (nongovernmental organizations), QUANGOs (quasi-autonomous nongovernmental organization) und GONGOs (government-organized nongovernmental organization were of an ambivalent nature. They ranged from a general "valuation of international civil society" to "neoliberal privatization visions."[14] This individualization of international law coincided with a melting away of the principle of state immunity. High-ranking politicians, military officers, civilian officials, and subordinates carrying out orders all had to reckon with a heightened possibility that they might one day be subject to criminal trials. The victims of state human rights violations were increasingly enshrined as legal subjects, which for political reasons had not been possible during the postwar Allied trials. With help from legal experts and support committees, many formerly targeted persons were able to use national courts to enforce restitution claims. Those who succeeded in this did not only achieve official recognition of the wrongs done to them; in many cases, they were also able to anchor their individual or collective experiences in the official memory cultures of their countries.

Given that these developments were consummated within the span of a few years, many Western commentators in the early 1990s believed the world was on the brink of a move from "the law of states to the law of world citizenship."[15] This view was also common among the Eastern European counter-elites, the former dissidents, who had sought to soften the old state monopolies on opinion and information by using legalist strategies and independent political languages.[16] Most actors within this group, though, took it as self-evident that common referents were being employed when, after the fall of the Communist one-party regimes, calls went up for "justice" and "truth" for the victims of the former ideological and educational dictatorships.

"Transitology" and Samuel Huntington's "Third Wave"

At the end of 1989, Samuel P. Huntington was busy working on a remarkable book. As "velvet revolutions" swept across several Eastern European countries, and as social scientists called these events "historically unprecedented" but also saw them as lacking a recognizable "revolutionary theory,"[17] the Harvard political scientist was seeking to identify an overarching pattern that would explain why the last quarter of the twentieth century was witnessing a series of collapses in dictatorial regimes. About fifteen years earlier, Huntington and two fellow political scientists had published the much-noticed *The Crisis of Democracy: On the Governability of Democracies*, originally as a report to the Trilateral Commission. The earlier book presented the finding that a high point in democratic participation via mass politics had been reached by the mid-1970s, above all in the United States.[18] According to the authors, the United States and other Western democracies had experienced an "excess" of political participation after World War II. The democratic pressures this unleashed had given rise to unfulfillable demands, and by the 1960s and 1970s the affected countries were becoming increasingly ungovernable.[19]

In his new book, *The Third Wave*, published in 1991, Huntington remained true to his predilections for grand narrative and normative judgments.[20] Regarding the historical significance of the liberal democratic model, however, he reached entirely different conclusions than one might have expected given his earlier pessimistic assessments. Now he instead observed a quasi self-reinforcing process of democratization, dating its start to the April 1974 military putsch by the young Portuguese officers who overthrew the forty-year dictatorship known as Estado Novo.[21] Huntington's history outlined the rise of democracy as occurring in three great waves starting in the early nineteenth century. Each wave, however, had been interrupted by phases of authoritarianism or totalitarianism. The ongoing "third wave" had seen a long sequence of collapses in thirty nondemocratic systems of differing political orientations, signaling that the efficacy of typically Western concepts and ideas was prevailing worldwide. The gradual decline of Marxism-Leninism had played a decisive role in this development, Huntington argued: even states within the Soviet sphere of power had made increased use of the language of freedom, equality, and human rights for legitimation purposes and thus at least indirectly advanced the dissemination of Western ideas.[22]

In its theoretical approach, Huntington's study employs a minimal understanding of democracy that foregrounds the procedural elements of building a political will.[23] In a manner typical of Anglo-American democracy studies, he constructs essential oppositions between democracy and dictatorship, and between liberal and authoritarian regimes.[24] Yet his argument is also defined by a general skepticism about the history-making power of democratic processes from below. This can be seen, for example, in how his outline of successes in implementing democracy leaves little room for any identifiable historical actors to whom an individual success can be attributed. He relies instead on a Hegelian stage model. The treatments of national case histories serve mostly to illustrate a timeless, universal desire for freedom and self-determination, one that seems to proceed from a natural drive. In Huntington's telling, however, this elementary will to freedom is able to unfold itself fully only in response to preceding experiences of "unfreedom."

The latter idea shows the enduring influence of dialectic explanatory models. It also indicates the persistence of the Cold War "system conflict," which was still far from overcome intellectually, and highlights Huntington's own role as a leading adviser to US policy makers. By reducing its dictatorial character to an episode, and by presenting it as a prerequisite for later democratic breakthroughs, his analysis appears more or less consistent with ideas he had postulated in the 1980s regarding the "Third World" and South America. At that time, when numerous Latin American dictatorships in particular were pursuing economic modernization under bureaucratic-authoritarian auspices, conservative democracy studies scholars in the United States had become more interested in questions of political stability and security.[25]

In retrospect, history scholars did not find Huntington's three-wave model particularly useful as a means of explaining the epochal upheavals in the Eastern European people's democracies.[26] The broader influence of the study was not because of its heuristic perspective, however, or any of its specific analytical interventions. Nevertheless, the book became a kind of reference work for the transitional justice networks forming just then, in the 1990s, and the most important reason was its usefulness for practitioners. Huntington's ambition was to provide a normative, programmatic set of social science guidelines for the transition from dictatorship to democracy. *The Third Wave* can be said to have sprung from the same US tradition, dating back to the early post–World War II years, that had produced an arsenal of "civil affairs guides" and "civil affairs handbooks" as contract research works funded by the Washington bureaucracy (see chapter 2). It was with such works that the US military administration and its advisers prepared themselves for the mission of building a stable democracy in their own occupation zone within western Germany.[27] In its close imbrication of scientific expertise with practical implementation of a specific model of political order, the American occupation authority stood out as a conspicuous example of what Lutz Raphael diagnosed as the "scientification of the social."[28]

A similarly prescriptive and technocratic understanding of science can be found in precincts of the Anglo-American "transition to democracy" research of the outgoing twentieth century. These works tend to share an underlying assumption that so-called transition processes—which in the case of the former Communist states included the parallel implantation of political institutions, legal systems, and market economies—are subject to rational planning despite their complexity; that they can be steered to some extent through the application of social science methods. While there was no historical precedent on which to model Allied occupation policy after World War II, Huntington's study operated in a highly conscious way with the tools of "precedent cases" and "historical comparison," the latter above all being understood in instrumental terms. The book offered up a bird's eye, whirlwind tour of twentieth-century global history, overflowing with national case examples, all of which qualified as successful democratization processes by the author's criteria.

The spectrum of cases ran from the early postwar democracies of West Germany, Japan, and Italy to the Mediterranean democratizations of the 1970s (Portugal, Greece, Spain), to the countries that underwent system change starting in the 1980s in South America (Argentina, Brazil, Chile, Paraguay), and, finally, to the formerly Communist countries of Eastern Europe in the late 1980s (USSR, Poland, Hungary, Czechoslovakia, Bulgaria, Romania, and East Germany). In the discipline of comparative history, international comparisons usually aim to identify problems, constellations, or common causes,[39] but Huntington's country briefs above all served as building blocks in an overarching outline that was meant to get a conceptual grip on the continuing processes of transformation in Eastern Europe, South Africa, and several Latin American states.

Implicit in the approach was a revival of the controversial, decidedly anti-Marxist modernization theory that had emerged in the 1950s as one of the most important legitimating ideas of the Western world. Developed primarily by US-based reformers, the theory usually defined modernization by a simplified checklist of attributes of industrial societies considered worthy of imitation. These were presented as the normative standards for the development of supposedly backward states and societies.[30] However, as the political scientist Nicolas Guilhot especially has stressed, the later rise of comparative democracy research brought about an important shift in meaning: the idea of "transition" was no longer mainly a matter of building socioeconomic structures, but rather denoted a process of institutional change to be handed down from the state and its elites.[31]

Despite these problematic premises, or perhaps because of them, Huntington's theses were met with success within and without the social science field. Over the course of the 1990s, his neologism of a "third wave" went global as a term general enough to obscure the overly complex and contradictory individual experiences and longer-term causes of upheavals that might be buried in the historical depths. Much like Francis Fukuyama's formulation of the "end of history," Huntington's book indicated a zeitgeist of greatly increased "Western" self-confidence and optimistic expectations about the malleability of political and societal development processes.[32] But *The Third Wave* is not only a particularly vivid example of how triumphalist historical discourse achieved a temporary hegemony following the implosion of Soviet communism. The reception history of the book also makes obvious how both the perception of organized violence and the standards for judging it began to change during this time. Contrary to the canonical self-historicization of the TJ field down to this day, a uniform pattern for explaining state and non-state mass crimes had already formed before the rediscovery of humanitarian international criminal law, and it was to be taken up beyond the countries that underwent systemic upheavals.

Conspicuous in hindsight is that during this early phase of TJ studies in the 1990s, a leveling perspective on problems of political violence predominated (although the trend was toward greater sophistication over time). Also recognizable now is the era's tendency to entangle historical reconstruction with juridical assessment. This came at the expense of historical complexity, insofar as the histories of violence in states and societies and their various manifestations were often perceived through a "judicial" filter and analyzed with a view to their potential as possible objects of criminal law.[33] Huntington's work foreshadowed both these phenomena—insofar as his observations on various cases intentionally concentrated on "serious" human rights violations like murder, kidnapping, torture, rape, and detention without trial—while completely omitting other forms of violence regarded as not actionable.[34]

This understanding of state violence as episodic and driven by events largely echoes the pragmatic line of the official US human rights policy of the time. The latter can be traced back to the early 1970s initiatives of US Representative Donald M. Fraser, chair of the Subcommittee on International Organizations and Movements, later taken up by President Jimmy Carter's administration starting in 1977.[35] Huntington's view of state violence also aligns with the approach of many of the new NGOs that arose around the world starting in the 1970s. Their self-concept, only superficially "unpolitical," was articulated in human rights campaigns that concentrated on the archetypical techniques of state persecution: those targeting dissidents and opposition activists. Such injustices were condemned in individual case campaigns aimed at capturing attention and broad appeal. While Huntington drew the dubious conclusion that the civil society-based human rights activism of the 1970s was concerned not with the "illegality of the regime" but only with the "illegal actions of its agents," human rights groups actually adopted these tactics in a conscious attempt to break out of the mutual blockades of the East-West conflict and the reigning anti-Communist ideology of "national security."[37] The latter trope in particular had posed an obstacle for decades to any serious criticism in the Western democracies of (pro-Western) military dictatorships.

Although the very serious crimes that were catalogued and in part described in detail in Huntington's book seemed to call for criminal prosecutions against perpetrators, the political scientist advocated a cautious approach. In contrast to his panorama of democratization processes shining out brilliantly in nearly all regions of the world, his depiction of national efforts at processing the past was sober, indeed somber. Although Huntington was among the first scholars who were writing about the upheavals of the time to recall as a precedent the largely forgotten national trials of the Greek junta and of Greek perpetrators of torture in 1974 and 1975,[38] his chapter on the uses of criminal law urged minimalism. Starting with the programmatic title "The Torturer Problem: Prosecute and Punish vs. Forgive and Forget," it is devoted mainly to the serious problems that supposedly arise when democratic successor regimes give in to popular demands for a judicial reckoning against the deposed perpetrators of fallen dictatorships.

Huntington was convinced that the practices employed against dissidents by the power elites of European and Latin American dictatorships in the 1960s and 1970s were similar to those of other epochs and regions. He did not view the politics of massive "disappearances," the systematic use of torture methods based on modern medical findings, or the measures of isolation and psychic torment that were usual in the Soviet sphere as phenomena conditioned by history. He instead posited that the 1970s saw a fundamental and near-global moral shift regarding what forms of state repression were acceptable; in the case of Greece, an Amnesty International report had after all contributed to the downfall of the regime.[39] To the extent that the US Congress, international NGOs, and bodies established by the Organization for Security and Co-operation in Europe had increasingly stressed human rights, this also raised the pressure on democratic successor regimes to feel responsible for the human rights violations of their predecessors and to take up demands that perpetrators be punished.[40]

Huntington argued that this would necessarily produce ambiguous results because a large part of the population in each case had supported the rise of the authoritarian regime, believing it would protect them from the political terror of leftist liberation movements. Criminal trials and personnel purges contributed only minimally to the establishment of democratic structures; where such measures were implemented, juridical and moral considerations were usually secondary among the true reasons. Rhetorical protestations to the contrary, whether a given former functionary would be held accountable, would be determined mainly by the real relations of political power obtaining at a given time and place.[41]

Finally, Huntington used a cursory comparison of the two examples of Greece and Argentina to derive points that he considered decisive in regard to the problem of retributive justice. His "Guidelines for Democratizers" recommend the reintegration of earlier power elites, mainly focusing on the role of the military.[42] He considered the Argentinean experiment to have failed, and therefore rejected nonpunitive options like lustrations or truth commissions as ineffective. He found that criminal investigations were advisable only in those countries that had undergone a thorough, comprehensive break with the old system.

But even in countries that combined system change with a full exchange of elites, Huntington counseled that deposed political and security elites should be prosecuted only if the trials could be carried out "promptly," defining this as no more than a year after the change of regimes.[43] His skepticism regarding judicial "processing" experiments proceeded from an altogether hypothetical assumption that criminal trials constitute one of the worst possible obstacles to democratization. Because political transitions in dictatorial regimes were often set off by people from within the inner circle of power, Huntington argued that such actors would want to avoid having to justify their own earlier acts after a completed transition.[44] What was true of public demands to achieve "justice" also applied to calls for "truth." Too much generosity in opening the archival legacies of fallen dictatorships might seriously delay the creation of democratic structures. As examples, Huntington turned to the post-Communist states of Eastern Europe, above all the reunited Germany. The uncontrolled release of information from the archives of the Communist secret services had set off fears that even the otherwise stable Federal Republic of Germany would be pulled into a whirlpool of suspicions and revelations, he asserted. Thus, before opening archives, political leaders should consider carefully whether "justice" and "truth" are the only possible alternatives. Historical experience instead showed that "in some respects, truth as well as justice was a threat to democracy."[45]

Although Argentina and Chile were experiencing periods of rollback in amnesty policy at the time,[46] Huntington's plea to let politically motivated perpetrators of violence off the hook was diametrically opposite to the zeitgeist. The early 1990s saw the formation of civil society movements to prosecute state mass violence using the tools of the law, not only in the Latin American states but also in parts of Asia and Africa and numerous intellectual circles in Eastern Europe.[47] "Individual accountability" became a global leitmotif for the reform and institutionalization of international criminal law based on a transnational understanding of human rights. Not least because this project was now also supported massively by the United Nations, the decade became a high-flying time for asserting the jurisdiction of international criminal courts. One after the next, there followed the two international ad hoc courts for Yugoslavia (1993) and Rwanda (1994), and a series of "special hybrid courts" that focused on mass crimes in Sierra Leone, Cambodia, and East Timor, among other cases. This set off a drive to realize the long-delayed plan for an International Criminal Court by the end of the decade.[48]

During this same time, several transitioning states conducted national experiments that were intended to prevent the past from becoming an obstacle to the formation of a lawful state. Several adopted the well-known model of "truth commissions," based on older Latin American and African examples.[49] These had the main task of documenting past acts of violence but also the explicit purpose, in each case, of contributing to reconciliation between hostile camps by identifying both the perpetrators and victims of state repression. The hope, ultimately, was to avoid a backslide into traditional patterns of violence.[50] Truth commissions gave many previously anonymous victims an opportunity to speak about their suffering in public, but also gave perpetrators who were ready to confess in full an opportunity for limited immunity from prosecution.[51] In a few cases, such as in South Africa, the victims also received modest restitution sums.[52] By comparison, the criminal trials against former party and state officials that were conducted in a few Eastern Bloc states received relatively little international attention (with the exception of the Christmas 1989 kangaroo trial of the Ceaușescus). This was in contrast to the Western European court cases against the Vichy functionaries Paul Touvier and Maurice Papon and against the SS officers Klaus Barbie and Erich Priebke, both of which served to crystalize the changing public memory of the Holocaust.[53]

Huntington thus did not share the mainstream scholarly and journalistic views on the uses of criminal trials, but his arguments exercised a substantial influence over the discourses and practices of "transitology" just as it began to emerge. *The Third Wave* postulated a categorical incompatibility between truth and justice, between retributive "processing" and societal "reconciliation."[54] Huntington viewed processing the past as a project that should be limited to national elites. Societal elites, new and old, were capable of claiming a hegemony over the interpretation of human rights violations committed under the old regimes. Elites were in a position to decide how and in what forms the state should initiate historical education—in place of criminal prosecution. We will describe below how this elitist approach was received positively in some quarters of the reunified Germany, even though the theorems of "transitology" had initially met with hesitation in German public discussions.

The Third Wave shaped discourse in a second way by linking political system changes to democratic processing of the past in a brisk, paradigmatic way. But Huntington sees the question of how best to process the past in purely functional terms. It should be an adjustable parameter, so as to allow the smoothest possible system transition.[55] All his case studies involve countries that more or less successfully effected a transition from dictatorship to democracy, reinforcing a perspective already tending to self-affirmation. Such a view was prevalent in many Western democracies during the early 1990s.

In this version of the world, the state mass violence of the twentieth century necessarily appears as a phenomenon exclusive to totalitarian and authoritarian regimes. Dealing with its aftermath is a problem particular to states in transition. In almost covert fashion, this attitude serves to reproduce the same self-idealizing image of the "West" that had been established around the world during the preceding decades of ideological conflict between the liberal democracies, Eastern Bloc states, and the states of the "Third World."

The protagonists of transitional justice in the 1990s thus took no account of the reality that the apparently stable democracies of the "First World"—several of which had only recently shed their status as colonial masters—had also engaged in serious, state-initiated human rights violations, right into the 1980s, with their own resulting accumulation of deficits in truth and justice.[56] TJ also tended to ignore the fact that the dictatorships had committed their crimes in an international context shaped by the friend-enemy distinctions of the Cold War and the associated economic, military, and ideological entanglements. This backdrop undermined transitological ambitions of assigning clearly defined responsibilities, which in many cases was possible only at the price of a clumsy historical reductionism. This also became clear during the South African Truth and Reconciliation Commission (TRC). The TRC concentrated on documenting serious human rights violations by the executive organs of the South African apartheid regime, but avoided questions about how this system of racial segregation, built over nearly a century's time, was also the basis for a major economic power that allowed the country to become a favored trade partner—precisely and especially in the West.

A third reason for the influence of Huntington's study of democratization, finally, lay in its claims of taking a nonideological, progress-oriented approach. Despite pronounced reservations about grassroots traditions, the book provided arguments that at least superficially seemed to have been tailored to the activism of the many human rights initiatives and the idealistic zeitgeist of the early 1990s. This was reinforced through its semantics, which consistently invoked the vision of a united world and posited a jointly pursued global project, a shared horizon of problems that would be overcome mutually. This all differed greatly from Huntington's much-critiqued publication, five years later, of *The Clash of Civilizations*,[57] which was perceived instead as positing the division of the world into conflicting camps.[58] Insofar as the regulatory theses of *The Third Wave* rested on the projection of Western power, these were put vaguely enough or camouflaged by a rhetoric that combined utopian human rights talk with rational technocratic flavors. Just this form of rhetoric would soon become a trademark of early TJ literature. It was one reason why historians for many years would participate only marginally in the research discussions of transitology.

Social scientists like Huntington, John H. Herz, Guillermo O'Donnell, and Philippe C. Schmitter[59]—the "democracy doctors" of the right and left, whom Guilhot holds responsible for the voluntaristic turn in recent American scholarship on democracy[60]—played a decisive role in the boom and massive institutionalization experienced by transition studies in the early 1990s. A series of gatherings marked the most important steps on the way to creating an international TJ network, starting in March 1992 with the Project on Justice in Times of Transition inaugural conference held in Salzburg.[61] Tellingly, it was not the United Nations but a private NGO that initiated and helped to fund this endeavor. The Charter 77 Foundation was founded in 1990 with a headquarters in New York and the mission of observing and providing scholarly support for transition processes in former Eastern Bloc states.[62] The organizational focus was on Czechoslovakia (still extant at the time, but in the process of breaking up into the independent nations of the Czech Republic and Slovakia). Czechoslovakia was treated as a model for processing the past that was suitable for export to other post-Communist countries.[63] The organizers of the Salzburg conference hoped to lay the groundwork for a multiyear research project that would bundle and systematize the practical experiences of various transitional countries.[64] Concretely, the societies of central and eastern Europe would also share in the "useful lessons" that Latin American states had gathered since the 1980s in their own treatments of violent pasts.[65] The conference brought together about fifty participants from more than twenty countries as prospective multipliers whose ranks included scientists, jurists, politicians, and members of civil society organizations. They came from the United States, France, Lithuania, Poland, Hungary, Spain, Argentina, Chile and Czechoslovakia. Notably underrepresented at this gathering were Germans (whether their backgrounds were from the East or West) and delegates from the just-dissolved Soviet Union.

In terms of their self-image, the first generation of transitologists tended to follow the example of American political advisers à la Huntington. He was also present at the gathering. The Salzburg organizers upheld the blanket view that even late Communist states were systemically "totalitarian" without differentiation[66] while at the same time viewing the problems of the post-Communist successor states as comparable to those in the new Latin American democracies.[67] This became evident in the introduction to the conference report, later published by Neil J. Kritz, which seemed to follow Huntingtonian theses closely in outlining the agenda of the nascent research subdiscipline:

> Recent political changes in Eastern and Central Europe, the Soviet Union and Latin America have led to the collapse of a number of totalitarian and authori-

tarian regimes. While the political, social and economic consequences of these transformations differ significantly from country to country, each of the new democracies in these regions face a common and pressing problem: how to deal with individuals who served the former oppressive regimes.[68]

With regard to "processing the past," most participants upheld a model predicated on the idea that certain instruments of transitional justice could be implanted quasi "from above," for example, by a panel of experts. This necessarily fosters the impression that states and governments are largely autonomous in their treatment of serious human rights violations. This premise simply did not apply after the spread of a universalized Holocaust memory culture and the formation of the first ad hoc tribunals by the United Nations.[69] Again aligning with Huntington's theses, the report assumes that postdictatorial societies have the freedom to apply calculations based on rational choice and that they can decide, autonomously, whether to pursue "processing" and "memory" or whether to hold criminal trials. The report remains vague on what criteria should be applied, however:

> The question of responsibility—in its moral, legal and political dimensions—for the abuses of the prior regimes is one which emerging democracies must address in order to allow their societies to move forward. The two key issues in this regard are *acknowledgment*—whether to "remember" or "forget" the abuses—and accountability—whether or not to prosecute or otherwise impose sanctions on the perpetrators.[70]

As a first opportunity for international exchange and closer networking among practitioners of the emerging discipline, the Salzburg symposium evinced many fundamental mistakes from the start, and these have accompanied TJ research ever since. To put it simply, the gathering displayed an obvious preponderance of more or less representative, country-specific experiential reports and a deficit of theoretical concepts. Among the symptoms of the missing conceptual framework was the lack of an intensive consideration of the IACHR's prior work on international criminal law. Also missing was any reflection on the experiences with the trials against leaders of the Argentinian junta.

As mentioned earlier, the work of the IACHR jurists in the 1970s and 1980s had set up the legal and theoretical prerequisites for conducting national trials in Argentina and other countries, making it possible for individual functionaries of the deposed regime to be convicted of systemic crimes under a principle of individual culpability.[71] By decisively weakening the principle of immunity, the Argentinians had solved an unavoidable problem that was confronting any attempt to criminally prosecute perpetrators of human rights violations—several years before the fall of the Iron Curtain.

Eastern Europeans could have doubtlessly profited from learning about this real-world case.[72] The Salzburg organizers did not see it as an opportunity to introduce delegates from post-Communist states to humanitarian international criminal law, however, or to the rapidly changing scene in modern international law generally. This was possibly never the intent. At the time of the conference, the original pioneers of juridical "processing," Argentina and Chile, had for the moment turned to "restorative justice" and a policy of far-reaching impunity for perpetrators.[73]

The consequences of this blind spot are well known. By the early 1990s, most Eastern European states started criminal investigations strictly as national solo efforts and did so more half-heartedly than out of an inner conviction. Within a few years, almost all the cases were bogged down in the courts or had been mooted by political or legislative interventions.[74] In the history of criminal approaches to Communist system crimes, Germany poses a relative exception, but there as well the debate on prosecution of SED injustice continued for years without almost any explicit reference to the concurrent international developments.[75]

In practice, the hope of establishing under the umbrella of transitional justice a transnational culture that could process histories of serious human rights violations ran into major obstacles. One reason undoubtedly was TJ discourse's failure to adequately understand and reflect on the extremely dynamic developments in humanitarian international law during the 1980s and 1990s. Another was that the first generation of transitologists adhered to a silent but apparent consensus to uphold the fiction of a pristine new start or "Zero Hour." As more effort has gone into historicizing the transition and transformation processes in Europe, recent literature has shown that the early 1990s system changes were usually associated with specific foundational myths. These were designed to facilitate a successful mastery of the "liminal" phase of each transition.[76] Although useful, such findings still tend to arise from analyses of domestic controversies and to neglect the importance of transnational "processing" discourses and their feedback effects on national developments. These are still treated in isolated fashion.[77] As I have repeatedly stressed, the rise of transitology as a new, consciously international research field itself counts among the external factors that influenced postdictatorial societies. It provided an armory of legal and other instruments that could be adapted and reinterpreted within national frameworks, as well as a canon of new and old "master narratives" that, at least in the middle term, offered potentials for new identity formation.

To the extent that the neologism Transitional Justice has become a fixed part of political thought and communication in recent years, the critique of its normative premises and assumptions has also intensified. One point of criticism has been the discipline's understanding of history as indicated by the often cavalier usage of terms like "historical truth" and "truth telling." From the perspective of historical theory as informed by the cultural turns, this comes across as naive at best.[78] As the sociologist John Torpey put it some years ago, TJ as a subdiscipline is weighed down by the discrepancy between its emphasis on explanation and its "historical shallowness":

> Against the background of the spreading worldwide preoccupation with righting historical injustices, however, the main difficulty with the transitional justice paradigm has been its foreshortened time horizons, its tendency to view the past as having begun only the day before yesterday. Dominated as this approach has been by lawyers, political scientists, and human rights activists, the disproportionate attention to regime changes of the very recent past is perhaps not surprising.[79]

A longer view allows the observation that the "truth" discourse of transitology is rooted in several phenomena. Among these are the commissions that arose in several Latin American states in the early 1980s. These were semi- or quasi-judicial bodies, in each case appointed by national governments. All possessed an independent status, however, often with parity between representatives of the state and of civil society. One of these early commissions' main tasks was to reconstruct the fates of innumerable "disappeared" persons and to make information about them public. Although most of these bodies lacked executive powers, they still employed forensic methods. Witness interrogations, documentation of evidence, and site inspections were customary. All these are among the investigative actions normally undertaken in court-trial discovery. Typical of the dual function of these institutions was that their investigative activity and simple fact-finding was always combined with the production of an authoritative historical narrative.

In the Latin American context of the 1980s, "truth" therefore primarily meant the publication of the most coherent possible chronology of individual acts of murder, in a report intended to become ineluctable going forward.[80] But this understanding of historical truth entailed a largely depoliticized version of the events it described. To reinforce public acceptance of the work, some individual cases were emphasized precisely because the targeted parties were coincidental victims of state repression. For similarly tactical reasons, the fact that most political prisoners were associated with leftist guerilla movements was concealed.[81]

Many have stressed that the appointment of the South African TRC in 1995 brought an important turn in the history of transitional justice. Usually forgotten are the two earlier and highly unusual truth commissions of 1992, both appointed by Nelson Mandela as the leader of the African National Congress (ANC). These had investigated not the crimes of the apartheid regime but cases of prisoner mistreatment by armed forces of the ANC itself during its resistance against apartheid.[82] The later TRC, called to life on 26 July 1995 based on the Promotion of National Unity and Reconciliation Act, originated in an initiative by the human rights activist Alex Boraine. As the founder in 1987 of the Institute for a Democratic Alternative for South Africa, the jurist Boraine was also among the most important pioneers of the early TJ networks.

The TRC consisted of three committees, each of which covered a nominally different concept of truth. The Amnesty Committee and the Reparation and Rehabilitation Committee were intended to deal with forensic and factual truth. The Human Rights Violations (HRV) Committee, led by the archbishop Desmond Tutu, was charged with the mission of determining "social, narrative and healing truth."[83] The HRV Committee's mandate was restricted to the exposure of serious acts of violence in the period between the Sharpeville massacre of 21 March 1960 and the country's first democratic elections in April 1994.

The TRC occupies an outstanding place in transitology because of its particular model for processing the past. Given the fragile state of South African society, criminal trials were seen as an unpredictable risk. The decision, therefore, was made to sacrifice legal "justice" in the cause of historical "truth" and social "peace."[84] While this bespeaks the "truth versus justice" dichotomy often found in transitional justice, it reflected how the TRC founders understood their role. Their vision was to initiate a societal reconciliation process and assist in constituting a "rainbow nation." From April 1996 to June 1997, the TRC held seventy-six public hearings, with testimonies from about two thousand victims and their relatives. They were chosen from about thirty-eight thousand available individual cases. Concurrently, the TRC issued rulings on 1,600 "amnesty" applications submitted by white agents of the former security apparatus, radical right-wing whites, and ANC activists.[85] The TRC possessed the power to release confessed suspects from the threat of prosecution, making it the first nonjudicial agency of this kind. The same model would later be adopted in several other countries.[86]

The historical significance of the South African truth commission is found not only in its status as a new instrument for dealing with serious human rights violations, or even in the diffusion of the model internationally in the following years. The TRC is also of interest to historical scholarship because it displays pronounced characteristics of the postmodern, transnational "processing" discourse that began to form at the turn of the millennium. This seemed in part to refer back to older models such as the Eichmann trial. That too had involved the cooptation of selected Holocaust victims, was motivated by identity politics, and adopted a "phenomenological" conception of history, one that relied on the public effects of engendering horror.[87] The TRC adopted a specific tradition of state-driven history politics and public history management, adapting both historical and legal methods and combining them into a new, hybrid form. In his comparative analysis of truth commissions, Berber Bevernage concludes that these methods in practice prove inadequate to the criteria of either historical or judicial truth finding. In reality, Bevernage argues, the "facts" that these commissions ostensibly produce were already known to the public beforehand. The true mission of the commissions should actually be described as the "procedural articulation of the known."[88]

That may sound like a blanket conclusion, given the variety of such bodies. It is nevertheless worth considering Bevernage's basic thesis that the commissions' fundamental function is theatrical. On the one hand, bodies like the TRC employ the judicial mode of case solving, lending the appearance of incontestability and unrevisability to their historical interpretations. On the other, great effort is invested in giving the public the impression that the resulting investigative reports rely on historiographic standards, although in reality these constitute active interventions of historical and memory politics. The rhetorical invocation of the victims mainly has a legitimating purpose, drawing up a forward-looking master narrative that will allow the nation to leave the conflicts and the violence of the past behind. Those victims who are not prepared to submit to these demands, who are unwilling to "forget" and "forgive," must therefore run the risk of being excluded from the national collective:

> Since forgiveness and reconciliation are considered defining features of the present, those unwilling to forgive or reconcile cannot be considered as fully simultaneous or contemporaneous with the rest of the nation, as fully belonging to the "new" South Africa or in the "new" Sierra Leone. Thus there is the tendency for truth commissions to identify uncooperative perpetrators and rancorous victims equally as living anachronisms, locked into the past and impeding the future progress of the nation.[89]

Elazar Barkan, who praises truth commissions as essential forums for conflict resolution and as a new form of "historiographic advocacy," also admits that in practice there is usually a strong tension between the demand for historiographic objectivity and the memory-politics goal of achieving "shared narratives."[90]

As the examples of the Latin American and South African truth commissions show, the transitology of the outgoing twentieth century had developed into an influential transnational dispositive covering some very different aspects of state and societal processing of the past. During the 1990s, its analytical framework was still fluid and diffuse enough to allow space for universalist, as well as particular, national-historic interpretations. The fact that the victims of state crime as such took a prominent place in TJ discourses, however, did not in itself suffice to achieve an overarching denationalization of historical conceptions.[91] This last point may be important in answering the question of why (and in what form) TJ instruments were taken up in some of the post-Communist states but played an altogether secondary role in others. In this regard there emerged a dividing line separating Russia and most of the earlier Eastern Bloc states on the one side from unified Germany and the Czech Republic on the other.[92]

In short, most of the former Eastern Bloc countries initially displayed a conspicuous reluctance to pursue criminal trials and truth commissions. Many TJ researchers have posited that, after suffering through decades in which information and opinion were monopolized by the Communist elites, the peoples of these countries had developed a strong aversion to state-sanctioned historical narratives of any kind. The legal scholar Ruti G. Teitel, a pioneer of TJ, is among those to have made this argument:

> Truth commissions are most popular where the predecessor regime disappeared persons or repressed information about its persecution policy, as was typical in Latin America. In contrast, truth commissions have been of less interest in post-Communist Europe, where the use of history by various governments was itself a destructive dimension of Communist repression. Accordingly, in Eastern Europe, the main critical response by the successor regime was not to create official histories but rather to guarantee access to the historical record.[93]

One may object that state-driven history and memory politics with strong antipluralist tendencies have, in fact, remained predominant in many of the same former Eastern Bloc states.[94] Teitel also overlooks that TJ networking efforts tended to bear the most fruit in countries like the Czech Republic. After its early passage of a lustration law to purge the ranks of the civil service, the Czech example was packaged and sold to an international scholarly public as an exemplary model for a more comprehensive TJ program.[95] A further factor lies in TJ's frequent employment of a schematic model of totalitarianism. Huntington and his fellow conservative democracy researchers obviously did not invent this concept, but they helped to revive and rehabilitate it. Even today, it continues to play a central role in the master narratives of the post-Communist states, paradoxically accompanied by the belief that most of these countries have no "indigenous totalitarianism" of their own to overcome.[96]

Given that after 1989 most countries in eastern and central Europe saw a return to national historical narratives, combined with often strong defensive reactions against universalist Holocaust memorializations,[97] a rather different explanation arises—albeit one that, in the final analysis, is not susceptible to an empirical proof. The political and academic elites in these countries likely view transitology as yet another universalist processing concept, one that harbors an attendant risk of reducing national autonomy and the possible loss of the nation's "right" to its own history.[98] Starting in 1993, those holding such views could point to the appointment of the ad hoc tribunal for the former Yugoslavia as an example of a supranational authority that, next to its prosecutorial mission, made an explicit historiographic claim that it would provide the conclusive version of the causes of the Balkan conflict.[99]

By contrast, transitology opened the door for the FRG and the Czech Republic to display their universalist profiles to the world. This came at a low risk that either country would be forced to give up on national "processing" strategies or to compromise on domestic political orientations. The expanded FRG became the only (partly) post-Communist country to make public use of the entire spectrum of TJ tools (with exceptions due to amnesty packages passed by the parliament). This was not only thanks to the established West German tradition of "critical self-examination of its *own* negative past."[100] Of equal relevance surely was that the Western European narrative for understanding the Holocaust until 1989 had been internalized within the "old" West Germany, while the "new" eastern Germany until then had had almost no connection to humanitarian international law or to a larger international human rights context. The German approach to system injustice under Communism therefore displayed a paradox, at least in the early years. Even as foreign observers at times praised the German developments as posing a "laboratory" case of transitology—exactly as a part of the German elites wished to present things to domestic and international publics[101]—the concurrent transnational discourses on processing the past were barely reflected within the national discourse.

The Politics of the Past after German Unification

In recent years, the literature has taken to speaking (once again) of a "special path" or *Sonderweg* that the expanded FRG supposedly struck in its treatment of the East German Communist past. Two general reasons are usually given for this characterization.[102] First, it is said that no other post-Communist country pursued "processing of the past" as thoroughly and systematically as the unified FRG did with the legacy of the former GDR. The measures taken were unique in their breadth, intensity, and sophistication. Nearly all the instruments of "transitology" were applied. This argument is supportable insofar as the territory of the former GDR became the site of criminal trials for injustices committed under the dictatorship. A comprehensive vetting was applied to former public personnel, especially of those who had worked for the GDR Ministry for State Security (commonly known as the Stasi) in an official capacity, or in its army of "unofficial employees" and informants. In a less spectacular process, other East German state personnel—employees of the former civil administration, schools and universities, justice system and police, army, railways, and post office—were transferred into the public service of the FRG. A few organizations, such as the army, civil service, and justice agencies, saw a substantial change in elites. Many officials were transferred from the West, and many GDR civil servants were found to lack qualifications and were retired, demoted, or made redundant.[103] In addition, compensations were quickly made available to victims of the SED dictatorship who had suffered unjust prison sentences. Most of the verdicts delivered by the GDR's political courts were annulled. One of the most controversial issues was the restitution of expropriated properties. Despite the June 1990 agreement between the governments of Bonn and East Berlin on the principle of "return before compensation," exceptions were allowed for several categories, such as expropriations under postwar occupation law and "fair acquisitions." Finally, there was an exceptional degree of archival transparency. Access was allowed to the controversial files left by the former Stasi. Two "truth commissions" on SED "injustice" were appointed by the parliament.

The second argument for the special path thesis is of a more qualitative sort. Many social scientists have viewed the collapse of the GDR as a kind of test for the normative premises of democracy research. The two societies were themselves formerly the objects of the "transitional justice" enacted after World War II by the Allied victor powers. More than forty years later, under completely different conditions, were they able to succeed in overcoming the consequences of a dictatorship without requiring help from the outside?[104] One the one hand, the FRG before 1990 is posed as a "fortunate special case" because the society had undergone several decades of an intensive political and moral debate about the NS past. This seemed almost to predestine the FRG for a self-reflexive treatment of the GDR's past.[105] On the other hand, by 1990 a liberal pattern for processing the past—predicated on the triad of democracy, predictable rule of law, and remembrance—was predominant in the West. Even as this system was applied more or less smoothly to the GDR, many critics raised fundamental doubts that the West's "memory" paradigm would be compatible with the total socioeconomic upheaval in eastern Germany. Such concerns did, in fact, motivate the second amnesty controversy of 1994–1995, which is covered below.[106]

There are good reasons to critically regard the application of topoi from the West German culture of debate—which was once largely unreflective but increasingly became self-reinforcing—to the German-German unification process. The continued use after 1989 of well-known terms like "special path," "overcoming the past," and "processing"—all key concepts in West German postwar history—served to encourage the image of a "processing" that was simply continuous with the West German past. This concealed the fundamental transformations in the "new" Federal Republic. Applying these terms anachronistically, to an eastern region that bore little relation to its pre-1989 predecessor, created a narrative frame that influenced the practical politics of the past and its public perception. This set putative aims for the "processing," including the expectation that it would follow a recognizable pattern established long before 1989.[107]

Despite these problematic implications, there is little argument that the German processing of the dictatorial past differed qualitatively from the experience in the other post-Communist states. More than any other post-Communist country, unified Germany met an early and firm decision to pursue a criminal justice strategy. The French historian Guillaume Mouralis, in his study on the *Épuration allemande*, convincingly shows that this was rooted in the German history of mentality and identity politics. He finds that soon after the fall of the Berlin Wall, elites in both Germanys came to a more-than-tacit consensus that the juridical confrontation with NS mass crime had been a failure. For this reason, they had a special obligation to get things right the second time, to conduct a more thorough processing of Communist injustice. West German jurists especially believed that the GDR "processing" would constitute a second German "overcoming of the past," one that would have to improve on the history of the immediate post-World War II decades.[108] Any initial reservations among them fell away as these jurists came to identify strongly with the mission of a criminal justice program. The idea at first was generally unpopular. But political and legal opinion leaders, such as the Berlin state justice minister Jutta Limbach, adopted the discursive strategy of casting it as a historic and moral national mission of the highest order. The delicate question of their own professions' moral legitimacy, however, would remain obscured for many years.[109]

A wave of criminal prosecutions had already begun in the final months of the GDR, after the collapse of the SED regime in November 1989 and the March 1990 elections that empowered a pro-unification coalition. This was expanded greatly after the unification treaty came into effect in October 1990. According to the most up-to-date estimates, authorities initiated about seventy-five thousand investigations, including twenty-five thousand in Berlin and the surrounding state of Brandenburg. Of these, however, only about one thousand cases actually went to court.[110] The structural conditions were difficult, as the unification treaty required equal application of both GDR and FRG law in investigations of GDR-era crimes. This caused major headaches for jurists trained in highly specialized legal doctrines. Despite this, and thanks to a tremendous political effort, qualified personnel were recruited and functional institutions were created basically overnight and from the ground up.

Once this massive effort was complete, a constellation arose that would persist throughout the judicial and administrative treatment of the GDR past: generally speaking, jurists who were socialized and educated in West Germany now sat in judgment over GDR system crime. It was primarily those from the West who could "set the standards, demand the punishments, allow exceptions to ex post facto, and postulate the reconstruction of a legal state without getting themselves into danger."[111] As the CDU politician Kurt Biedenkopf put it candidly in 1992 to an international public of TJ experts, the imbalance was bound to awaken the impression among former East Germans that they were subject to "judgment by foreigners."[112] Born in the East but raised and educated in the West, Biedenkopf was elected after unification the first premier of the Free State of Saxony. Nearly all his civil-service expert and advisory appointments were West Germans, a fact he left out of his 1992 speech.[113]

Another unusual feature of the German case lay in the combination of political rupture with a form of legal continuity. During the unification negotiations, the sides agreed that the territory of the GDR would join the FRG as five new states under Article 23 of the Basic Law. This meant that the existing West German constitution would apply to the new eastern states immediately, without changes. Article 146, which would have required the ratification of a new constitution for Germany as a whole, was not invoked. This had the effect of defining the parameters of actionability for prosecuting human rights violations.[114] While there were good reasons for union under Article 23, there were two key disadvantages. First, the prosecution of GDR-era injustice was expanded along a broad front without a prior society-wide debate on the necessity of criminal prosecutions or the aims that these were meant to pursue.[115] Second, avoiding a society-wide discussion on the future constitution of Germany also avoided the issue of whether the constitutional ban on retroactive law should be lifted to legally secure prosecutions of state crimes under the deposed regime.[116] As an alternative, the "core state" (*Kernstaat*) theory predominant in West German constitutional thinking was applied. According to this, the FRG, and not the GDR, had been the legitimate successor to the German Reich. Thus, in the eyes of the constitutional law, a true *re*unification had occurred, of two territories that had always belonged together in a single country. This meant that prosecutors were free to invoke a "continuity of prosecutions" that had begun in the FRG;[117] for example, to use evidence gathered by the special West German law enforcement agency charged with investigating Communists, which had first been set up in 1961 at Salzgitter. In other words, the trials of the former East German leader Erich Honecker and other SED high functionaries would rely on practices that originated in the heyday of the Cold War. In a sense, the old FRG was imposing its public order on the fallen East German state.

The contradiction between the legal premises of unity and the political transformation in the German-German relationship gave rise to nearly unresolvable tension. The advocates of a punitive treatment of the past did not deny the anti-Communist case law of the old FRG but took pains to play it down.[118] The defendants naturally went the opposite way. At their trials for state crime, accused GDR functionaries and their lawyers repeatedly stressed that the prosecutions were based on an anachronism, that the new "Berlin Republic" had thrown itself back into the darkest days of West German persecution of Communists. (For example, West Germany had maintained a blacklist of its own citizens identified as "Communist," barring them from licensed professions and public sector employment into the 1970s.) The image of a politically motivated "ideological justice" was also invoked by writers with sympathies for the SED and by the leaders of the Party of Democratic Socialism (PDS), the reform-Communist party that had arisen out of former SED circles.[119]

From the start, the debates over the GDR past thus were entangled in a web of discourses that had originated during the division into two states. As Dirk van Laak would put it, the processing of the state Communist past occurred at the intersection of law, politics, and historical scholarship.[120] This was typical of the old West German "overcoming of the past." The GDR "processing" was prestructured, consciously or unconsciously, by West German discourses dating back long before 1989. At the same time, the FRG was also increasingly subject to international factors. At first, these had little to do with the treatment of governmental crime but influenced intellectual reflections on how the GDR past should be treated.

In the keynote address to the annual conference of German judges at Cologne in September 1991, the federal justice minister, Klaus Kinkel (FDP), delivered an appeal that was rather unusual for a member of the liberal party. Incanting in a rhetoric that recalled the propagandistic self-mobilization of the 1950s, he declared:

> I believe in German justice. We must succeed in delegitimizing the SED regime, which until the bitter end had cobbled justifications together out of antifascist professions, supposedly higher values, and claims of absolute humanity. But under the smokescreen of Marxism-Leninism, it built a state that in many ways was as terrible as that of the fascist Germany that had been fought and—rightly so—was never supposed to arise again.[121]

Kinkel's appeal was a variation on the thesis of the "double perversion of the law," a post-1990 motif linking the historical and political treatment of NS *and* GDR criminal cases.[122]

The intervention was not unexpected. A year after it had begun, the criminal processing of SED injustice was in danger of falling apart. The prosecutors in Berlin had suffered a serious setback in their efforts to try the former general secretary of the SED for issuing general orders to shoot people attempting to cross into West Germany. In March 1991, during a stay at a Soviet military hospital in the Brandenburg town of Beelitz, the gravely ill Honecker managed to slip away from his refuge unnoticed. He departed for Moscow. Meanwhile, Erich Mielke, the former chief of the Stasi, was being tried on charges dating back to the Weimar era. He was alleged to have been a gunman in the 1931 revenge killing of two police officers in Berlin, as ordered by his superiors in the Communist Party of Germany (KPD). The trial was the source of widespread unease because it used evidence from investigations conducted in the Nazi era.[123] GDR judges and prosecutors were profiting from an old ruling by the FRG Federal Court of Justice. In assessing judicial injustice conducted under the NS regime, they had introduced a "judges' privilege," granting almost complete immunity for Nazi-era jurists. GDR jurists more or less enjoyed the same judicial standards. The border and Berlin Wall guards accused of shootings were also able to invoke immunity. Convictions of either group were possible only for "blatant" and "grave" human rights violations, and even then only on charges of "perversion of justice."[124]

The greatest problems, however, arose from the complicated legal environment.[125] Within a few months of the unification on 3 October 1990, it was obvious that aside from a handful of "excesses," many GDR system crimes would remain unpunishable under the new conditions. Kinkel called on the judges to take the legal reunification into their own hands and "not allow the statute of limitations to lapse on the political crimes" of the GDR. The justice minister asserted that legislators were helpless to act as long as the constitutional ban on retroactivity remained in effect.[126] Most likely without realizing it, the FDP politician was reviving a stance held by his party colleague and predecessor in office about thirty-five years earlier, Ewald Bucher. As it happens, he had died in 1991 at the age of seventy-seven, just a few weeks before Kinkel's speech to the judges. During the 1965 Bundestag debate over a proposal to extend the statute of limitations pertaining to NS-era crimes, Minister of Justice Bucher had argued that it would violate the constitutionally untouchable ban on retroactivity. Bucher resigned soon after, after a clear majority of CDU-CSU and SPD deputies had voted against him on this matter.[127]

With his encroachment on the statute of limitations issue, Kinkel had touched on a well-known problem from West German history. Overcoming retroactivity was also an issue in the international discourses of transitional justice, but these played no role in the German debate. Many prominent German legal scholars stepped up to point out that the unification treaty provisions upholding the ban on retroactivity were unambiguous. Others objected that compared with the Third Reich, the human rights violations of the East German "workers and farmers' state" were relatively tame.[128] The latter argument was almost tantamount to enshrining the Nazi genocide as the absolute standard for determining the actionability of state crimes. It would achieve the status of orthodoxy in public and scholarly discourse. It united all political camps and was hardly ever seriously questioned.[129] From a domestic perspective, the human rights issue in the FRG appeared to be stalled. Unexpectedly, Kinkel's intervention did cause a turn. Soon after his speech, the justice ministers of the German states submitted a bill to the Bundestag that would suspend the statute of limitations for SED injustice cases. It fundamentally corresponded to the statute of limitations compromise of 1965.

Nearly two years after the last of the Politburo resigned, the controversy over the GDR past was threatening to turn into an academic discussion among legal experts. Concurrently, sociopolitical tensions intensified as a wave of xenophobic mob violence swept the eastern states. This was the context as more and more voices called for the appointment of a societal "tribunal."[131] In retrospect, one can identify this as the hour when the first parliamentary Enquete Commission on the Processing of the SED Dictatorship was born. One of the first statements calling for such a body was issued in August 1991 by the Wittenberg pastor Friedrich Schorlemmer. He proposed that the ongoing criminal trials be supplemented by an extrajudicial "tribunal" that would bring together representatives of the executive, legislature, judiciary, universities, and civil society.[132] According to Schorlemmer, the members would collaborate in exposing the fundamentals of SED rule to encourage moral purification or, as he put it, a "catharsis." They would aim to reach a judgment of the GDR past that could be accepted equally in east and west.[133]

Another approach was suggested by Wolfgang Thierse, who published his comments one week later in the influential Hamburg weekly newspaper *Die Zeit*. The deputy leader of the SPD at the time, the former GDR dissident proposed the appointment of a "tribunal on the past of the SED and the Stasi state" to act in the name of "former GDR citizens." There was an evident danger, Thierse wrote, that the haphazard course of judicial processing would gradually alienate former East Germans from their own history. While he considered "turnabout" (*Wende*, a term often used to reference the fall of the Berlin Wall) a "doleful word," it did describe the "massive turning away from our own history." Thierse then cited the historian Martin Broszat, who had died in 1989, describing an analogous case. Broszat had written of the negative consequences when a society delegates the task of processing its own history. Those who would "talk the citizens out of a self-critical approach to their own recent history" would rob them of "one of the best elements of political civility."[134]

In the tradition of Marxist historical thinking, Thierse understood the tribunal as an opportunity to assist the revolutionary subject—although he seemed uncertain of its concrete historic significance—to once again determine its own history, an opportunity to supply the appropriate categories for interpreting it.[135] On the events of 1989 and 1990, he wrote:

> The inconsequence of the Fall 1989 revolution (if that is what it was) cannot be compensated through criminal law. Rather, we have yet to draw out its consequences: Once again, the forces of Fall '89, the civil rights movement and the social democrats, need to demonstrate what they have in common—their rebellion against elementary injustice and the desire for self-determined freedom.

From a Social Democrat with an East German background, one might have expected that the verdict on forty years of GDR history would proceed from the classic parameters of social inequality, level of socioeconomic modernization, or perhaps a Gramscian model of political-cultural hegemony. Instead, the former member of the GDR civil rights movement proposed that "GDR injustice" should be treated using a few exemplary cases, with human rights and the "Nuremberg principles" as the applicable standards of "political-moral judgment."[136]

While the diagnoses of Schorlemmer and Thierse agreed that the prosecutions to date were more problem than solution, Wolfgang Ullmann demurred. The theologist was a member of parliament for Bündnis 90/ Die Grünen (Alliance 90/The Greens), the party unifying the West German Greens with a like-minded East German formation. Ullmann was convinced that judicial processing had run into difficulties mainly because it was pursued as a national project, without connection to international norms and laws. The provocative title of his article, published in the weekly paper *Freitag*, posed the question "Trial of the King or Nuremberg Tribunal?" (a reference to the French national trial of King Louis XVI as the less desirable of the two alternatives). Ullmann called for a radical change of course in processing the GDR past.[137] The justice system of unified Germany with its clumsy prosecutions was entangling itself "in ever-deeper embarrassments." Every new indictment raised the risk of further disgrace for "an administration of justice clearly overwhelmed by the particulars of the cases." A new beginning was needed. Ullmann proposed delegating the processing of SED injustice to an international legal authority, a tribunal along the lines of Nuremberg, one that could deal with "state criminality" rather than "government criminality":

> Where the destruction of law has reached the level of state criminality, national courts are no longer sufficient to rebuild the destroyed law. An international effort is required to create a new forum, before which the affected can appear

and expect a verdict that upholds human rights. I do not believe that the existing international courts are up to the task. How should the full extent of the crimes committed by the Communist secret services be investigated, if not through a new form of communication between those who suffered and those who possess the capacity to judge the case precisely because they did not suffer?[138]

The political class took almost no notice of Ullman's plea for an international solution. His argument was not wholly beyond the pale; the government of Helmut Kohl, a coalition of CDU-CSU and FDP that had been in power since 1982, seemed to have revised the traditional reticence about international criminal law in a few important ways. They supported calls to revitalize the Nuremberg principles and establish an international criminal court. There were also opposite tendencies: in late 1988, West Germany had joined the United States, Great Britain, France, and Israel at the UN General Assembly in voting against a proposal that would the International Law Commission to resume its interrupted work on the so-called Draft Code.[139]

Some three years later, the page seemed to have turned. Following the 1990 invasion of Kuwait and the 1991 Gulf War, the United States and Great Britain floated a proposal that the Iraqi dictator Saddam Hussein should be tried before an international tribunal for grave violations of human rights. The German foreign minister, Hans-Dietrich Genscher (FDP), soon expressed his support. In April 1991, the German government submitted several statements to the UN Security Council that characterized Hussein's actions against Iraqi Kurds as a "genocide" threatening the peace and stability of the region as a whole.[140] At Genscher's initiative, the chair of the council of EU-member foreign ministers wrote to UN Secretary General Javier Pérez de Cuéllar, calling on him to initiate studies on the establishment of an international court to prosecute Iraqi crimes under international law. This amity for international law continued after Klaus Kinkel replaced Genscher the next year. A visibly sobered Kinkel related how the difficulties he encountered while dealing with the SED past as justice minister were among the reasons why now, as foreign minister, he hoped to promote a stronger institutionalization of international law. He expressed "fascination with the idea of helping to secure world peace using the means of the rule of law."[141]

It can be argued that the abrupt shift in attitudes about an international law solution was related to exposure of West Germany's role as one of the main arms suppliers to the Bagdad dictator during the eight-year Iran-Iraq War in the 1980s. This became a foreign policy embarrassment only after Iraq invaded Kuwait in August 1990.[142] It escalated further into controversy during Operation Desert Storm in January 1991, when Iraq fired its SCUD missiles at Israel, although it was not part of the military coalition fighting

Iraq, and furthermore threatened to launch poison gas attacks against Israel. Of course, the rhetorical turn was also related to the failures up to that point in the attempted judicial treatment of Communist state violence. But the reflex against anything that remotely smacked of "Nuremberg" remained strong enough in the early 1990s to prevent any serious consideration of using international law as the means of dealing with GDR injustice. A leading international law expert in Austria, Otto Trifterer, argued that the fatal shootings at the Berlin Wall could qualify as a "special form" of crimes against humanity prosecutable under international law principles, but in the FRG this remained an isolated minority opinion.[143]

For the most part, the public was also skeptical about the idea of a societal "tribunal."[144] Especially among FDP-style liberals like *Die Zeit* columnist Robert Leicht, both the word and the underlying concept awakened unappetizing associations with the "real-socialist peoples' justice" of East Germany.[145] Speaking at an awards ceremony in December 1991, the president of the FRG, Richard von Weizsäcker, greeted the idea of putting the discussion about the GDR past on a broader basis. But he strongly rejected a tribunal, for such an institution "would have to work without the powers of the justice system and would rely on voluntary participation. . . . It could not punish, nor confer absolution, but only have the impact of presenting findings." At the same time, he considered the public controversy about it helpful in developing a moral consciousness by asking, "Who then is in a position regarding the past to definitively distinguish between good and evil in all cases?"[146] Weizsäcker also dismissed the proposal of an international tribunal for GDR criminality as unworthy of serious consideration.[147] It must remain an open question whether his rejection was related to resentment against "Nuremberg"—where Weizsäcker himself had served as an assistant counsel to his accused father[147]—or actually intended as an implicit criticism of those who would equate National Socialism with "real-existing Socialism."

Even if analogies to the Communist show trials were not entirely without merit, most critics seem to overlook a different, far more democratic tradition of tribunals: that of the mock trial. One held in 1934 at Madison Square Garden in New York, in response to the Reichstag fire trial, also condemned the racially motivated persecution of German Jews. In the late 1960s, leftist intellectuals like Bertrand Russell and Jean-Paul Sartre led a revival of this form of social protest against state-initiated acts of violence.[148]

By the fall of 1991, the history politics controversies about the GDR past started to heat up further. The domestic climate was being poisoned by an insistent drumbeat of media exposés of former collaboration with the Stasi, mostly by politicians, academics, and artists from the new German states.[149] The harsh criticism of the tribunal idea from leaders of the old "West" caused the eastern German advocates of a "societal treatment" to look for alternatives. On 28 November, the SPD politicians Markus Meckel and Martin Gutzeit, in a memorandum distributed among their fellow Bundestag deputies, raised the call for the appointment of a parliamentary commission on GDR history. In their view, this seemed to banish the danger of a "self-appointed quasi justice" while also guaranteeing that a confrontation with the GDR would receive the greatest possible domestic stage.[150]

Most parliamentarians agreed that "processing" was good, even if "tribunals" were bad, so a majority in favor of the proposal came together quickly, including among the ruling parties. The key vote in swaying the latter was that of Wolfgang Schäuble, leader of the CDU-CSU group in the parliament since 1991. In December, he formally asked his party to support a parliamentary commission on the history of the forty years of division and the "SED injustice state."[151] Rolf Schwanitz (SPD) and Jürgen Rüttgers (CDU) announced a concord among their parties, stating that the commission's purpose would be to "process the history in East Germany" and not to engage in "political trench warfare."[152] This harmony would diminish rapidly, and the announcement was made without a more precise specification of the project's aims and ground rules. But the more important factor for the participants was presumably to reach an agreement before the law allowing access to Stasi documents came into effect in January 1992. Since this would doubtless start a new wave of revelations about collaboration, it bolstered hopes of embarrassing the PDS group in parliament (who opposed the new commission) as the party of "processing blockers."

A month after the SPD-CDU declaration, however, there still was no clarity about what kind of processing the commission would pursue, and to what end. A group of prominent veterans of the GDR civil rights movement (including several who had backed the tribunal idea) stepped forward with a long statement in *Frankfurter Allgemeine Zeitung* in which they distanced themselves from the supposedly "problematic" term but reiterated their support for the original concept.[153] Now that the GDR had obviously not survived the "tribunal of history," it was time for a "tribunal" about its history to illuminate the responsibility for its failure and help in determining levels of "guilt." On the one hand, primary responsibility self-evidently lay with the SED leadership and the apparatus they conducted for the "disintegration of economy and nature, of towns and countrysides, government and law, education and science, human communication and thought." But a share of the blame also lay with the countless "followers" who had supported the system in "covert and overt collaboration."

Since the rule of law had been unable to help many of the disadvantaged and penalized victims "experience vindication through the verdict of an orderly court," a different way was needed to achieve public satisfaction.

A "just acknowledgment" was owed to all who had "opposed the despotism, resisted the naked power interests, and fought for people":

> In the final analysis, to illuminate the connections of personal responsibility under the changing conditions and historical situations of the GDR also means gaining insights into the structures and mechanisms by which democracy was undermined and well-intentioned social engagement was perverted. The people who lived in the GDR in good faith and under difficult circumstances do not stand empty-handed in the united Germany. Their experience with dictatorship and how it was overcome, and the stubbornness and the force of critical minorities are, in the long run, the most important dowry that the history of the GDR has to give to a democratic Germany.

In their "Appeal for a Tribunal," the signatories also described the practical details of how they envisioned this illumination of GDR "injustice." They foresaw a three-stage process. The first would draw on the "historic experiences" from the time immediately after 1945 and place these in a comparative juxtaposition to the forty years of GDR history proper. In the second phase, local, regional, and state-level forums and discussion circles would be held, in which independent experts on given subjects would also participate. The final phase would be to document the resulting findings and make them available to a broader public. The most desirable aspect, according to the tribunal supporters, would be the "public dimension of the process." Only in public communication could victims, responsible parties, and experts present their narratives and counternarratives toward "formation of an opinion" about GDR history.

Although the proposed format was highly specific and clear, the methods and standards of assessment underlying the procedure remained rather nebulous. The authors appeared to be skeptical whether anything much could be accomplished through law, especially through the criminal justice system. Nevertheless, they believed it was necessary to judge GDR history in the terms of (international) legal-punitive categories. The relevant part of the statement seems more mystifying than precise:

> Beyond the applicable law, there is no objective standard for judging the legality of acts. . . . Therefore, standards to judge the behavior of persons arise from insight and the assessment of behaviors under comparable conditions. The legal situation applicable at a given time should be considered, as should the ways in which legal practice often deviated. That human rights are valid was not unknown within the general sense of justice in the GDR. Their fundamental principles, specified in its constitution and in its international treaty obligations, provided a generally known framework at all times.

In the voices who raised the idea of a societal "tribunal" starting in the summer of 1991, one can see the attempt of a fragmented East German civil rights movement to regain a degree of interpretative authority over their former country's history, after the project of a free and democratic GDR had been flattened irretrievably by the German unification train. The various proposals imagine that they would narrate their own, East German counter to the reading of the Federal Republic's history as a "success story" that had gained such hegemonic force since 1990.[154] Their shared story's central motifs would be the forty years of dictatorship and the history of how it was overcome. But measured against the historical findings that East Germany developed a powerful opposition only after the regime had entered its terminal agony, this narrative is no less harmonized and teleological than its West German foil. Unlike the latter, its historical understanding was more national than postnational. A strongly moralizing perspective, it fed from the binary categories of the contemporary human rights discourse and the old totalitarianism theory that remained quite popular among Eastern European dissidents.

As understandable as it is in retrospect that the civil rights activists, duped and politically marginalized, now sought to rewrite their genuine contribution to the East German revolution as a linear history of resistance and liberation, this does not yet explain why their tribunal effort of 1991 and 1992 found an echo not only among the West German elites but even with the post-Communist PDS. With the exception of two abstentions, the parliament—still in Bonn but preparing the later move to Berlin—overwhelmingly approved the appointment of an Enquete Commission on Working through the History and Consequences of the SED Dictatorship in Germany. Although the East German pastor Rainer Eppelmann—a CDU deputy waved into the chairperson's spot on Schäuble's initiative—announced in his speech to open the commission that its goals were to achieve "inner unity" and Germany-wide "reconciliation," the boilerplate could hardly disguise his party's actual priorities. The "people," said Eppelmann, should recognize that the "divisive talk of an East-West contradiction" was reckless and irresponsible. Once the second Enquete Commission began its hearings, all ongoing problems in the eastern German territories were attributed to the "misdeeds of yesteryear," blamed on "the narrow-minded socialism, the partisan and ideological arrogance of the SED Communists and their helpers."[155] The governing coalition saw the commission mainly as a chance to regain electoral terrain lost in the new eastern states amid the economic turbulence of the unification process. The planned parliamentary "processing" doubled as a highly welcome field for governmental history management.

That being said, the two Enquete Commissions of 1992 and 1995 were monumental projects, featuring a variety of actors with a huge range of interests. It comes as no surprise that each developed its own dynamics and forces. The practical course of these projects nevertheless remained remote from what the tribunal supporters originally envisioned, and this was not only because of the political forces in play but also structurally unavoidable. Political scientists have often stressed that neither commission fulfilled its announced goal of helping SED victims achieve more "justice," which remained little more than rhetoric. The drive to establish a more consensual narrative of GDR history also failed, and mainly because of differences regarding history policy between the two big parties, CDU and SPD.[156] Without discounting any these points, however, these criticisms are analytically insufficient, because they do not go beyond the mental map of the actors in 1991 and 1992. They accept the normative standards of the time, without asking where the novelty of a "history processing" run by a parliamentary committee should be located in the longer run of history management, or of the historical discipline itself. The analyses furthermore tend to proceed from an ideal typology of the "truth commission," against which the two German commissions are measured retrospectively.[157]

Andrew H. Beattie was the first to approach the phenomenon from a historicizing perspective. He understands the two commissions as instruments of transitional justice, but also embeds them in a *longue durée* of national dictatorship processing, which the more recent literature has analyzed as cases of politics of the past, "memory politics," and history politics or management.[158] Although he stresses the "contingent, tentative and rather experimental character of the endeavor"[159] and the difficulties this poses for historical assessment, he ascribes to it a big role in the officious history politics of the "Berlin Republic." The commissions' work guarantees to this day that GDR history is discussed in the German public sphere mainly within the power-political rubric of "SED dictatorship." Issues of social and everyday history remain relatively underexamined.

Practically all the actors in the two commission projects who participated as members of political parties agree that their lasting achievement was to establish an "antitotalitarian consensus" and that this represented great progress over the West German "Historians' Argument" (*Historikerstreit*) of 1986, in which genuine revisionists of Nazi history had gained a new platform. Beattie sees the commissions as only a partial success, however, and on second look he relativizes that even further. He stresses that the "antitotalitarian" consensus in many ways existed only in a shared rhetoric.[160] The commissions' proclaimed identity politics aim, of reconciling the antitotalitarianism of conservatives in both parts of the country with the critical and reflective mode of the West German leftists, failed mostly because large parts of the eastern German population were intentionally left out of the proceedings altogether. In Beattie's words:

> In fact, the commission produced a highly politicized analysis that was intended to delegitimize the GDR and support a renewed "antitotalitarian

consensus," to which it hoped all Germans would subscribe. However, the commission was quite content to leave not inconsiderable sections of the population, such as anyone who thought there was anything positive about the GDR, and of the political spectrum, that is, the PDS, outside the consensus, and thus beyond the democratic pale.... The commission was thus both an instrument of and a site for conducting politics with history.[161]

The fragility of the antitotalitarian narrative frame became evident in a subsequent controversy sparked by the Saxon Memorial Foundation, the publicly funded organization that maintained history monuments in the new eastern state of Saxony. The law empowering the foundation and its organizational policy initially watered down distinctions between the victims of Nazism and the victims of the SED, prompting the Central Council of Jews in Germany temporarily to withdraw from the foundation's scientific advisory board in 2004.[162]

Beattie's work shows that over the course of the 1990s, the metanarrative of the "Federal Republic success story" was increasingly anchored in the national mentality, while anti-Communist narratives also gained momentum. The parliamentary commissions had effectively contributed to the exclusion of professions to the contrary. The broad-brush devaluation of GDR antifascism indirectly boosted the old West German narrative of "overcoming the past." The public discourse about the GDR's "state of injustice" and Germany's "double totalitarian past" and methodologies that failed to distinguish between the dictatorships allowed entry to revisionist historiography. Conservative West German historians, like Alexander Fischer and Horst Möller, saw the debate about the GDR's "totalitarian" character and the unified country's "double overcoming of the past" as the latest round in a culture war that had begun with the 1980s *Historikerstreit*, which, in their view, had ended in a "victory" for the left. Beattie writes, "These strident anticommunists were not interested in the differences between the dictatorships; they treated their comparison primarily as an avenue for highlighting what they had in common."[163] On this point, the positions of German conservatives east and west would diverge sharply. While the chair of the first commission, Eppelmann, saw the Nazi mass crimes as a factor "limiting" comparisons between the NS regime and the GDR, Möller—who at the time was serving as the director of the Institute of Contemporary History—stated that the political systems of the Third Reich and the GDR could be compared straightforwardly, since mass crimes were not intrinsic to the NS state. Both Möller and Friedrich-Christian Schroeder, a prominent expert on GDR law, used the strategy of including Soviet Stalinism in the comparison.[164] This overstretch of comparative method is regarded as unacceptable among most historians of dictatorships but found its way into the commission's final report.[165]

Beattie presents good empirical grounding for his thesis that the two Enquete Commissions were part of a larger cultural rollback set into motion by old conservatives of the FRG with support from East German civil rights activists, and designed to break the predominance of the left that they perceived in media, science, and culture. The picture is complicated, however, if we contextualize it within the transnational developments of the time. As with the field of "memory governance"[166] as a whole, the two German truth commissions raised the question of new and old, of continuity and rupture. Do these parliamentary experiments in history writing really represent a regression from prior achievements, as Norbert Frei, among others, postulates? Did the expanded FRG thus deviate from the "societal-discursive" standard of the 1980s and return to a "normative, state-anchored understanding of history"?[167]

Both commissions showed certain inherent contradictions that also reflect the hybrid forms of transitology, further confusing things. The étatist and elitist self-understanding behind the attempt to produce and disseminate an official version of GDR history stands in contradiction to the emancipatory claim of processing the past "from below" and with participation of the victims. This form of history processing continued with the late 1990s establishment of the Federal Foundation for the Reappraisal of the SED Dictatorship, which belonged to a new generation of publicly funded foundations on a typically neoliberal model. The state was no longer involved directly in decisions, management, or control but instead divided various functions among civil society actors who were expected to more or less faithfully follow a particular philosophical stance. However, the basic credo of "truth," "justice," and "memory" harbored a variety of very different political aims. One was to give stronger representation to victims' interests, for example, by supporting oral history projects or organizing archives of victims' documents. Another was to manufacture "replacement conflicts" for the mass-media public so as to cover up the "consequences of the political, social, and economic transformation process."[168]

Another change compared with the 1980s came thanks to the continuing global decay of the old "soft law" separating law, history, and political morality. While the silos were still up and strong in the age of West German "overcoming of the past," now even the institutional actors within the disciplines were bringing them down. The South African and German "truth commission" experiences, as described earlier, make it clear that the increased transnational and interdisciplinary networking—which can no longer be described simply as a "juridification of history" or politics, or as a "politicization" of the law[169]—make for altogether ambivalent results. When history writing uses the binary categories of the law, it may hope for greater public acceptance because that is simpler and pithier. In a few cases, this may produce satisfaction in the short term. The hazards of this approach are also obvious. The first Enquete Commission attempted to deliver a final "verdict" on East German history. But its authors soon found the critics rejecting their delivery of simple judgments based on little more than abstract legal categories and popular labels ("SED dictatorship," "state of injustice") that cannot replace a deeper historical understanding.[170]

"Mercy Before Justice"? The Amnesty Debate of 1994–1995

"Who demands to be exonerated has no need of amnesty." As lightning from the pen of a celebrated jurist, the maxim illuminates the character of the German-German debate over the East German past.[171] The public discussion about the fallen GDR was oft phrased in legal semantics and codes. But the time was scant before the question of amnesty came on the agenda. This was predictable in several ways, as amnesties—derived from the ancient Greek for forgetting and forgiving—have served since time immemorial as a proven means for putting a symbolic end to wars among states and for pacifying domestic social conflicts.[172] Generally, these actions not only follow a concrete political aim but also pose a wide-ranging intervention in the routine course of criminal justice, allowing response to significant political ruptures.[173] Independently of whether one had recognized the GDR as a sovereign state before the events of 1989 or saw it instead as the most vivid expression of a long-standing state of emergency that abruptly ended with East Germany's entry into the FRG in 1990, an amnesty law might seem like the right way to reckon with the epochal dimensions of the breaching of the Berlin Wall.[174]

In the months between the fall of the SED Politburo starting in November 1989 and the coming into force of the second German-German treaty that unified East and West into a single FRG in October 1990, various sides had in fact called for a political amnesty. But none of the proposals gained momentum. The reasons lay in the history of the two German states and in the different ways in which West and East Germany had used this legal instrument in the past. Over the course of the forty years following its founding in May 1949, the FRG had issued four political amnesties.[175] Soon after the state came into being, a coalition of the CDU-CSU, FDP, and DP passed two different exemptions from punishment to cover the much-discussed "black market" delinquents, small-time criminals, and lower-level Nazis and regime perpetrators who had been deceptive during their de-Nazification proceedings (who in a play on words were called "*Braun-Schweiger*," those silenced their "brown" past). This presumably worked out to the benefit of tens of thousands of more or less incriminated perpetrators of the NS regime and order.[176] Intentionally kept vague because of concerns about Allied reactions, these first two FRG amnesties served a dual purpose: to recapture the room for action open to the state and institutions and to regain a measure of interpretative authority over the meaning of the Nazi past.

The political need for amnesties declined noticeably in the years that followed. First among the reasons, the political criminal justice of the 1950s and to an extent even the 1960s was directed mainly against the left.[177] The FDP in 1956 submitted legislation to allow exemptions from punishment that would have mainly benefited persons from KPD circles who had been convicted based on retroactive national security regulations. It failed against the united opposition of the CDU-CSU, which at the time was the sole ruling party. The conspicuous reluctance to amnesty also arose from the intensified "totalitarianism" discourse. By then the SED in East Berlin had extensively used political amnesties, hardening a West German perception that such instruments belonged to the arsenal of rule typical of "totalitarian" states.[178]

Only toward the end of the 1960s did two consecutive and larger waves of West German amnesty follow. Both exemption acts—the first passed in July 1968 at the time of the grand coalition government of the CDU-CSU and SPD, the second in 1970 by the "social-liberal" coalition of the SPD and FDP—were seen as combinations of "legal correction" and "pacification amnesty."[179] They expressed a general liberalization of the national security law, the reform of which began in 1968 with the passage of amendments to the criminal code and proceeded in a series of other reforms. The last of the cases still pending against Communists were dropped, and the student protest culture was largely decriminalized.[180]

After a longer dormancy, an early 1980s party-finance scandal briefly raised the prospect of new exemptions. This ended in a fairly big fiasco, especially for the SPD. With its attempt to sweep under the rug the scandal of bribes paid by the Flick concern to politicians of the CDU-CSU, FDP, and SPD by the means of an ad hoc law granting exemptions from punishment, the social-liberal coalition contributed to its own demise, in 1982.[181] Various legal initiatives undertaken on the regional state level by the newly arrived Green Party, intended to grant exemptions to opponents of the Frankfurt airport and members of the West Berlin squatters' scene, also failed.[182]

In contrast to the FRG, the GDR could look back on a long tradition of amnesties that, however, were burdened with the stigma of what the criminal law expert Klaus Marxen has called "as-if law." To underline their claim to absolute political leadership, the SED command issued amnesties and wide-ranging clemency orders at fairly regular intervals. These were the expression of a "real-socialist dialectic" in which expansive exemptions from punishment were combined with simultaneous intensifications of criminal justice laws.[183] This continued after the 1971 passage of power from Walter

Ulbricht to Erich Honecker. For example, as a flanking maneuver to the ongoing German-German talks of October 1972, Honecker used the celebrations around the twenty-third anniversary of the GDR's founding to order amnesty for nearly one hundred thousand persons, including about forty-two thousand prisoners and detention inmates whom the SED leadership categorized as "political and criminal perpetrators."[184] The "amnesty" was in fact a general commutation of all the sentences to a term of three years' probation. Western observers at the time treated the move as a sensation, because the SED deviated from its usual diction by acknowledging for the first time the existence of "political" prisoners.

Amnesties and commutations became scarcer in the next fifteen years, with ever-greater intervals between them. This was not because of a decline in the population of inmates at the GDR's prisons. On the contrary, the incarceration rate rose constantly after Honecker's assumption of power. To relieve the pressure on overflowing prisons and pretrial detention centers, the GDR turned increasingly to the business of releasing prisoners to the West in exchange for payoffs of hard currency, which helped alleviate the East's ever more difficult balance of payments.[185] The country's domestic and foreign situation had clearly deteriorated by July 1987, when the most expansive reprieve action in East German history was initiated. Finalized in October 1987, in time for the thirty-eighth anniversary of the country's founding, this "general amnesty"—once again a collective probation measure—was meant to benefit all persons convicted before that date. Exceptions remained for "Nazi and war crimes," "crimes against humanity," and espionage and murder.[186] These measures and the parallel abolition of the death penalty, however, met with little enthusiasm among the East German people.

Nevertheless, the Politburo clung to its controversial "social experimentation" (Johannes Raschka), which can be read as a sign of its growing alienation from the Soviet Communist Party under Mikhail Gorbachev, and the state's mounting economic dependence on the West. With a visit by Honecker in Bonn imminent, the GDR leadership was being forced into making certain concessions on human rights issues. The phase of political upheaval that followed in 1989 saw a quick succession of two additional amnesties. Ten days after Honecker's resignation, on 17 October 1989, the Politburo under Egon Krenz issued a clemency for all persons who had been arrested and convicted for border violations or in connection with the mass "Monday demonstrations" that had driven the regime's retreat. After the fall of the Berlin Wall on 9 November and the resignations of Krenz and Stasi chief Mielke in December, the Council of State issued what came to be known as the "Gerlach Amnesty." It was named after the last chairman of the council, and thus the country's final head of state, Manfred Gerlach of the SED's subsidiary or "bloc" party, the Liberal Democratic Party of Germany.

The comprehensive amnesty would empty out the GDR's carceral facilities almost completely in the months that followed.[187]

In the summer of 1990, after the first open GDR parliamentary elections but before completion of the second German-German treaty that would effect full unification with the FRG, it became obvious that political amnesties had become very unpopular with a large portion of the East German people. Most of the population saw these actions as the expressions of an obsolescent state authority. To the civil rights activists and intellectuals who had criticized the old system, however, amnesties represented a key means by which the SED leadership had secured its own power for decades. Despite these rejections from the East, various alliances in the old FRG had already formed in 1990 in support of amnesty or partial amnesty for GDR system criminality. These involved political linkages: in the Bundestag, the "black-yellow" coalition of the CDU-CSU and FDP submitted legislation in August 1990 with the aim of linking the negotiations over the unification treaty with an amnesty for East German agents and "small-time" Stasi informants.[188] Among members of the West German SPD and parts of Alliance 90/The Greens (which had just emerged from the joining of the West German Greens with an East German civil rights party), there was also no fundamental aversion to a limited exemption from punishment for GDR spies.[189] SPD and Greens both wanted to link this with amnesty for political-criminal charges against activists of the left-alternative milieu. The idea of amnesty for West German leftists had been anathema to the government ever since Helmut Schmidt's SPD-FDP coalition had been replaced by Helmut Kohl's CDU-FDP coalition back in 1982. In the end, none of these initiatives were reflected in the unification treaty, as the East German delegation to the talks issued a clear rejection of any such measures.

Although widely supported by the West German government and opposition parties, these plans failed largely because of unrelenting resistance to them among a relatively small group of long-time GDR civil rights activists. Their stance arose from a concept of democratization that rested more on the idea of a cultural change "from below" than on institutional reforms "from above."[190] Driven by a powerful desire for democratic self-determination, these GDR opposition discourses placed fundamental value on ethical standards like authenticity, transparency, integrity, and trust. This was not merely a reaction to the propagandistic ideological dictatorship of the Communist regimes, which Václav Havel had diagnosed as the culture of "the lie."[191] The same discourse also saw the domestic tensions of the old FRG as the product of an only half-hearted treatment of historical truth: an incomplete "processing of the past." As historical models, the obstructed "overcoming of the past" in the West and the instrumental antifascism of the East were both good only as examples of wrong paths to follow.[192] Ever since the 1973–1975 origins of the Conference for Security and Cooperation in Europe and the "Helsinki Process" of international human rights monitoring, the East German opposition had mainly used the legalistic strategies that these bodies offered. They now sought to continue in the same vein after the end of the GDR.[193] They rejected any amnesty proposal that laid out a generic definition for a group to be pardoned (which would have conformed to the principles of a generalizable rule of law as understood in the West) rather than specifying exactly which individuals were to benefit from it.[194] Anything else was meaningless, they believed, because individual responsibilities had yet to be determined through proper court processes.

The public debate over an amnesty for GDR state injustices was first revived again in late 1994. Meanwhile, two laws, passed in March and September 1993, had set a statute of limitations on misdemeanors to go into effect at the end of 1995, and one on serious crimes to take force two years later. The exception was for homicide, in keeping with GDR law.[195] Only in retrospect is it obvious that the subsequent argument, concerning the pressure to bring charges before the statutes of limitations expired, was conducted in absurd fashion and often as a delaying tactic. Amnesty supporters often attempted to construct a supposed urgent need for it, when in fact the statutes of limitations were about to obviate it. This smoke-and-mirrors approach went together with an avoidance of specifying exactly which crimes should be subject to amnesty. Much evidence, therefore, speaks for the view that the debate was set off not so much by the coming statute of limitations dates but by the results of the Bundestag elections of October 1994. Kohl's coalition prevailed for a fourth time, but the CDU-CSU suffered losses to the SPD and Greens, and the FDP share of the vote plunged. The post-Communist PDS, meanwhile, while falling short of the minimum of 5 percent of the national vote required for entry as a party with proportional representation in the parliament, still managed to secure Bundestag seats by winning pluralities directly in thirty eastern German districts.

The much-discussed "crisis of unification" (Jürgen Kocka) brought a relatively moderate winning share of only 41.5 percent nationwide for the CDU-CSU, with losses in the eastern German states of more than 3 percent compared to the 1990 elections. Despite their risky back-and-forth regarding "Germany policy" and an exceptionally weak candidate for chancellor in Rudolf Scharping, the SPD had climbed to a respectable 36.4 percent. While this was insufficient for building a governing coalition with third parties, it was considered an indisputable victory compared with the traumatic defeat four years earlier, and this was thanks mostly to gains for the SPD in the eastern states. The party's ruling "troika" of Scharping, Oskar Lafontaine, and (future chancellor) Gerhard Schröder were confounded, however, by the PDS's phenomenal performance in capturing almost 20 percent of the eastern vote. This camouflaged their mere 1 percent share in the old FRG and established them as a player within an expanded, five-party system.[196] It prompted one sarcastic observer to comment that "left of the center," the fourth year of German unity saw a clump of "old [SED] functionaries, Stasi informants, and nostalgic fans of the GDR, all those who should have melted into insignificance under the bright lights of freedom and democracy."[197]

In late October, *Der Spiegel* ran an interview about the SPD's electoral near-miss by two of its editors with Egon Bahr, long-time adviser to the late Willy Brandt and architect in the early 1970s of Brandt's Ostpolitik—under which FRG and GDR had first established diplomatic relations, and restrictions on travel from West to East Germany had been eased. Bahr minced no words, stating that he hoped to see his party engage in a rapprochement with the PDS that would eventually lead to the latter's complete disappearance. Concretely, he expressed support for wider adoption of the ongoing "Magdeburg model." Named for the capital of Saxony-Anhalt, this phrase described the arrangement under which the regional SPD under Reinhard Höppner had formed a minority government in the state with the tolerance by abstention of the PDS. Bahr attributed the post-Communists' success in capturing a large part of the SPD's potential base in eastern Germany to their use of populist rhetoric. Now was the time to win back these alienated voters with a politics of "reconciliation." Asked if by this he meant the same kind of "reconciliation" that Konrad Adenauer had once practiced with many major and smaller "old Nazis," Bahr shot back: "The external symbol of reconciliation with the collaborators of the NSDAP was of course the presence of [Hans] Globke as a top adviser in [Adenauer's] chancellery" from 1953 to 1963. "At the time, I thought that was wrong." (As a leading jurist in the NS era, Globke had helped to author the Nuremberg race laws of 1935 and issued the official guidelines for their enforcement; see also chapter 3.) "But looking back today, I must say I consider [Globke's appointment] to be one of Adenauer's greatest achievements as a statesman."[198]

Bahr had already made clear in the previous year that his concept of "reconciliation" above all meant the generous reintegration of the former dictatorship's elites. In a public discussion with the justice minister of Saxony, Steffen Heitmann (CDU), Bahr had related that the idea of an amnesty had first come to him in 1990 while talking to recently decommissioned officers of the East German National People's Army. Their fate, he said, reminded him of the successful reintegration of former Wehrmacht generals under the early FRG:

> I was also convinced we would find proven people among the [East German] generals, given the good experiences of the past with high officers [of the Wehrmacht] in building the Bundeswehr [West German postwar military].

These former officers of the Wehrmacht had taken their oath to the Führer and Reich Chancellor. [After 1990,] reconciliation, domestic unity, and equality of opportunity should have been placed on the foundation of an amnesty for violations related to the country's former division, with the exception of capital crimes and cases in which people were harmed. Instead, the Gordian knot was sundered, and [every East German military officer] from the level of colonel on up was fired. This created a number of personal injustices.[199]

In the *Spiegel* interview, the SPD politician stuck firmly to the line that the early FRG should be treated as a blueprint for the successful treatment of a dictatorial past. He spoke out for a "closure law" that would put an end to the judicial if not the political and historical confrontation with the GDR:

> In the history of the Federal Republic we have had several closure laws regarding the NSDAP. Now we must do it again. We know today that we cannot create a just situation because the justice system is incapable—it is objectively incapable—of achieving justice. In the end, any justice that comes will only be coincidental, and that is terrible.

Bahr called on the new Bundestag to make one of its first acts an amnesty law that would go into effect in October 1995, on the fifth anniversary of German unity. This would grant freedom from culpability to all persons "who did not harm any person, did not commit capital crimes, do not have blood on their hands. Above all, thousands of petty crimes can be laid to rest overnight."[200]

It is impossible to say if Bahr was merely pursuing the tactical aim of breaking resistance to amnesty proposals on the right wing of the CDU-CSU or whether he was convinced of the accuracy of his own historical reminiscences. He conspicuously avoided mentioning another twentieth-century tradition of amnesties, that among Social Democrats, which had mainly (although not exclusively) accrued to the benefit of the political left. The first coalition of the Weimar Republic had issued an amnesty for participants in the 1919 uprising against the Kaiser,[201] but Bahr made no mention of that, or of the 1970 exemption from punishment law adopted by the "social-liberal" government under Brandt. Bahr himself, as a state secretary in the Chancellery in 1970, bore a measure of political responsibility for the latter. His bold comparisons instead seemed to adopt and exaggerate a much older narrative, one deployed by conservatives in the old FRG against the rebellious "1968 generation," in the days when the latter had protested old Nazis in high office.[202] In Bahr's telling, Adenauer's rollback of personnel purges conducted under Allied occupation and the FRG's reintegration of hundreds of thousands of collaborators in the NS regime—which was partly implemented in spite of the Allies—was hypostasized into a foundation myth, into the story of how the FRG had enacted a successful democratic reconstruction while neutralizing radical forces.

Like the other leading Social Democrats of the older generation, Bahr in 1993 and 1994 was of course fully aware that Adenauer's postwar integration policy was not and never could have been the work of a single man. Bahr glossed over the indisputable fact that the leadership of the SPD also supported this policy to some extent at the time, causing great friction within the party. But this found its way into his narrative for amnesty only insofar as he described his new position as the result of a personal conversion. His most disconcerting move, however, was in presenting the 1966–1969 grand coalition government as a further example of "reconciliation," because it featured the partnership at the top of a former NSDAP member (Chancellor Kiesinger) and an opponent of the Nazis who had fled into exile and returned as a remigrant (Vice Chancellor Brandt). The implicit suggestion behind this argument was that victims of the NS regime had a duty, as good citizens, to demonstrate their willingness to make up with the former perpetrators. Bahr's explicitly stated conclusion, however, was that the former GDR civil rights activists who were now opposing amnesty were not acting as good citizens.[203] The East German opposition movement, in Bahr's estimation, had hardly achieved anything—"We have no German Wałesa, and we have no German Havel"—and was therefore now all the more obligated to support the national reconciliation project. Bahr felt the SPD also owed a debt in this regard, attributing the party's defeat—regardless of its improved showing in the eastern German states—to the clumsy rejectionism of GDR civil rights activists like Bärbel Bohley and Stephan Hilsberg.[204]

For all this, Bahr's proposals for amnesty were markedly vague. They largely ignored the legal reality that the statutes of limitations would soon enough put to rest any issue about the majority of less serious injustices. Above all, they were based on the rather doubtful premise that the signs of social disintegration in eastern Germany, which had helped the PDS gain an unexpectedly high increase in votes, were attributable to the trials of the SED cadre. In addition, Bahr's initiative evinced a troubling view of democracy and the role of an opposition. By claiming the prosecutions were endangering the foundations of "domestic unity," and by saying that this unity had to be placed beyond differences of political opinion, he was giving a quasi-sacral meaning to an easily misunderstood phrase. As a term, "amnesty" itself allowed the semantic maneuver of defusing contemporary problems by positioning the "Berlin Republic" within a longer series of "states of exception." Its public invocation in 1994 conveyed the diffuse feeling that the country was once again in the midst of a historical exception that required truces among parties and solutions handed down from above, as though from an authoritarian state. Finally, the concept of amnesty was also a medium for memory culture interventions aimed at papering over the rising conflicts over historical policy among the various forces of the center-to-left camp with a national reconciliation narrative. This also explains why Bahr advocated the anachronistic idea of a "jubilee amnesty," with its roots in a premodern political understanding—a circumstance that before 1989 had been a source of amusement to Western observers who attributed it to the SED.[205]

Despite these rather problematic implications, Bahr's proposals were not met with particularly strong resistance. The following weeks and months saw some hustle and bustle in the highest bodies of his party. By Christmastime, an internal round had been convened at the invitation of the deputy party chief, Wolfgang Thierse, to consult on drafting a law that would grant amnesty for SED perpetrators. The initiative appears to have begun with the independent justice minister of Brandenburg, Hans Otto Bräutigam. The former diplomat and first director of the West German delegation in East Berlin had been appointed to the state cabinet in 1990 by the state's SPD premier, Manfred Stolpe, following controversies over the latter's alleged contacts to the Stasi. Since then, by virtue of his office Bräutigam was responsible for Brandenburg's retention of former GDR judges and prosecutors at a rate higher rate than that of any of the other eastern states.[206] Even before the process of evaluating these rehirings had begun, Bräutigam had signaled that he expected a high rate of retention, justifying it by pointing to the chronic shortage of jurists but also saying that after the era of "serious German division," there was a need for more integration and "as little exclusion as possible."[207] He also proposed that Brandenburg pass its own amnesty for "system-dependent crimes," like election rigging and denunciations, which was seen as a symbolic gesture to the former functional elites. He intended to "make it apparent that even in a system of injustice, loyalty should not be seen as fundamentally condemnable."[208]

As the year turned, even as the SPD continued to deliberate in closed meetings over amnesty for East German system crimes,[209] a more public discussion on the issue broke out. By January, practically every week saw pro and contra columns published in widely distributed press organs. A Berlin legal historian and former member of the Russell-Sartre Tribunal, Uwe Wesel, who had by then argued repeatedly against prosecutions for SED injustice, got the trend going with a column in *Die Zeit* titled "Appeal for a Closure Law." Adopting Bahr's demand for limited exemption from punishment for GDR functionaries, Wesel deployed the same mode of diachronous comparison. He, too, went back to the early FRG and its "131 Law" as a worthy model,[210] in the process mangling the historical facts:

> After many old Nazis were given a rather harsh treatment in the first four years after the war, [Adenauer] turned to integration. The start of a democracy

cannot be burdened with the exclusion of millions of citizens. Adenauer's intent with the implementation law for Article 131 of the Basic Law reflects this. All old Nazis were allowed to return to public service, except those from the Gestapo. . . . The principle was correct. Integration, not exclusion. And success proved Adenauer right. The Federal Republic became a stable democracy, despite former Nazis in the justice system, in the government, and at the universities.[211]

The arbitrariness of Wesel's historical argumentation, which brims with "great men" like Thrasyboulos (who issued the Athenian amnesty of 403 BC) and features its far-seeing helmsman in Adenauer, could not conceal Wesel's main concern: he wanted to put the East German civil rights activists back in their place. Characteristically, he spoke not of law but of "history," and of a metaphysical ideal of mercy derived from history. The victims, he demanded, must also pay their dues for the new start. Already "back then in Athens," the victims were forced to forego "vengeance for the sake of a common future." For the first time in a quarter-century, the FRG was called on once again to put "mercy before justice."[212]

One week later, the journalist Marion Gräfin Dönhoff became the next long-prominent figure to join the amnesty train. In its tendency, her proposal was the most wide-ranging of all. Instead of a partial amnesty, the editor of *Die Zeit* demanded nothing less than a "general amnesty" for SED crimes, one that would exclude only capital crimes like murder, manslaughter, and torture. She found this justified above all because the justice system of unified Germany had so far failed to show that it could process the "acts of an unjust system" using the means of a state under rule of law. While jurists like the Berlin attorney general, Christoph Schaefgen, had argued that failure to investigate SED injustices might have dire future consequences for society as a whole, Dönhoff was not convinced. While she agreed that the West German prosecution of Nazi crimes had been "highly inadequate," her argument was that this had not posed a fundamental obstacle to building a stable democracy.[213]

A committed Liberal, Dönhoff in making her case for amnesty avoided mythologizing the Adenauer-era restoration policy, in contrast to the Social Democratic critics Bahr and Wesel. Instead, she credited the collapse of Communism with revitalizing her understanding of dictatorship. In many ways, however, her new understanding reiterated the popular totalitarianism concept of the 1950s. She referred to the victims of Communist repression as those who were "tortured, outlawed, disenfranchised, and murdered," and spoke of "accomplices," "opportunists," and the "indifferent" among the East German people. Dönhoff accordingly also saw the problem of politically motivated criminality as a dilemma of the "common man." Her prototypical example were the border guards, who in her telling had become culpable only through their "loyalty" to their "socialist fatherland."[214] Her view of GDR state injustice also reflected the political discourses of the 1960s, although these had become increasingly anachronistic starting with the era of détente. It remains an open question whether Dönhoff's approach was meant to compensate for the "perceptual deficit regarding the repressive character of the SED dictatorship" that had been in the pages of *Die Zeit* until the late 1980s.[215]

Undoubtedly, Dönhoff's actual frame of reference for judging developments in the expanded FRG was not the period of the two German states but rather the preceding occupation by the Allies. Her fundamental opposition to any form of judicial treatment (in which she even included the orderly release of the Stasi files) was rooted in the immediate postwar experience. In 1993, during the less-heated debate about the statutes of limitations, Dönhoff had published an inflamed editorial in which she compared the criminal trials of SED functionaries to the Allied postwar trials. The latter had been a "terrifying example" because the Allies had used "special law" against "citizens" who could be accused of nothing worse than "not providing enough resistance." At the postwar trials, she argued, the political leaderships of the Allied powers, none of whom other than the Soviets had experienced what it was like to live under a dictatorship, had raised "heroism to the status of a norm."[216] Instead of the "true oppressors"—the Nazi "Gauleiters, district leaders, and local leaders"—Nuremberg had put "industrialists and high officials of the Foreign Office" in the dock.[217] These trials, which could have "overcome" the NS-era crimes, instead often resulted in "new injustices."[218]

In the late 1940s, a younger Dönhoff had been among the thought leaders in the West German clemency campaigns directed against the Allied High Commission. Her 1994 commentary is illuminating for mirroring the language of this earlier work.[219] She clearly saw parallels between the historic ruptures of 1945 and 1989, and discerned similarities in the governmental reactions. In both cases, she claimed to see an intrusion of the law in the sphere of politics, and a "moralization of history" to the detriment of historical truth.[220] Her harsh criticism of the Nuremberg punitive program, published in 1993, also served to bolster her opposition to a judicial reckoning with the SED functionaries in the present day. She overlooked that forty years later this argument could only sound cynical to those former East Germans who had, in fact, stood against the GDR system. In the new eastern German states, where the former official state antifascism of the GDR was still the glue of a regional identity,[221] her equation of the Communist Party and state functionaries with the defendants at Nuremberg could be understood only as a provocation. Instead of achieving "reconciliation," these misfired comparisons reinforced reservations and resentments against the all-powerful "West." They fomented the suspicion that incorrigible intellectuals of the old West were using the FRG's "first overcoming of the past" as a way to dispense with the problems of both the "second overcoming" after unification—*and* the old trauma of "Nuremberg."

This suspicion did not entirely lack a basis. It could not be seen as coincidence that other persons from the milieu of the 1950s "Nuremberg clemency" lobby began to join the 1990s campaign to grant amnesty to SED system perpetrators. Now retired, the former ministerial councillor Johann-Georg Schätzler showed exceptional engagement on behalf of the Communist functionaries and their helpers. Schätzler had served for years as a prosecutor and judge in West Berlin before he was hired in 1960 by the Ministry of Justice in Bonn, where he worked at the criminal justice department as an expert adviser for clemency questions. Immediately after the war, however, he had been a member of the defense team under Alfred Seidl for Hitler's former deputy, Rudolf Hess, at the International Military Tribunal. In the years that followed, Seidl had maintained relations with two men prominent in the history of West German prosecutions of Nazis: Ernst Achenbach and Hans Gawlik. During his time as the highest-ranking legal official at the West German foreign ministry, Gawlik (see chapter 3) had assured that many men suspected of NS-era crimes escaped the investigators' scrutiny. Achenbach, a former diplomat and a Bundestag member with the FDP after the war, defended many high-ranking NS perpetrators in court. Together with Werner Best (the former second in command to Reinhard Heydrich), Achenbach had coordinated the campaign for a "general amnesty" after the war.

Schätzler had also belonged to an informal association of former Nuremberg defenders who were also ministerial servants in Bonn. As late as the mid-1960s, they were still united by a common plan to protect former SiPo and SD functionaries and Reich military administrators from investigations by French authorities.[222] Unlike Achenbach and others in this circle, however, Schätzler was interested less in protecting perpetrators than in what he saw as the restoration of national legal jurisdiction. Once this goal was met in his eyes, Schätzler helped West German prosecutors with arranging a deal to gain the extradition of the last suspects in France. But the clemency lobby around Achenbach kept up a ferocious resistance and played a role in delaying the extraditions until 1975.[223]

As the writer of a West German handbook for clemency law, Schätzler was conscious of the ambivalent meaning of abolition laws in the workings of a state.[224] Unlike most of the non-jurists supporting an SED amnesty, he realized that amnesty would generally be received by the public as a straightforward "rehabilitation," although in reality it only signified the state's tactical decision to relinquish its power to prosecute. Under what circumstances was an amnesty obviously necessary? What determined the best timing for announcing one? Answering such questions was an "art of state," Schätzler wrote. When in doubt, he advised a country's political leadership to choose "functionality" over "justice," should overarching concerns demand it. During the Cold War, the Adenauer government had also "clearly decided in favor of political functionality. The German people must be united; it cannot be divided. Functionality goes before justice."[225]

Schätzler described the entry of former GDR territories into the FRG as a normal procedure of "state fusion," comparable to the integration of the Saarland in the German Reich in 1935, and again in the FRG after a referendum of 1956.[226] Regarding these two cases, Schätzler attested that both the Nazi leadership and the Adenauer government had been adequate in the "art of state." Both issued amnesties to those who had opposed the German annexation of the province. But the FRG had failed to enact a comparable solution for the case of German unification. In 1989 and 1990, a historic opportunity was missed to agree with the incoming new states on a comprehensive amnesty "for the purpose of legal peace in united Germany."[227] This break with what Schätzler regarded as a proven tradition was mainly because of two factors, he wrote. First, the East German delegation at the unification talks had been full of "Protestant pastors" who had opposed "reconciliation through amnesty," and the West German politicians there had been too "fainthearted" to push the amnesty question forward against the pastors.[228] Since then, West German opinion leaders had acquired a widespread prejudice that now solidified into nothing less than a "reckoning mentality." Those who shared it "want to tell us we must now make up for everything we failed to do during the prosecutorial treatment of the NS past."[229] Schätzler's conclusion? With the entry of the new eastern states, the moral rigor of Protestantism had pushed aside the Catholic tradition of reconciliation. Furthermore, the left was dominating public opinion and the virtues of the old "art of state" were therefore in danger of extinction.

From these crude findings, Schätzler moved on to the question of whether the Nuremberg prosecution program and the West German trials of Nazis could serve as historical models for overcoming the GDR past. Here he argued against comparisons of the two processes following 1945 and 1989. First, the GDR had been responsible for "crimes against humanity, but not for an extermination policy or a genocide," so it was not right to compare the prosecution of SED injustice with the prosecutions of the Nazis.[230] Second, the history of the earlier prosecutions had proved that criminal justice was fundamentally ill-equipped to deal with the overwhelming job of assessing historical conjunctures:

> The clemencies [issued by US High Commissioner for Germany John McCloy] coming just six years after the war prove two things: the impetus to punish

those guilty for the war and its atrocities in the name of justice and human rights had played itself out. The declared war aims of the Allies had been satisfied with the convictions. . . . German criminal justice convicted about six thousand defendants for NS crimes and war crimes by 1958, but just around then began to investigate charges more systematically and thoroughly. That only produced a few hundred additional criminal trials, but these were endless: The Frankfurt Auschwitz trial (twenty defendants) lasted for two years, the Treblinka trial (ten) for one, the Majdanek trial (four) for more than five and a half. These data show how poorly suited German criminal procedures and courts are for dealing with the legacies of an injustice state. At the same time, there was no solution other than orderly trial procedures.[231]

Schätzler's interventions in legal policy pointed to a national particularity of the German debate about a GDR amnesty. While the pronouncements might read as though from the perspective of neutral experts, they were often written from personal experience and on behalf of personal interests. The aim often was to fit the contradictory primary experiences of the postwar period into an overarching narrative guided by vague terms like "inner unity" or "national reconciliation," not unlike the common trope of "*re*unification."[232] The stereotypical references to events like "Nuremberg" and Adenauer's amnesty moves was meant not only to reinforce the claim of expertise in the matter but also to establish conservative, state-authoritarian, and personalistic interpretations of the aftermath of 1945. This framework reduced "Nuremberg" to a historical episode and raised up the West German leniency policies to the status of a medium for the country's cultural self-transformation.

The amnesty supporters' accord around these historically revisionist interpretations took aim above all at the "political-moral overflow" of the 1968 generation, but it also involved a tacit departure from another hegemonic framework, even if none of the participants in this discourse made an explicit issue of it. The styling of the early FRG as a "success story" and the narrative of integration necessarily involved a move away from the patterns and commandments of the Cold War. This related first of all to West German definitions of political crime and the decades-long official practice of employment bans on Communists, which in its time had grown out of a multiparty anti-Communist consensus.[234] Following the West German failure to engage with the demands of the GDR opposition before 1989, the post-unification calls for prosecutions and political purges raised fears among western German elites that the FRG would return to the old repressive structures that had been overcome. These worries were not entirely baseless, but the real need was for an open political debate on how to find an adequate treatment of SED criminality despite the past failure to deal with NS injustice and without allowing a kind of general absolution for the East German dictators and their helpers. The western German amnesty supporters tended to lack an answer for these questions; presumably, they feared playing into the hands of the PDS. Instead, they renovated the barely disputable failures of the old FRG into a new history of political success, in the process making the exculpatory phrases of the Nazi elites once again acceptable in polite society.

By no means did all the leading advocates of amnesty emerge from the Social Democratic camp, nor did they all belong to the earlier 1968ers. Those who were from either group, however, were accused of executing an abrupt historical U-turn in the face of German reunification. Decisively, that accusation came from those who had formed and sharpened their political self-understandings through critical confrontations with the FRG's failures of history policy. Under the provocative headline "1968ers in the Service of Dictators," Falco Werkentin read the riot act to some of his long-term political comrades:

> The effort to squeeze this apologia into legal garb brings with it a sudden new assessment of the treatment of the Nazi legacy. The example of the old Federal Republic is now supposed to demonstrate the impossibility of dealing with the crimes of totalitarian regimes via the means of criminal law; or so have many old comrades preached since 1990. Imperiously, we are advised to be extremely sparing about the use of criminal law. Until 1989–1990, our analysis had always been that too few Nazi perpetrators were held responsible before the law because the old West German society and its legal staff lacked the political will to do it. Now the failure of the old FRG is transformed into an argument for continuing the poor practice of the past. And still that is not enough. Overnight we have discovered the historical wisdom of the Adenauer era, with its consistent integration of party members, profiteers, accomplices, and perpetrators of the Nazi era. This was a contribution toward building a stable democracy in the Federal Republic, Uwe Wesel and Egon Bahr now tell us. They seem to forget, however—and this is hard to believe with a college professor like Uwe Wesel, who always stuck close to my generation albeit as a participant-observer—the *dis*integrating effects of the old FRG policy. It was the reason why so many in my generation came to see in the GDR the "better postwar Germany, because it is more thoroughly antifascist." For a few, this disintegration went so far that they turned to political murder—and finally suicide—hoping that armed struggle would tear the mask off the face of the "prefascist Federal Republic."[235]

The last sentence of the passage referred to the Red Army Fraction and would have required no clarification at the time.

At the turn of 1994 to 1995, support for a limited amnesty surprisingly was expressed by two leading figures of the former GDR civil rights movement and founders in 1990 of Alliance 90 and the New Forum, the first East German parties not approved by the SED. Bärbel Bohley had led the

December 1989 occupation of the Stasi headquarters to prevent the destruction of documents. Joachim Gauck, a former Lutheran pastor, had been appointed as the first federal commissioner for the Stasi records on 4 October 1990, one day after unification (and would eventually be elected president of the Republic in 2012). But Bohley and Gauck distanced themselves from the idea soon after. Mouralis attributes this turnaround to fears among the civil rights activists that they might lose their influence over interpretation of the dictatorship's history. Their party had lost political influence ever since its near wipeout in the first GDR elections of March 1990 and subsequently merged with the West German Greens, who also failed to make the 5 percent cut in the Bundestag elections of December 1990.[236] Presumably, a further concern was that the European Parliament in Strasbourg had taken an interest in the domestic German debate, as was revealed when *Focus* magazine got hold of a draft report being prepared by the parliament's interior committee. The European parliament found that criminal prosecutions of former GDR injustice would be a violation of the "norms and practices of IL" and "discrimination . . . of GDR citizens."[237]

Up to that point, the Kohl government had avoided taking a position on the amnesty issue. Now it made clear that it was strictly against a "general amnesty," because this would rob SED victims of their opportunity to gain their measure of justice. At the same time, the chancellor indicated that he could envision excluding GDR misdemeanors from prosecution in the future.[238] The debate would continue for several months, but it was clear that the SPD's intervention on legal policy had failed. It resulted in a lasting and deep alienation between the SPD and the former East German dissidents, not so much because of the debate itself but because of the historical understanding that it had expressed. Gauck brought it to a point with his observation that the West German left continued to suffer from historical blind spots:

> A self-enlightened anti-Communism continues to be unacceptable for many intellectuals, although in concrete historical situations it should have been a sibling to antifascism—an appeal for universal freedom and human rights. Instead, there was a substantial measure of refusal to show solidarity with those who rebelled within Socialism. That would have disturbed the well-cultivated dialogue of the West with the old ruling elites of the East. In the absence of a serious self-correction, this attitude will remain (not only the east, the west also must rethink!). Today more understanding and indulgence is displayed for the psyches and interests of the former privileged strata than for the mass of those who were once oppressed. In the amnesty debate, Uwe Wesel demanded that the victims show a readiness for reconciliation, before any of the perpetrators had so much as signaled a recognition of their guilt or a willingness to accept responsibility.[239]

Conclusion

With the election victory of the Alliance for Germany pro-unification party in the GDR's first democratic elections of March 1990, no one was left to deny that the days of the East German partial state were numbered. Among countless other issues, this made immanent the problem of how to treat the fallen dictatorship's past. Despite many differences about the details, the negotiators from both East and West quickly agreed on one point: there would be no general amnesty for GDR system crimes. An ambitious decision was made, not only to continue the prosecutions against SED functionaries and GDR officials that had already begun in East German courts in December 1989, but to greatly expand these. The many motives involved in this related to the history of the German division into two states, the particularities of the ideological system conflict, and the processes of rupture underway in 1989 and 1990.

The East German civil rights activists who had helped lead the movement for change hoped mainly to gain some measure of satisfaction for the victims of SED injustice and to avoid a premature "lazy peace" with the perpetrators. The West German side acted in the belief that their country had "failed" in its treatment of the Nazi past. Elites in politics and the justice system almost universally shared the belief that the punishment of the Nazis had been "too late" and "too half-hearted," leading to the conclusion that it was now urgent to prosecute GDR state criminality systematically and decisively. In their search for a responsible treatment of the dictatorship's legacy, decision-makers on both sides at first concentrated almost entirely on national-historical or German-German connections. Above all, the political class of the "old" FRG took it as practically self-evident that the negative experience of a largely "suppressed" Nazi past entailed a kind of historic obligation to devote themselves to a judicial reckoning with the SED dictatorship.

These priorities in the German discourse were the result of a decades-long process of critical self-reflection on the aftereffects of the Third Reich. But they also reflected a particular sense for the politics of the past that had already developed in West Germany during the immediate postwar period. As a kind of defensive reflex, prompted above all by the punitive programs of the US occupation authorities and the Nuremberg follow-up trials, West German elites came to see domestic control over NS crime prosecutions and the "making good again" policy (*Wiedergutmachung*, i.e., restitutions and reparations) as essentials of national "honor." The resulting and persistent tension between the reality of national self-absorption and the ideal self-image of postnationality would also shape the FRG's treatment of the GDR's past. It is notable that the possibility of an international law approach never once entered internal discussions of the matter, although it was during this same period that the foreign minister, Hans-Dietrich Genscher, lobbied the United Nations to demand an international tribunal against the Iraqi dictator Saddam Hussein.

Similarly notable is the role representatives of reunified Germany assumed in the field of Transitional Justice. Originating during the political upheaval processes of Central and South America in the late 1970s, "transitology" grew within a few years into a highly attractive research field, in no small part thanks to generous help from American third-sector funders such as the Ford Foundation. Its rapid rise and worldwide spread also rested on the catchall appeal[240] of combining human rights activism with scientific political consulting. Transitology stood in the American tradition of democracy research, upholding the normative-programmatic ambition not just to analyze processes of rupture but also to actively shape them. Based on a democracy concept that stressed the strategic role of experts and state elites, transitology especially in its early years strongly emphasized legal forms of "processing the past." Other than the punishment of actionable violations, this was supposed to cover every form of judicial or administrative process that aimed at compensating victims and returning confiscated property after a system change. With the development of a comparative research design, the creation of a set of instruments (criminal trials, truth commissions) and the formation of a specialized jargon (repurposing truth, reconciliation, and justice), transitology also influenced the discourse in the post-Communist states of eastern and central Europe. This development was reinforced by the professionalization wave that followed the collapse of Soviet Communism.

Many West German experts were also involved in these developments. Among those who participated in planning and speaking at international conferences were politicians like Kurt Biedenkopf, members of the GDR civil rights scene like Joachim Gauck, the former chief justice of the Constitutional Court, Helmut Steinberger, and a series of renowned social scientists including Jürgen Habermas, Ralf Dahrendorf, and Claus Offe. But others active in the transitology communications networks also represented the German "case," such as John H. Herz. Originally from Dusseldorf, the political scientist and leading international relations theorist in a sense embodied the still nascent discipline's claim of translating the "lessons" of the German reconstruction under US occupation rule to the situation in the post-Communist states. In the early stages, texts by Karl Jaspers and Otto Kirchheimer were also received with great interest in the community. These gatherings of the pioneers made for a unique forum in which representatives of the former occupation government, East German opposition leaders, and West German democracy researchers engaged in exchanges on the problems of "processing" the experience of a dictatorship.

Seen from the outside, the efforts of unified Germany to deal with the GDR past appeared to be a "transition under laboratory conditions," as György Bence would put it. At least during the early 1990s, however, the ongoing international debates about the new Germany transpired almost completely without a critical reception in the reunified country itself. While little direct reference to transitology can be found, its standards and categories did permeate into the German discourse. This can be seen, for example, in how the German criminal justice system felt the pressure of high expectations regarding its treatment of SED system injustice. The demand not merely to mete out justice but to speak historical "truth" through rulings was manifest, for example, in an extraordinary appeal by Minister of Justice Kinkel to the conference of German judges. By the mid-1990s, it was also evident in the lively debates about a limited amnesty for GDR crimes. The amnesty debate rested on a schematic opposition of "justice" against "reconciliation," a dichotomy typical of the judicially flavored discourses of transitology during the 1990s.

In the final analysis, the persistent criticism of the meager results of the prosecutions and trials prompted the political public to take an interest in other forms of processing the past. Here too it was notable that the immediate resort was to a format that at least superficially resembled the truth commissions in Latin America and South Africa. The self-definition of the two Enquete Commissions of the German Bundestag was based on the idea that "processing" should investigate the repressive structures of the SED dictatorship above all to benefit its "victims." In practice, this promise proved hard to fulfill. The rhetorical invocation of the victims in the end served mainly to package a relatively conventional history of power politics in the GDR as a foil demonstrating the "success story" of the FRG. It was thus symptomatic of the German situation after 1989 and 1990 that certain outward forms of transitology were adopted but that their utopian and emancipatory roots were forgotten in the treatment of the GDR past.

Final Reflections

～⊙•⊙～

"We are all Germans now." The American sociologist John Torpey's not entirely ironic bon mot captures a perspective on the "extreme twentieth century" as seen at the turn of the twenty-first. Common among exponents of the young research field of transitional justice, this view employs a specific model of state violence. More than any other country, Germany once represented the new and exceptional forms of state-orchestrated violence that engulfed the European continent during the first half of the twentieth century. The country's name alone tended to invoke the mass murder of the European Jews by the National Socialist regime, a crime combining conventional means of killing with an industrial division of labor. The German state's violent tendencies were considered so exceptional that its acts over the course of the twentieth century prompted their criminalization under international law. Interstate wars of aggression and a series of racially motivated practices targeting foreign civilians and prisoners of war were declared illegal because of these acts. In the liberal and often Eurocentric worldview of "transitology," the Germany from 1914 to 1945 in some sense represented the paradigmatic incarnation of a modern "rogue state."

By the end of the century, this could be counterposed to a different image, one no less selective and broad-brush in its omissions and exaggerations. TJ scholars classified the postwar history of (West) Germany as the exemplary case for the successful application of the field's methods and standards. Models worthy of emulation were identified in the Nuremberg trials, in the de-Nazification programs of the Western occupation zones, in the later West

German national prosecutions as supported by the Ludwigsburg agency, in the FRG's policies of reparations for and reconciliation with Israel, and in a memory culture focused on the Holocaust. All of these were elevated retrospectively as exemplary instruments—textbook cases of transitional justice as a progressive, teleological trinity: democracy, predictable rule of law, an enlightened memory culture. To this series of achievements, some representatives of Anglo-American democratization research also added the FRG's reckoning with East German Communism via prosecutions and history politics. Of course, more than a few critics saw the latter as little more than a continuation of the Cold War by other means.

Critics on various sides have pointed out the narrow perspective and omissions of this liberal metanarrative, especially to the extent that the German experience was presented as the model for a new, integrated Europe. The projection back on the early postwar era of the values, norms, and practices of post-1989 transitology smacks of an inadmissible anachronism. In the years after World War II, the Western allies were less concerned about the murder of the Jews and the biologistic ethnopolitics of the NS regime than is today commonly assumed. The advancement of Geneva and Hague human rights law proceeded only imperfectly and in fits and starts. The idea that the victorious powers at Nuremberg had for the first time laid down the foundations for a system to restrain state violence and support human rights is based on an essentialist understanding of the law. It reflects the historical reality far less than the ahistorical self-image of a younger generation of international law experts and professional human rights activists, who are so committed to inheriting a juridical tradition of liberal internationalism for themselves that they will invent it if necessary. Given that the ambitious political and institutional demands of the juridical interventionists of the 1990s were often met with weak democratic support, it is not surprising that they sought to draw additional legitimation from history. Especially in the neoliberal version of TJ research, the misinterpretation of the IMT as a "Holocaust trial" may seem attractive precisely because the paradoxical combination of the trial's imperfect legal basis with its morally justified and globally accepted verdicts seem to raise it above history.

The longitudinal history presented in this book has revealed many reasons why the "German case" is mostly unsuitable as a building block in constructing the tradition for a new international criminal law animated by human rights ideals.[1] One of the main findings of this study has been that such ambitious claims for the German case float only at the cost of thorough historical decontextualization. The German rapprochement with the discourse of humanitarian law at best can be described as a long-term process, one with many breaks and false starts. If the entire period since the late 1940s is considered, the German encounter with international law and human rights concepts has been ambivalent and tense. A cautious opening took place only over the course of more than four decades, and even then was established only in a context that was shaped by postnational tendencies and the emergence of an international community of remembrance.

For the same reasons, the postwar history of West Germany is of limited use in current debates among political and legal scholars about how to persuade states to follow universalist rules and norms.[2] During the entire period studied here, it is clear that human rights thinking was peripheral to German state policy on German state crimes (although the same state invoked human rights in regard to Soviet, Polish, and Czechoslovakian expulsions of German populations). Instead of engaging in the international debate about how to limit belligerence and genocide through international law, the relevant German institutions and actors for decades invested their efforts in limiting or blocking interference from "outsiders," whether these were defined as the international community, other states, or the victims of historic German state violence. As shown in chapter 3, the question remains to what extent this vehement defensive posture may have also impelled a dialectic by which Germany eventually adopted and adapted itself to human rights thinking.

Despite these difficulties, the categories of transitology are useful as heuristic instruments that can help us better understand the history of transnational responses to German state violence, as the above research work has also revealed. Although the various situations and contexts presented in this book are separated by time, if a single arc connects them it is this: the institution of humanitarian international law, juridical understandings of public history, and the human rights politics of state and nonstate actors always came into relation with each other. But they did so in different ways in each period. This is unlike the normative premises of transitions research, which often assume that these three factors collaborate in harmony or else that they must compete with each other for territory. The actual constellations in each period prove to be far more complex and tense than any simple model can describe. The encounters between various cultures of knowledge, expert discourses, and styles of thinking created unexpected frictions and sustained extended political and social confrontations in each case. Contemporary discussions not only were typified by interpretative struggles over the question of what constituted legitimate or illegitimate state violence, but also usually involved conflicting historical interpretations and moral-political valuations.

This study has shown how the controversies over specific forms of violence were often defined by a focus on exemplary cases or on highly particular "sets of facts." Selective approaches were necessitated by juridical logic and the specific legal interests of given actors. At the same time, many participants intentionally engaged and implemented public relations strategies. The juridification of historical processes often served an agenda-setting function or was intended to mobilize the collective moral feelings of both actual and imagined publics. By the early twentieth century forward, politicians, scholars, and activists were all prepared to appeal to the court of public opinion and were aware of its importance. In World War I, the early debate on German war crimes and German war guilt gave rise to a plethora of official, semiofficial, and private institutions ready to place their juridical-historical research works in the service of decidedly moral-political aims. The various commissions and investigative committees understood that their purpose was in part to convert historical narratives into proofs of juridical truths by discursive-performative means and thus to achieve moral clarity on behalf of a cause. Through public debates and juridical forums, historical evidence was structured to satisfy the public demand for recognizable dramaturgy with identifiable actors and tangible acts.

If one considers the example of the early Weimar Republic, the institutions of official and semiofficial history management were already up and running well before the Allies had even made any concrete proposals for the peace. It is probably impossible at this point to establish clearly whether the wave was set off by the USPD politicians' leaks and demands for punishment or by fears that the Treaty of Versailles would include a guilt clause. While Allied discussions at first focused on "German atrocities," the German debate was almost entirely fixated on the issue of real or presumed German "war guilt." Leftists and the national-conservative officials at the imperial ministries both took an early interest in the causes of the war's outbreak. An important difference between these two political camps was that the latter projected the "prewar" phase all the way back to the 1870s. This historiographic operation was in part intended to assure that the files from the 1914 July Crisis, overall more compromising than not, would not serve as the basis for indictments. It was also an attempt to gain precious time in the hope of eventually launching a historical-political and legal counteroffensive.

Although the pacifist voices were many in the defeated German empire immediately after the war's end, and there was even a measure of popular sympathy for the prosecutorial aims of the USPD, the framing of the problem by the foreign and war ministries soon assured that the question of war crimes came to be seen solely as an expression of the Allied "guilt dictate." A broad resistance within civil society thus was roused not against the official legend of innocence but against the Entente powers' demanded extradition of 850 to 1,500 German war criminals. In summary, the conclusion cannot be avoided that by debating the war, its history, and human rights, the Allies had opened a transnational sphere of communication that within Germany was successfully dominated and exploited by the old imperial elites. Presumably, the ministerial bureaucrats would not have been as successful if so many prestigious liberal academics had not thrown their full support behind the

German countercampaign. The prominent men who came together as the Heidelberg Association to call for a "politics of the law" were correct when they claimed that there was no international law precedent for the planned combination of a peace treaty with a retroactive punishment of the war enemy. At the same time, they relied on a concept of historical-truth discovery that came at the cost of preventing a legal assessment. They danced around a position that was tantamount to a negation of international law.[3]

The debate on German violations of international law in World War II started at a relatively much later point than it had in World War I. This can partly be understood as a belated effect of the earlier Allied failure. It also helps explain why the debate at first was conducted mostly as an academic discourse within an international scientific community, while government officials were conspicuous in their absence. Researchers continue to debate how much influence to attribute to the relatively unmediated human rights rhetoric delivered by President Franklin D. Roosevelt in the months after the German invasion of the Soviet Union. But it is safe to assume it did influence perceptions of German crimes of violence. It was impossible to ignore Roosevelt's explicit rehabilitation of the Treaty of Versailles provisions as declared to Congress: "We should remember that the peace of 1919 was far less unjust than that kind of pacification [of Germany by the later Allies] which began even before Munich." He also upheld human rights as a guiding principle for a future moral world order.

Regardless of these official statements, international law debates seldom made direct references to the human rights ideal. However, this did not mean that the judicial experts were not inclined to go beyond the traditional limits of international law and to arrive at innovative solutions for punishing the mass crimes of the NS regime. Given the Nazi leadership's efforts to conceal the wide-ranging aims of their ideologically driven war of destruction from the international public, it is extraordinary in hindsight how many academics were already aware, during the war, that a large part of the German acts of violence in Eastern Europe were not directly related to war needs. The mounting recognition that an unprecedented form of state-orchestrated mass violence was being carried out apparently also helped spark the efforts to conceptualize the debate, beginning above all among Jewish international lawyers who had emigrated from the European continent.

Despite all their theoretical and methodological differences, the writings of the international lawyer Raphael Lemkin, the New York IJA director Jacob Robinson, and the German social scientists working for the OSS displayed several common features. Generally, it can be said that each of these authors' professional specializations and legal-policy aims were reflected in their respective analyses of the NS system of rule. They each sought to construct empirical models of the German Reich's ruling intentions and techniques of persecution. In each case, their attempts at historical classification and assessment of the Reich's wartime occupation practices were influenced by a state-centered perspective and a forensic approach. Each tended to proceed from the premise that the old institution of the European nation-state was in "crisis." Each saw its progressive erosion since the turn of the century as having created a vacuum that allowed the intrusion of the NS system with its hostility to the state. With their scientific findings that this was a "non-state" under a "non-law," these analyses were quite early in discovering a way to justify the punishment of German functionaries despite the principle of state immunity. Although the German leftist intellectuals who had left the New York Institute for Social Research for the OSS initially distanced themselves from that aim, their work on the regime's sociology of power paradoxically provided an important basis for the later indictments at Nuremberg.

Among the many innovations introduced to international law by the Nuremberg prosecution was its combination of an experiment in "didactic legality" (Lawrence Douglas) with a sophisticated agenda of "history politics." Today the literature is still far from identifying all the various concepts and influences on which the participants as individuals may have drawn. The case of the German international law expert Hermann Jahrreiß (chapter 2) serves to show the insights that can be gained by more closely examining the growth of historical tropes in the hothouse of the Nuremberg trials. Next to the defendants themselves, their lawyers were in the best position to influence the production and communication of historical models through their choice of defense strategy. The example of the Cologne legal scholar Jahrreiß shows that the historicizing approach of the Allied prosecutors prompted unintended dialectical effects. Compromised German functionaries were able to access an arena for self-presentation that was respectable and prestigious in the eyes of the international public. Having shown an ever-willing readiness to conform to the Third Reich's conditions, the exponents of German international legal scholarship had experienced international isolation and a loss of academic autonomy. The trial gave them the chance to portray the problematic role of their profession as the consequence of the Allies' contradictory international law policy since World War I. In the Allied charges against the defendants, they discovered a starting point for creating new metanarratives of German national history. They proved willing to adopt the prosecution's idea of a "Führer principle" so that they could reinterpret it, through an equally deterministic and simplified totalitarianism theory, into an image of active, top-down oppression against a passive following. In other words, Nuremberg became the stage for the discursive and performative formation of a new German "community of destiny and victimhood." Not coincidentally, this topos maintained undertones of hostility to international law that echoed the "war innocence" debate of 1918–1919.

The ambivalence of the Nuremberg program's signals regarding history politics became evident by the late 1940s. As (West) Germans gradually acquired sovereignty over the prosecutorial enterprise, they increasingly moved toward wrapping up the criminal trials while also trying to scrub the memory culture of their effects. In portraying the history of NS-era crime, criminal justice agencies and professional historiography alike began to follow the same guidelines that the government and justice agencies had taken in regard to the Nuremberg legacy: NS mass crimes were considered punishable only in those cases wherein prior German criminal law would have also applied. In the new field of contemporary history, the view predominated that a deeper understanding of the Third Reich could come only from those who formerly witnessed it as members of the "people's community."

This front against the Nuremberg program later meant that the FRG would enter the European Convention on Human Rights only given the caveat that it would not be required to enforce retroactive criminal law, even in the case of serious crimes of state. It therefore comes as a paradox that, with American human rights idealism already past its zenith, the German government in Bonn began to show interest in joining the Genocide Convention. One factor behind the FRG's entry to the convention in 1953 was that West German international law experts had already developed an ethnicizing discourse of human rights, one that presented Germans as the victims of a contradictory "Western" idea of human rights. This discourse suggested the German people were both the actual inventors of the human rights idea and the primary victims of state human rights violations in the twentieth century. A key role in creating a West German consensus on the Genocide Convention was played by the Jewish Polish international law scholar Raphael Lemkin, who led efforts at gaining ratification from New York. By persuading his West German interlocutors that the convention could serve as a robust legal instrument against Communist crimes of expulsion, he inspired false expectations about its true real-world applicability among the German expellee associations.

Following a latency phase of several years, the country's growing international involvements and an increased sensibility for moral-political matters contributed toward formation of a West German culture of "overcoming the past" in regard to NS mass crimes. As this encroached on sensitive domestic as well as foreign issues, however, the responsible politicians found it advisable to put the resumption of NS crime investigations in the charge of newly created independent justice and police structures, such as the Ludwigsburg agency. The West German Holocaust trials of the 1950s and 1960s characteristically strove to avoid direct or even indirect reference to humanitarian international law, or to human rights in general. The murder of the European Jews was generally pressed into a narrow interpretative frame, although the special prosecutors tended to have far better knowledge of the reality. The wartime shift to systematic mass killings was attributed to a secret central order to kill that was executed within a highly limited circle of perpetrators. This intentionalist interpretation, which rested on testimonies from defendants and perpetrators at the Nuremberg trials, entered into the West German criminal court rulings of the late 1950s through the back door of historians' expert witness briefs.

Contemporary history and criminal justice continued to mutually reinforce a limited view of the murderous reality into the 1960s, as the West German reaction to the Eichmann trial made clear. Despite a few dissonant voices, this event caused no change of course in West German prosecution policy or in the FRG's treatment of so-called ideological perpetrators. On the contrary, the leveling historical perspective of the Israeli prosecutors only reinforced the West German prosecutors' identification with their own strategy of pursuing "on the spot" perpetrators exclusively and of placing the criminal acts of individuals in the broadest possible historical context. In legitimating this selective approach to a still largely skeptical West German public, resort was made to a vulgarized functionalist view of the perpetrators. This drew on the original analyses of fascism among the exile scholars and was popularized in the course of the "Einsatzgruppen trial" (Case 9 in the Nuremberg follow-up trials) by the US judge, Michael Musmanno. The exonerating image of the perpetrator—for example, of Eichmann as a pale gray bureaucrat and pedantic administrative specialist—did not prevail in West Germany because of Hannah Arendt's report but had arisen earlier from the interaction between juridical "processing" strategies and mass media representations of the murder of the Jews. Long before the Eichmann trial, a kind of division of labor on this question had formed between West German historians and the criminal justice system. This was self-evidently among the reasons that Arendt's thesis of the "banality of evil" and Raul Hilberg's comprehensive history of the annihilation were both conspicuously ignored in West German contemporary history research.

Compared with the immediate postwar era, the controversies about state crimes under the GDR took place in a very different political and cultural environment. The victims had a strong public presence, the justice system was much more self-assured, and the international climate was much more friendly to human rights. With the rise of a "cosmopolitan" remembrance of the Holocaust (in the words of Daniel Levy and Natan Sznaider) and the emergence of transitional justice, public awareness for the domestic repercussions of state violence had developed in most Western countries. A series of West German experts had participated enthusiastically in TJ's conceptualization. But in dealing with SED crimes, the unified FRG initially avoided any linkage to the international discourses. Prosecutions of Communist state crimes tended to follow along the same lines laid down by West German case law long before 1989. And at least for the first couple of years of the "Berlin Republic," historical processing of the GDR's dictatorial past remained the domain of the juridical experts.

As the limits of this approach became increasingly clear, the government turned to instruments other than criminal trials. On the surface, the Enquete Commissions called forth by the German Bundestag in 1992 and 1995 were based on the models of the Latin American and South African truth commissions. The 1992 commission especially sought legitimation for its activity through rhetorical references to the victims of Communist rule. This reflected the increased influence of international processing models and a human rights discourse that had taken to postulating a supranational "duty to the truth."[4] Against the original ambition of writing an inclusive as well as victim-centered German-German history of the entire postwar era, the final report presented a rather conventional political history, reading the GDR as an "SED state." In the style of West German scholarship on Communism during the Cold War, the report catalogued the differences between East German dictatorship and West German democracy, claiming legitimacy for one and illegitimacy for the other. The history of the "old" FRG was covered only as the positive foil for the negative depiction of the GDR.

The tendency to use juridical and historical debates over East German history to reinforce the idea of West German development as a history of success was also expressed in the 1994–1995 amnesty controversy. On the left-liberal side of the political spectrum, the terms and categories of transitology were mustered in part to recapitulate the 1980s debates about West Germany's "self-assurance" in the world. Amnesty supporters employed almost premodern concepts of amnesty in evoking the supposed "state of emergency" under the GDR. They also linked amnesty demands to an affirmative view of the early West German policy of amnesty and integration for NS-era actors, even reducing the Nuremberg trials to a mere episode: a failed sociopolitical experiment. This approach both threatened the moral-political antifascist consensus of the 1968 generation and ignored the strong turn back to human rights that had occurred in the meantime. Just as the unified FRG in defining its foreign policy was looking to engage more vigorously in international discourses on humanitarian law, the domestic debate about how to deal with SED injustices paradoxically adopted a hermeneutic, national-historical perspective in which, furthermore, the traditional lines of left and right began to lose salience.

Assuming a perspective that accepts the partly fictitious separation between German and non-German actors, much of the transnational debate on German state violence feels like the proverbial "speeches among the mute." Humanitarian international law attempts the innovation of interweaving state crimes with individual culpability, as well as of linking these to a specific historical interpretation of the state crimes. In Germany, this has usually prompted rejection and defensiveness, which reflects a long tradition of skepticism about the universalist claims of international law and human rights. But it also manifests the long-term effects of the national-history culture that predominated starting in the nineteenth century and went without major challenge before the 1960s: a culture defined by historicism, by the theorem of a German "special path," and by a traditional, state-centered understanding of political historiography. It should be noted, however, that the German view on the violence question was never as uniform as politicians, the media, and scholars generally claimed, and the turn away from the international legalism of the early postwar years was hardly limited to the FRG.[5]

While the coordinates of international politics have shifted fundamentally and though contexts may differ radically, many of the same problems remain that have always accompanied the idea of establishing an international-law regime grounded in human rights. One indicator for the changing power relations since the end of the bipolar world order is apparent in the FRG's adoption of the permanent International Criminal Court (ICC) as its own trademark cause. In the late 1990s, the German delegation at the UN Preparatory Committee talks in Rome, where the ICC statute was drafted, joined other "middling" powers like Canada, Argentina, and Australia in demanding that the new court not be placed under the authority of the UN Security Council. At home, this stance had the support of international law scholars, most of whom by then were strong advocates of human rights regimes, and by a veritable army of human rights activists.[6] Top diplomat Hans-Peter Kaul, at the time leading the German delegation in Rome on behalf of the Kohl government, would later look back and uphold this position as the result of a "cosmopolitan" learning process that grew out of Germany's history of violence in the twentieth century. Given a special "German guilt" for unprecedented international crimes, united Germany had a "historical obligation" to advocate for the establishment of the ICC.

However, this did not mean that the reservations characterizing the "old" FRG's forty-odd years of international law discourse had all been swept away. Soon enough, German foreign and security policymakers were preparing the country's first foreign military deployment since World War II, in former Yugoslavia, and this raised the prospect that one day German soldiers or government officials might themselves once again have to answer before a supranational court. The "idealistic" paradigm shift in German international law policy, though energetically pursued by Kaul and several other liberal legal experts, became possible only after the defense ministry was satisfied that enough precautions had been taken to assure the country would never have to extradite a German citizen to the ICC in The Hague. The first barrier to such an eventuality was included in the act on international law passed by the German Bundestag in 2002. The second was worked into the ICC statute itself, which defined war crimes far more restrictively than the standard of "criminal offenses" given in the 1977 additional protocols to the Geneva Convention.[8] After Germany underwent a relatively abrupt "transformation from the object to the subject of international criminal justice"[9] at the end of the twentieth century, the political influence thus gained on the international stage was used to cast US human rights and international law policy—traditionally more idealistic—in the role of an outsider and "blocker," even as Germany insured itself against the eventuality of future war crimes charges under international law. Yet another remarkable moment in the long German journey "from The Hague to The Hague" that calls for more research in the future, when the time comes again to reexamine the breaks and continuities of the twentieth century.

ABBREVIATIONS

AA	Auswärtiges Amt (Foreign Office), German foreign ministry
AJC	American Jewish Congress
ANC	African National Congress
BArch	Bundesarchiv (FRG Federal Archives)
BfV	Bundesamt für Verfassungsschutz (Federal Office for the Protection of the Constitution), FRG domestic security agency
BGBl	*Bundesgesetzblatt (Federal Law Gazette)*
BGH	Bundesgerichtshof (FRG Court of Justice)
BKA	Bundeskriminalamt (FRG Criminal Police Office), Bonn
BMJ	Bundesministerium der Justiz (FRG Ministry of Justice)
BND	Bundesnachrichtendienst (FRG Intelligence Service)
BNV	Bund Neues Vaterland (New Fatherland Alliance)
BP	Bayernpartei (Bavarian Party), post–World War II era
BPA	Bundespresseamt (Federal Press Office)
BT	Bundestag (Parliament of the FRG)
CAD	Civil Affairs Division, US Department of War
CCL	Control Council Law (joint Allied occupation forces in Germany)
CDU	Christlich-Demokratische Union (Christian Democratic Union)
CPSU	Communist Party of the Soviet Union
CSCE	Conference on Security and Co-operation in Europe
CSSF	Charter 77 Foundation, Czechoslovakia
CSU	Christlich-Soziale Union (Christian Social Union), Bavarian sister party of the CDU
DASR	Akademie für Deutsches Recht (Academy for German Law)
DDP	Deutsche Demokratische Partei (German Democratic Party), Weimar era
DFG	Deutsche Forschungsgemeinschaft (German Research Foundation)

DHfP	Deutsche Hochschule für Politik (German Academy for Politics)
DNVP	Deutschnationale Volkspartei (German National People's Party), Weimar era
DP	Deutsche Partei (German Party), post–World War II era
ECHR	European Convention of Human Rights
EU	European Union
FBI	Federal Bureau of Investigation
FDP	Freie Demokratische Partei (Free Democratic Party), post–World War II era
FRG	Federal Republic of Germany, West Germany (Bundesrepublik Deutschland)
FZ	*Frankfurter Zeitung*
GDR	German Democratic Republic, East Germany (Deutsche Demokratische Republik)
GG	Grundgesetz (Basic Law), FRG constitution
GONGO	government-organized nongovernmental organization
HStA	Hauptstaatsarchiv (FRG Main State Archives)
IACHR	Inter-American Commission on Human Rights
ICC	International Criminal Court
ICRC	International Committee of the Red Cross
IDASA	Institute for a Democratic Alternative for South Africa
IfZ	Institut für Zeitgeschichte (Institute of Contemporary History)
IJA	Institute of Jewish Affairs
IL	International Law (referring to the discipline)
ILC	International Law Commission
IM	Inoffizielle Mitarbeiter ("unofficial employee" of the Stasi)
IMT	International Military Tribunal
KPD	Kommunistische Partei Deutschlands (Communist Party of Germany)
LJV	Landesjustizverwaltung (State Justice Agency)
MfS	Ministerium für Staatssicherheit, "the Stasi" (GDR Ministry for State Security)
MSPD	Majority Social Democratic Party of Germany, World War I and post–World War I-era
MWG	*Max-Weber-Gesamtausgabe*, collected works of Max Weber in original German
NGO	nongovernmental organization
NS	National Socialist
NSDAP	National Socialist German Workers' Party

NSG	"National Socialist Crimes of Violence," an official category under West German law
NVA	Nationale Volksarmee (GDR National People's Army)
NYPL	New York Public Library
OAS	Organization of American States
OCCWC	(US) Office of the Chief of Counsel for War Crimes
OGHBZ	Oberster Gerichtshof für die britische Zone (Supreme Court for the British Zone)
OKW	Oberkommando der Wehrmacht (High Command of the Armed Forces, NS-era)
OSS	Office of Strategic Services
OStA	Oberstaatsanwalt (attorney general)
PAAA	Politisches Archiv des Auswärtigen Amtes (Political Archive of the Foreign Office)
PDS	Partei des Demokratischen Sozialismus (Party of Democratic Socialism), post-1989 era
QUANGO	quasi-autonomous nongovernmental organization
R&A	Research and Analysis Branch, Central European Division, OSS
RSHA	Reichssicherheitshauptamt (Reich Main Security Office)
SA	Sturmabteilung (Storm Division)
SBZ	Sowjetische Besatzungszone (Soviet Occupation Zone)
SD	Sicherheitsdienst des Reichsführers-SS (Security Service of the Reich Führer of the SS)
SED	Sozialistische Einheitspartei Deutschlands (Socialist Unity Party of Germany)
SiPo	Sicherheitspolizei (Security Police), NS era
SPD	Social Democratic Party of Germany
SS	Schutzstaffel der NSDAP (Security Echelon of the NSDAP)
Stasi	Ministerium für Staatssicherheit (GDR Ministry for State Security)
TJ	Transitional Justice (referring to the discipline)
TRC	Truth and Reconciliation Commission
TTP	Telford Taylor Papers
UN	United Nations
UNO	United Nations Organization
UNWCC	United Nations Commission for the Investigation of War Crimes
USPD	Unabhängige Sozialdemokratische Partei Deutschlands (Independent Social Democratic Party of Germany), World War I and post–World War I-era
USSR	Union of Soviet Socialist Republics

WJC	World Jewish Congress
ZRS	Zentrale Rechtsschutzstelle (Central Office for Legal Protection), post–World War II era
ZSL	Zentrale Stelle der Landesjustizverwaltungen zur Aufklärung nationalsozialistischer Verbrechen (Central Office of the State Justice Administrations for the Investigation of National Socialist Crimes (Ludwigsburg), aka Ludwigsburg Office)

Select Chronology

The "Long Nineteenth Century": A term of art in historiography that covers the period from the upheavals of the American and French revolutions to the outbreak of World War I. By convention, this is dated from 1789 to 1914.

The "Short Twentieth Century": Coined by the historian Eric Hobsbawm to refer to the period from the Russian Revolution to the end of the Cold War (1917–1991), as marked by the grand state-ideological competition among liberalism, communism, and fascism.

The "Long Twentieth Century": A period from the mid-to-late nineteenth century until recent times, shaped by economic and sociopolitical modernization and characterized among many other factors by the generally rising hegemony of liberal ideas and systems and by the development of modern international legal thinking and humanitarian law.

1864	Establishment of the International Committee for Relief to the Wounded, later the International Committee of the Red Cross (ICRC); negotiations of the first Geneva Conventions "for the Amelioration of the Condition of the Wounded in Armies in the Field."
1873	Foundation of Institut de Droit International (Institute for International Law) in the town hall of Ghent, Belgium.
1899	First Hague Conference of major powers negotiates the Hague Conventions (I–IV).
1907	Second Hague Conference negotiates additional Hague provisions including confirmation and revision of Convention IV, "respecting the Laws and Customs of War on Land."
1914	The July Crisis leads to the outbreak of World War I between the Central Powers and the Entente Powers in August; military forces of imperial Germany invade neutral Belgium and Luxembourg, prompting a British declaration of war.

1918	9–11 November: The imperial German government collapses in the face of widespread mutiny as Kaiser Wilhelm II is forced to flee to Holland; a German republic is declared and the Council of People's Deputies assumes power in Berlin as its first provisional government. 11 November: Signing of armistice ends fighting in World War I.
1919	19 January: Elections to the first National Assembly in Germany; start of the Weimar Republic. 28 June: Signing of the Treaty of Versailles.
1928	27 August: Germany, France, and the United States are the first of many states to sign the "Kellogg-Briand Pact," the General Treaty for Renunciation of War as an Instrument of National Policy.
1929	27 July: Second Geneva Convention "relative to the Treatment of Prisoners of War."
1933	In the months after Adolf Hitler is appointed chancellor of Germany in January, forces of the National Socialists conduct a rapid seizure of state and societal power and establish what will come to be known as the Third Reich.
1939	August: NS state initiates quasi-secret medical murder of hundreds of thousands of patients at hospitals and asylums for the mentally ill and disabled, an action that comes to be called the "euthanasia." September: German invasion of Poland begins World War II in Europe.
1941	6 January: President Franklin D. Roosevelt delivers the State of the Union address, known as the Four Freedoms speech, declaring that people "everywhere in the world" should enjoy freedoms of speech, of worship, from want, and from fear. 22 June: German Reich launches surprise invasion of the Soviet Union; SS-led "Einsatzgruppen" enter German-occupied territories and begin to round up and murder all Jewish men, women, and children without exception. 14 August: US and UK governments declare the Atlantic Charter, which provides the basis for later Allied war goals and the founding of the United Nations.
1942	January: In London, the governments-in-exile of European countries occupied by German forces deliver the Declaration of St. James' Palace.
1943	October: Allies issue the Moscow Declarations specifying Allied war goals and calling for trials of perpetrators of Axis war crimes.

1945	November: Several months after the end of World War II, the International Military Tribunal (IMT) is convened at Nuremberg. (The IMT will deliver verdicts convicting NS regime and party leaders and military officers of crimes against peace, war crimes, and crimes against humanity in October 1946.)
1945–1946	An estimated twelve million ethnic German residents are expelled from Czechoslovakia (Sudetenland), former East Prussian territories within the new borders of Poland, and other eastern European countries, with most of them arriving in western Germany as refugees.
1948	December: The United Nations votes to approve the Universal Declaration of Human Rights and the Genocide Convention.
1949	May: Foundation of a West German state, the Federal Republic of Germany (FRG).
	August: Third and fourth Geneva Conventions.
1950	European Convention of Human Rights (ECHR).
1954	November: West Germany ratifies the UN Genocide Convention.
1958	April: Opening of the Einsatzgruppen Trial at Ulm.
	May: The last four German prisoners at Landsberg Castle (War Criminal Prison No. 1) receive early release.
1961	April: Trial of Adolf Eichmann convenes in Jerusalem.
1964	Publication of the German edition of Hannah Arendt's *Eichmann in Jerusalem*.
1965	April: Hans Egon Holthusen reviews Arendt's book in *Vierteljahrshefte für Zeitgeschichte*.
1985	April: Trial of the Juntas start in Argentina.
1989	9 November: Fall of the Berlin Wall.
1990	April: The parliament of the German Democratic Republic claims co-responsibility for persecution of Jews under National Socialism and asks for Israel's pardon for the GDR's previously hostile foreign policy.
	August: German Unification Treaty; the end of the GDR follows in October as the territories of East Germany are joined to the Federal Republic of Germany.
1991	Publication of Samuel Huntington's *The Third Wave*.
1992	March: International Salzburg Conference.
	April: The first Enquete Commission for Working through the History and Consequences of the SED Dictatorship convenes in the FRG.
1994	Public debate resumes in Germany on how to deal with crimes committed under the GDR.

1995	July: Second Enquete Commission for the Overcoming of the Consequences of the SED Dictatorship in the Process of German Unity.
1996	April: South African Truth and Reconciliation Commission convenes its first hearings.

NOTES

Introduction

1. On the terms "modernity" and "high modernity" and on the conceptualization of a comparative European history of the twentieth century, see Ulrich Herbert, "Europe in High Modernity: Reflections on a Theory of the 20th Century," *Journal of Modern European History* 5 (2007): 5–20; more critically, Lutz Raphael, "Ordnungsmuster der 'Hochmoderne'? Die Theorie der Moderne und die Geschichte der europäischen Gesellschaften im 20. Jahrhundert," in *Dimensionen der Moderne: Festschrift für Christof Dipper*, ed. Lutz Raphael and Ute Schneider, 73–91 (Frankfurt, 2008). According to Christoph Dipper, historiographers often use modernity synonymously with the modern period or the present. Christoph Dipper, "Die Epoche der Moderne: Konzeption und Kerngehalt," in *Vergangenheit und Zukunft der Moderne*, ed. Ulrich Beck and Martin Muslow (Frankfurt, 2014), 105; see also Christoph Dipper, "Moderne, Version: 1.0," *Docupedia-Zeitgeschichte*, 25 August 2010, http://docupedia.de/zg/Moderne?oldid=106453.
2. The characterization of the nineteenth century as a "long" phase with relatively fewer cases of interstate and intrastate violence, followed by extreme violence in the first half of the twentieth century, has shaped the literature on this issue since the early 1990s. See, e.g., Eric Hobsbawm, *The Age of Empire, 1875–1975* (London, 1987); Eric Hobsbawm, *The Age of Extremes Extremes: The Short Twentieth Century, 1914–1991* (London, 1994); Volker H. Berghahn, *Europa im Zeitalter der Weltkriege: Die Entgrenzung und Entfesselung der Gewalt* (Frankfurt, 2002); Mark Mazower, *Dark Continent: Europe's Twentieth Century* (London, 1998); Ian Kershaw, "War and Political Violence in Twentieth Century Europe," *Contemporary European History* 14, no. 1 (2005): 107–123; James J. Sheehan, *Kontinent der Gewalt: Europas langer Weg zum Frieden* (Bonn, 2008). By contrast, a younger generation of historians in recent years has not only stressed the entrenchment of state-based violence in the latter third of the nineteenth century, but has also called into question the paradigmatic meaning of the two world wars, as well as the usual division of the twentieth century into violent and largely peaceful halves. See Benjamin Ziemann, "Germany after the First World War: A Violent Society? Result and Implications of Recent Research on Weimar Germany," *Journal of Modern European History* 1, no. 1 (2003): 80–95; Donald Bloxham and Robert Gerwarth, *Political Violence in Twentieth-Century Europe* (Cambridge, 2011).
3. The concept of a "culture of war" (*Kriegskultur*), which goes back to the social and cultural history turns in recent military scholarship, has focused especially on the role of intermediary institutions like churches, political parties, and civil associations.

John Horne, ed., *State, Society and Mobilization in Europe during the First World War* (Cambridge, 1997).
4. The historiographic narrative of the twentieth century as one of "total" or "unlimited" violence has not gone without contradiction. In his alternative outline for a periodization of the century, Charles Maier has fundamentally questioned the criterion of politically motivated mass violence, arguing that this is a moral and metaphorical category—not a sociopolitical one. Charles S. Maier, "Consigning the Twentieth Century to History: Alternative Narratives for the Modern Era," *American Historical Review* 105, no. 3 (2000): 807–831.
5. On the term "international criminal law politics" (*Völkerstrafrechtspolitik*), which also aims at overcoming traditional definitions as shaped by national state law, see the instructive contribution by Andreas Fischer-Lescano and Philipp Liste, "Völkerrechtspolitik: Zur Trennung und Verknüpfung von Politik und Recht der Weltgesellschaft," *Zeitschrift für internationale Beziehungen* 12, no. 2 (2005): 209–249. According to Eckart Conze, "international criminal law politics" refers to every political action that involves international criminal law and its norms, as well as its development and application. Eckart Conze, "Völkerstrafrecht und Völkerstrafrechtspolitik," in *Dimensionen internationaler Geschichte*, ed. Jost Dülffer and Wilfried Loth (Munich, 2012), 189.
6. A few historians instead assume an intrinsic, mutually reinforcing relationship between the two manifestations of European high modernity. Thus, Eric Weitz considers protections of minority rights as the sign of a deep political transformation, since traditional diplomacy and the dynastic-territorial principle of the Congress of Vienna was supplanted by an ethnic or possibly racially based population politics. The discourse in the legal scholarship also partly supports the view that the new respect for international criminal law in fact effected a "mystification" of law, because its specific "framework" above all served to legitimate state violence. Eric Weitz, "From Vienna to the Paris System: International Politics and the Entangled Histories of Human Rights, Forced Deportation and Civilizing Missions," *American Historical Review* 113 (2008): 1313–1343; see Chris af Jochnik and Roger Normand, "The Legitimation of Violence: A Critical History of the Laws of War," *Harvard International Law Journal* 35, no. 1 (1994): 49–95.
7. On this approach, see Eckart Conze, "Zwischen Staatenwelt und Gesellschaft: Die gesellschaftliche Dimension der Internationalen Geschichte," in *Internationale Geschichte: Themen—Ergebnisse—Aussichten*, ed. Wilfried Loth and Jürgen Osterhammel (Munich, 2009), 117–140; Eckart Conze, "Abschied von Staat und Politik? Überlegungen zur Geschichte der internationalen Politik," in *Geschichte der internationalen Beziehungen: Erneuerung und Erweiterung einer historischen Disziplin*, ed. Eckart Conze, Ulrich Lappenküper, and Guido Müller (Cologne, 2004), 15–43.
8. See Susan Zimmermann, "International—Transnational: Forschungsfelder und Forschungsperspektiven," in *Transnationale Netzwerke im 20. Jahrhundert. Historische Erkundungen zu Ideen und Praktiken, Individuen und Organisationen*, ed. Berthold Unfried, Jürgen Mittag, and Marcel van der Linden (Leipzig, 2008), 27–46.
9. See Madeleine Herren, *Internationale Orgasinationen seit 1865: Eine Globalgeschichte der internationalen Ordnung* (Darmstadt, 2009); Dieter Gosewinkel, Dieter Rucht, Wolfgang van den Daele, and Jürgen Kocka, eds., *Zivilgesellschaft: National und transnational* (Berlin, 2004).
10. On "liberal internationalism," see Fred Halliday, "Three Concepts of Internationalism," *International Affairs* 64 (1988): 187–198; from a conceptual history perspective, see Peter Friedemann and Lucian Hölscher, "Internationale, International,

Internationalismus," in *Geschichtliche Grundbegriffe: Historisches Lexikon zur politisch-sozialen Sprache in Deutschland*, vol. 3, 1st reprinted ed., ed. Otto Brunner, Werner Conze, and Reinhart Koselleck (Stuttgart, 1995), 367–397.

11. See Friedrich Kießling, "(Welt-)Öffentlichkeit," in Dülffer and Loth, *Dimensionen internationaler Geschichte*, 85–105

12. Stefan-Ludwig Hoffmann, ed., *Moralpolitik: Geschichte der Menschenrechte im 20. Jahrhundert* (Göttingen, 2010).

13. On the constitution of reality as a concept within the terminology of Niklas Luhmann's systems theory, see Frank Becker and Elke Reinhardt-Becker, *Systemtheorie: Eine Einführung für die Geschichts- und Kulturwissenschaften* (Frankfurt, 2001).

14. See Susanne Buckley-Zistel and Anika Oettler, "Was bedeutet: Transitional Justice?" in *Nach Krieg, Gewalt und Repression: Vom schwierigen Umgang mit der Vergangenheit*, ed. Susanne Buckley-Zistel and Thomas Kater (Baden-Baden, 2011), 21–37.

15. Norbert Frei, *Vergangenheitspolitik: Die Anfänge der Bundesrepublik und die NS Vergangenheit* (Munich, 1996); Petra Bock and Edgar Wolfrum, "Einleitung," in *Umkämpfte Vergangenheit: Geschichtsbilder, Erinnerung und Vergangenheitspolitik im internationalen Vergleich*, ed. Petra Bock and Edgar Wolfrum (Göttingen, 1999), 7–14; Christoph Cornelißen, "Errinnerungskulturen, Version: 1.0," *Docupedia-Zeitgeschichte*, 11 February 2010, https://docupedia.de/zg/Erinnerungskulturen?oldid=75513.

16. Taking up an analysis by Frank Bösch and Constantin Goschler, public history is understood here not as a part of memory culture but rather as an autonomous production site of historical bodies of knowledge, characterized by interests and modes of presentation specific to intended publics. Frank Bösch and Constantin Goschler, "Der Nationalsozialismus und die deutsche Public History," in *Public History: Öffentliche Darstellungen des Nationalsozialismus jenseits der Geschichtswissenschaft*, ed. Frank Bösch and Constantin Goschler (Frankfurt, 2009), 7–23. On the relationship between memory culture and juridical processing, see also Sabine Horn, *Erinnerungsbilder: Auschwitz-Prozess und Majdanek-Prozess im westdeutschen Fernsehen* (Essen, 2009).

17. Donald Bloxham and Robert Gerwarth, whose book on the history of political violence in Europe rests on a broad concept, distinguish four forms of state and nonstate violence: (1) violence in military conflicts; (2) projects of genocidal policy and "ethnic cleansing"; (3) terrorism and state repression; (4) revolutionary and counterrevolutionary violence. Bloxham and Gerwarth, "Introduction," in Bloxham and Gerwarth, *Political Violence in Twentieth-Century Europe*, 1.

18. A sophisticated and problem-oriented introduction to the material can be found in Hannah Franzki, "Mit Recht Erinnern: Völkerrechtliche Ahndung von Kriegsverbrechen zwischen Aufarbeitungsimperativ und selektiver Geschichtsschreibung," *Geschichte in Wissenschaft und Unterricht* 63, nos. 7–8 (2012): 448–464.

19. A great number of recent publications explore the tense relationship between law, history, and memory: Tzvetan Todorov, "The Touvier Affair," in *Memory, the Holocaust and French Justice: The Bousquet and Touvier Affairs*, ed. Richard J. Golsan (Hanover, 1996), 114–121; John Borneman, *Settling Accounts: Violence, Justice, and Accountability in Postsocialist Europe* (Princeton, NJ, 1997); Mark Osiel, *Mass Atrocity, Collective Memory, and the Law* (New Brunswick, NJ, 1997); Martha Minow, *Between Vengeance and Forgiveness: Facing History after Genocide and Mass Violence* (Boston, 1998); Henry Rousso, *The Haunting Past: History, Memory, and Justice in Contemporary France* (Philadelphia, 1998); Carlo Ginzburg, *The Judge and the Historian: Marginal Notes on a Late-Twentieth-Century Miscarriage of Justice* (London, 1999); Norbert Frei, Dirk van Laak, and Michael Stolleis, eds., *Geschichte vor Gericht: Historiker, Richter und die*

Suche nach Gerechtigkeit. (Munich, 2000); Lawrence Douglas, *The Memory of Judgment: Making Law and History in the Trials of the Holocaust* (New Haven, CT, 2001); Donald Bloxham, *Genocide on Trial: War Crimes Trials and the Formation of Holocaust History and Memory* (Oxford, 2001); Richard J. Evans, "History, Memory and the Law: The Historian and Expert Witness," *History and Theory* 41, no. 3 (2002): 326–345; Martti Koskenniemi, "Between Impunity and Show Trials," *Max Planck Yearbook of United Nations Law* 6 (2002): 1–35; Paul Ricœur, *History, Memory, Forgetting* (London, 2004); Martin Schulze Wessel, "Geschichte vor Gericht: Zum juristischen und geschichtswissenschaftlichen Umgang mit dem Unrecht untergegangener Staatsordnungen in Deutschland und im östlichen Europa," in *Bewusstes Erinnern und bewusstes Vergessen*, edited by Angelika Nussberger and Caroline von Gall (Tübingen, 2011), 9–26; Richard Ashby Wilson, *Writing History in International Criminal Trials* (Cambridge, 2011); Kim Christian Priemel and Alexa Stiller, *Reassessing the Nuremberg Military Tribunals: Transitional Justice, Trial Narratives, and Historiography* (New York, 2012); Priemel, "Der Sonderweg vor Gericht."
20. Hannah Arendt, *Eichmann in Jerusalem: A Report on the Banality of Evil* (New York, 1963); Hannah Arendt, *Eichmann in Jerusalem: Ein Bericht von der Banalität des Bösen*, 2nd ed. (Munich, 2007).
21. See Ruti Teitel, "Transitional Justice Genealogy," *Harvard Human Rights Journal* 16 (2003): 69–94; Elazar Barkan, *The Guilt of Nations: Restitution and Negotiating Historical Injustices* (New York, 2000); Anne K. Krüger, "Transitional Justice, Version: 1.0," *Docupedia-Zeitgeschichte*, 25 January 2013, http://docupedia.de/zg/Transitional_Justice?oldid=85576.
23. See Michel Feher, "Terms of Reconciliation," in *Human Rights in Political Transitions*, ed. Carla Hesse and Robert Post (New York, 1999), 325–338.
24. Critically, see Paige Arthur, "How 'Transitions' Reshaped Human Rights: A Conceptual History of Transitional Justice," *Human Rights Quarterly* 31, no. 2 (2009): 321–367; Stefan-Ludwin Hoffmann, "Einführung: Zur Genealogie der Menschenrechte," in Hoffmann, *Moralpolitik*, 7–37.
25. In tendency, this is the argument presented in Henry Rousso, "Égo-Histoire: Vichy in Geschichte, Erinnerung und Recht," in *Frankreich und die "dunklen Jahre": Das Regime von Vichy in Geschichte und Gegenwart*, ed. Henry Rousso (Göttingen, 2010), 163.
26. In this vein, see Volkhard Knigge, "Gesellschaftsverbrechen erinnern: Zur Entstehung und Entwicklung des Konzepts seit 1945," in *Der Kommunismus im Museum: Formen der Auseinandersetzung in Deutschland und Ostmitteleuropa*, ed. Volkhard Knigge and Ulrich Mählert (Weimar, 2005), 19–30; see also Paul Betts, "Germany, International Justice and the Twentieth Century," *History and Memory* 17, nos. 1–2 (2005): 45–86.
27. One such approach is followed by Isabel Hull's pathbreaking comparative study on German, British, and French international law politics in World War I. Isabel V. Hull, *A Scrap of Paper: Breaking and Making International Law during the Great War* (Ithaca, NY, 2014).
28. In unison with Philipp Sarrazin, "discourses" here are understood as the regularity and schematics of "generative structures." Philipp Sarrazin, "Diskursanalyse," in *Geschichte: Ein Grundkurs*, ed. Hans-Jürgen Goertz (Reinbek, 2007) 199–217; Achim Landwehr, *Historische Diskursanalyse* (Frankfurt, 2008).
29. See Lora Wildenthal, *The Language of Human Rights in West Germany* (Philadelphia, 2013).
30. Regarding the 1990s, Gross speaks of the emergence of a new phenomenon of "historability" (*Geschichtsbarkeit*), which for him points to not only the growing entanglement

but also the increasing interchangeability between jurisprudence, historical scholarship, and ethics. Raphael Gross, "Mächtiger als die Gerichte? Geschichte und historische Gerechtigkeit," in Frei et al., *Geschichte vor Gericht*, 166.
31. See Waldemar Hummer and Jelka Mayr-Singer, "Internationale Strafgerichtsbarkeit," in *Handwörterbuch Internationale Politik*, ed. Wichard Woyke (Bonn, 2008), 216–228; Annette Weinke, *Die Nürnberger Prozesse* (Munich, 2006); Norbert Frei, "Nach der Tat: Die Ahndung deutscher Kriegs- und NS-Verbrechen in Europa—eine Bilanz," in *Transnationale Vergangenheitspolitik: Der Umgang mit deutschen Kriegsverbrechern in Europa nach dem Zweiten Weltkrieg*, ed. Norbert Frei (Göttingen, 2006), 7–36.
32. See Elizabeth Borgwardt, *A New Deal for the World: America's Vision for Human Rights* (Cambridge, MA, 2005); Tim B. Müller, "Die epistemischen Bedingungen der Macht: Wissenschaft, Staatsapparate und Stiftungen im frühen Kalten Krieg—Der institutionelle Kontext Otto Kirchheimers, Herbert Marcuses und Franz Neumanns in Amerika," in *Kritische Verfassungspolitologie: Das Staatsverständnis von Otto Kirchheimer*, ed. Robert Christian van Ooyen and Frank Schale (Baden-Baden, 2011), 35–66; Ralf Ahrens, "Kartelle und Verschwörungen: Franz Neumanns 'Behemoth' und die Nürnberger Prozesse," in *Unternehmen im Nationalsozialismus: Zur Historisierung einer Forschungskonjunktur*, ed. Norbert Frei and Tim Schanetzk (Göttingen, 2010), 26–35.
33. A trenchant contribution from Rüdiger Graf and Kim Christian Priemel recently drew attention to the epistemological traps that can arise in the historicization of social science theories and terms. See Rüdiger Graf and Kim Christian Priemel, "Zeitgeschichte in der Welt der Sozialwissenschaften: Legitimität und Originalität einer Disziplin," *Vierteljahrshefte für Zeitgeschichte* 59, no. 4 (2011): 479–508; see the response in Bernhard Dietz and Christopher Neumann, "Vom Nutzen der Sozialwissenschaften für die Zeitgeschichte: Werte und Wertewandel als Gegenstand historischer Forschung," *Vierteljahrshefte für Zeitgeschichte* 60, no. 2 (2012): 293–304.
34. Peter J. Opitz, *Menschenrechte und Internationaler Menschenrechtsschutz im 20. Jahrhundert: Geschichte und Dokumente* (Munich, 2002), 11; see also Klaus Dicke and Manuel Fröhlich, "Menschenrechte," in Woyke, *Handwörterbuch Internationale Politik*, 326–334.
35. See Michael Ignatieff, *Human Rights as Politics and Idolatry* (Princeton, NJ, 2001); Fisch, "Die Menschenrechte als Politik-Ersatz," *Süddeutsche Zeitung*, 19 June 1993.
36. On this, refer to the model by John Torpey, who conceives of transnational justice as a large field of measures relating to the past. John Torpey, "Introduction," in *Politics and the Past: On Repairing Historical Injustices*, ed. John Torpey (Lanham, MD, 2003) 6.
37. See Arthur, "How 'Transitions' Reshaped Human Rights."
38. The intended role of transnational justice can perhaps best be compared to that of sociology as a guiding discipline in the preunification German Federal Republic. Paul Nolte, "Soziologie als kulturelle Selbstvergewisserung: Die Demokratisierung der deutschen Gesellschaft nach 1945," In *Soziale Konstellation und historische Perspektive: Festschrift für M. Rainer Lepsius*, ed. Steffen Sigmund (Wiesbaden, 2008), 18–40.
39. See Jan Eckel and Samuel Moyn, eds., *Moral für die Welt? Menschenrechtspolitik in den 1970er Jahren* (Göttingen, 2012).
40. See Arthur, "How 'Transitions' Reshaped Human Rights."
41. See Buckley-Zistel and Oettler, "Was bedeutet: Transitional Justice?"
42. See Guillaume Mouralis, *Une épuration allemande: La RDA en procès 1949–2004* (Paris, 2008).
43. See Barbara Stollberg-Rilinger, *Was heisst Kulturgeschichte des Politischen?* (Berlin, 2005); Thomas Mergel, "Kulturgeschichte der Politik, Version: 1.0," *Docupedia-Zeitgeschichte*,

11 Feburary 2010, https://docupedia.de/zg/Kulturgeschichte_der_Politik_Version _1.0_Thomas_Mergel/Text.
44. See Hoffmann, "Einführung"; Hans Joas, *Die Sakralität der Person: Eine neue Genealogie der Menschenrechte* (Berlin, 2011). For an instructive overview of the literature, see Jan Eckel, "Utopie der Moral, Kalkül der Macht: Menschenrechte in der globalen Politik seit 1945," *Archiv für Sozialgeschichte* 49 (2009): 437–484.
45. See Michel Foucault, "Nietzsche, die Genealogie, die Historie," in *Michel Foucault: Schriften in vier Bänden—Dits et Ecrits II*, ed. Daniel Defert, François Ewald, and Jacques Lagrange (Frankfurt, 2002), 166–191. Comparative analyses on the concepts of "archaeology" and "genealogy" can be found in Andrew G. Neal, "Foucault in Guantánamo: Eine Archäologie des Ausnahmezustand," in *Rationalitäten der Gewalt: Staatliche Ordnungen vom 19. bis zum 21. Jahrhundert*, ed. Susanne Krasmann and Jürgen Martschukat (Bielefeld, 2007), 47–74.
46. Hoffmann, "Einführung," 30.
47. Accordingly, some newer histories of human rights give secondary status to events that have been seen as key milestones of humanitarian international law history, like the Nuremberg trials or the Genocide Convention. Samuel Moyn, *The Last Utopia: Human Rights in History* (Cambridge, MA, 2010).
48. Samuel Moyn, "On the Genealogy of Morals," *The Nation*, 16 April 2007.
49. See Peter Maguire, *Law and War: An American Story* (New York, 2011).
50. Michael Ignatieff in this connection has spoken of a "revolution" in human rights discourses after 1945, one that he attributes both to the experience of violence in the war and to the rise of psychoanalysis to a globally leading discipline. Michael Ignatieff, "Human Rights," in Hesse and Post, *Human Rights in Political Transitions*, 313–324. A pithy case study is offered in the essay by Tara Zarah, "'The Psychological Marshall Plan': Displacement, Gender, and Human Rights after World War II," *Central European History* 44 (2011): 37–62.
51. Most firmly, Moyn, *The Last Utopia*, 7; Eckel, "Utopie der Moral," 471.
52. Hoffmann, "Einführung," 32.
53. Teitel, "Transitional Justice Genealogy."
54. The frequent conflict between the aims of stabilizing society and achieving historical justice often causes intentional avoidance of prosecutions. It cannot be overlooked that transitional justice differentiates itself greatly from the conventional administration of justice, in regard to both its claims of meeting standards of formality and its philosophical foundations. See Ibid., 81.

Chapter 1

1. On this current of internationalism, see Akira Irye, "Nationale Geschichte, Internationale Geschichte, Globale Geschichte," in *Deutschland und die USA in der internationalen Geschichte des 20. Jahrhunderts: Festschrift für Detlef Junker*, ed. Manfred Berg and Philipp Gassert (Stuttgart, 2004) 38; for a political science treatment, see Joannes Varwick, "Völkerrecht/Internationales Recht," in Woyke, *Handwörterbuch Internationale Politik*, 557–564.
2. See Matthias Schulz, "Macht, internationale Politik und Normenwandel," in *Macht und Recht: Völkerrecht in den internationalen Beziehungen*, ed. Ulrich Lappenküper and Reiner Marcowitz (Paderborn, 2010), 133–134.

3. On the term "preemptive historiography," see Erich J. C. Hahn, "The German Foreign Ministry and the Question of War Guilt in 1918–1919," in *German Nationalism and the European Response, 1890–1945*, ed. Carole Fink, Isabel Hull, and MacGregor Knox (Norman, OK, 1985), 49.
4. Article 1 of the Statutes of the Institute for International Law (Institute de Droit International), adopted at Ghent, Belgium, on 10 September 1873, describes the "exclusively learned society" as "striving to formulate the general principles of the subject, in such a way as to correspond to the legal conscience of the civilized world." On the dual sense of conscience as also entailing consciousness, see Martti Koskenniemi, *The Gentle Civilizer of Nations: The Rise and Fall of International Law 1870–1960* (Cambridge, 2002), 47.
5. See Jörg Fisch, *Das Selbstbestimmungsrecht der Völker: Die Domestizierung einer Illusion* (Munich, 2010).
6. See Koskenniemi, *The Gentle Civilizer of Nations*, 53. As the Ottoman Empire declined in power, the originally symmetrical relations between the Muslim world and Christian Europe slipped into asymmetry. See Klaus Schlichte, "Das formierende Säkulum: Macht und Recht in der internationalen Politik des 19. Jahrhunderts," in Lappenküper and Marcowitz, *Macht und Recht*, 161–177.
7. As in Moyn, *The Last Utopia*, 178.
8. Jürgen Osterhammel, *Die Entzauberung Asiens: Europa und die asiatischen Reiche im 18. Jahrhundert* (Munich, 1998), 1183; Milos Vec, "Universalization, Particularization, and Discrimination: European Perspectives on a Cultural History of 19th Century International Law," *InterDisciplines* 3, no. 1 (2012): 79–102.
9. Schlichte, "Das formierende Säkulum," 176, speaks of the "internal space of European domestic morality."
10. See A. Dirk Moses, "Besatzung, Kolonialherrschaft und Widerstand: Das Völkerrecht und die Legitimierung von Terror," *Peripherie: Zeitschrift für Politik und Ökonomie in der Dritten Welt* 29, no. 116 (2009): 399–424. In reducing modern international law to its functions as an instrument of power and repression in the hands of strong states, Moses's sketches from the history of ideas provide a reverse image of the idealizing narratives common in international law studies and political science, but his argument is just as teleological. On the term "civilization," see Gerrit W. Gong, *The "Standard of Civilization" in International Society* (Oxford, 1984).
11. See Daniel Marc Segesser, *Recht statt Rache oder Rache durch Recht? Die Ahndung von Kriegsverbrechen in der internationalen wissenschaftlichen Debatte 1872–1945* (Paderborn, 2010), 131.
12. See Osterhammel, *Die Entzauberung Asiens*, 1188.
13. See Antony Anghie, "Finding the Peripheries: Sovereignty and Colonialism in Nineteenth Century International Law," *Harvard International Law Journal* 40, no. 1 (1999): 1–80, 4.
14. See Koskenniemi, *The Gentle Civilizer of Nations*, 57–58.
15. Segesser, *Recht statt Rache oder Rache durch Recht?* 78.
16. See Christian Jansen, "Pazifismus in Deutschland: Entwicklung und innere Widersprüche (1800 bis 1940)," in *Recht ist, was den Waffen nützt: Justiz und Pazifismus im 20. Jahrhundert*, ed. Helmut Kramer and Wolfram Wette (Berlin, 2004), 59–78; Hauke Brunkhorst, "Kritik am Dualismus: Hans Kelsen und die Völkerrechtsrevolution des 20. Jahrhunderts." in *Transnationale Verrechtlichung: Nationale Demokratien im Kontext globaler Politik*, ed. Regina Kreide and Andreas Niederberger (Frankfurt, 2008), 37.

17. Moltke, quoted in Segesser, *Recht statt Rache*, 28, emphasis added.
18. Moltke, quoted in Johannes Caspar Bluntschli, *Denkwürdiges aus meinem Leben, Teil III/2 ("Heidelberg 1861–1881")* (Nördlingen, 1884), 472. The Saint Petersburg Declaration of 1868 banned the use of artillery shells under four hundred grams. Jost Dülffer, "Regeln im Krieg? Kriegsverbrechen und die Haager Friedenskonferenzen," in *Frieden stiften: Deeskalations- und Friedenspolitik im 20. Jahrhundert*, ed. Jost Dülffer and Marc Frey (Cologne, 2008), 80n7.
19. Jochnik and Normand, "The Legitimation of Violence," 81.
20. Moyn, *The Last Utopia*, 210–211.
21. See Holger Nehring, "Transnationale soziale Bewegungen," in Dülffer and Loth, *Dimensionen internationaler Geschichte*, 129–149; Hillard von Thiessen and Christian Windler, eds., *Akteure der Außenbeziehungen: Netzwerke und Interkulturalität im historischen Wandel* (Cologne, 2010).
22. Schlichte, "Das formierende Säkulum," 170; Jörg Requate and Martin Schulze Wessel, eds., *Europäische Öffentlichkeit: Transnationale Kommunikation seit dem 18. Jahrhundert* (Frankfurt, 2002). On typologies and characteristics of transnational and international publics, see Kießling, "(Welt-)Öffentlichkeit," 96–97.
23. Dieter Riesenberger, *Geschichte der Friedensbewegung in Deutschland: Von den Anfängen bis 1933* (Göttingen, 1985), 89.
24. See Jansen, "Pazifismus in Deutschland"; Segesser, *Recht statt Rache oder Rache durch Recht?* 172.
25. Riesenberger, *Geschichte der Friedensbewegung in Deutschland*, 77–78.
26. Schlichte, "Das formierende Säkulum," 170. Following Max Weber's theory of law and rights, which viewed international law as a set of "conventions" rather than "laws," Schlichte considers the term *Verrechtlichung* (juridification or legalization) as an exaggeration concerning events of the nineteenth century.
27. A thorough treatment can be found in Dieter Fleck, *Handbuch des humanitären Völkerrechts in bewaffneten Konflikten* (Munich, 1994).
28. See Frank Feidel, "Francis Lieber and the Codification of the International Law of War," in *Préludes et Pionniers: Les Précurseurs de la Croix-Rouge 1840–1860*, ed. Roger Durand and Jacques Meurant (Geneva, 1991), 31–45.
29. In his compact longitudinal treatment of the history of US punitive policy, Frank M. Buscher interprets the sense of mission and the feeling of superiority of the Union in the Civil War as constants that remain through the epochs. See Buscher, "Bestrafen und Erziehen."
30. See Segesser, *Recht statt Rache oder Rache durch Recht?* 85.
31. On the Wirz case, see Willis, *Prologue to Nuremberg The Politics and Diplomacy of Punishing War Criminals of the First World War* (Westport, CT, 1982), 46, 76.
32. This debate over Moynier's proposal of a tribunal to investigate violations during the Franco-Prussian War is outlined in Segesser, *Recht statt Rache oder Rache durch Recht?* 90–91.
33. In an overview of the terminological history, Heinhard Steiger views the Hague Conventions as a key stage in the path from European international law to "world international law." see Steiger, "Art. Völkerrecht," in *Geschichtliche Grundbegriffe: Historisches Lexikon zur politisch-sozialen Sprache in Deutschland*, vol. 7, ed. Otto Brunner, Werner Conze, and Reinhart Koselleck (Stuttgart, 1992) 125.
34. Prologue, Hague Convention (IV), Respecting the Laws and Customs of War on Land, The Hague, 18 October 1907, entered into force 26 January 1910, http://avalon.law.yale.edu/20th_century/hague04.asp; Segesser, *Recht statt Rache oder Rache durch Recht?* 127.

35. Mark Lewis is of the opinion that the German delegation advanced this proposal as a means of mitigating the international criticism of the Reich military memo "Kriegsbrauch im Landkrieg" ("Wartime Conduct in Landwar") after its 1902 publication. His book, however, shows no evidence for this. Mark Lewis, *The Birth of the New Justice: The Internationalization of Crime and Punishment, 1919–1950* (Oxford, 2014), 18.
36. Quoted in Dülffer, *Regeln im Krieg*, 83–84.
37. Article 3, Hague Convention (IV); see note 34.
38. Quoted in Steiger, "Art. Völkerrecht," 132. The contemporary discussion already noted that Bethmann Hollweg apparently confused the terms *Notwehr* (literally self-defense, as a legal term meaning the state of mind justifying personal acts of self-defense) and *Notstand* (a national or collective state of emergency); see Hull, *A Scrap of Paper*, 44–45. The paradoxes of this speech are discussed in Schulz, "Macht, internationale Politik und Normenwandel," 132, who relies therein on Michael Walzer's thinking in regard to a ban on interventions under international law.
39. In her analysis of the speech, Hull, *A Scrap of Paper*, 43–44, argues that Bethmann Hollweg did not himself write the passage on obligations for future compensation. She attributes it to the press officer of the Federal Foreign Office, Otto Hammann, whose intent was to make it easier for the Social Democrats to vote in favor of the war budget.
40. On the terminological history of *Wiedergutmachung* ("making good again," which can be used in the sense of literally material compensation, reparations, restitutions, and the like, but also as atonement, expiation, redemption, amends, etc.), see Constantin Goschler's compact overview, which, however, does not treat its longer prehistory in international law. Constantin Goschler, *Schuld und Schulden: Die Politik der Wiedergutmachung für NS-Verfolgte seit 1945* (Göttingen, 2005), 11–17.
41. See Segesser, *Recht statt Rache oder Rache durch Recht?* 136.
42. Lassa Oppenheim, *International Law: A Treatise*, vol. 2: *War and Neutrality* (London, 1906), 263–266.
43. Among the states that did not ratify the 1907 Hague Conventions were Bulgaria, Montenegro, Romania, Serbia, und Turkey.
44. Hull, *A Scrap of Paper*, 83.
45. Großer Generalstab (German General Staff), *Kriegsbrauch im Landkriege* (Berlin, 1902).
46. Segesser, *Recht statt Rache oder Rache durch Recht?* 139.
47. James M. Spaight, *Bombing Vindicating* (London, 1944).
48. Quoted in Hull, *A Scrap of Paper*, 82.
49. Ibid., 88.
50. John Horne and Alan Kramer masterfully illuminate the transnational, imaginary and intellectual adoption processes of the intellectuals' mobilization using the example of German atrocities in World War I. John Horne and Alan Kramer, *Deutsche Kriegsgreuel 1914: Die umstrittene Wahrheit* (Hamburg, 2004); see also Flasch, *Die geistige Mobilmachung: Die deutschen Intellektuellen und der Erste Weltkrieg—ein Versuch* (Berlin, 2000).
51. Michael Jeismann, "Propaganda," in *Enzyklopädie Erster Weltkrieg*, ed. Gerhard Hirschfeld, Gerd Krumeich, and Irina Renz (Paderborn, 2003), 199.
52. Quoted in Willis, *Prologue to Nuremberg*, 13.
53. On this, see Margrit Szöllösi-Janze, *Fritz Haber: 1868–1934—Eine Biographie* (Munich, 1998), 316–321.
54. Horne and Kramer, *Deutsche Kriegsgreuel 1914*, 319.

55. As in Jeismann, "Propaganda," 198, who sees German war aims policy and Allied demands for punishment as equally expressions of a propagandistic self-delusion.
56. See Willis, *Prologue to Nuremberg*.
57. See Schulze Wessel, "Geschichte vor Gericht"; see also Ginzburg, *The Judge and the Historian*, 14.
58. On the Belgian priests' attempt to involve the Vatican, see Horne and Kramer, *Deutsche Kriegsgreuel 1914*.
59. Quoted in ibid., 389.
60. Ibid., 392.
61. Belgium and Official Commission of the Belgian Government, *Reports on the Violation of the Rights of Nations and of the Laws and Customs of War in Belgium* (London, 1914); Ministére des affaires Ètrangères, *Les violations des lois de la guerre par líAllemagne* (Paris, 1915).
62. Committee on Alleged German Outrage, *Report of the Committee on Alleged German Outrages Appointed by His Britannic Majesty's Government and Presided Over by the Right Hon. Viscount Bryce* (London, 1914).
63. On the history of the commission directed by James Bryce in a close collaboration with historian H. A. L. Fisher and the legal historian Sir Frederick Pollock, see Trevor Wilson, "Lord Bryce's Investigation into Alleged German Atrocities in Belgium, 1914–1915," *Journal of Contemporary History* 14 (1979): 369–383; Segesser, *Recht statt Rache oder Rache durch Recht?* 160; Gary S. Messinger, *British Propaganda and the State in the First World War* (Manchester, 1992), 71.
64. Horne and Kramer, *Deutsche Kriegsgreuel 1914*, 347.
65. See Segesser, *Recht statt Rache oder Rache durch Recht?* 160–165; Horne and Kramer, *Deutsche Kriegsgreuel 1914*, 421–422, point out that Bédier's methodology may no longer be reconstructable, since the originals war diaries have not been passed down. Bédier's conclusions are often essentialist and exaggerated, but his critics do not question the veracity of the documented events as such.
66. Horne and Kramer, *Deutsche Kriegsgreuel 1914*, 347.
67. Wilson, "Lord Bryce's Investigation," 381.
68. Sacha Zala, *Geschichte unter der Schere politischer Zensur: Amtliche Aktensammlungen im internationalen Vergleich* (Munich, 2001).
69. Quoted in Immanuel Geiss, ed., *Julikrise und Kriegsausbruch 1914*, vol. 1 (Hannover, 1963), 29.
70. *Vorläufige Denkschrift zum Kriegsausbruch*, 3 August 1914; Reichstag printed matter, 13th Legislative Period, Session II, no. 19. The text was published in 1914 under two other titles, *German White Book* and *Wie Russland Deutschland hinterging und den Europäischen Krieg entfesselte* (*How Russia Deceived Germany and Unleashed the European War*). *Aktenstücke zum Kriegsausbruch: Mit nachträglichen Ergänzungen auch in Buchform*.
71. Zala, *Geschichte unter der Schere politischer Zensur*, 31.
72. Quoted in Willis, *Prologue to Nuremberg*, 10.
73. The term goes back to the German-British international law jurist Oppenheim. See Segesser, *Recht statt Rache oder Rache durch Recht?* 51.
74. On the history of the August 1914 white book, see Horne and Kramer, *Deutsche Kriegsgreuel 1914*, 349–363.
75. Auswärtiges Amt, *Die völkerrechtswidrige Führung des belgischen Volkskrieges: Denkschrift* (*The Illegal Conduct of the Belgian Popular War*) (Berlin, 1915).

76. On the topos of the *franc-tireur* war, see Segesser, *Recht statt Rache oder Rache durch Recht?*, 157–170.
77. Hull coined the term to describe the concept of national self-defense derived from analogous concepts in national criminal law and the associated and extremely flexible concept of "military necessity" with its tendency to lift all self-imposed limits on conduct. Hull, *A Scrap of Paper*, 60–94.
78. In the 1950s, the historian Peter Schöller was able to show in his research on the events at Louvain/Leuven that the Federal Foreign Office and the Ministry of War had suppressed a large number of incriminating witness testimonies. Peter Schöller, *Der Fall Löwen und das Weißbuch: Eine kritische Untersuchung der deutschen Dokumentation über die Vorgänge in Löwen vom 25. bis 28. August 1914* (Cologne, 1958).
79. On the "Manifesto of the Ninety-Three" and other manifestoes by German academics, see Wolfgang J. Mommsen, "Die kulturellen Eliten im Ersten Weltkrieg," in *Bürgerliche Kultur und politische Ordnung: Künstler, Schriftsteller und Intellektuelle in der deutschen Geschichte 1830–1933*, 2nd ed., ed. Wolfgang J. Mommsen (Frankfurt, 2002), 178–195; Klaus Böhme, ed., *Aufrufe und Reden deutscher Professoren im Ersten Weltkrieg* (Stuttgart, 1975); Bernhard vom Brocke, "Wissenschaft und Militarismus Der Aufruf der 93 'An die Kulturwelt!' und der Zusammenbruch der internationalen Gelehrtenpolitik im Ersten Weltkrieg," in *Wilamowitz nach 50 Jahren*, ed. William L. Calder III, Helmut Flashar, and Theodor Lindken (Darmstadt, 1985), 649–719; Jürgen Ungern-Sternberg and Wolfgang von Ungern-Sternberg, *Der Aufruf "An die Kulturwelt!" Das Manifest der 93 und die Anfänge der Kriegspropaganda im Ersten Weltkrieg* (Stuttgart, 1996), 144–145, which includes a facsimile print of the document.
80. The periodical title translates simply as "Journal of International Law." Wehberg's open letter to his colleague Joseph Kohler was first published in 1915 in *Berliner Tageblatt*. The letter was reprinted in the *American Journal of International Law* 9 (1915), 924–927.
81. On the positions taken by various German international law jurists, see Segesser, *Recht statt Rache oder Rache durch Recht?* 166–167.
82. On the petition by the renowned legal scholar Heinrich Triepel and other Berlin professors on 26 January 1915, see Hull, *A Scrap of Paper*, 242.
83. Conservative estimates number the victims at about 300,000; see Jay Winter, "Some Paradoxes of the First World War," in *The Upheaval of War: Family, Work and Welfare in Europe, 1914–1918*, ed. Jay Winter and Richard Wall (Cambridge, 1988), 30. A contemporary inquiry by the German Federal Ministry of Health presented a figure of more than 750,000 deaths. Hull, *A Scrap of Paper*, 169.
84. The most thorough discussion of German war conduct in regard to international legality is offered in Hull, *A Scrap of Paper*.
85. Quoted in Segesser, *Recht statt Rache oder Rache durch Recht?* 179, 184.
86. Quoted in Hull, *A Scrap of Paper*, 108.
87. See Binoy Kampmark, "'No Peace with the Hohenzollerns': American Attitudes on Political Legitimacy towards Hohenzollern Germany, 1917–1918," *Diplomatic History* 34, no. 5 (2010): 769–791.
88. See John C. G. Röhl, *Wilhelm II: Der Weg in den Abgrund 1900–1941* (Munich, 2008).
89. He was apparently repulsed by the idea of killing innocent women and children by dropping bombs on them. See Hull, *A Scrap of Paper*, 228.
90. Quoted in Segesser, *Recht statt Rache oder Rache durch Recht?* 199.
91. Quoted in Hull, *A Scrap of Paper*, 77.

92. Ibid., 176.
93. See Ibid., 145.
94. Ibid., 94.
95. Ibid., 321.
96. John Coogan, review of Hull, *A Scrap of Paper*, H-Diplo, 12 December 2014, https://networks.h-net.org/node/28443/discussions/55267/h-diplo-essay-121-review-essay-scrap-paper-breaking-and-making; Samuel Moyn, review of Hull, *A Scrap of Paper*, *Wall Street Journal*, 5 June 2014, www.wsj.com/articles/book-review-a-scrap-of-paper-by-isabel-v-hull-1402010920.
97. Josef Kohler, "Das neue Völkerrecht," *Zeitschrift für Völkerrecht* 9 (1916), 6–7; on Kohler's transformation from a pacifist to a fiery supporter of the war, see Koskenniemi, *The Gentle Civilizer of Nations*, 215.
98. One of the first to take an editorial position, in October 1914, was the *Edinburgh Review*. See Hull, *A Scrap of Paper*, 312
99. On the course of the discussion, see ibid., 213. On the US international legal policy see also Brunkhorst, "Kritik am Dualismus des internationalen Rechts."
100. In the opinion of the Army Council, such trials would be more trouble than they were worth, posing "a precedent which might involve us in difficulties in similar cases in the future." Quoted in Hull, *A Scrap of Paper*, 313.
101. See Willis, *Prologue to Nuremberg*, 50.
102. Quoted in ibid., 57.
103. This problem was treated in detail only by the crown jurists in their report for the British cabinet. See Fritz Dickmann, "Die Kriegsschuldfrage auf der Friedenskonferenz von 1919," *Historische Zeitschrift* 197 (1963): 23.
104. See Walter Schwengler, *Völkerrecht, Versailler Vertrag und Auslieferungsfrage Auslieferungsfrage: Die Strafverfolgung wegen Kriegsverbrechen als Problem des Friedensschlusses 1919/20* (Stuttgart, 1982), 88–89.
105. See Binoy Kampmark, "Sacred Sovereigns and Punishable War Crimes: The Ambivalence of the Wilson Administration towards a Trial of Kaiser Wilhelm II," *Australian Journal of Politics and History* 53, no. 4 (2007): 519–537.
106. On the US president's position, see Willis, *Prologue to Nuremberg*, 68, 77–79; Schwengler, *Völkerrecht, Versailler Vertrag und die Auslieferungsfrage*, 84–85.
107. Quoted in Willis, *Prologue to Nuremberg*, 78.
108. On the activities of the first commission, see Ellinor von Puttkamer, "Die Haftung der politischen und militärischen Führung des Ersten Weltkriegs für Kriegsurheberschaft und Kriegsverbrechen," *Archiv des Völkerrechts* 1 (1948/1949): 424–449; Heiko Ahlbrecht, *Geschichte der völkerrechtlichen Strafgerichtsbarkeit im 20. Jahrhundert* (Baden-Baden, 1999); Willis, *Prologue to Nuremberg*; Schwengler, *Völkerrecht, Versailler Vertrag und die Auslieferungsfrage*; Lewis, *The Birth of the New Justice*.
109. See Willis, *Prologue to Nuremberg*, 72; Lothar Albertin, *Liberalismus und Demokratie am Anfang der Weimarer Republik* (Düsseldorf, 1972), 212–215.
110. Schwengler, *Völkerrecht, Versailler Vertrag und die Auslieferungsfrage*, 124.
111. Ahlbrecht, *Geschichte der völkerrechtlichen Strafgerichtsbarkeit*, 36–38; Segesser, *Recht statt Rache oder Rache durch Recht?* 218. Hull, *A Scrap of Paper*, 9–10, mistakenly suggests that the concept of crimes against humanity is found in the treaty; Article 227 of the Treaty of Versailles actually charges Wilhelm with "a supreme offence against international morality and the sanctity of treaties." The first use of "crimes against humanity" appears to occur in a note from the Allies to German negotiator and Foreign Minister Brockdorff-Rantzau on 16 June 1919.

112. The enumeration of war crimes was later taken on by the United Nations War Crimes Commission; its thirty-two concrete accusations are listed in Schwengler, *Völkerrecht, Versailler Vertrag und die Auslieferungsfrage*, 100–101.
113. Dickmann, "Die Kriegsschuldfrage auf der Friedenskonferenz," 29.
114. Robert Lansing, "Cruel and Inhuman Acts of War," in *The Diary of Robert Lansing*; quoted in Willis, *Prologue to Nuremberg*, 41.
115. Willis, *Prologue to Nuremberg*, 41.
116. Schwengler, *Völkerrecht, Versailler Vertrag und die Auslieferungsfrage*, 105, is more of the opinion that Lansing was so concerned about achieving a stable peace that he considered the call for sanctions to be secondary.
117. Lewis, *The Birth of the New Justice*, 47–49, names three main motives behind Lansing's attitude of rejection: fear of a Bolshevik revolution in a destabilized postwar Germany, the burdens that an international tribunal would place on the United States, and the protection of US freedom to act on behalf of imperial interests in Mexico and the Philippines.
118. Thomas Würtenberger and Gernot Sydow, "Versailles und das Völkerrecht," in *Versailles 1919: Ziele—Wirkung—Wahrnehmung*, ed. Gerd Krumeich (Essen, 2001), 35–52, provide a well-balanced assessment of the Treaty of Versailles from the perspective of international law.
119. Schwengler, *Völkerrecht, Versailler Vertrag und die Auslieferungsfrage*, 138. By contrast, Dickmann, "Die Kriegsschuldfrage auf der Friedenskonferenz," 61, assumes the German leadership strata had not shared in the late nineteenth-century turn to a "popular sense of justice" and thus lacked any understanding for the international law demands posed by the victorious Allied powers.
120. Quoted in Schwengler, *Völkerrecht, Versailler Vertrag und die Auslieferungsfrage*, 138.
121. Michael Salewski, "Das Weimarer Revisionssyndrom," *Aus Politik und Zeitgeschichte*, 30 (1980): 2, 14–25; Konrad H. Jarausch, "World Power or Tragic Fate? The Kriegsschuldfrage as Historical Neurosis," *Central European History* 5 (1972): 73.
122. Quoted in Schwengler, *Völkerrecht, Versailler Vertrag und die Auslieferungsfrage*, 138–139. The Special Office was officially renamed the War Guilt Department in 1920; on its activities, see Ulrich Heinemann, *Die verdrängte Niederlage: Politische Öffentlichkeit und Kriegsschuldfrage in der Weimarer Republik* (Göttingen, 1983), 37–38; Holger Herwig, "Clio Deceived: Patriotic Self-Censorship in Germany after the Great War," in *Forging the Collective Memory: Government and International Historians through Two World Wars*, ed. Keith Wilson (Providence, RI, 1996), 91–92; also Immanuel Geiss, "Die manipulierte Kriegsschuldfrage: Deutsche Reichspolitik in der Julikrise 1914 und deutsche Kriegsziele im Spiegel des Schuldreferats des Auswärtigen Amtes, 1919–1931," *Militärgeschichtliche Mitteilungen* 34 (1983): 31–60.
123. See Dickmann, "Die Kriegsschuldfrage auf der Friedenskonferenz," 17.
124. On the two notes in the autumn of 1918, see Schwengler, *Völkerrecht, Versailler Vertrag und die Auslieferungsfrage*, 139.
125. See Heinemann, *Die verdrängte Niederlage*, 255; Horne and Kramer, *Deutsche Kriegsgreuel 1914*, 520.
126. Quoted in Schwengler, *Völkerrecht, Versailler Vertrag und die Auslieferungsfrage*, 141.
127. Eisner's private secretary, Felix Fehrenbach, soon after published one of the documents in a French periodical, for which he would be convicted in 1922 by a Bavarian "popular court" and sentenced to eleven years in prison. The drift of the Weimar-era justice system is evident in the fact that Admiral von Tirpitz also made an unauthorized publication of a document from his time as a state secretary at the Imperial Naval Office,

but never faced charges for it. The case of Fehrenbach is treated in Heinemann, *Die verdrängte Niederlage*, 104. Friz Klein, *Deutschland im Ersten Weltkrieg*, 3 vols. (Berlin, 1968).
128. Pius Dirr, *Bayerische Dokumente zum Kriegsausbruch und Versailler Schuldspruch*, 3rd ed. (Munich, 1925). On the methods of publication, see Dickmann, "Die Kriegsschuldfrage auf der Friedenskonferenz," 62–63; Allan Mitchell, *Revolution in Bavaria 1918–1919: The Eisner Regime and the Soviet Republic* (Princeton, NJ, 1965).
129. Quoted in Schwengler, *Völkerrecht, Versailler Vertrag und die Auslieferungsfrage*, 144.
130. Heinemann, *Die verdrängte Niederlage*, 25.
131. Quoted in Schwengler, *Völkerrecht, Versailler Vertrag und die Auslieferungsfrage*, 144.
132. Quoted in Heinemann, *Die verdrängte Niederlage*, 27.
133. Horne and Kramer, *Deutsche Kriegsgreuel 1914*, 391.
134. Heinemann, *Die verdrängte Niederlage*, 35.
135. See ibid.; Wolfgang Jäger, *Historische Forschung und politische Kultur in Deutschland: Die Debatte 1914–1980 über den Ausbruch des Ersten Weltkriegs* (Göttingen, 1984); Bernd-Jürgen Wendt, "Über den geschichtswissenschaftlichen Umgang mit der Kriegsschuldfrage," in *Wissenschaftliche Verantwortung und politische Macht*, ed. Klaus Jürgen Gantzel (Berlin, 1986), 1–63; Christoph Cornelißen, "'Schuld am Weltfrieden': Politische Kommentare und Deutungsversuche deutscher Historiker zum Versailler Vertrag," in Krumeich, *Versailles 1919*, 237–258; Gerd Krumeich and Gerhard Hirschfeld, "Die Geschichtsschreibung zum Ersten Weltkrieg," in Hirschfeld et al., *Enzyklopädie Erster Weltkrieg*, 304–313; Klaus Große Kracht, "Kriegsschuldfrage und zeithistorische Forschung in Deutschland: Historiographische Nachwirkungen des Ersten Weltkriegs." *Zeitgeschichte Online*, May 2004, http://www.zeitgeschichte-online.de/thema/kriegsschuldfrage-und-zeithistorische-forschung-deutschland; Jan Eckel, *Hans Rothfels: Eine intellektuelle Biographie im 20. Jahrhundert* (Göttingen, 2005). See also the contemporary overview "Überblick über 'Deutsche Kriegsschuldforscher,'" *Berliner Monatshefte* 7 (1929): 552–590.
136. Regarding the term "history management," see Sacha Zala, "Geltung und Grenzen schweizerischen Geschichtsmanagements," in *Zeitgeschichte als Streitgeschichte: Grosse Kontroversen seit 1945*, ed. Martin Sabrow, Ralph Jessen, and Klaus Große Kracht (Munich, 2003), 306–325.
137. The historian Hans Rothfels described the effects of the Treaty of Versailles on the profession in idealized terms in 1927, writing: "The political and moral charge unintentionally proved to be a heuristic principle of the first rank, a divining rod that causes hidden sources to spring up." Quoted in Große Kracht, "Kriegsschuldfrage und zeithistorische Forschung in Deutschland," 10.
138. See Michael Stolleis, *Geschichte des öffentlichen Rechts in Deutschland, Bd. 3: Staats- und Verwaltungsrechtswissenschaft in Republik und Diktatur 1914–1945* (Munich, 1999), 86–89.
139. On the conception of the network, see Rüdiger Hachtmann, *Wissenschaftsmanagement im "Dritten Reich": Geschichte der Generalverwaltung der Kaiser-Wilhelm-Gesellschaft*, vol. 1 (Göttingen, 2007), 26–31. The categories of "social space" and "field" as developed by Bourdieu are treated well in Markus Schwingel, *Pierre Bourdieu zur Einführung* (Hamburg, 2003), 69–71, 80–83.
140. Lutz Raphael, *Geschichtswissenschaft im Zeitalter der Extreme: Theorien, Methoden, Tendenzen von 1900 bis zur Gegenwart* (Munich, 2003), 83.
141. See Manfred Hettling, ed., *Volksgeschichten im Europa der Zwischenkriegszeit* (Göttingen, 2003).

142. Markus Pöhlmann, *Kriegsgeschichte und Geschichtspolitik: Der Erste Weltkrieg—Die amtliche deutsche Militärgeschichtsschreibung 1914–1956* (Paderborn, 2002), 76.
143. Writing on the composition of a parliamentary investigations committee of 1919, Max Weber, "Zur Zusammensetzung des Parlamentarischen Untersuchungsausschusses, Oktober/November 1919," in *Max-Weber-Gesamtausgabe, Bd. I/16: Zur Neuordnung Deutschlands: Schriften und Reden 1918–1920*, ed. Wolfgang J. Mommsen and Wolfgang Schwentker (Tübingen, 1988), 569 (hereafter the collection will be referred to as *MWG*). This memorandum and several other documents were destroyed by Marianne Weber.
144. Pöhlmann, *Kriegsgeschichte und Geschichtspolitik*, 94–95.
145. "Die Grausamkeit der Kriegführung," *Norddeutsche Allgemeine Zeitung*, 20 November 1918; on the declaration, see Horne and Kramer, *Deutsche Kriegsgreuel 1914*, 495; Schwengler, *Völkerrecht, Versailler Vertrag und die Auslieferungsfrage*, 164.
146. Hans Delbrück, "Die deutsche Kriegserklärung 1914 und der Einmarsch in Belgien," *Preussische Jahrbücher* 175 (1919): 272.
147. On Delbrück's role with the 4th subcommittee of the 15th commission of the German National Assembly of 21 August 1919, see Heinemann, *Die verdrängte Niederlage*, 177–185.
148. The official name of the office was Zentralstelle für Erforschung der Kriegsursachen. After Rassow passed, the job went to a Swiss doctor, Ernst Sauerbeck, whose apparent qualification was that he had drawn attention with his pro-German publications during the war. Ibid., 67.
149. On the history of *Große Politik der Europäischen Kabinette*, see Heinemann, *Die verdrängte Niederlage*, 78–87; Zala, *Geschichte unter der Schere politischer Zensur*, 51–52.
150. On historical engineering, a term coined originally by Noam Chomsky, see Wilson, "Introduction: Governments, Historians and 'Historical Engineering,'" in Wilson, *Forging the Collective Memory*, 1–27.
151. See Herwig, "Clio Deceived," 100.
152. Heinemann, *Die verdrängte Niederlage*, 29–33. Heinrich August Winkler argues that deep-seated differences among the leaders of the party were why they did not heed their comrade Bernstein's passionate appeal. Delivered before the first party congress after the war, the leading party theoretician had claimed that they had to "finally get out of this dungeon" (a reference to the SPD's infamous vote to approve the war budget on 4 August 1914). Heinrich August Winkler, "Die verdrängte Schuld," in *Auf ewig in Hitlers Schatten? Über die Deutschen und ihre Geschichte*, 2nd ed., ed. Heinrich August Winkler (Munich, 2007), 58–71. The Hindenburg biographer Wolfgang Pyta instead adopts the premise that the MSPD leaders wanted to return a favor to Hindenburg for his constructive role in the November revolution by scrupulously avoiding controversial questions about the role of the wartime military leadership. Wolfgang Pyta, *Hindenburg: Herrschaft zwischen Hohenzollern und Hitler* (Munich, 2007), 386.
153. Gerd Krumeich, "Die Dolchstoß-Legende," in *Deutsche Erinnerungsorte*, vol. 1, ed. Etienne François Hagen Schulze (Munich, 2001), 585–599.
154. Horne and Kramer, *Deutsche Kriegsgreuel 1914*, 497.
155. Quoted in Heinemann, *Die verdrängte Niederlage*, 36.
156. Quoted in ibid., 30–31; see also Robert A. Wheeler, "The Failure of 'Truth and Clarity' at Berne: Kurt Eisner, the Opposition, and the Reconstruction of the International," *International Review of Social History* 18 (1973): 173–201.
157. Dickmann, "Die Kriegsschuldfrage auf der Friedenskonferenz," 77–86.

158. The first published resolution from the side of legal scholars appeared on 24 February 1919 in the right-wing conservative *Kreuzzeitung* and predictably rejected the planned tribunal against Wilhelm II. The Heidelberg Association included several leading German legal scholars: Gerhard Anschütz, Karl Binding, Otto von Gierke, Erich Kaufmann, Josef Kohler, Otto Koellreuter, Herbert Kraus, Franz von Liszt, Christian Meurer, Richard Schmidt, Walther Schücking, Rudolf Smend, Karl Strupp, Heinrich Triepel, and Philipp Zorn. See Harald Wiggenhorn, *Verliererjustiz: Die Leipziger Kriegsverbrecherprozesse nach dem Ersten Weltkrieg* (Baden-Baden, 2005), 14.
159. See Weber, *MWG* I/16, 180n3.
160. "Für eine Politik des Rechts," 7 February 1919, in ibid., 523–525.
161. See Dirk Kaesler, *Max Weber: Preusse, Denker, Muttersohn—eine Biographie* (Munich, 2014), 870–873; also Wolfgang J. Mommsen, *Max Weber und die deutsche Revolution 1918/19* (Heidelberg, 1994), 10.
162. Max Weber, "Zum Thema der 'Kriegsschuld,'" in *MWG* I/16, 179–190.
163. Ibid., 182.
164. Ibid., 183.
165. See Gotthart Schwarz, *Theodor Wolff und das "Berliner Tageblatt": Eine liberale Stimme in der deutschen Politik 1906–1933* (Tübingen, 1968), 69. On Weber's concept of "Caesarian leader democracy," see Albertin, *Liberalismus und Demokratie*, 250–256.
166. Regarding Weber's position on the war guilt question, see Joachim Radkau, *Max Weber: Die Leidenschaft des Denkens* *Munich, 2005), 767–768; also Wolfgang J. Mommsen, *Max Weber und die deutsche Politik 1890–1920* (Tübingen, 1974). Fritz Ringer adopts a premise I regard as mistaken, arguing that Weber's engagement on the war guilt question proceeded above all from his alleged belief that the activities of German pacifists were predicated on a recognition of Germany as the sole party bearing guilt for the war. Fritz Ringer, *Max Weber: An Intellectual Biography* (Chicago, 2004), 74.
167. On the handling of the Fryatt case by the Schücking commission, see Schwengler, *Völkerrecht, Versailler Vertrag und die Auslieferungsfrage*, 172–175.
168. Radkau, *Max Weber*, 769, instead argues that Weber's stance against the pacifists' calls for a historical processing was distinct from that of the militant right wing. In Radkau's view, Weber held contempt for people like Eisner, but did not brand them as "traitors."
169. Max Weber, "Parlament und Regierung im neugeordneten Deutschland," *MWG* I/16, 351.
170. Foreign observers saw Weber's stance as part of a "campaign of sedition and lies" and as currying favor with the political right. The *Nationalzeitung* of Basel wrote: "Weber, like Naumann and Solf—and here we are intentionally naming the supposed moderates, the democrats, the conciliators, the non-imperialists—will never understand that there is only one hope for Germany, and it lies in the path struck by Lichnowsky, Förster, and Eisner: acknowledge the truth!" Weber, *MWG* I/16, 178.
171. Heinemann, *Die verdrängte Niederlage*, 23.
172. Quoted in Schwengler, *Völkerrecht, Versailler Vertrag und die Auslieferungsfrage*, 150. According to Reinhart Koselleck, the historical thinking of German idealism is marked by a "consistent temporalization" and the invocation of a "higher law" that would realize itself in world history. Koselleck, "Geschichte, Recht und Gerechtigkeit," in *Zeitschichten: Studien zur Historik*, ed. Reinhart Koselleck (Frankfurt, 2000), 347.
173. See Eberhard Kolb, *Deutschland 1918–1933: Eine Geschichte der Weimarer Republik* (Munich, 2010), 48–49; Kalus Schwabe, "'Gerechtigkeit für die Großmacht Deutschland': Die deutsche Friedensstrategie in Versailles," in Krumeich, *Versailles 1919*, 71–86. For two treatments that show far more understanding for Brockdorff-Rantzau's

position, see Dickmann, "Die Kriegsschuldfrage auf der Friedenskonferenz," 77–109; Udo Wengst, *Graf Brockdorff-Rantzau und die außenpolitischen Anfänge der Weimarer Republik* (Frankfurt, 1973).

174. Led by Walter Lippmann, the team of experts brought together as the Inquiry was given the job of gathering reliable data on the ethnographic situation in Europe that could be used in guiding US nationalities policy. Mark Mazower, *Governing the World: The History of an Idea* (London, 2012), 127.

175. The most prominent of such groups started in Germany were the Paxkonferenz (Peace Conference) and the Komitee für Friedensverhandlungen (Committee for Peace Negotiations). See Alma Luckau, *The German Peace Delegation at the Paris Peace Conference* (New York, 1971), 27–53.

176. In German, the name of the group was Heidelberger Arbeitsgemeinschaft für Politik des Rechts. Until now, the history of the Heidelberg Association has only been superficially examined. A short treatment, based in part on personal discussions, is provided in ibid., 47. Other cursory looks are given in Schwengler, *Völkerrecht, Versailler Vertrag und die Auslieferungsfrage*, 164–169; Mommsen, *Max Weber und die deutsche Politik*, 348–350; Albertin, *Liberalismus und Demokratie*, 212–215.

177. The editors of the collected works of Max Weber are inclined to the view that the Heidelberg Association was founded without any particular coordination with the Foreign Office. See Weber, *MWG* I/16, 197. Originally writing in 1941, Alma Luckau, *The German Peace Delegation*, 46–53, presents a different picture, contextualizing the Heidelberg Association within a series of other lobbying groups, but without being able to measure their influence clearly. It is revealing that the single version of the minutes from the association's original meeting, which in the meantime has been lost, was found by Luckau among the legacy papers of the top legal counsel to the Foreign Office, Walter Simons. On the source history of the minutes, see Weber, *MWG* I/16, 200.

178. "Für eine Politik des Rechts." Declaration of the Heidelberger Vereinigung, 7 February 1919. The statement was published in several German dailies on 13 February and later reprinted in *Preußische Jahrbüchern* [PJ] 175 (1919): 319–320. On the creation and reception of this text, see Weber, *MWG* I/16, 518–522.

179. Ibid., 523–525. Days earlier, on 3 February 1919, Max von Baden had delivered a lecture to announce the founding in which he strongly condemned the Entente Powers' German policy and attributed a central role to Germany in defending against Bolshevism. See Prinz Max von Baden, *Völkerbund und Rechtsfriede* (Berlin, 1919).

180. The editors of Weber's collected works are of the opinion that the article was published only under his name because other Heidelberg Association members were government officials. Weber, *MWG* I/16, 228.

181. See ibid., 229.

182. Max Weber, "Begleitschreiben vom 20.3.1919 an die *Frankfurter Zeitung*," in *Max Weber: Gesammelte Politische Schriften*, 5th ed., ed. Johannes Winckelmann (Tübingen, 1988), 503.

183. Max Weber, "Die Untersuchung der Schuldfrage," in *MWG* I/16, 230–232.

184. Max Weber, "Politik als Beruf," in Winckelmann, *Gesammelte Politische Schriften*, 549.

185. Ibid., 551. The American sociologist Jeffrey Olick provides an analysis of Karl Jaspers's 1946 work, *Schuldfrage* (The guilt question), in which Jaspers wrote about the Allied policy of de-Nazification after World War II. Olick concludes that Jaspers was strongly influenced the argument in Weber, "Politik als Beruf" (Politics as a profession), *Gesammelte Politische Schriften*, 505–560. According to Olick, Jaspers interpreted

Weber's polemics against the Weimar coalition's pacifism as the direct consequence of Weber's particular understanding of modernity and rationality. Jaspers had also adopted Weber's identity construction of a German *Kulturnation*, Olick avers. Jeffrey K. Olick, *In the House of the Hangman: The Agonies of German Defeat* (Chicago, 2005), 314–317. In an earlier work Olick wrote together with Brenda Coughlin, the authors conclude that Weber had viewed any recognition of war guilt as a flight from responsibility, and rejected it on those grounds. Jeffrey K. Olick and Brenda Coughlin, "The Politics of Regret: Analytical Frames," in Torpey, *Politics and the Past*, 37–62.

186. Starting during the war, blaming czarist Russia for its outbreak was already a common trope in the war-guilt discourse of German liberals and leftists, while conservatives preferred to lay the blame mainly on the English. See Michael Dreyer and Oliver Lembcke, *Die deutsche Diskussion um die Kriegsschuldfrage 1918/19* (Berlin, 1993), 41.
187. Eckel, *Hans Rothfels*, 42.
188. The historian Hermann Oncken wrote at the time that the task of the historian after 1919 would be to expand the image of history both forward and backward. See Cornelißen, "Schuld am Weltfrieden."
189. Mommsen, *Max Weber und die deutsche Politik*, 339, has a different explanation for Weber's recognizably ambiguous attitude on the question of document disclosures, by arguing that the proposal should actually be attributed to Prince Max von Baden, with Weber as his proxy.
190. See James McMillan, "War," in Bloxham and Gerwarth, *Political Violence in Twentieth-Century Europe*, 50.
191. Quoted in Heinrich August Winkler, *Weimar, 1918–1933: Die Geschichte der ersten deutschen Demokratie* (Munich, 1993), 87.
192. Quoted in ibid., 87; on this same controversy, see also Winkler, *Auf ewig in Hitlers Schatten?* 58–71.
193. Quoted in Winkler, *Weimar, 1918–1933*, 88.
194. On 12 March 1919, the justice minister, Otto Landsberg, submitted legislation to convene a state court. See Schwengler, *Völkerrecht, Versailler Vertrag und die Auslieferungsfrage*, 157–158; Heinemann, *Die verdrängte Niederlage*, 22.
195. This was the Parlamentarische Untersuchungsausschuss für die Schuldfragen des Weltkriegs (Parliamentary Inquiry on Questions of Guilt of World War I). On the origins and reception of the "stab in the back" thesis, see Oksana Nagornaja, "Einführung," *Erklärung des Generalfedlmarschalls von Hindenburg vor dem Parlamentarischen Untersuchungsausschuß ["Dolchstoßlengende"], 18. November 1919.* 1000 deutsche Schlüsseldokumente. www.1000dokumente.de/index.html?c=dokument_de&dokument=0026_dol&object=context&st=&l=de.
196. Heinemann, *Die verdrängte Niederlage*, 41.
197. Quoted in Schwengler, *Völkerrecht, Versailler Vertrag und die Auslieferungsfrage*, 166.
198. Heinemann, *Die verdrängte Niederlage*, 77.
199. See Weber, *MWG* I/16, 306. Edited by Roderich Gooß, the Austrian documentary collection was published in 1919, presenting an image of Wilhelm II and his government not as calm tacticians but as careless actors. Zala, *Geschichte unter der Schere politischer Zensur*, 55.
200. Graf Max Montgelas and Walther Schücking, eds., *Die deutschen Dokumente zum Kriegsausbruch 1914: Vollständige Sammlung der von Karl Kautsky zusammengestellten Aktenstücke mit einigen Ergänzungen im Auftrage des Auswärtigen Amtes nach gemeinsamer Durchsicht mit Karl Kautsky*, 4 vols. (Charlottenburg, 1919).

201. Karl Kautsky, *Wie der Weltkrieg entstand: Dargestellt nach dem Aktenmaterial des Deutschen Auswärtigenf Amts* (Berlin, 1919), 11.
202. See Weber, *MWG* I/16, 302.
203. This is at least indicated in a comment Weber made in a letter to his wife, in which he declared that he would "not take part in the guilt note" if "indignities" were planned or allowed. Ibid., 309; see also Mommsen, *Max Weber und die deutsche Politik*, 340–341.
204. Quoted in Weber, *MWG* I/16, 309.
205. Max Weber, "Bemerkungen zum Bericht der Kommission der alliierten und assoziierten Regierungen über die Verantwortlichkeiten der Urheber des Krieges" (the "Professors' Memorandum"), in ibid., 324–351.
206. Quoted in Dickmann, "Die Kriegsschuldfrage auf der Friedenskonferenz," 100.
207. This is the conclusion in Horne and Kramer, *Deutsche Kriegsgreuel 1914*, 491.
208. Max Weber, "Editorischer Bericht zu den Bemerkungen der Viererkommission" [Editors' report on comments by the four members of the commission], in Weber, *MWG* I/16, 311. Dreyer and Lembcke, *Die deutsche Diskussion um die Kriegsschuldfrage 1918/19*, 133–153, also provide a thorough look at the difficult process of drafting the memorandum. Both treatments stress that the professors maintained a high share of autonomy in creating the document, and judge their role in it mainly as positive.
209. Weber, "Editorischer Bericht zu den Bemerkungen der Viererkommission," 313–314.
210. Weber, "Bemerkungen zum Bericht der Kommission der Alliierten," 342.
211. Weber, "Editorischer Bericht zu den Bemerkungen der Viererkommission,", 312; Mommsen, *Max Weber und die deutsche Revolution*, 17, expects that the Foreign Office engaged in chicanery by enlisting the professors in support of Brockdorff-Rantzaus's strategy without informing them about the actual stance of the government in Berlin.
212. As stressed by Dreyer and Lembcke, *Die deutsche Diskussion um die Kriegsschuldfrage 1918/19*.
213. See Horne and Kramer, *Deutsche Kriegsgreuel 1914*, 491.
214. It may be assumed that the two jurists among the four professors, aware that the charter of the League of Nations was in preparation, did not want to expose themselves to charges of insufficient patriotism. On the position of the organized pacifist movement in the Weimar Republic, see Gerd Hankel, "Auf verlorenem Posten: Friedenspolitik und Völkerrecht in der Weimarer Republik," in Kramer and Wette, *Recht ist, was den Waffen nützt*, 176–189.
215. On Schücking's position, see Segesser, *Recht statt Rache oder Rache durch Recht?* 267–268.
216. After the French occupation of the Rhineland, the Heidelbergers also took part in the German propaganda campaign against the "Black Dishonor" (*Schwarze Schmach*), which condemned the French above all for deploying regiments from their African colonies in Germany, calling it a "violation of civilized norms." See Iris Wigger, "'Gegen die Kultur und Zivilisation aller Weissen': Die internationale rassistische Kampagne gegen die 'Schwarze Schmach," in *Grenzenlose Vorurteile: Antisemitismus, Nationalismus und ethnische Konflikte in verschiedenen Kulturen*, ed. the Fritz Bauer Institute (Frankfurt, 2002), 101–128.
217. Quoted in Weber, *MWG* I/16, 545, 553; see Mommsen, *Max Weber und die deutsche Politik*, 348–350.
218. Ibid., 351.
219. Horne and Kramer, *Deutsche Kriegsgreuel 1914*, 498.
220. Noske, quoted in ibid., 501–502.

221. On the Leipzig War Crimes Trials, see Gerd Hankel, *Die Leipziger Prozesse: Deutsche Kriegsverbrechen und ihre strafrechtliche Verfolgung nach dem Ersten Weltkrieg* (Hamburg, 2003); Wiggenhorn, *Verliererjustiz*; Horne and Kramer, *Deutsche Kriegsgreuel 1914*, 498–520; Jürgen Matthäus, "The Lessons of Leipzig: Punishing German War Criminals after the First World War," in *Atrocities on Trial: Historical Perspectives on the Politics of Prosecuting War Crimes*, ed. Patricia Heberer and Jürgen Matthäus (Lincoln, NE, 2008), 3–23; Segesser, *Recht statt Rache oder Rache durch Recht?* 225–231.

Chapter 2

1. Bösch and Goschler, "Der Nationalsozialismus und die deutsche Public History," give a good overview of literature on the tensions between academic researchers of the subject and other actors in the "contemporary history arena."
2. Ernst Fraenkel, *The Dual State*, was first published in New York in 1941 and much later retranslated into German and published as *Der Doppelstaat* (1974).
3. See Laura Jockusch, *Collect and Record! Jewish Holocaust Documentation in Early Postwar Europe* (Oxford, 2012); Michael Marrus, "A Jewish Lobby at Nuremberg: Jacob Robinson and the Institute of Jewish Affairs, 1945–46," in *The Nuremberg Trials: International Criminal Law Since 1945*, ed. Herbert R. Reginbogin and Christoph Safferling, 63–71. Munich, 2006.
4. Quoted in Segesser, *Recht statt Rache oder Rache durch Recht?* 304. On the negationist doctrine among German international law scholars, see Mazower, *Governing the World*, 180–187.
5. An example of this progressive narrative can be found in Fabian Klose, *Menschenrechte im Schatten kolonialer Gewalt: Die Dekolonisierungskriege in Kenia und Algerien 1945–1962* (Munich, 2009).
6. On the Allies' war crimes policy, above all see Arieh J. Kochavi, *Prelude to Nuremberg: Allied War Crimes Policy and the Question of Punishment* (Chapel Hill, NC, 1998).
7. On the background to Roosevelt's speech, see Borgwardt, *A New Deal for the World*, 48–53.
8. See Mazower, "The Strange Triumph of Human Rights, 1933–1950," *Historical Journal* 47, no. 2 (2004): 379–398.
9. Borgwardt, *A New Deal for the World*, 56.
10. Ibid., 21.
11. See Anson Rabinbach, "Totalitarismus: Konjunkturen eines Begriffs," in *Begriffe aus dem Kalten Krieg: Totalitarismus, Antifaschismus, Genozid*, ed. Anson Rabinbach (Göttingen, 2009), 7–27; Moyn, *The Last Utopia*, 65.
12. See Annette Weinke, "'Von Nürnberg nach Den Haag'? Das Internationale Militärtribunal in historischer Perspektive," in *Vom Tribunal zum Weltgericht: Neue Fragestellungen zum Verhältnis von Menschenrechtsverbrechen und Völkerstrafrecht 60 Jahre nach dem Nürnberger Hauptkriegsverbrecherprozess*, ed. the Justice Department of Nordrhein-Westfalen and Villa ten Hompel (Geldern, 2008), 20–33; Samuel Moyn, "Personalismus, Gemeinschaft und die Ursprünge der Menschenrechte," in Hoffmann, *Moralpolitik*, 63–91.
13. See Klose, *Menschenrechte im Schatten kolonialer Gewalt*, 24–25.
14. Arguing along these lines, see Mazower, "The Strange Triumph of Human Rights," 387.

15. The "phrase meant different things to different people from the beginning. And therefore, it meant nothing specific as various parties tried to give it sense." Moyn, *The Last Utopia*, 50–51.
16. See Segesser, *Recht statt Rache oder Rache durch Recht?* 315; Lewis, "The World Jewish Congress and the Institute of Jewish Affairs at Nuremberg: Ideas, Strategies, and Political Goals, 1942–1946," *Yad Vashem Studies* 36, no. 1 (2008): 185.
17. Along these lines, for example, Winston Churchill suggested handling the Nazi leadership after their capture as "outlaws." On this, see Kochavi, *Prelude to Nuremberg*, 73–80; Weinke, *Die Nürnberger Prozesse*, 11.
18. On the history of the Cambridge Commission and the London International Assembly, see Segesser, *Recht statt Rache oder Rache durch Recht?* 318–319.
19. The Cambridge Commission brought together Arnold Duncan McNair, Hersch Lauterpacht, Václav Beneš, René Cassin, Marcel de Baer, and Stefan Baer. The London International Assembly included jurists like Bohuslav Ecer, René Cassin, Sheldon Glueck, and Georg Lelewer. Ibid., 318.
20. With a positivistic approach and a relatively narrow definition of human rights, Moyn, *The Last Utopia*, 176–211, seems to miss that human rights concepts played a role in the international law of war discourse. This is especially true of the controversies over a judicial response to German occupation crimes. Moyn argues instead that the discovery of human rights first came about with the rise of new social movements in the 1970s. In his view, international lawyers benefitted from this but had done as good as nothing to bring it about.
21. Segesser, *Recht statt Rache oder Rache durch Recht?* 323.
22. Active in the Cambridge Commission, Hersch Lauterpacht pleaded for the creation of new stipulations to criminalize persecution measures taken against German and Austrian Jews before the war. He wanted to describe these as "crimes against humanity." Marrus, "A Jewish Lobby at Nuremberg," 63.
23. Viktor Fischl, "The Jews and the Conscience of the World," *Spirit of Czechoslovakia* 4 (1943): 11, quoted in Segesser, *Recht statt Rache oder Rache durch Recht?* 327.
24. So goes the argument of Glueck, "Trial and Punishment of the Axis War Criminals," *Free World* 4 (1942): 138–146.
25. Quoted in Segesser, *Recht statt Rache oder Rache durch Recht?* 322–323.
26. Quoted in ibid., 355; Glueck, "Trial and Punishment of the Axis War Criminals," 39–40.
27. The writings of the Austrian emigrant Hans Kelsen are a perfect example of this. Kelsen, *Peace through Law* (Chapel Hill, NC, 1944).
28. See Dan Diner, "Rassistisches Völkerrecht: Elemente einer nationalsozialistischen Weltordnung," *Vierteljahrshefte für Zeitgeschichte* 37, no. 1 (1989): 23–56.
29. John Cooper, *Raphael Lemkin and the Struggle for the Genocide Convention* (London, 2008); A. Dirk Moses, "The Holocaust and Genocide," in *The Historiography of the Holocaust*, ed. Dan Stone (London, 2004), 533–551; Anson Rabinbach, "Genozid Genese eines Konzepts," in Rabinbach, *Begriffe aus dem Kalten Krieg*, 43–72.
30. Moses, "The Holocaust and Genocide," 537.
31. For a short biographical treatment, see Claudia Kraft, "Völkermord als delictum iuris gentium: Raphael Lemkins Vorarbeiten für eine Genozidkonvention," *Jahrbuch des Simon-Dubnow-Instituts* 4 (2005): 79–98; also instructive is the overview of Lemkin's scattered legacy in Tanya Elder, "What You See Before Your Eyes: Documenting Raphael Lemkin's Life by Exploring His Archival Papers, 1900–1959," *Journal of Genocide Research* 7, no. 4 (2005): 469–499

32. As argued by Kraft, "Völkermord als delictum iuris gentium"; by contrast, Moses, "The Holocaust and Genocide," 536, describes Lemkin's understanding of the law as "irreducibly particular."
33. Raphael Lemkin, *Axis Rule in Occupied Europe: Laws of Occupation, Analysis of Government, Proposals for Redress* (New York, 1944), 79.
34. On this discussion, see Moses, "The Holocaust and Genocide," 540.
35. Lemkin, *Axis Rule in Occupied Europe*, 77.
36. Ibid., 22, 89.
37. Ibid., 75.
38. Lewis, *The World Jewish Congress*, 186. On the ambivalence in contemporary perception of whether to view Jews as a religious group or as a "race," see also Marrus, "A Jewish Lobby at Nuremberg," 66.
39. See Mark Mazower, "Nations Refugees, and Territory," in *No Enchanted Palace: The End of Empire and the Ideological Origins of the United Nations* (Princeton, NJ, 2009), 128–131.
40. Rabinbach, "Genozid," 54.
41. Reasons for the fairly reserved approach to law-of-war issues in *Axis Rule* are discussed in Daniel Segesser and Myriam Gessler, "Raphael Lemkin and the International Debate on the Punishment of War Crimes (1919–1947)," in "The 'Founder of the United Nations' Genocide Convention' as a Historian of Mass Violence," special issue, *Journal of Genocide Research* 7, no. 4 (2005): 453–468, 460–462. Dan Stone, "Raphael Lemkin on the Holocaust," *Journal of Genocide Research* 7, no. 4 (2005): 539–550, instead emphasizes the presentist orientation of *Axis Rule*.
42. The Moscow Conference, October 1943, "Statement on Atrocities, Signed by President Roosevelt, Prime Minister Churchill and Premier Stalin," Joint Four-Nation Declaration, Shlomo Aronson http://avalon.law.yale.edu/wwii/moscow.asp; see Kochavi, *Prelude to Nuremberg*, 57.
43. Stone, "Raphael Lemkin on the Holocaust," 546.
44. Alexa Stiller by contrast assumes that Lemkin saw the praxis of "forced cultural assimilation" and "biological extermination" as equivalent. Alexa Stiller, "Semantics of Extermination: The Use of the New Term of Genocide in the Nuremberg Trials and the Genesis of a Master Narrative," in Priemel and Stiller, *Reassessing the Nuremberg Military Tribunals*, 107.
45. According to Rabinbach, "Genozid," 57, Lemkin's genocide concept attempts to combine two different but closely related historical processes in one term: the annihilation of the Jews and the destruction of Poland as an independent nation. With this "semantic bridge," he was pleading for an integrated view of two legal questions that diplomats and international lawyers until then had regarded separately.
46. Lemkin, *Axis Rule in Occupied Europe*, 80.
47. The postulate by Jürgen Zimmerer and others that the Nazi system of rule was "colonial" remains controversial. Jürgen Zimmerer, "Nationalsozialismus postkolonial: Plädoyer zur Globalisierung der deutschen Gewaltgeschichte," *Zeitschrift für Geschichtswissenschaft* 57, no. 6 (2009): 529–548; Dietmut Majer, "Das besetzte Osteuropa als deutsche Kolonie (1939–1944): Die Pläne der NS-Führung zur Beherrschung Osteuropas," in *Gesetzliches Unrecht: Rassistisches Recht im 20. Jahrhundert*, ed. Fritz Bauer Institut (Frankfurt, 2005), 111–134; Robert Gerwarth and Stephen Malinowski, "Der Holocaust als kolonialer Genozid," *Geschichte und Gesellschaft* 33, no. 3 (2007): 439–466; Birthe Kundrus, "Kolonialismus, Imperialismus, Nationalsozialismus? Chancen und Grenzen eines neuen Paradigmas," in *Kolonialgeschichten: Regionale Perspektiven*

auf ein globales Phänomen, ed. Claudia Kraft, Alf Lüdtke, and Jürgen Martschukat (Frankfurt, 2010), 187–210; Wendy Lower, "Hitler's 'Garden of Eden': Nazi Colonialism, Volksdeutsche and the Holocaust 1941–1944," in *Gray Zones: Ambiguity and Compromise in the Holocaust and Its Aftermath*, ed. Jonathan Petropoulos and John Roth (New York, 2005),185–204.
48. Hannah Arendt, *Elemente und Ursprünge totaler Herrschaft*, 2nd ed. (Munich, 1986), 307–309; see also Richard H. King and Dan Stone, *Hannah Arendt and the Uses of History: Imperialism, Race, Nation and Genocide*, ed. Richard H. King and Dan Stone (New York, 2007).
49. Lemkin, *Axis Rule in Occupied Europe*, 80.
50. Ibid., 93.
51. Ibid., 24.
52. Ibid., 23.
53. Fraenkel, *Der Doppelstaat*; Michael Wildt, "The Political Order of the Volksgemeinschaft: Ernst Fraenkel's Dual State Revisited," in *On Germans and Jews under the Nazi Regime: Essays by Three Generations of Historians—A Festschrift in Honor of Otto Dov Kulka*, ed. Moshe Zimmermann (Jerusalem, 2006), 143–160.
54. Mark Mazower, "Ende der Zivilisation und Aufstieg der Menschenrechte: Die konzeptionelle Trennung Mitte des 20. Jahrhunderts," in Hoffmann, *Moralpolitik*, 49.
55. After the war, Lemkin turned to the problems of European and North American colonialism and considered these as cases within his concept of genocide. See Michael A. McDonnell and A. Dirk Moses, "Raphael Lemkin as Historian of Genocide in the Americas," *Journal of Genocide Research* 7, no. 4 (2005): 501–529. Dominik Schaller points out instead that Lemkin's attitude toward the old European colonialism was ambivalent and influenced by the ideas of British Victorianism. Dominik Schaller, "Raphael Lemkin's View of European Colonial Rule in Africa: Between Condemnation and Admiration," *Journal of Genocide Research* 7, no. 4 (2005): 532–538.
56. Lewis, "The World Jewish Congress," 187.
57. Biographical information is supplied by Omry Kaplan-Feuereisen, "Jacob Robinson," *The YIVO Encyclopedia of Jews in Eastern Europe*, 18 November 2010, http://www.yivoencyclopedia.org/article.aspx/Robinson_Jacob; Omry Kaplan-Feuereisen, "Geschichtserfahrung und Völkerrecht: Jacob Robinson und die Gründung des Institute of Jewish Affairs," *Leipziger Beiträge zur jüdischen Geschichte und Kultur* 2 (2004): 307–327; Omry Kaplan-Feuereisen, "Im Dienste der jüdischen Nation: Jacob Robinson und das Völkerrecht," *Osteuropa: Impulse für Europa—Tradition und Moderne der Juden Osteuropas* 58, nos. 8–10 (2008): 279–293.
58. See Lewis, "The World Jewish Congress."
59. On this, see esp. Bloxham, *Genocide on Trial: War Crimes Trials and the Formation of Holocaust History and Memory* (New York, 2001); Donald Bloxham, "From Streicher to Sawoniuk: The Holocaust in the Courtroom," in Stone, *The Historiography of the Holocaust*, 397–419; Donald Bloxham, "Milestones and Mythologies: The Impact of Nuremberg," in Heberer and Matthäus, *Atrocities on Trial*, 263–282; Michael Marrus, "History and the Holocaust in the Courtroom," in *Lessons and Legacies: The Holocaust and Justice*, vol. 5, ed. Ronald Smelser (Evanston, IL, 2002), 215–239; Daniel Levy and Natan Sznaider, *Erinnerung im globalen Zeitalter: Der Holocaust* (Frankfurt, 2001).
60. "St. James's Conference of the Allied Governments in London and Nazi Anti-Jewish Crimes," Documents Exchanged with the World Jewish Congress, London 1942, 6; quoted in Lewis, "The World Jewish Congress," 185.

61. On this, see Lewis, "The World Jewish Congress"; Marrus, "A Jewish Lobby at Nuremberg"; Kaplan-Feuereisen, "Geschichtserfahrung und Völkerrecht." Shlomo Aronson's history puts the IJA in a much more peripheral role. Schlomo Aronson, "Preparations for the Nuremberg Trial: The OSS, Charles Dwork, and the Holocaust," *Holocaust and Genocide Studies* 12, no. 2 (1998): 257–281.
62. Quoted in Marrus, "A Jewish Lobby at Nuremberg," 65.
63. Lewis, *The Birth of the New Justice*, 159.
64. Ibid., 65.
65. Quoted in Lewis, "The World Jewish Congress," 192.
66. Quoted in Aronson, "Preparations for the Nuremberg Trial," 264.
67. Ibid., 260–263; Donald Bloxham calls the stipulations for conspiracy a "brainchild" of Bernays, without mentioning the influence of Jewish NGOs. Donald Bloxham, *Genocide on Trial: The World Wars, and the Unweaving of Europe* (London, 2008), 19.
68. Lewis, "The World Jewish Congress," 195–199.
69. See Weinke, *Die Nürnberger Prozesse*, 48.
70. Bloxham, *Genocide, the World Wars, and the Unweaving of Europe*, 57–63.
71. Ibid., 69.
72. Franz Leopold Neumann, *Behemoth: Struktur und Praxis des Nationalsozialismus 1933–1944*, 5th ed. (Frankfurt, 2004). On the creation and reception history of the book, see Jürgen Bast, *Totalitärer Pluralismus: Zu Franz L. Neumanns Analyse der politischen und rechtlichen Struktur der NS-Herrschaft* (Tübingen, 1999); Armin Nolzen, "Franz Leopold Neumanns 'Behemoth': Ein vergessener Klassiker der NSForschung, Version: 1.0." *Docupedia-Zeitgeschichte*, 30 May 2011, https://docupedia.de/zg/Nolzen_-_Neumann.2C_Behemoth?oldid=79047.
73. Barry M. Katz, *Foreign Intelligence: Research and Analysis in the Office of Strategic Services 1942–1945*. Cambridge, MA, 1989, 52.
74. Neumann, *Behemoth: Struktur und Praxis*, 415.
75. Thomas Hobbes, *Leviathan*, ed. Richard Tuck (Cambridge, 2005).
76. See Samuel Salzborn, "Leviathan und Behemoth: Staat und Mythos bei Thomas Hobbes und Carl Schmitt," in *Der Hobbes-Kristall: Carl Schmitts Hobbes-Interpretation in der Diskussion*, ed. Rüdiger Vogt (Stuttgart, 2009), 152.
77. Franz Leopold Neumann, *Behemoth: The Structure and Practice of National Socialism, 1933–1944*, intro. Peter Hayes (Chicago, 2009), 160.
78. Neumann, *Behemoth: Struktur und Praxis*, 196.
79. Ibid., 211.
80. Neumann, *Behemoth: The Structure and Practice*, 167, emphasis in original.
81. From the Institute for Social Research, the OSS Research and Analysis (R&A) Branch recruited Neumann, the constitutional lawyer Otto Kirchheimer, and the philosopher Herbert Marcuse. Other émigrés who were hired at R&A included the international jurist Hans Herz, the philosopher Hans Meyerhoff, the historian Felix Gilbert, the former Prussian ministerial officials Oskar Weigert and Robert Eisenberg, and the Austrians Robert Neumann und Henry Kellermann. Alfons Söllner, "Wissenschaftliche Kompetenz und politische Ohnmacht: Deutsche Emigranten im amerikanischen Staatsdienst 1942–1949," in *Deutsche Politikwissenschaftler in der Emigration: Studien zu ihrer Akkulturation und Wirkungsgeschichte*, ed. Alfons Söllner (Opladen, 1996), 125. For a thorough history of the R&A, see Alfons Söllner, *Zur Archäologie der Demokratie in Deutschland: Analysen politischer Emigranten im amerikanischen Geheimdienst, Bd. 1: 1943–1945* (Frankfurt, 1982); Petra Marquardt-Bigman, *Amerikanische Geheimdienstanalysen über Deutschland 1942–1949* (Munich, 1995), 67–73.

82. See Barry M. Katz, "The Criticism of Arms: The Frankfurt School Goes to War," *Journal of Modern History* 59, no. 3 (1987): 441.
83. John H. Herz, *Vom Überleben: Wie ein Weltbild entstand—Autobiographie* (Düsseldorf, 1984), 136.
84. On knowledge production at R&A, see Söllner, "Wissenschaftliche Kompetenz," 126; Tim B. Müller, *Krieger und Gelehrte: Herbert Marcuse und die Denksysteme im Kalten Krieg* (Hamburg, 2010), 49–59.
85. Neumann, "Vorwort" (in first ed. of 23 December 1941), in *Behemoth: Struktur und Praxis*, 18.
86. Müller, *Krieger und Gelehrte*, 50.
87. Katz, "The Criticism of Arms," 465.
88. Söllner, "Wissenschaftliche Kompetenz," 121.
89. Neumann, *Behemoth: Struktur und Praxis*, 581–583.
90. Müller, *Krieger und Gelehrte*, 56.
91. Quoted in Katz, "The Criticism of Arms," 454.
92. See ibid. On the Association of Free Germans, see also Marjorie Lamberti, "German Antifascist Refugees in America and the Public Debate on 'What Should Be Done with Germany after Hitler, 1941–1945," *Central European History* 40, no. 2 (2007): 285.
93. Quoted in Katz, "The Criticism of Arms," 458.
94. See Söllner, *Zur Archäologie der Demokratie in Deutschland*, 145–148; Marquardt-Bigman, *Amerikanische Geheimdienstanalysen*, 196–203; Katz, "The Criticism of Arms," 466–473; Joachim Perels, "Franz L. Neumanns Beitrag zur Konzipierung der Nürnberger Prozesse," in *Kritische Theorie der Politik: Franz L. Neumann—eine Bilanz*, ed. Matthias Iser and David Strecker (Baden-Baden, 2002), 83–94; Raul Hilberg, "Die bleibende Bedeutung des Behemoth," in Iser and Strecker, *Kritische Theorie der Politik*, 75–82; Michael Salter, *Nazi War Crimes, US Intelligence and Selective Prosecution at Nuremberg: Controversies Regarding the Role of the Office of Strategic Services* (London, 2007); Müller, *Krieger und Gelehrte*, 52–59; Ahrens, "Kartelle und Verschwörungen."
95. On the phenomenon of "judicial activism," see Aronson, "Preparations for the Nuremberg Trial," 258.
96. See Salter, *Nazi War Crimes*, 315–320.
97. Quoted in ibid., 316–317.
98. Katz, "The Criticism of Arms," 468; similar reading in Alfons Söllner, "Jüdische Emigranten in den USA: Ihr Einfluss auf die amerikanische Deutschlandpolitik 1933–1949," in *"Gegen alle Vergeblichkeit": Jüdischer Widerstand gegen den Nationalsozialismus*, ed. Hans Erler, Arnold Paucker, and Ernst Ludwig Ehrlich (Frankfurt, 2003), 384–385.
99. Söllner, *Zur Archäologie der Demokratie in Deutschland*, 146.
100. Quoted in Katz, "The Criticism of Arms," 470. A German translation of this text can be found in Söllner, *Zur Archäologie der Demokratie in Deutschland*, 163–172.
101. "Memorandum for the President," 22 January 1945, reprinted in Bradley F. Smith, *The American Road to Nuremberg: The Documentary Record 1944–1945* (Stanford, CA, 1982), 117–122; see also Weinke, *Die Nürnberger Prozesse*, 15.
102. See Marquardt-Bigman, *Amerikanische Geheimdienstanalysen*, 198–199.
103. On the concept of "terrorist technocracy," see Herbert Marcuse, "Some Social Implications of Modern Technology," *Studies in Philosophy and Social Science* 9 (1941): 414–439.
104. See Marquardt-Bigman, *Amerikanische Geheimdienstanalysen*, 201.

105. Otto Kirchheimer, "Nazi Plans for Dominating Germany and Europe. Domestic Crimes." Draft for War Crimes Staff, 13 August 1945; quoted in Katz, "The Criticism of Arms," 471.
106. This is the interpretation of Müller, "Bearing Witness to the Liquidation of Western Dasein: Herbert Marcuse and the Holocaust 1941–1948," special issue on "Intellectuals," *New German Critique* 85 (2002): 152; see also Martin Jay, "Die Antisemitismusanalyse der Kritischen Theorie," in *Die Frankfurter Schule und Frankfurt: Eine Rückkehr nach Deutschland*, ed. Monika Boll and Raphael Gross (Göttingen, 2009), 136–149; Mitchell G. Ash, "Learning from Persecution: Emigré Jewish Social Scientists' Studies of Authoritarianism and Anti-Semitism after 1933," in *Jüdische Welten: Juden in Deutschland vom 18. Jahrhundert bis in die Gegenwart*, ed. Marion Kaplan and Beate Meyer (Göttingen, 2005), 271–294.
107. Herbert Marcuse, "Nazi Plans to Dominate Europe," memorandum of 12 June 1945; quoted in Katz, "The Criticism of Arms," 473.
108. For an opposite interpretation, see Söllner, *Zur Archäologie der Demokratie in Deutschland*, 148, which speaks of an overwhelming agreement.
109. Franz Leopold Neumann, "The War Crimes Trials," *World Politics* 2, no. 1 (1949): 135–147.
110. Robert H. Jackson, *Report of Robert H. Jackson, United States Representative to the International Conference on Military Trials* (Washington, DC, 1949), 331.
111. On the German policy planning of R&A, see Joachim Perels, "Pläne der US-Administration für ein anderes Deutschland: Die Arbeiten der Neumann-Gruppe," *Das juristische Erbe des "Dritten Reiches": Beschädigungen der demokratischen Rechtsordnung*, ed. Joachim Perels (Frankfurt, 1999), 39–46.
112. Robert M. W. Kempner and Jörg Friedrich, *Ankläger einer Epoche: Lebenserinnerungen* (Frankfurt, 1986), 223.
113. Ahrens, "Kartelle und Verschwörungen," 32.
114. On the concept of "purified memory," see Manfred Messerschmidt, "Vorwärtsverteidigung: Die 'Denkschrift der Generäle' für den Nürnberger Gerichtshof," in *Vernichtungskrieg: Die Verbrechen der Wehrmacht 1941–1944*, ed. Hannes Heer and Klaus Naumann (Hamburg, 1995), 532.
115. Despite the great importance of this group of more than several dozen men on the German defense team at Nuremberg, their collective biographical background remains underresearched. Little is known about the style of thinking, ways of perception, and patterns of action—the factors that commonly form a group's political self-understanding and worldview. This is above all because of the lack of access to relevant ego documents, but also because research interest until now has focused almost exclusively on the defendants themselves. A first overview can be found in Christoph Safferling and Philipp Graebke, "Strafverteidigung im Nürnberger Hauptkriegsverbrecherprozess: Strategien und Wirkung," *Zeitschrift für die Gesamte Strafrechtswissenschaft* 123 (2011): 47–81; see also the short summary in Weinke, *Die Nürnberger Prozesse*, 37–39.
116. The tendency is especially pronounced in Hans Laternser, defender of the Wehrmacht General Staff at the IMT, and Hellmut Becker, the lawyer of Richard von Weizsäcker in the eleventh follow-up trial. Kerstin von Lingen, *Kesselrings letzte Schlacht: Kriegsverbrecherprozesse, Vergangenheitspolitik und Wiederbewaffnung—Der Fall Kesselring* (Paderborn, 2004), 123–131; Eckart Conze, Norbert Frei, Peter Hayes, and Moshe Zimmermann, eds., *Das Amt und die Vergangenheit: Deutsche Diplomaten im Dritten Reich und in der Bundesrepublik* (Munich, 2010), 401–435.

117. In addition, an internal working paper details that the twelve Nuremberg follow-up trials employed 375 defense attorneys (373 German citizens and two Americans), Office of Chief of Counsel for War Crimes, Public Information Office, "List of Defense Counsel," 27 January 1949, Telford Taylor Papers (TTP), 20-I-LC3.
118. Overall, we can assume the accuracy of Kempner's retrospective assessment that in the recruitment of the defense personnel, only the Soviets had worked to assure a degree of distance from the regime. See Kempner and Friedrich, *Ankläger einer Epoche*, 239.
119. The group of German defense attorneys included Walter Ballas, Ludwig Babel, Friedrich Bergold, Georg Böhm, Rudolf Dix, Franz Exner, Hans Flaechsner, Heinz Fritz, Hans Gawlik, Carl Haensel, Martin Horn, Hermann Jahrreiß, Kurt Kauffmann, Theodor Klefisch, Otto Kranzbühler, Ernst Wolgast, Herbert Kraus, Egon Kubuschok, Hans Laternser, Martin Loeffler, Otto Freiherr von Lüdinghausen, Hanns Marx, Rudolf Merkel, Otto Nelte, Otto Pannenbecker, Horst Pelckmann, Günther von Rohrscheidt, Fritz Sauter, Alfred Schilf, Alfred Seidl, Robert Servatius, Walter Siemers, Otto Stahmer, Gustav Steinbauer, and Alfred Thoma. See Safferling and Graebke, "Strafverteidigung im Nürnberger Hauptkriegsverbrecherprozess," 48–50. Not named in the list by Safferling and Graebke is the lawyer Georg Fröschmann, who defended Joachim von Ribbentrop.
120. See Andreas Toppe, *Militär und Kriegsvölkerrecht: Rechtsnorm, Fachdiskurs und Kriegspraxis in Deutschland 1899–1940* (Munich, 2007), 207.
121. Office of Chief of Counsel for War Crimes, Public Information Office, List of Defense Counsel, 27 January 1949, TTP, 20-I-LC3. In the literature, estimates of the number of NSDAP, SA, or SS members on the defense team vary between eight and fourteen. See Safferling and Graebke, "Strafverteidigung im Nürnberger Hauptkriegsverbrecherprozess," 51n14.
122. Ernst Klee, *Das Personenlexikon zum Dritten Reich: Wer war was vor und nach 1945* (Frankfurt, 2007), 142.
123. For example, in the second edition of his textbook on criminal biology, Franz Exner attributed the crime rate among Jews to "a Jewish racial characteristic." This passage was first revised in the 1949 edition; quoted in Immanuel Baumann, *Dem Verbrechen auf der Spur: Eine Geschichte der Kriminologie und Kriminalpolitik in Deutschland 1880 bis 1980* (Göttingen, 2006), 153.
124. See Weinke, *Die Nürnberger Prozesse*, 37–39.
125. On Nipperdey's role as the first presiding judge on the 1954 FRG Labour Court, see Thomas Henne, "Die neue Wertordnung im Zivilrecht: Speziell im Familien- und Arbeitsrecht," in *Das Bonner Grundgesetz: Altes Recht und neue Verfassung in den ersten Jahrzehnten der Bundesrepublik Deutschland (1949–1969)*, ed. Michael Stolleis (Berlin, 2006), 13–37.
126. Hans Carl Nipperdey, "Bericht über den Zustand der juristischen Fakultät," August 1945, UAK Sec. 44/205, 8, quoted in Leo Haupts, *Die Universität zu Köln im Übergang vom Nationalsozialismus zur Bundesrepublik* (Cologne, 2007), 43n133; see also the mildly hagiographic work by Frank Golczewski, *Kölner Universitätslehrer und der Nationalsozialismus: Personengeschichtliche Ansätze* (Cologne, 1998), 412; Franz Dillmann, "Beschweigen ist unverfänglicher als Aufdeckung: Die juristische Fakultät im Nationalsozialismus." in *Nachhilfe zur Erinnerung: 600 Jahre Universität zu Köln*, ed. Wolfgang Blaschke (Cologne, 1988), 98–110. Hermann Jahrreiß, like many other scholars after the war, pointed to his nonmembership in the Nazi Party as evidence of his dissent. Historical research has refuted this simplistic equivalence in a great many cases. Wolfgang Bialas and Anson Rabinbach, "Introduction: The Humanities in Nazi

Germany," in *Nazi Germany and the Humanities*, ed, Wolfgang Bialas and Anson Rabinbach (Oxford, 2007), xi.
127. "Protokoll der Juristischen Fakultätssitzung," November 1946, UAK Sec. 308/2, quoted in Haupts, *Die Universität zu Köln*, 43.
128. Numerous essays and monographs published in recent years have treated the situation of the international legal discipline in Germany before and after the National Socialist seizure of power. Among these are Diner, "Rassistisches Völkerrecht"; Detlef F. Vagts, "International Law in the Third Reich," *American Journal of International Law* 84, no. 3 (1990): 661–704; Mathias Schmoeckel, *Die Großraumtheorie: Ein Beitrag zur Geschichte der Völkerrechtswissenschaft im Dritten Reich, insbesondere der Kriegszeit* (Berlin, 1994); Anna Maria Gräfin von Lösch, *Der nackte Geist: Die Juristische Fakultät der Berliner Universität im Umbruch von 1933* (Tübingen, 1999); Ingo J. Hueck, "Die deutsche Völkerrechtswissenschaft im Nationalsozialismus Das Berliner Kaiser-Wilhelm-Institut für ausländisches öffentliches Recht und Völkerrecht, das Hamburger Institut für Auswärtige Politik und das Kieler Institut für Internationales Recht," in *Geschichte der Kaiser-Wilhelm-Gesellschaft im Nationalsozialismus: Bestandsaufnahme und Perspektiven der Forschung*, vol. 2, ed. Doris Kaufmann (Göttingen, 2000), 490–527; Ingo J. Hueck, "The Discipline of the History of International Law: New Trends and Methods on the History of International Law," *Journal of the History of International Law / Revue d'Histoire du Droit International* 3 (2001): 194–217; Koskenniemi, *The Gentle Civilizer of Nations*; Mayo Moran, "'In the Glass Darkly': Legacies of Nazi and Fascist Law in Europe," *University of Toronto Law Journal* 54, no. 4 (2004): 449–463; Stolleis, "International Law under German National Socialism: Some Contributions to the History of Jurisprudence," in *East Asian and European Perspectives on International Law*, ed. Michael Stolleis and Masaharu Yanagihara (Baden-Baden, 2004), 203–213; Toppe, *Militär und Kriegsvölkerrecht*.
129. The dissertation was not published. Hermann Jahrreiß, "Sich mühen um Recht und Gesetz," in *Festschrift der Rechtswissenschaftlichen Fakultät zur 600-Jahr-Feier der Universität zu Köln* (Cologne, 1988), 704.
130. See Karl Carstens, "Hermann Jahrreiß," *Festschrift für Hermann Jahrreiß zu seinem siebzigsten Geburtstag*, ed. Karl Carstens and Hans Peters (Cologne, 1964), 1.
131. Hermann Jahrreiß, *Das Problem der rechtlichen Liquidation des Weltkrieges für Deutschland* (Leipzig, 1924).
132. See Hueck, "Die deutsche Völkerrechtswissenschaft"; Gideon Botsch, *"Politische Wissenschaft" im Zweiten Weltkrieg: Die "Deutschen Auslandswissenschaften" im Einsatz 1940–1945* (Paderborn, 2006).
133. Carl Schmitt, *Völkerrechtliche Großraumordnung mit Interventionsverbot für raumfremde Mächte: Ein Beitrag zum Reichsbegriff im Völkerrecht* [Grand Area Order under International Law with a ban on intervention by powers foreign to the area: A contribution to the concept of the Reich in international law] (Berlin, 1939).
134. Quoted in Frank-Rutger Hausmann, *"Deutsche Geisteswissenschaft" im Zweiten Weltkrieg im Zweiten Weltkrieg: Die "Aktion Ritterbusch" (1940–1945)* (Dresden, 1998), 62.
135. The titles published during the war in the Wandel der Weltordnung series included Axel Freiherr von Freytagh-Loringhoven, *Völkerrechtliche Neubildungen im Kriege* [New formations of international law during wartime] (Hamburg, 1941); Hermann Jahrreiß, *Paris 1919 und Europa: Die Ordnungsversuche der atlantischen Weltmächte* (Hamburg, 1943); Walter Hamel, *Reich und Staat im Mittelalter* [Kingdom and state in the middle ages] (Hamburg, 1944); Theodor Maunz, *Das Reich der spanischen Großmachtzeit* [The Spanish empire in the sixteenth and seventeenth centuries] (Hamburg, 1944); Ulrich

Scheuner, *Das europäische Gleichgewicht und die britische Seeherrschaft* [The European balance of power and British naval rule] (Hamburg, 1944).
136. Hermann Jahrreiß, "Wandel der Weltordnung: Zugleich eine Auseinandersetzung mit der Völkerrechtslehre von Carl Schmitt," *Zeitschrift für öffentliches Recht* 21 (1941): 516.
137. Ibid., 533.
138. See Ulrich Herbert, *Best: Biographische Studien über Radikalismus, Weltanschauung und Vernunft, 1903–1989* (Bonn, 1996).
139. Safferling and Graebke, "Strafverteidigung im Nürnberger Hauptkriegsverbrecherprozess," 75, derived this number from an evaluation of the IMT minutes; these render moot the estimates in Weinke, *Die Nürnberger Prozesse*, 38.
140. Felix Römer, "Richtlinien für die Behandlung politischer Kommissare [Kommissarbefehl], 6. Juni 1941,". *100(0) Schlüsseldokumente zur deutschen Geschichte*, http://www.1000dokumente.de/index.html?c=dokument_de&dokument=0088_kbe&object=context&st=&l=de.
141. International Military Tribunal, Secretariat, *Der Prozess gegen die Hauptkriegsverbrecher vor dem Internationalen Militärgerichtshof: Nürnberg 14. November 1945–1. Oktober 1946—Amtlicher Text in deutscher Sprache*, 42 vols., vol. 17: *Verhandlungsniederschriften 25. Juni 1946 bis 8. Juli 1946* (Nuremberg, 1947), 520.
142. Ibid., 521.
143. Hans Kelsen, "Collective and Individual Responsibility in International Law with Particular Regard to the Punishment of War Criminals," *California Law Review* 31, no. 5 (1943): 530–571. Kelsen reiterated his criticism of international legal punishability for crimes during peacetime soon after the Nuremberg verdicts in "Will the Judgment in the Nuremberg Trial Constitute a Precedent in International Law?" *International Law Quarterly* 1, no. 2 (1947): 153–171; Slaughter, "Defining the Limits: Universal Jurisdiction and National Courts," in *Universal Jurisdiction and the Prosecution of Serious Crimes Under International Law*, ed. Stephen Macedo (Philadelphia, 2004), 176.
144. On the defense strategy in the I.G. Farben trial, see Weinke, "Hintergründe der justiziellen 'Aufarbeitung' des KZ Buna/Monowitz: Möglichkeiten, Probleme und Grenzen—Informationstext im Rahmen des Projektes 'Ort des Gedenkens und der Information Norbert Wollheim.'" http://docplayer.org/11729999-Annette-weinke-hintergruende-der-justiziellen-aufarbeitung-des-kz-buna-monowitz-moeglichkeiten-probleme-und-grenzen-alliierte-strafverfolgung.html.
145. See Danilo Zolo, "Hans Kelsen: International Peace Through International Law," *Jura Gentium* 3, no. 1 (2007), http://www.juragentium.org/topics/thil/en/kelsen.htm.
146. More on this discursive device will follow in chapter 3.
147. IMT, Secretariat, *Verhandlungsniederschriften 25. Juni 1946 bis 8. Juli 1946*, 523.
148. Using the example of the legal theoretician Fritz von Hippel, Raphael Gross presents a lucid explication of the topos of the "Führerwillen" (Führer's will) as a principle of rule. Raphael Gross, "Der Führer als Betrüger" Moral und Antipositivismus in Deutschland 1945/46 am Beispiel Fritz von Hippels," in *Anständig geblieben: Nationalsozialistische Moral*, ed. Raphael Gross (Frankfurt, 2010), 124–142.
149. "Wider den Sinn der Anklage: Die Haltung der Verteidiger in Nürnberg," *Der Tagesspiegel*, 21 July 1946.
150. Annette Wieviorka, "Die Entstehung des Zeugen," in *Hannah Arendt Revisited: "Eichmann in Jerusalem" und die Folgen*, ed. Gary Smith (Frankfurt, 2000), 142.

151. On the sociopsychological importance of the collective guilt thesis after 1945, see Nortbert Frei, "Von deutscher Erfindungskraft, oder: Die Kollektivschuldthese in der Nachkriegszeit," *Rechtshistorisches Journal*, no. 16 (1997): 621–634.
152. See Christoph Burchard, "The Nuremberg Trial and Its Impact on Germany," *Journal of International Criminal Justice* 4, no. 4 (2006): 808.
153. On Case 3, see Weinke, *Die Nürnberger Prozesse*, 68–72.
154. On CCL 10, see Weinke, "Gesetz Nr. 10 des Alliierten Kontrollrats vom 20. Dezember 1945," *100(0) Schlüsseldokumente zur deutschen Geschichte im 20. Jahrhundert*, 17 August 2011, http://www.1000dokumente.de/index.html?c=dokument_de&dokument=0229_kri& object=context&st=&l=de
155. See Salter, "Neo-Fascist Legal Theory on Trial: An Interpretation of Carl Schmitt's Defence at Nuremberg from the Perspective of Franz Neumann's Critical Theory of Law," *Res Publica* 5 (1999): 161–194.
156. Quoted in P. A. Steiniger and Kazimierz Leszczynski, eds. *Fall 3: Das Urteil im Juristenprozess vom 4.12.1947* (East Berlin, 1969), 156–157.
157. See Manfred Walther, "Hat der juristische Positivismus die deutschen Juristen wehrlos gemacht?" in *Die juristische Aufarbeitung des Unrechts-Staats*, ed. Redaktion Kritische Justiz (Baden-Baden, 1998), 299–322.
158. See Conze et al., *Das Amt*, 391–401.
159. See Devin O. Pendas, "Auf dem Weg zu einem globalen Rechtssystem? Die Menschenrechte und das Scheitern des legalistischen Paradigmas des Krieges," in Hoffmann, *Moralpolitik*, 226–255
160. Neumann, "The War Crimes Trials," 145.
161. "Information Control Intelligence Summary," no. 15, 20 October 1945, quoted in Krösche, "Abseits der Vergangenheit: Das Interesse der deutschen Nachkriegsöffentlichkeit am Nürnberger Prozess gegen die Hauptkriegsverbrecher," in *NS-Prozesse und deutsche Öffentlichkeit*, ed. Jörg Osterloh and Clemens Vollnhals (Göttingen, 2011), 102; A. J. Merrit and R. L. Merrit, *Public Opinion in Occupied Germany: The OMGUS Surveys 1945–1949* (Urbana, IL, 1970), 33–39; J. Merrit and R. L. Merrit, *Public Opinion in Semisovereign Germany: The HICOG Surveys 1949–1955* (Urbana, IL, 1980), 11, 101. Susanne Karstedt analyzes the survey results from the standpoint of legal sociology. Susanne Karstedt, "The Nuremberg Tribunal and German Society," in *The Legacy of Nuremberg: Civilizing Influence or Institutional Vengeance?* ed. David A. Blumenthal and Timothy L. H. McCormack (Leiden, 2008), 13–35.
162. Quoted in Maguire, *Law and War*, 246.
163. As argued in Frei, *Vergangenheitspolitik*, 402.
164. See Lora Wildenthal, "Rudolf Laun und die Menschenrechte der Deutschen im besetzten Deutschland und in der frühen Bundesrepublik," in Hoffmann, *Moralpolitik*, 125.
165. See Cooper, *Raphael Lemkin and the Struggle for the Genocide Convention*, 180. Cooper's version is in part suspect by standards of source criticism, since he often relies exclusively on ego documents found in Lemkin's extensive legacy.
166. Trygve Lie, Secretary General of the United Nations, to FRG Chancellor Adenauer, 20 December 1950, PAAA, B80, vol. 202.
167. Memorandum from Sanne, Department V, for Mosler, 20 February 1952, PAAA, B80, vol. 202.
168. See Burchard, "The Nuremberg Trial and Its Impact on Germany," 813; Gerhard Werle, "Die Entwicklung des Völkerstrafrechts aus deutscher Perspektive," in *Die Macht und das Recht: Beiträge zum Völkerrecht und Völkerstrafrecht am Beginn des 21.*

Jahrhunderts, ed. Gerd Hankel (Hamburg, 2000), 104; Boris Krivec, "Von Versailles nach Rom: Der lange Weg vom nullum crimen, nulla poena sine lege: Bedeutung und Entwicklung des strafrechtlichen Gesetzesvorbehalts im völkerrechtlichen Strafrecht," PhD diss. (Hamburg, 2004).

169. On Heidelberger Kreis, see Frei, *Vergangenheitspolitik*, 163–166; Lingen, *Kesselrings letzte Schlacht*, 241–242; Günther Buchstab, "Die Nürnberger Prozesse und der 'Heidelberger Kreis' (1949–1955)," in *Macht und Zeitkritik: Festschrift für Hans-Peter Schwarz zum 65. Geburtstag*, ed. Peter Weilmann et al. (Paderborn, 1999), 61–74.

170. See Rabinbach, "Genozid," 58–63.

171. See Lewis, *The Birth of the New Justice*, 281; Cooper, *Raphael Lemkin and the Struggle for the Genocide Convention*, 224–229.

172. An example was Lemkin's suspicion of Vespasian Pella, an international lawyer of Romanian ancestry and a former diplomat in the Fascist Antonescu regime, whom he accused of conspiring together with the Polish American and Lithuanian American lobbying groups to represent Soviet interests in the ILC. Lewis, *The Birth of the New Justice*, 282.

173. Julius Epstein to Konrad Adenauer, 28 July 1953, PAAA, B80, vol. 202.

174. Interview with Lemkin, *Volkszeitung-Tribüne*, 16 July 1953; *Tagesspiegel*, 16 August 1953.

175. On the difficult negotiations with regarding clemency for Allied-held prisoners, see Frei, *Vergangenheitspolitik*, 266–306.

176. "StS Hallstein an den Präsidenten des Deutschen Bundestages betr. Genocide-Konvention" [State Secretary Hallstein to the President of the German Bundestag Re: Genocide Convention], 23 October 1953, *Deutsche Bundestag, 2. Wahlperiode 1953*, BT-Drucksache no. 31, in PAAA, B80, vol. 202.

177. "Sudetendeutsche Landsmannschaft, Kreisverband Holzminden, an das Auswärtige Amt" [Sudeten German Compatriots' Association, Holzminden District, to the Federal Foreign Office], 18 September 1953, in PAAA, B80, vol. 202.

178. The legislative draft was distributed to the cabinet meeting of 17 November 1953 by FRG Minister of Justice Fritz Neumayer (FDP). The justice and foreign ministries submitted a joint text on 26 November 1953. BArch, B136/2115, B141/10601.

179. "Gesetz über den Beitritt der Bundesrepublik Deutschland zu der Konvention vom 9. Dezember 1948 über die Verhütung und Bestrafung des Völkermordes," in BGBl vol. 2, no. 15 (1954):, 729.

180. Lemkin's contact to Eduard Wahl, who served as the chair of the Heidelberg Circle, was mediated by the diplomat Horst Pelckmann, who had served as a defense counsel in the trial of Friedrich Flick and other leading wartime industrialists (Nuremberg post-IMT "Case 5"). See Lemkin to Wahl, 4 May 1953, NYPL, Lemkin Papers, Reel 1.

181. Lemkin to Globig, 6 May 1953, NYPL, Lemkin Papers, Reel 1.

182. Lemkin to Wahl, 4 May 1953, NYPL, Lemkin Papers, Reel 1.

183. Ibid., emphasis in original.

184. Note from Schmoller, Department V, 3 November 1953, in PAAA, B80, vol. 202.

185. Robert Merrill Bartlett, "Pioneer vs. an Ancient Crime," *The Christian Century*, 18 July 1956, 854.

186. See Pendas, "Auf dem Weg zu einem globalen Rechtssystem?" 232.

187. Christoph Gusy is of the view that the legal costs and benefits for the FRG of entering the ECHR (EMRK) were calculable, since the basic rights guaranteed in FRG Basic Law were largely identical to those specified in the ECHR. Christoph Gusy, "Die Rezeption der EMRK in Deutschland," in *Menschenrechte in der Bewährung: Die*

Rezeption der Europäischen Menschenrechtskonvention in Frankreich und Deutschland im Vergleich, ed. Constance Grewe and Christoph Gusy (Baden-Baden, 2005), 135.

Chapter 3

1. Wulf Kansteiner defines *Vergangenheitsbewältigung*, the "overcoming of the past," as a type of public intervention that seeks to gain in legitimation by thematizing the past. Kansteiner, "Losing the War, Winning the Memory Battle: The Legacy of Nazism, World War II, and the Holocaust in the Federal Republic of Germany," in *The Politics of Memory in Postwar Europe*, ed. Richard Ned Lebow, Wulf Kansteiner, and Claudio Fogu (Durham, NC 2006,) 102; on the term, see also Peter Reichel, "Vergangenheitsbewältigung," in *Deutsche Geschichte im 20. Jahrhundert: Ein Lexikon*, ed. Axel Schildt (Munich, 2005), 375–378.
2. Kansteiner, "Losing the War, Winning the Memory Battle," 115.
3. On the amnesty acts, see esp. Norbert Frei, "Amnestiepolitik in den Bonner Anfangsjahren: Die Westdeutschen und die NS-Vergangenheit," *Kritische Justiz* 29, no. 4 (1996): 484–494.
4. See Ulrich Brochhagen, *Nach Nürnberg: Vergangenheitsbewältigung und Westintegration in der Ära Adenauer* (Hamburg, 1994), 166–167. A short outline on CCL 10 is available in Weinke, "Gesetz Nr. 10 des Alliierten Kontrollrats vom 20. Dezember 1945."
5. Quoted in Brochhagen, *Nach Nürnberg*, 167.
6. See Karl Kroeschell, *Rechtsgeschichte Deutschlands im 20. Jahrhundert* (Göttingen, 1992), 108.
7. Quoted in Richard J. Evans, *Rituale der Vergeltung: Die Todesstrafe in der deutschen Geschichte 1532–1987* (Berlin, 2001), 930; see Hans Heinrich Jescheck, "Die Todesstrafe im ausländischen Recht," in *Die Frage der Todesstrafe: Zwölf Antworten*, ed. Reinhart Maurach, Eberhard Schmidt, and Wolfgang Preiser (Munich, 1992), 49–54. On human rights and the German Basic Law, see Stolleis, *Geschichte des öffentlichen Rechts in Deutschland*, vol. 4, 211. The reversal of the classic front lines continued as a small group of SPD deputies, including the prominent legal policy spokespersons Georg August Zinn and Adolf Arndt, demanded keeping the death penalty for NS crimes. Gosewinkel, *Adolf Arndt: Die Wiederbegründung des Rechtsstaats aus dem Geist der Sozialdemokratie (1945–1961)* (Bonn, 1991), 124; Kristina Meyer, *Die SPD und die NS-Vergangenheit 1945–1990* (Göttingen), 138–143.
8. See Frei, *Vergangenheitspolitik*, 195–233.
9. See Weinke, *Die Nürnberger Prozesse*, 62.
10. Lawrence Douglas, "Was damals Recht war ... Nulla Poena and the Prosecution of Crimes Against Humanity in Occupied Germany," in *NMT: Die Nürnberger Militärtribunale zwischen Geschichte, Gerechtigkeit und Rechtsschöpfung*, ed. Kim Christian Priemel and Alexa Stiller (Hamburg, 2013), 727.
11. In 1933, Hodenberg had opposed the incorporation of the German lawyers' association into the Alliance of National Socialist German Jurists. He also spoke out against the suspension of licenses to practice for Jewish lawyers. Tillmann Krach, *Jüdische Rechtsanwälte in Preußen: Über die Bedeutung der freien Advokatur und ihre Zerstörung durch den Nationalsozialismus* (Munich, 1991), 221.
12. Hodo von Hodenberg, "Zur Anwendung des Kontrollratsgesetzes Nr. 10 durch deutsche Gerichte," 120. An unpublished draft of this October 1946 article can be found in the files of the central justice agency of the British occupation zone in

the FRG federal archives, Bundearchiv, Koblenz (BArch, Z21). Devin O. Pendas, "Retroactive Law and Proactive Justice," *Central European History* 43, no. 3 (2010): 428–463, 445–446. Regarding this debate, also see Martin Broszat, "Siegerjustiz oder strafrechtliche 'Selbstreinigung': Aspekte der Vergangenheitsbewältigung der deutschen Justiz während der Besatzungszeit 1945–1949," *Vierteljahrshefte für Zeitgeschichte* 29, no. 4 (1981): 477–544.

13. On CCL 10, see Pendas, "Retroactive Law and Proactive Justice," 445.
14. On these premises rested the "separation thesis," the predominant interpretation of NS law after 1949. Anders, "Kontinuität oder Diskontinuität? Plädoyer für eine rechtshistorische Persektive bei der Nutzung von Strafakten als Quellen," in *Vom Recht zur Geschichte: Akten aus NS-Prozessen als Quellen der Zeitgeschichte*, ed. Jürgen Finger, Sven Keller, and Andreas Wirsching (Göttingen, 2009), 27–37.
15. Radbruch, formerly a professed legal positivist, began the third part of his much-praised essay on "legal injustice and right above law" as follows: "In reality, positivism, with its conviction that 'law is law,' rendered German jurists defenseless against laws of arbitrary and criminal content." Gustav Radbruch, "Gesetzliches Unrecht und übergesetzliches Recht" (1946), 10 (original edition in *Süddeutsche Juristen-Zeitung*, vol. 1, 1946, 105–108). The otherwise profound introduction by Winfried Hassemer unfortunately lacks anything about the reception history of this one sentence, which was in inverse proportion to that of Radbruch's essay generally in connection with the judicial treatment of NS injustice after 1949. On the "positivism thesis" regarding the NS-era justice system, see also Walther, "Hat der juristische Positivismus die deutschen Juristen wehrlos gemacht?"; Walter Ott and Franziska Buob, "Did Legal Positivism Render German Jurists Defenseless during the Third Reich?" *Social and Legal Studies* 2 (1993): 91–104; and Hubert Rottleuthner, "Das Nürnberger Juristenurteil und seine Rezeption: In Ost und West," *Neue Justiz* 12 (1997): 617–624.
16. See Christian Meyer-Seitz, *Die Verfolgung von NS-Straftaten in der Sowjetischen Besatzungszone* (Berlin, 1998), 102.
17. Pendas, "Retroactive Law and Proactive Justice," 32.
18. See Judith N. Shklar, *Legalism: Law, Morals, and Political Trials* (Cambridge, 1986), 168–170; David Cohen, "Transitional Justice in Divided Germany after 1945," in *Retribution and Reparation in the Transition to Democracy*, ed. Jon Elster (Cambridge, 2006), 62.
19. See Gosewinkel, *Adolf Arndt*, 117–125.
20. See Adolf Arndt, "Das Verbrechen der Euthanasie (Probleme der Frankfurter Euthanasie-Prozesse)," in *Der Konstanzer Juristentag* (Tübingen, 1947), 188.
21. Occupation zones differed in their practices for authorizing German courts. See Edith Raim, "NS-Prozesse und Öffentlichkeit: Die Strafverfolgung von NS-Verbrechen durch die deutsche Justiz in den westlichen Besatzungszonen 1945–1949," in Osterloh and Vollnhals, *NS-Prozesse und deutsche Öffentlichkeit*, 33–51.
22. See Heinz Boberach, "Die strafrechtliche Verfolgung der Ermordung von Patienten in nassauischen Heil- und Pflegeanstalten nach 1945," in *Euthanasie in Hadamar: Die nationalsozialistische Vernichtungspolitik in hessischen Anstalten*, ed. Christina Vanja and Martin Vogt (Kassel, 1991), 165–174; Matthias Meusch, "Die strafrechtliche Verfolgung der Hadamarer 'Euthanasie'-Morde," in *Hadamar: Heilstätte—Tötungsanstalt—Therapiezentrum*, ed. Uta George (Marburg, 2006), 205–326; Patricia Heberer, "Early Postwar Justice in the American Zone: The 'Hadamar Murder Factory' Trial," in Heberer and Matthäus, *Atrocities on Trial*, 25–47.
23. Gosewinkel, *Adolf Arndt*, 98.

24. Ibid., 111.
25. Arndt, "Das Verbrechen der Euthanasie," 192.
26. Ibid., 195.
27. Paul Julian Weindling, *Nazi Medicine and the Nuremberg Trials: From Medical War Crimes to Informed Consent* (London, 2004); Marrus, "The Nuremberg Doctors' Trial and the Limitations of Context," in Heberer and Matthäus, *Atrocities on Trial*, 103–122.
28. According to the most recent estimates, the "euthanasia" killed approximately 196,000 people within the German Reich. In addition, 80,000 died at facilities in occupied Polish, Soviet, and French territories, and about 20,000 concentration camp prisoners were murdered at "euthanasia" facilities. Hans-Walter Schmuhl, "'Euthanasie' und Krankenmord," in *Medizin und Nationalsozialismus: Bilanz und Perspektiven der Forschung*, 2nd ed., ed. Robert Jütte, Hans-Walter Schmuhl, and Winfried Süss (Göttingen, 2011), 214.
29. See Lamberti, "German Antifascist Refugees."
30. Marrus, "The Nuremberg Doctors' Trial," 113, made this point in his criticism of the prosecutorial approach in Nuremberg follow-up Case 3: "The prosecution regularly drew attention to non-German victims, ignoring the powerful ideological thrust of the campaign and presenting Nazi 'euthanasia' in simple utilitarian terms—removing 'useless eaters' from a country fully mobilized for war (presented as 'the principal rationale') and pursuing the struggle against Germany's enemies."
31. Regarding the discourses of the European and Transatlantic eugenicists, who can be seen as having provided the scaffolding in the prehistory of the National Socialist eugenics policy, see Stefan Kühl, *Die Internationale der Rassisten: Aufstieg und Niedergang der internationalen Bewegung für Eugenik und Rassenhygiene im 20. Jahrhundert* (Frankfurt, 1997).
32. Regarding the memory-politics implications of the "particularist" and "universalist" victim models, respectively, see Natan Sznaider, "Suffering as a Universal Frame for Understanding Memory Politics," in *Clashes in European Memory: The Case of Communist Repression and the Holocaust*, ed. Muriel Blaive, Christian Gerbel, and Thomas Lindenberger (Innsbruck, 2011), 239–254
33. Devin Pendas wrote in this vein regarding the absence of human rights dicourse during the West German Holocaust trials: "Such an account treats the victims of the Holocaust and other German crimes as passive objects of German moral reflection, not as subjects in their own right. Paradoxically, such an approach unintentionally recapitulates the disenfranchisement and the objectification of the victims initiated by the Nazis themselves." Devin O. Pendas, "'Law, Not Vengeance': Human Rights, the Rule of Law, and the Claims of Memory in German Holocaust Trials," in *Truth Claims: Representation and Human Rights*, ed. Mark Philip Bradley and Patrice Petro (New Brunswick, NJ, 2002), 36.
34. See Willi Dressen, "NS-'Euthanasie'-Prozesse in der Bundesrepublik Deutschland im Wandel der Zeit," in *NS-"Euthanasie" vor Gericht: Fritz Bauer und die Grenzen juristischer Bewältigung*, ed. Hanno Loewy and Bettina Winter (Frankfurt, 1996), 36.
35. Karl Teppe, "Bewältigung von Vergangenheit? Der westfälische 'Euthanasie'-Prozess," in *Nach Hadamar: Zum Verhältnis von Psychiatrie und Gesellschaft im 20. Jahrhundert*, ed. Franz-Werner Kersting, Karl Teppe, and Bernd Walter (Paderborn, 1993), 232.
36. Ibid., 251.
37. See Schmuhl, "Nürnberger Ärzteprozess und 'Euthanasie'-Prozesse," in Jütte et al., *Medizin und Nationalsozialismus*, 267–282.

38. Quoted in Fralk Pingel, "Die NS-Psychiatrie im Spiegel des historischen Bewußtseins und sozialpolitischen Denkens in der Bundesrepublik," in Kersting et al., *Nach Hadamar*, 185.
39. Ibid., 188.
40. Hans Buchheim, "Das Euthanasieprogramm," in *Gutachten des Instituts für Zeitgeschichte* (Munich, 1958), 61–84.
41. Unlike historical inquiry, truth finding in a criminal court is generally restricted to simple questions: "Who did what? Is the fact generally known? Who saw it, and who can prove it? What were the clues, and what was the evidence? Is there a confession?" See Michel Foucault, "Theorien und Institutionen des Strafvollzugs," in Defert et al., *Michel Foucault*, 488.
42. Rousso, "Justiz, Geschichte und Erinnerung in Frankreich: Überlegungen zum Papon-Prozess," in Frei et al., *Geschichte vor Gericht*, 141–163.
43. Klaus-Michael Mallmann and Andrej Angrick describe the consequences on juridical and historiographic scholarship as "doubly devastating." Mallmann and Angrick, "Die Mörder sind unter uns: Gestapo-Bedienstete in den Nachfolgegesellschaften des Dritten Reichs," in *Die Gestapo nach 1945: Karrieren, Konflikte, Konstruktionen*, ed. Klaus-Michael Mallmann and Andrej Angrick (Darmstadt, 2009), 22.
44. In an affidavit from 24 April 1947, Ohlendorf still spoke of the "killing of all captured racially and politically undesirable element," but in October 1948 revised himself to suggest it applied only to groups considered to be security risks; quoted in Helmut Krausnick, *Hitlers Einsatzgruppen: Die Truppen des Weltanschauungskrieges 1938–1942* (Frankfurt, 1985), 137.
45. See Michael Wildt, "Differierende Wahrheiten: Historiker und Staatsanwälte als Ermittler von NS-Verbrechen," in Frei et al., *Geschichte vor Gericht*, 46–59.
46. See Hilary Earl, *The Nuremberg Einsatzgruppen Trial, 1945–1958: Atrocity, Law, and History* (Cambridge, 2009).
47. Nicholas Berg, "Lesarten des Judenmords," in *Wandlungsprozesse in Westdeutschland: Belastung, Integration, Liberalisierung 1945–1980*, ed. Ulrich Herbert (Göttingen, 2002), 96.
48. Gerald Reitlinger, *The Final Solution: The Attempt to Exterminate the Jews of Europe, 1939–1945* (London, 1953). The book was published in German by Colloquium Verlag in West Berlin a few years later under the misleading title *Die Endlösung: Hitlers Versuch der Ausrottung der Juden Europas 1939–1945*. In 1954, the advisory board of the Institute of Contemporary History in Berlin had rejected a translation of the book. Nicholas Berg, *Der Holocaust und die westdeutschen Historiker: Erforschung und Erinnerung*, 3rd rev. ed. (Göttingen, 2004), 284–285.
49. Reitlinger, *Die Endlösung*, 90.
50. León Poliakov, *Brèviaire de la Haine: Le Troisième Reich et les Juifs*. Paris, 1951; Wolfgang Scheffler, *Die nationalsozialistische Judenpolitik* (Berlin, 1960); Artur Eisenbach, *Hitlerowska polityka zaglady Zydów* (Warsaw, 1961); Raul Hilberg, *The Destruction of the European Jews* (New York, 1961). The German historian Joseph Wulf, originally from Kraków, also worked mainly with this archival material. Berg, *Der Holocaust und die westdeutschen Historiker*, 339–342.
51. Ian Kershaw, *Der NS-Staat Geschichtsinterpretationen und Kontroversen im Überblick*, rev. ed. (Reinbek, 1999), 150–162.
52. See Jockusch, *Collect and Record!*
53. Berg, *Der Holocaust und die westdeutschen Historiker*. In a different vein, and without reference to Berg, see also Sybille Steinbacher, "Martin Broszat und die Erforschung

der nationalsozialistischen Judenpolitik," in *Martin Broszat, der "Staat Hitlers" und die Historisierung des Nationalsozialismus*, ed. Norbert Frei (Göttingen, 2007), 130–145.
54. See Sebastian Conrad, *Auf der Suche nach der verlorenen Nation: Geschichtsschreibung in Westdeutschland und Japan, 1945–1960* (Göttingen, 1999), 227–228.
55. Ibid., 238.
56. On the prehistory and founding of the institute, see John Gimbel, "The Origins of the Institut für Zeitgeschichte Scholarship, Politics, and the American Occupation, 1945–1949," *American Historical Review* 70, no. 3 (1965): 714–731; Winfried Schulze, *Deutsche Geschichtswissenschaft nach 1945* (Munich, 1993).
57. Rudolf Holzhausen, "Vorschlag zur Gründung eines deutschen Forschungs- und Aufklärungsausschusses," 19 July 1945, IfZ Hausarchiv, ID1, vol. 1.
58. Anton Pfeiffer, Bayerische Staatskanzlei, to Siegert, archive of the former Reich finance ministry (RFM), 23 August 1948, IfZ Hausarchiv, ID1, vol. 1.
59. Gerhard Ritter to the scientific advisory board, 12 May 1949, IfZ Hausarchiv, ID1, vol. 1.
60. Theodor Heuss to Gerhard Kroll, 24 June 1949, IfZ Hausarchiv, ID1, vol. 1.
61. Astrid Eckert, *Kampf um die Akten: Die Westalliierten und die Rückgabe von deutschem Archivgut nach dem Zweiten Weltkrieg* (Stuttgart, 2004), 405.
62. Gerhard Kroll to Lucius D. Clay [n.d.], IfZ Hausarchiv, ID1, vol. 1.
63. Hermann Mau, "Die Akten des großen Nürnberger Kriegsverbrecherprozesses als Geschichtsquelle," lecture of 22 December 1950, IfZ Hausarchiv, ID101/8, 3.
64. See Klaus-Dietmar Henke and Claudio Natoli, eds., *Mit dem Pathos der Nüchternheit: Martin Broszat, das Institut für Zeitgeschichte und die Erforschung des Nationalsozialismus* (Frankfurt, 1991).
65. For this reason, Conrad, *Auf der Suche nach der verlorenen Nation*, 264–271, attributes to structural history the function of a "palliative."
66. The term was coined later by the British historian Donald Bloxham. Bloxham, *Genocide on Trial*, xi.
67. On Mau's appointment, see Schulze, *Deutsche Geschichtswissenschaft nach 1945*, 237-239.; also Hermann Graml, "Zur Frage der Demokratiebereitschaft des deutschen Bürgertums nach dem Ende der NS-Herrschaft Hermann Maus Bericht über eine Reise nach Munich im März 1946," in *Miscellanea: Festschrift für Helmut Krausnick*, ed. Wolfgang Benz in collaboration with Ino Arndt, Hellmuth Auerbach, Martin Broszat, Hermann Graml, and Lothar Gruchmann (Stuttgart, 1980), 149–168; Helmut Becker, "Das Arbeitsprogramm vor 25 Jahren," in *25 Jahre Institut für Zeitgeschichte: Statt einer Festschrift* (Stuttgart, 1975), 25–29.
68. Eckert, *Kampf um die Akten*, 404.
69. For example, after a reception at the house of the military governor, Lucius D. Clay, Mau reported to Becker in September 1948 disparagingly that the American professors present had served up the "intellectual comfort food" that was typical of the "banquets at American colleges." Mau to Becker, 29 September 1949, PAAA, Becker Legacy, vol. 9/2. On Becker, see Conze et al., *Das Amt*, 405–406.
70. Quoted in Berg, *Der Holocaust und die westdeutschen Historiker*, 534–535.
71. Hermann Mau, "Die Akten des großen Nürnberger Kriegsverbrecherprozesses als Geschichtsquelle," lecture of 22 December 1950, IfZ Hausarchiv, ID101/8, 3.
72. Ibid., 8.
73. Ibid., 10.
74. Ibid., 15.
75. Ibid., 19, emphasis in original.

76. Ibid., 20.
77. This document was also introduced in the Nuremberg trial under the signature PS-170. Heydrich's memorandum to the four highest-ranking SS and police chiefs of 2 July 1941 was not yet known as the time. Helmut Krausnick, "Judenverfolgung: Schriftliches Sachverständigengutachten für den Auschwitz-Prozess," in *Anatomie des SS-Staates*, vol. 1, ed. Hans Buchheim, Broszat, Martin, Hans-Adolf Jacobsen, and Helmut Krausnick (Olten, 1965), 364. On the context of the document see also Raul Hilberg, *Unerbetene Erinnerung: Der Weg eines Holocaust-Forschers* (Frankfurt, 1994), 70–71.
78. As presented in Berg, *Der Holocaust und die westdeutschen Historiker*, 542–548.
79. See Weinke, *Eine Gesellschaft ermittelt gegen sich selbst: Die Geschichte der Zentralen Stelle Ludwigsburg 1958–2008* (Darmstadt, 2008).
80. See Steinbacher, "Martin Broszat und die Erforschung."
81. Krausnick was originally hired as an expert assessor for the trial, but later stepped back in early 1958 after "thorough consideration" and consultation with the IfZ management. He would appear as a witness in the Ulm trial, however. Andreas Eichmüller, *Keine Generalamnestie: Die Strafverfolgung von NS-Verbrechen in der frühen Bundesrepublik* (Munich, 2012), 368.
82. See Christopher Browning, *Die Entfesselung der "Endlösung": Nationalsozialistische Judenpolitik 1939–1942* (Munich, 2003), 318–332; Dieter Pohl, *Holocaust: Die Ursachen—das Geschehen—die Folgen*. Freiburg, 2000, 44–57; Christoph Dieckmann, "Der Krieg und die Ermordung der litauischen Juden," in *Nationalsozialistische Vernichtungspolitik 1939–1945: Neue Forschungen und Kontroversen*, ed. Ulrich Herbert (Frankfurt, 1998), 292–329; Peter Longerich, *Politik der Vernichtung: Eine Gesamtdarstellung der nationalsozialistischen Judenverfolgung 1933–1945* (Munich, 1998), 326–334; Konrad Kwiet, "Rehearsing for Murder: The Beginning of the Final Solution in Lithuania in June 1941," *Holocaust and Genocide Studies* 12, no. 1 (1998): 3–26; Jürgen Matthäus, "Jenseits der Grenze: Die ersten Massenerschiessungen von Juden in Litauen (Juni–August 1941)," *Zeitschrift für Geschichtswissenschaft* 44, no. 2 (1996): 101–117; Henrik G. van Dam and Ralph Giordano, *KZ-Verbrechen vor deutschen Gerichten, Bd. II: Einsatzkommando Tilsit—Der Prozess zu Ulm* (Frankfurt, 1966), 11–53.
83. Alfred Streim, "Zur Eröffnung des allgemeinen Judenvernichtungsbefehls gegenüber den Einsatzgruppen," in *Der Mord an den Juden im Zweiten Weltkrieg: Entschlussbildung und Verwirklichung*, ed. Eberhard Jäckel and Jürgen Rohwer (Stuttgart, 1985), 107–119.
84. Van Dam and Giordano, *KZ-Verbrechen vor deutschen Gerichten*, 53, 115–118.
85. Ibid.
86. Klaus-Michael Mallmann, "Die Türöffner der 'Endlösung': Zur Genesis des Genozids," in *Gestapo im Zweiten Weltkrieg: "Heimatfront" und besetztes Europa*, ed. Gerhard Paul and Klaus-Michael Mallmann (Darmstadt, 2000), 439; see also the overview by Dieter Pohl, "Prosecutors and Historians: Holocaust Investigations and Historiography in the Federal Republic 1955–1975," in *Holocaust and Justice: Representation and Historiography of the Holocaust in Post-war Trials*, ed. David Bankier and Dan Michman (Jerusalem, 2010), 117–129.
87. Ulrich Herbert, "Vernichtungspolitik: Neue Antworten und Fragen zur Geschichte des 'Holocaust,'" in Herbert, *Nationalsozialistische Vernichtungspolitik*, 13.
88. See Krausnick, "Judenverfolgung," 364; Krausnick, *Hitlers Einsatzgruppen*, 129–150. Remarkably, it was Krausnick's successor as IfZ director after 1972, Martin

Broszat, who finally questioned the thesis of a "secret order." This came in Broszat, "Hitler und die Genesis der 'Endlösung': Aus Anlass der Thesen von David Irving," *Vierteljahrshefte für Zeitgeschichte* 25, no. 4 (1977): 739–775, a broadside aimed at thoroughly debunking David Irving's contemporary apologetics for Hitler. However, Broszat avoided reference to his predecessor Krausnick's work in support of the thesis. See also the critical response by Christopher R. Browning, "Zur Genesis der 'Endlösung': Eine Antwort an Martin Broszat," *Vierteljahrshefte für Zeitgeschichte* 29, no. 1 (1981): 97–109

89. A selection of relevant court rulings is listed in Longerich, *Politik der Vernichtung*, 664n72–73.
90. Alfred Streim, *Die Behandlung sowjetischer Kriegsgefangener im "Fall Barbarossa": Eine Doukmentation* (Heidelberg, 1981), 74–93.
91. Ibid., 93.
92. See Ralf Ogorreck, *Die Einsatzgruppen und die "Genesis der Endlösung"* (Berlin, 1996); Dieckmann, "Der Krieg und die Ermordung der litauischen Juden"; Longerich, *Politik der Vernichtung*, 292–329; Johannes Hürter, *Hitlers Heerführer: Die deutschen Oberbefehlshaber im Krieg gegen die Sowjetunion 1941/42* (Munich, 2006), 520.
93. Streim, "Zur Eröffnung des allgemeinen Judenvernichtungsbefehls gegenüber."
94. Berg, *Der Holocaust und die westdeutschen Historiker*, 652–661, regards the conference as the start of the later conflict between Saul Friedländer und Martin Broszat. Steinbacher, "Martin Broszat und die Erforschung."
95. In a newspaper report, the historian Götz Aly, "Die volle Wahrheit und die reine Wissenschaft," *Die Tageszeitung*, 7 May 1984, wrote that the single positive thing about the conference was that Jäckel's initiative had prompted the first public exchange of opinions between historians and criminal investigators. Aly's view of the substance of the Krausnick/Streim debate, however, was far more negative: he regarded it as a typical case of German "counting of flies' legs" and shrugged it off as a one-track dispute about sites and proofs. The treatment of the conference in scholarship usually fails to mention that both historians and jurists were present. See John Fox, "The Final Solution: Intended or Contingent? The Stuttgart Conference of May 1984 and the Historical Debate," *Patterns of Prejudice* 18, no. 3 (1984): 27–39.
96. The commentary following Streim's lecture was productive, as Wolfgang Scheffler, Christopher Browning, and Adalbert Rückerl all possessed many years of experience with NS-era investigation files. Jäckel and Rohwer, *Der Mord an den Juden im Zweiten Weltkrieg*, 120–124.
97. Some years later, Streim expressed disappointment at the ignorance of the historians' guild in an English-language journal: "It is incomprehensible and deplorable that despite all these findings historians have adopted Professor Krausnick's thesis uncritically. Even today, after the publication of my critique, some of those who accepted Professor Krausnick's interpretation without criticism still seem unwilling critically to reexamine his thesis. They are of the opinion that the question concerning the disclosure of the general destruction order is a question of detail that does not matter. It is certain, they argue, that an order to kill all Jews did exist and that many people were killed under such orders. I cannot share this view; it contradicts the task of historical scholarship, which demands that we attempt as complete an explanation of the past as the sources permit." Alfred Streim, "Correspondence," *Simon Wiesenthal Center Annual* 6 (1988): 311–347; see Alfred Streim, "The Task of the SS Einsatzgruppen," *Simon Wiesenthal Center Annual* 4 (1987): 309–328; Helmut Krausnick, "Correspondence," *Simon Wiesenthal Center Annual* 6 (1989): 311–329.

98. See Johannes Tuchel, "Die NS-Prozesse als Materialgrundlage für die historische Forschung: Thesen zu Möglichkeiten und Grenzen interdisziplinärer Zusammenarbeit," in *Vergangenheitsbewältigung durch Strafverfahren? NSProzesse in der Bundesrepublik Deutschland*, ed. Jürgen Weber and Peter Steinbach (Munich, 1984), 134–144.
99. Beyond the question of how the genocide of the European Jews was set into motion, there has been greatly increased interest in the role of the civilian administration of occupied areas and the role of the Wehrmacht in the murder of the Eastern European Jewish population.
100. The legal scholar Ernst Forsthoff had already provided a short overview of the problems in the mid-1960s. Ernst Forsthoff, "Der Zeithistoriker als gerichtlicher Sachverständiger," *Neue Juristische Wochenschrift* 13 (1965): 574–575.
101. See the contributions in Johannes Heil and Rainer Erb, eds., *Geschichtswissenschaft und Öffentlichkeit: Der Streit um Daniel J. Goldhagen* (Frankfurt, 1998); Christopher R. Browning, "German Memory, Judicial Interrogation, and Historical Reconstruction: Writing Perpetrator History from Postwar Memory," in *Probing the Limits of Representation: Nazism and the "Final Solution,"* ed. Saul Friedländer (Cambridge, MA, 1992), 22–36.
102. See Marc von Miquel, *Ahnden oder amnestieren? Westdeutsche Justiz und Vergangenheitspolitik in den sechziger Jahren* (Göttingen, 2004), 205.
103. Quoted in Aldalbert Rückerl, *NS-Verbrechen vor Gericht, Versuch einer Vergangenheitsbewältigung*. 2nd ed. (Heidelberg, 1984), 155.
104. See Weinke, "Amnestie für Schreibtischtäter: Das verhinderte Verfahren gegen die Bediensteten des Reichssicherheitshauptamtes," in Mallmann and Angrick, *Die Gestapo nach 1945*, 200–220.
105. The Ludwigsburg agency chaired weekly meetings to hash out public relations strategies with representatives from the German Chancellery, the Federal Press Office (BPA), the Federal Intelligence Service (BND), the Federal Office for the Protection of the Constitution (BfV), and the federal ministries for justice, defense, and interior. A representative from the Institute for Contemporary History sat in as an adviser. Conze et al., *Das Amt*, 615.
106. Quoted in Raphael Gross, "Moralität des Bösen: Adolf Eichmann und die deutsche Gesellschaft," in Gross, *Anständig geblieben*, 197. More recent research has found that an "ostentatious cluelessness" prevailed in the latter stages of the war, motivated by the dread of collective responsibility; see, e.g., Peter Longerich, *"Davon haben wir nichts gewusst!" Die Deutschen und die Judenverfolgung* (Munich, 2006), 327.
107. Hilberg, *The Destruction of the European Jews*; see also Nicholas Berg, "'Phantasie der Bürokratie Raul Hilbergs Pionierstudie zur Vernichtung der europäischen Juden,'" in *50 Klassiker der Zeitgeschichte*, ed. Jürgen Danyel-Holger Kirsch, and Martin Sabrow (Göttingen, 2007), 71–83.
108. Gerhard Schoenberner, *Der gelbe Stern: Die Judenverfolgung in Europa 1933 bis 1945* (Hamburg, 1960); Wolfgang Scheffler, *Judenverfolgung im Dritten Reich* (Berlin, 1960). The first study on the "dejudaization" of the German economy first came out in 1966 and similarly relied on Nuremberg documents. Helmut Genschel, *Die Verdrängung der Juden aus der Wirtschaft im Dritten Reich* (Göttingen, 1966).
109. Reitlinger, *Die Endlösung*.
110. León Poliakov and Joseph Wulf, *Das Dritte Reich und die Juden: Dokumente und Aufsätze* (Berlin, 1955).
111. Jürgen Matthäus, "Der Eichmann-Prozess und seine Folgen: Strafverfolgung von NS-Verbrechen und Geschichtsschreibung," In *Interessen um Eichmann: Israelische*

Justiz, deutsche Strafverfolgung und alte Kameradschaften, ed. Werner Renz (Frankfurt, 2012), 226.
112. See Herbert, *Best*, 501–508; Norbert Frei, "Abschied von der Zeitgenossenschaft: Der Nationalsozialismus und seine Erforschung auf dem Weg in die Geschichte," in *1945 und wir: Das Dritte Reich im Bewusstsein der Deutschen*, ed. Nortbert Frei (Munich, 2009), 43.
113. Gross, "Moralität des Bösen," 199.
114. Dan Diner, "Hannah Arendt Reconsidered: Über das Banale und das Böse in ihrer Holocaust-Erzählung," in Smith, *Hannah Arendt Revisited*, 127.
115. Theo Sommer, "Adolf Eichmann, Ostubaf. a. D.," *Die Zeit*, 3 June 1960.
116. In one of his early works on Herbert Marcuse, Barry Katz pointed out the parallelization of Fordism and totalitarianism: "In a telling analogy, Marcuse observed that just on a modern assembly line, where it is the conveyor belt that dictates the pace of production and not the morale of the worker, so in Nazi Germany the totalitarian machinery of society sweeps along the Nazi and anti-Nazi alike; it is like factory system, he concluded, except that the worker cannot quit." Katz, "The Criticism of Arms," 452.
117. Quoted in Michael Bock, "Metamorphosen der Vergangenheitsbewältigung," in *Die intellektuelle Gründung der Bundesrepublik: Eine Wirkungsgeschichte der Frankfurter Schule*, ed. Clemens Albrecht, Günter C. Behrmann, Michael Bock, Harald Homann, and Friedrich H. Tenbruck (Frankfurt, 1999), 561.
118. Habbo Knoch, "Verschobene Schuld: Täterbilder und historische Fotografien in einem Illustriertenbericht zum Eichmann-Prozess," in *History: Ein Studienbuch*, ed. Gerhard Paul (Göttingen, 2006), 303.
119. On the impact of the Eichmann trial in the further development of international law and the so-called world law principle, see Leora Bilsky, David Bloxham, Lawrence Douglas, and Annette Weinke, "Forum: The Eichmann Trial Fifty Years On," *German History* 29, no. 2 (2011): 265–282.
120. See Annette Weinke, *Die Verfolgung von NS-Tätern im geteilten Deutschland: Vergangenheitsbewältigungen 1949–1969 oder—eine deutsch-deutsche Beziehungsgeschichte im Kalten Krieg* (Paderborn, 2002); Miquel, *Ahnden oder Amnestieren?*
121. Dreher of BMJ to the Hamburg state justice ministry, 10 June 1960, ZSL GA, 9-7 ("Israel"), vol. 1. The FRG and Israel did not maintain official diplomatic relations or a mutual legal aid treaty before 1965.
122. Schüle to justice ministry of Baden-Württemberg, 18 January 1961 (draft copy), ZSL GA, 9-7 ("Israel"), vol. 1.
123. Since its founding, the Ludwigsburg central office shared investigative tasks with the state prosecutor of Berlin; the latter was responsible for matters related to "RSHA and upper Reich ministries." Until the mid-1960s, responsibilities concerning deportation crimes were somewhat unclear. Ludwigsburg was only supposed to cover crimes outside the territory of the Reich, while deportations were planned and coordinated centrally in Berlin. Ludwigsburg therefore opened blank cases for given geographic regions in advance of gathering evidence. Rückerl, *NS-Verbrechen vor Gericht*; Weinke, "Amnestie für Schreibtischtäter."
124. Justice ministry notes by BW, 6 February 1961, "on discussion with Schüle of 6 February 1961"; HStA Stuttgart, EA 4/106, 1.
125. See Ruth Bettina Birn, "Staatsanwalt Zeug in Jerusalem: Zum Kenntnisstand der Anklagebehörde im Eichmann-Prozess und der Strafverfolgungsbehörden der Bundesrepublik," *Einsicht* 5 (2011): 26–32; Ruth Bettina Birn, "Der Prozess," *Frankfurter Allgemeine Zeitung*, 11 April 2011, 8.

126. Justice ministry notes of 11 January 1961, BArch, B141, 21887; quoted in Birn, "Staatsanwalt Zeug in Jerusalem," 26.
127. Notes of Marmann, Ref. 503, 12 January 1961 regarding discussion with Grützner, BMJ, PAAA, B83, 55.
128. Quoted in Conze et al., *Das Amt*, 613.
129. Although this is the view of Birn, "Staatsanwalt Zeug in Jerusalem."
130. Report of Zeug to State Prosecutor Wolf, 17 August 1961, ZSL GA, 9-7 ("Israel"), vol. 1.
131. Report of Zeug to State Prosecutor Wolf, 28 July 1961, ZSL GA, 9-7 ("Israel"), vol. 1.
132. Report of Zeug to State Prosecutor Wolf, 30 April 1961, ZSL GA, 9-7 ("Israel"), vol. 1.
133. Zeug to Anton Hoch of IfZ Archive, 2 May 1961, ZSL GA, 9-7 ("Israel"), vol. 1.
134. Bauer to Zeug, 24 May 1961, ZSL GA, 9-7 ("Supplementary").
135. Erwin Schüle, "Die strafrechtliche Aufarbeitung des Verhaltens in totalitären Systemen: Der Eichmann-Prozess aus deutscher Sicht," in *Möglichkeiten und Grenzen für die Bewältigung historischer und politischer Schuld in Strafprozessen*, ed. Karl Forster (Würzburg, 1962), 73.
136. On this interpretation going back to Franz Neumann and later updatd by Peter Hüttenberger, see the chapter in Kershaw, *Der NS-Staat*, 80–111.
137. Hannah Arendt, "Adolf Eichmann: Von der Banalität des Bösen" *Merkur* 186, no. 8 (1963): 759–776; Arendt, *Eichmann in Jerusalem*.
138. In a letter to her German publisher, Klaus Piper, Arendt wrote about her sources as follows: "I have here as elsewhere used material available in the 1961 book by Raul Hilberg. This is a standard work that makes all earlier studies like Reitlinger, Poljakoff [*sic*], etc. appear dated. The author has worked with the sources for fifteen years, and if he had not written a very misguided first chapter in which he shows that he does not understand very much of German history, the book would have so to speak been perfect. No one will be able to write on this subject without using it." Quoted in Hilberg, *Unerbetene Erinnerung*, 135. As Jürgen Matthäus writes, it may be considered certain that Arendt had delivered a negative assessment of Hilberg's book two years earlier for Princeton University Press, as a result of which it was not placed with a major publisher. Matthäus, "Der Eichmann-Prozess und seine Folgen," 235.
139. Hannah Arendt, *The Origins of Totalitarianism* (New York, 1951).
140. See Annette Vowinckel, *Geschichtsbegriff und historisches Denken bei Hannah Arendt* (Cologne, 2001), 70. Arendt's idea of racial imperialism originated with Franz Neumann. Berg, *Der Holocaust und die westdeutschen Historiker*, 470. In his analysis of *Origins of Totalitarianism*, Berg misunderstands Arendt's theoretical conception of National Socialism and therefore reaches false conclusions on her understanding of it. Arendt's claim of "decadence" would be often criticized in the literature, most recently in Diner, "Kaleidoskopisches Denken: Überschreibungen und autobiographische Codierungen in Hannah Arendts Hauptwerk," in Danyel et al., *50 Klassiker der Zeitgeschichte*, 39.
141. Arendt, *Elemente und Ursprünge totalitärer Herrschaft*, 308.
142. Ibid., 309.
143. See Konrad H. Jarausch, "Die Provokation des 'Anderen': Amerikanische Perspektiven auf die deutsche Vergangenheitsbewältigung," in *Doppelte Zeitgeschichte: Deutsch-deutsche Beziehungen 1945–1990*, ed. Arnd Bauerkämper, Martin Sabrow, and Bernd Stöver (Bonn, 1999), 432–447.
144. Robert Gerwarth and Stephan Malinowski, "Der Holocaust als 'kolonialer Genozid'?" *Geschichte und Gesellschaft* 33, no. 3 (2007): 445. For a broader perspective that also

draws on Arendt, see Christian Geulen, "Gouverneure, Gouvernementalität und Globalisierung: Zur Geschichte und Aktualität imperialer Gewalt," in Krasmann and Martschukat, *Rationalitäten der Gewalt*, 117–135.

145. This criticism of Arendt's "boomerang thesis" was given already in the mid-1970s by the American political scientist Margaret Canovan, *The Political Thought of Hannah Arendt* (New York, 1974). In the successive waves of reception for *Origins* since then, the postcolonial interpretation has proven especially fruitful for history scholarship, see Richard H. King and Dan Stone, "Introduction," in King and Stone, *Hannah Arendt and the Uses of History*, 1–17.

146. Arendt, *Eichmann in Jerusalem: A Report*, 126, emphasis in original.

147. Ibid., 57.

148. In this way, Arendt arrived at the following conclusions: "It is quite conceivable that in the automated economy of a not-too-distant future men may be tempted to exterminate all those whose intelligence quotient is below a certain level." Ibid., 58.

149. The attribution of a "functionalist" view to Arendt was first made by Saul Friedländer in the mid-1980s and was soon after taken on by Hans Mommsen. Saul Friedländer, "From Anti-Semitism to Extermination: A Historiographical Study of Nazi Policies toward the Jews and an Essay in Interpretation," *Yad Vashem Studies* 16, no. 1 (1984): 1–50; Hans Mommsen, "Hannah Arendt und der Prozess gegen Adolf Eichmann," in Arendt, *Eichmann in Jerusalem: Ein Bericht*, 9–48.

150. Regarding the long-term impact of the book, Herbert, *Best*, 16, writes that "historiographically it has had perhaps the fateful effect of causing one to see the National Socialist 'deskbound perpetrator' in the image of the assiduous follower of orders, Eichmann." In a similar vein, see Gerhard Paul, "Täterbilder—Täterprofile—Taten Ergebnisse der neueren Forschung zu den Tätern des Holocaust," Erler et al., *"Gegen alle Vergeblichkeit,"* 145.

151. See also Vowinckel, *Geschichtsbegriff und politisches Denken bei Hannah Arendt*, 77.

152. An example of the impressionistic way in which Arendt disseminated Hilberg's research results is in her description of the Wehrmacht role in the massacres of Jews in Serbia; Arendt, *Eichmann in Jerusalem: A Report*, 95–96.

153. Ibid., 87.

154. Ibid., 90.

155. A similar presumption often appears about Arendt's report on the trial, which is always assumed to have had an inestimable influence on West German perceptions, as though this assertion requires no further examination. Mommsen describes the reaction as generally negative; Krause credits the book with a paradigm shift on how the Holocaust was seen in the FRG. Mommsen, "Hannah Arendt und der Prozess gegen Adolf Eichmann," 34; Peter Krause, "'Eichmann und wir': Die bundesdeutsche Öffentlichkeit und der Jerusalemer Eichmann-Prozess 1961," In *NS-Prozesse und die Öffentlichkeit in Deutschland 1945–1969*, ed. Jörg Osterloh and Clemens Vollnhals (Göttingen, 2011), 283–306. See also, Weinke, "'Waning Confidence in Germany's Rehabilitation': Das gespaltene Krisenmanagement der bundesdeutschen Aussenpolitik zum Eichmann-Prozess," in Renz, *Interessen um Eichmann*, 201–215.

156. Mommsen seems to forget the difference between criminal law and history writing and ignores the selective nature of West German prosecutions when he claims that the trials had proven that "extreme subalternity" was typical of the majority of Nazi criminals. Mommsen, "Hannah Arendt und der Prozess gegen Adolf Eichmann," 25.

157. Report of Zeug to OStA Wolf vom 10 May 1961, ZSL GA, 9-7 ("Israel"), vol. 1.

158. Schüle, "Die strafrechtliche Aufarbeitung," 65.

159. Arendt, *Eichmann in Jerusalem: A Report*, 393.
160. See Krause, "'Eichmann und wir,'" 296.
161. On Jäger's *Makrokriminalität*, a pioneering study on the judicial treatment of state injustice, see Thomas Horstmann and Heike Litzinger, "Der Kreis von Königstein und die NS-Verbrechen: Eine Einführung," in *An den Grenzen des Rechts: Gespräche mit Juristen über die Verfolgung von NS-Verbrechen*, ed. Thomas Horstmann and Heike Litzinger (Frankfurt, 2006), 26.
162. Michael Wildt, *Generation des Unbedingten: Das Führungskorps des Reichssicherheitshauptamtes*, 2nd ed. (Hamburg, 2003), 797–813.
163. Friedrich A. Krummacher, *Die Kontroverse: Hannah Arendt, Eichmann und die Juden* (Munich, 1964).
164. Bruno Bettelheim, "Eichmann—das System—die Opfer," in Krummacher, *Die Kontroverse*, 91–113; Al Alvarez, "Es geschah nicht überall," in Krummacher, *Die Kontroverse*, 176–181; Schroers, "Der banale Eichmann und seine Opfer," in Krummacher, *Die Kontroverse*, 199–206.
165. Golo Mann, "Der verdrehte Eichmann," Krummacher, *Die Kontroverse*, 190–198, 194.
166. An extended review of a single book was a rarity for *Vierteljahrshefte für Zeitgeschichte*. The editors' standard practice was to publish reviews only covering several books on a specific issue. An earlier exception had been made for William Shirer's best seller *Rise and Fall of the Third Reich*, when *Vierteljahrshefte* published a translation of a review by Klaus Epstein that had appeared in the United States. See the editor's introduction to Klaus Epstein, "Shirers 'Aufstieg und Fall des Dritten Reichs,'" *Vierteljahrshefte für Zeitgeschichte* 10, no. 1 (1962): 95–112, here 95.
167. Recently, Eschenburg's activities during the Nazi era came under scrutiny in an essay by the political scientist Rainer Eisfeld. This prompted the advisory and executive boards of the German political science association to commission a study of Eschenburg's past. See Rainer Eisfeld, "Theodor Eschenburg: By the way, he forgot to mention. . ." *Zeitschrift für Geschichtswissenschaft* 59, no. 1 (2011): 27–44; Hannah Bethke, "Theodor Eschenburg in der NS-Zeit," Gutachten im Auftrag der DVPW, 3 September 2012; see Anne Rohstock, "Kein Vollzeitrepublikaner: Die Findung des Demokraten Theodor Eschenburg," in *Gesichter der Demokratie: Porträts zur deutschen Zeitgeschichte*, ed. Bastian Hein, Manfred Kittel and Horst Möller (Munich, 2012), 193–210.
168. Hans Egon Holthusen, *Der unbehauste Mensch* (Frankfurt, 1951).
169. Holthusen's apologetic memoir of his days with the SS, published in *Merkur* in 1966, provoked a public reply by Jean Améry. Hans Egon Holthusen, "Freiwillig zur SS," *Merkur* 20, no. 10 (1966): 921–939. On the controversy between Holthusen and Améry, see Ernst Klee, *Das Kulturlexikon zum Dritten Reich: Wer war was vor und nach 1945* (Frankfurt, 2003); Torben Fischer, "Jean Améry: Jenseits von Schuld und Sühne," in *Lexikon der "Vergangenheitsbewältigung" in Deutschland*, ed. Torben Fischer and Matthias N. Lorenz (Bielefeld, 2007), 159–161; see also Nicolas Berg, "Jean Améry und Hans Egon Holthusen. Eine Merkur-Debatte in den 1960er Jahren," in *Mittelweg 36, Zeitschrift des Hamburger Instituts für Sozialforschung*, 2012 no. 2, S. 28–48.
170. Regarding the controversy over Holthusen's appointment, Arendt wrote to her friends Gertrud and Karl Jaspers: "Here they have sent over Holthusen as director of the Goethe House. It became known for the first time that the fellow had been in the SS. And I, idiot, tried to get him out of trouble. But he had apparently given me false information." Karl Jaspers replied advising her to inform Klaus Piper about her experience with Holthusen, since the two were friends. Arendt to Jaspers, 1 November 1961, in Arendt and Jaspers, *Briefwechsel 1926–1969*, 495–497.

171. Hans Egon Holthusen, "Hannah Arendt, Eichmann und die Kritiker," *Vierteljahrshefte für Zeitgeschichte* 13, no. 2 (1965): 179; see Hans Egon Holthusen, "Plädoyer für den Einzelnen: Kritische Anmerkungen zu Hannah Arendt, Eichmann in Jerusalem," *Allgemeines Deutsches Sonntagsblatt*, 15 November 1964.
172. Holthusen, "Hannah Arendt, Eichmann und die Kritiker," 180.
173. Ibid., 181.
174. Ibid., 182
175. Ibid., 185.
176. See Helmut König, "Kein Neubeginn: Hannah Arendt, die NS-Vergangenheit und die Bundesrepublik," in *Streit um den Staat: Intellektuelle Debatten in der Bundesrepublik 1960–1980*, ed. Dominik Geppert and Jens Hacke (Göttingen, 2011), 113–134. The concept of "radical evil" originally goes back to Immanuel Kant's 1793 essay on "Religion innerhalb der Grenzen der bloßen Vernunft." Mark Arenhövel, *Demokratie und Erinnerung: Der Blick zurück auf Diktatur und Menschenrechtsverbrechen*. (Frankfurt, 2000), 87.
177. Holthusen, "Hannah Arendt, Eichmann und die Kritiker," 186.
178. Ibid., 187.
179. Ibid., 188, emphasis in original.
180. König, "Kein Neubeginn," 125.
181. As covered in Berg, *Der Holocaust und die westdeutschen Historiker*, 618.
182. This claim is given by Berg, "'Phantasie der Bürokratie,'" 74, citing Hilberg himself. In his autobiography, however, Hilberg makes it clear that he never saw this as anything other than a dubious excuse. Rather, he supposes that the publisher, Droemer Knauer, broke off the contract with him in 1965 because they feared that his book might become "a weapon in the hands of the prosecutors." Hilberg, *Unerbetene Erinnerung*, 140. According to David Engel, the actual debate among Jews about the role of the Judenräte during the Holocaust intensified a split that already existed between Holocaust historiography and Jewish history writing. David Engel, *Historians of the Jews and the Holocaust* (Stanford, 2010).
183. According to the British historian Ian Kershaw, the West German scholarship frequently received key impulses from abroad, but the resulting controversies always maintained a "uniquely West German" character; Kershaw, *Der NS-Staat*, 151.

Chapter 4

1. Knigge, "Gesellschaftsverbrechen erinnern," 23.
2. On the origins of this concept, see the discussion in Cornelißen, "Erinnerungskulturen, Version: 1.0." From a sociological perspective, see Levy and Sznaider, *Erinnerung im globalen Zeitalter*; Ulrich Beck, *Der kosmopolitische Blick oder: Krieg ist Frieden* (Frankfurt, 2004).
3. See Conrad, *Auf der Suche nach der verlorenen Nation*.
4. See Beck, *Der kosmopolitische Blick*; Bloxham, *Genocide on Trial: The World Wars, and the Unweaving of Europe*.
5. Below the top level of Communist state-regulated history politics, countries like Lithuania and Poland already saw a more pronounced confrontation with issues of collaboration starting in the 1980s, see Jan Eckel and Claudia Moisel, "Nachgeschichte und Gegenwart des Nationalsozialismus in internationaler Perspektive," in *Das "Dritte*

Reich": Eine Einführung, ed. Dietmar Süss and Winfried Süss (Munich, 2008), 333–353.
6. This is how it is formulated in Knigge, "Gesellschaftsverbrechen erinnern," 26.
7. Volkskammer of the German Democratic Republic, 10th term, 2nd session of 12 April 1990 (stenographic minutes), 23. The declaration is printed in *Deutschland-Archiv* 23 (1990), vol. 5, 794; see also Peter Reichel, *Vergangenheitsbewältigung in Deutschland: Die Auseinandersetzung mit der NS-Diktatur von 1945 bis heute* (Munich, 2001), 16.
8. Olick and Coughlin, "The Politics of Regret."
9. For this reason, the commission was called the National Commission on the Disappearance of Persons (CONADEP). Kathryn Sikkink, *The Justice Cascade: How Human Rights Prosecutions Are Changing World Politics* (New York, 2011), 63; Iain Guest, *Behind the Disappearances: Argentina's Dirty War Against Human Rights and the United Nations* (Philadelphia, 1990).
10. Sikkink, *The Justice Cascade*, 60–83.
11. See Moshe Zimmermann, "Die transnationale Holocaust-Erinnerung," in *Transnationale Geschichte: Themen, Tendenzen und Theorien*, ed. Gunilla Budde, Sebastian Conrad, and Oliver Janz (Göttingen, 2006), 202–216.
12. Stolleis, *Geschichte des öffentlichen Rechts*, vol. 4, 632.
13. Herren, *Internationale Organisationen seit 1865*, 121.
14. Ibid., 117.
15. In this vein, see Jürgen Habermas, "Hat die Konstitutionalisierung des Völkerrechts noch eine Chance?" in *Der gespaltene Westen*, ed. Jürgen Habermas (Frankfurt, 2004), 113–194.
16. This applies especially but not only to the dissident scene in Czechoslovakia. Jonathan Bolton, *Worlds of Dissent: Charter 77, the Plastic People of the Universe, and Czech Culture under Communism* (Cambridge, MA, 2012); Celia Donert, "Charta 77 und die Roma Menschenrechte und Dissidenten in der sozialistischen Tschechoslowakei," in Hoffmann, *Moralpolitik*, 397–423; Michal Kopeček, "The Rise and Fall of Czech Post-Dissident Liberalism after 1989," *East European Politics and Societies* 25, no. 2 (2011): 244–271. On use of language in the discourses of self-understanding, see Hartmut Fehr, "Öffentlicher Sprachwandel und Eliten-Konkurrenz Zur Rolle politischer Semantik in den Dekommunisierungskampagnen post-kommunistischer Gesellschaften (Tschechische Republik, Polen und Ostdeutschland)," in *Eliten, politische Kultur und Privatisierung in Ostdeutschland, Tschechien und Mittelosteuropa*, ed. Ilja Srubar (Konstanz, 1998), 65–96.
17. Claus Offe, *Der Tunnel am Ende des Lichts: Erkundungen der politischen Transformation im Neuen Osten* (Frankfurt, 1994), 58–59, critiques the "strangely 'untheoretical' character" of events from 1989 to 1991.
18. Michael Crozier, Samuel P. Huntington, and Joji Watanuki, *The Crisis of Democracy: the Governability of Democracies to the Trilateral Commission* (New York, 1975); regarding it, see Jan-Wertner Muller, *Contesting Democracy Political Ideas in Twentieth-Century Europe* (New Haven, CT, 2011), 204; W. Fitzhugh Brundage and Konrad H. Jarausch, "Massen: Mobilisierung und Partizipation," in *Wettlauf um die Moderne: Die USA und Deutschland 1890 bis heute*, ed. Christof Mauch and Kiran Klaus Patel (Bonn, 2008), 295–329.
19. Quoted in Muller, *Contesting Democracy*, 204. On the ungovernability debate, see also Gabriele Metzler, "Staatsversagen und Unregierbarkeit in den siebziger Jahren?" in *Das Ende der Zuversicht? Die siebziger Jahre als Geschichte*, ed. Konrad H. Jarausch (Göttingen, 2008), 243–260.

20. Samuel P. Huntington, *The Third Wave: Democratization in the Late Twentieth Century* (Norman, OK, 1991).
21. Caetano was the last dictator of the Estado Novo regime that had ruled in Portugal since 1933. Its end also brought the collapse of the last European overseas territorial colonial empire, a fact that Huntington neglects to mention in his book.
22. Ibid., 46–47.
23. On the essential differences between materialist and procedural concepts of democracy, see Offe, *Der Tunnel am Ende des Lichts*, 82–85.
24. From an early stage, the field of democracy studies was criticized for its tendency to present simplistic dichotomies and construct fictional alternatives. See Torpey, "Introduction," 9.
25. Myron Weiner, Samuel Phillips Huntington, and Gabriel Abraham Almond, *Understanding Political Development: An Analytic Study* (Glenview, IL, 1987). Nicolas Guilhot, *The Democracy Makers: Human Rights and the Politics of Global Order* (New York, 2005), 111–113, describes the ambivalence of modernization and development theory approaches.
26. For examples, see Andreas Wirsching, *Der Preis der Freiheit: Geschichte Europas in unserer Zeit* (Munich, 2012), 29.
27. The link to US occupation rule in postwar Germany is embodied literally in John H. Herz, who would play an important role in the origins of transitional justice. The social scientist had fled Europe to the United States in 1938 and later took part in the US delegation to Nuremberg and, as an adviser to the Department of State, planning for the occupation zone. John H. Herz, *From Dictatorship to Democracy: Coping with the Legacies of Authoritarianism and Totalitarianism* (Westport, CT, 1982).
28. Lutz Raphael, "Die Verwissenschaftlichung des Sozialen als methodische und konzeptionelle Herausforderung für eine Sozialgeschichte des 20. Jahrhunderts," *Geschichte und Gesellschaft* 22 (1996): 165–193.
29. See Heinz-Gerhard Haupt, "Historische Komparatistik in der internationalen Geschichtsschreibung." in Budde et al., *Transnationale Geschichte*, 137–149.
30. Dominant and normative in US scholarship in the 1950s and 1960s, modernization theory posited a mutually reinforcing rise of parliamentary democratization, market-driven industrial growth, and a rationalization of lifeworlds and values; a model of progress in stages oriented to Western Europe or North America as the precedents. Anselm Doering-Manteuffel and Lutz Raphael, *Nach dem Boom: Perspektiven auf die Zeitgeschichte seit 1970* (Göttingen, 2008), 60–61; Axel Schildt, "Modernisierung, Version: 1.0," *Docupedia-Zeitgeschichte*, 11 February 2010, http://docupedia.de/zg/Modernisierung?oldid=84640; Harmut Kaelble, "Historischer Vergleich, Version: 1.0," *Docupedia-Zeitgeschichte*, 14 August 2012, http://docupedia.de/zg/Historischer_Vergleich?oldid=84623. The mutation of Japan in the eyes of the American societal reformers who relied on modernization theory, from "problem child" to exemplary case, is described in Conrad, *Auf der Suche nach der verlorenen Nation*, 327–332.
31. "By focusing on democratic agents within authoritarian coalitions, political scientists located within the state the principle of its own transformation. It was hence possible to analyze political change as a process internal to the ruling elite and relatively unconstrained by structural patterns of state-society relations." Guilhot, *The Democracy Makers*, 146–147; see Nicolas Guilhot, "'The Transition to the Human World of Democracy': Notes for a History of a Concept of Transition, from Early Marxism to 1989," *European Journal of Social Theory* 5, no. 2 (2002): 219–243.
32. Francis Fukuyama, *The End of History and the Last Man* (London, 1992).

33. On the concept of legally actionable sets of facts and circumstances (*Sachverhalt*), see Michael Stolleis, "Der Historiker als Richter: Der Richter als Historiker," in Frei et al., *Geschichte vor Gericht*, 177.
34. Huntington, *The Third Wave*, 211.
35. See Jean H. Quataert, *Advocating Dignity: Human Rights Mobilizations in Global Politics* (Philadelphia, 2009); Daniel Sargent, "Eine Oase in der Wüste? Amerikas Wiederentdeckung der Menschenrechte," in Eckel and Moyn, *Moral für die Welt?* 259–289.
36. Huntington, *The Third Wave*, 212–213.
37. See Sikkink, *The Justice Cascade*, 37.
38. Ibid., 89.
39. On the impact of the 1975 Amnesty study on *Torture in Greece*, see Edward M. Peters, *Folter: Geschichte der Peinlichen Befragung* (Hamburg, 2003), 204–205.
40. Huntington, *The Third Wave*, 212. Mainstream US conservatives reservations' regarding the human rights discourse are emphasized in Mary Nolan, "Human Rights and Market Fundamentalism in the Long 1970s," in *Toward a New Moral World Order? Menschenrechtspolitik und Völkerrecht seit 1945*, ed. Norbert Frei and Annette Weinke (Göttingen, 2013), 115.
41. Huntington, *The Third Wave*, 215.
42. Ibid., 81.
43. Ibid.
44. "Is a system undemocratic because the government either lacks the power or the will to prosecute criminals in the predecessor regime? If it is, then no democratic system established through transformation is democratic because clearly no authoritarian leaders will make their system democratic if they expect themselves or their associates to be prosecuted and punished as a result. Governments that are strong enough to bring about transformations are strong enough to exact that price. If they had not been, possibly half of the pre-1990 third wave transitions would not have occurred. To reject amnesty in these cases is to exclude the most prevalent form of democratization." Ibid., 217.
45. Ibid., 231.
46. Already in 1986–1987, the Argentinian government under Raul Alfonsin passed the Full Stop Law and Due Obedience Law, which guaranteed impunity for junta crimes. See Arthur, "How 'Transitions' Reshaped Human Rights," 323; Arenhövel, *Demokratie und Erinnerung*, 91–92.
47. Quataert, *Advocating Dignity*, 223.
48. See Weinke, *Die Nürnberger Prozesse*; Lingen, "'Crimes against Humanity': Eine umstrittene Universalie im Völkerrecht des 20. Jahrhunderts," *Zeithistorische Forschungen / Studies in Contemporary History* 8, no. 3 (2011), http://www.zeithistorische-forschungen.de/16126041-vonLingen-3-2011.
49. An overview of various commissions and other bodies is given in Priscilla Hayner, *Unspeakable Truths: Facing the Challenge of Truth Commissions* (New York, 2002). See Krüger, "Transitional Justice, Version: 1.0."
50. Mark Freeman, *Truth Commissions and Procedural Fairness* (Cambridge, 2006), 18, defines the instrument of the truth commission as follows: "A truth commission is an ad hoc, autonomous, and victim-centered commission of inquiry set up and authorized by a state for the primary purposes of (1) investigating and reporting on the principal causes and consequences of broad and relatively recent patterns of severe violence of repression that occurred in the state during determinate periods of abusive rule or conflict, and (2) making recommendations for their redress and future prevention."

51. See Buckley-Zistel, "Einleitung: Nach Krieg, Gewalt und Repression," in Buckley-Zistel and Kater, *Nach Krieg, Gewalt und Repression*, 7–20.
52. Torpey, "Introduction," 10.
53. See Golsan, *Vichy's Afterlife: History and Counterhistory in Postwar France* (Lincoln, NE, 2000); Rousso, "Justiz, Geschichte und Erinnerung in Frankreich."
54. Sikkink, *The Justice Cascade*, 143, is also critical of Huntington on this point. Her study decisively refutes the argument that criminal trials must necessarily extend conflicts or have destabilizing effects.
55. Claudia Kraft, "Pacto de silencio und gruba kreska: Vom Umgang mit Vergangenheit in Transformationsprozessen," in *Aufarbeitung der Diktatur Normierungsprozesse beim Umgang mit diktatorischer Vergangenheit*, ed. Katrin Hammerstein, Ulrich Mählert, and Edgar Wolfrum (Göttingen, 2009), 101.
56. Following the postcolonial turn, historical scholarship has focused increasingly on the violent pacification strategies employed to suppress anticolonial liberation struggles. See McMillan, "War."
57. Samuel P. Huntington, *Kampf der Kulturen: Die Neugestaltung der Weltpolitik im 21. Jahrhundert* (Munich, 1996).
58. See Sebastian Conrad and Andreas Eckert, "Globalgeschichte, Globalisierung, Multiple Modernen," in *Globalgeschichte: Theorien, Ansätze, Themen*, ed. Sebastian Conrad, Andreas Eckert, and Ulrike Freitag (Frankfurt, 2007), 17.
59. Guillermo O'Donnell and Philippe C. Schmitter, *Transitions from Authoritarian Rule: Tentative Conclusions about Uncertain Democracies* (Baltimore, 2013).
60. Guilhot, *The Democracy Makers*, 134–165; a similar analysis in Arenhövel, *Demokratie und Erinnerung*, 26–33.
61. The 1994 conference was followed by an additional four gatherings. See Luc Hyse, "Justice after Transition: On the Choices Successor Elites Make in Dealing with the Past." *Law and Social Inquiry* 20, no. 20 (1995): 54. A few histories of the transitional justice movement also credit its origins partly to the 1988 conference held by the Aspen Institute, "State Crimes: Punishment or Pardon"—not, however, in the sense of a founding but as the beginning of an "intellectual framework." See Arthur, "How 'Transitions' Reshaped Human Rights," 327.
62. Weitere Sponsoren waren der German Marshall Fund of the United States, der National Endowment for Democracy, Open Society und die Rockefeller Foundation; Arthur, "How 'Transitions' Reshaped Human Rights," 367.
63. The association changed its name to the Foundation for a Civil Society in 1992, following the dissolution of Charter 77.
64. See Timothy Phillips, "The Project on Justice in Times of Transition," in *The New Humanitarians*, ed. Chris E. Stout. Westport, CT, 2008.
65. Neil J. Kritz, "The Dilemmas of Transitional Justice," in *Transitional Justice: How Emerging Democracies Reckon with Former Regimes*, vol. 1, ed. Neil J. Kritz (Washington, DC, 1995), xix.
66. A totalitarianism reading of Communism shorn of specifics can also be found in the Council of Europe's resolutions 1096 (1996) and 1481 (2006). In linking the condemnation of communism to contemporary demands for punishment of state acts of violence, the latter elevates the supposedly comprehensive prosecution of NS injustice to the level of a binding standard: "The totalitarian communist regimes which ruled in central and eastern Europe in the last century, and which are still in power in several countries in the world, have been without exception characterised by massive violations of human rights. The violations have differed depending on the culture, country

and the historical period and have included individual and collective assassinations and executions, death in concentration camps [sic], starvation, deportations, torture, slave labour and other forms of mass physical terror, persecution on ethnic or religious grounds, violation of freedom of conscience, thought and expression, of freedom of the press, and also lack of political pluralism." Parliamentary Assembly of the Council of Europe, "Need for International Condemnation of Crimes of Totalitarian Communist Regimes," Resolution 1481, adopted on 25 January 2006, http://assembly.coe.int/nw/xml/XRef/Xref-XML2HTML-en.asp?fileid=17403&lang=en.

67. This comparability was vehmently disputed in later research. See Torpey, "Introduction," 8.
68. Mary Albon, "Project on Justice in Times of Transition: Report of the Project's Inaugural Meeting," in Kritz, *Transitional Justice*, 42.
69. This emerged obviously in talks by the jurists Diane Orentlicher and Claudio Grossman, who both agreed that in the most serious cases there was a duty to prosecute under international law. Ibid., 47.
70. Ibid., 42, emphasis in original.
71. The Argentinian cases were pursued on the basis of not international but national criminal law, but the legal policy impetus to prosecute referred directly to Nuremberg. See Sikkink, *The Justice Cascade*, 67; Teitel, "Transitional Justice Genealogy," 76.
72. The resort to international law in Hungary came "through the backdoor," in that the statutes of limitation were extended retroactively for state crimes committed under Communist rule. See Julie Trappe, "Verjährung, Rückwirkungsverbot und Menschenrechtsschutz," in Hammerstein et al., *Aufarbeitung der Diktatur*, 130.
73. Daniel Stahl, *Nazi-Jagd: Südamerikas Diktaturen und die Ahndung von NS-Verbrechen* (Göttingen, 2013), 320–333, describes the "dual politics of the past" in Argentina under the government of the Peronist politician Carlos Menem.
74. See Albin Eser, Jörg Arnold, and Julie Trappe, *Strafrechtsentwicklung in Osteuropa Zwischen bewältigten und neuen Herausforderungen* (Berlin, 2005); Friedrich-Christian Schröder and Herbert Küpper, *Die rechtliche Aufarbeitung der kommunistischen Vergangenheit in Osteuropa* (Frankfurt, 2010); Jan Pauer, "Die Aufarbeitung der Diktaturen in Tschechien und der Slowakei," *Aus Politik und Zeitgeschichte* 56, no. B42 (2006): 25–32; Hyse, "Justice after Transition."
75. As one among many publications, see Bodo Pieroth, "Der Rechtsstaat und die Aufarbeitung der vor-rechtsstaatlichen Vergangenheit," *Veröffentlichungen der Vereinigung der Deutschen Staatsrechtslehrer* 51 (1992): 91–115
76. Kraft, "Pacto de silencio und gruba kreska," 102.
77. See my own review of Mouralis, Annette Weinke, *Une épuration allemande*, H-Soz-u-Kult, 1 December 2009, http://hsozkult.geschichte.hu-berlin.de/rezensionen/2009-4-189.
78. In his 1997 final report, Louis Joinet, the then Special Rapporteur of the Sub-Commission on Prevention of Discrimination and Protection of Minorities of the UN Commission on Human Rights, reiterated that there was a right to historic truth and a duty to remember historic crimes: The "right to know," he wrote, was "not simply the right of any individual victim or closely related persons to know what happened, a right to the truth. The right to know is also a collective right, drawing upon history to prevent violations from recurring in the future. Its corollary is a 'duty to remember,' which the State must assume, in order to guard against the perversions of history that go under the name of revisionism or negationism; the knowledge of the oppression it has lived through is part of a people's national heritage and as such must be preserved.

These, then, are the main objectives of the right to know as a collective right." Louis Joinet, *Question of the Impunity of Perpetrators of Human Rights Violations (Civil and Political)*, Revised Final Report, E/CN.4/Sub.2/1997/20/Rev.1, 2 October 1997, http://www.derechos.org/nizkor/impu/joinet2.html; see also Park, "Truth as Justice," *Harvard International Review* 31, no. 4 (2010), http://hir.harvard.edu/big-ideas/truth-as-justice.
79. Torpey, "Introduction," 8.
80. See Hayner, "Fifteen Truth Commissions—1974 to 1994: A Comparative Study," in Kritz, *Transitional Justice*, 225–261.
81. See Sikkink, *The Justice Cascade*, 73.
82. Hayner, "Fifteen Truth Commissions," 239.
83. Rita Schäfer, "Gender in der südafrikanischen Wahrheits- und Versöhnungskommission," in Buckley-Zistel and Kater, *Nach Krieg, Gewalt und Repression*, 155.
84. According to Torpey, "Introduction," 10: "The TRC thus famously traded justice for truth"; see also Robert I. Rotberg and Dennis Thompson, *Truth v. Justice: The Morality of Truth Commissions* (Princeton, NJ); Shane Darcy and William A. Schabas, eds., *Truth Commissions and Courts* (Dordrecht, 2004).
85. Schäfer, "Gender in der südafrikanischen Wahrheits- und Versöhnungskommission," 156.
86. The literature for the most part refers to "amnesties," but in reality these are measures of impunity that do not require a court ruling. Teitel, "Transitional Justice Genealogy," 79.
87. Annette Wieviorka sees these criteria as common to both the Eichmann trial and the history of genocide as written by Daniel J. Goldhagen, among others. Wieviorka, "Die Entstehung des Zeugen."
88. Berber Bevernage, "Writing the Past Out of the Present: History and Politics of Time in Transitional Justice," *History Workshop Journal* 69, no. 1 (2010): 112.
89. Ibid., 122.
90. Elazar Barkan, "Introduction: Truth and Reconciliation in History," *American Historical Review* 114, no. 4 (2009): 900.
91. This is the thesis in Henry Rousso, "Das Dilemma eines europäischen Gedächtnisses," *Studies in Contemporary History* 1, no. 3 (2004), http://www.zeithistorische-forschungen.de/16126041-Rousso-3-2004, 10.
92. An overview of the measures taken after 1989 is given in Wirsching, *Der Preis der Freiheit*, 102–113. His narrative is limited to national parallel stories without closer illumination of international context.
93. Ruti G. Teitel, *Transitional Justice* (Oxford, 2000), 79.
94. Next to Russia, perhaps the most obvious example here is Hungary. Muriel Blaive, "The Memory of the Holocaust and of Communist Repression in a Comparative Perspective: The Cases of Hungary, Poland and Czechoslovakia/the Czech Republic," in Blaive et al., *Clashes in European Memory*, 154–172.
95. On this, see the overview on the Salzburg Inaugural Meeting of 1992: Mary Albon, "Project on Justice in Times of Transition: Report of the Project's Inaugural Meeting," in Neil Kritz, ed., *Transitional Justice: How Emerging Democracies Reckon with Former Regimes*, vol. I (Washington, DC, 1995), 42–54. The practice of lustration in part followed the memory politics of constructing a "genealogy of betrayal" that would exclude from the national collective both former Communist functionaries as well as parts of the opposition. The criteria for this exclusion were often ethnically connoted against Jews, Sinti, and Romany, as well as Germans. Paul Gradvohl, "La maison de la

terreur-musèe ou Terror Háza Múzeum," in *Lieux de mémoire en Europe centrale*, edited by Antoine Marès (Paris, 2009), 114–115.
96. See Schulze Wessel, "Geschichte vor Gericht," 18.
97. On the problems of adapting Holocaust remembrance to nationalist motivations in post-Communist Bulgaria, see Stephan Troebst, "Rettung, Überleben oder Vernichtung? Geschichtspolitische Kontroversen über Bulgarien und den Holocaust," *Südosteuropa* 59, no. 1 (2011) 97–127; Oliver Rathkolb, "Historical Perceptions of the Repression of the Holocaust in Czech, Polish and Hungarian Public Opinion and the Austrian 'Special Case,'" in Blaive et al., *Clashes in European Memory*, 173–191.
98. As Michal Kopeček explicates, demands for a "right to history" (used in the title of a 1984 statement by the Czechoslovakian dissident group Charta 77) and references to a "national memory" were important for crystallizing opposition against the official history writing of the party, but they also defined the national perspective after 1989. Michal Kopeček, "Human Rights Facing a National Past: Dissident 'Civic Patriotism' and the Return of History in East Central Europe, 1968–1989," *Geschichte und Gesellschaft* 38 (2012): 601.
99. As part of his strategy, Chief Prosecutor Geoffrey Nice incorporated a monumental history of the Balkans in the trial, prompting much public critique. According to the *Financial Times*: "The court confused the need to bring one man to account with the need to produce a clear narrative of war crimes and atrocities for the history books." Quoted in Wilson, *Writing History in International Criminal Trials*, 1.
100. As in Knigge, "Gesellschaftsverbrechen erinnern," 26 (emphasis in original), which especially stresses the national prehistory of dealing with Communist injustice.
101. At the Salzburg conference, the Hungarian philosopher György Bence declared, "Germany is making the transition in laboratory conditions"; quoted in Albon, "Project on Justice in Times of Transition," 48.
102. See A. James McAdams, "Vergangenheitsaufarbeitung nach 1989: Ein deutscher Sonderweg?" *Deutschland Archiv* 36, no. 5 (2003): 851–860; Christoph Cornelißen, "'Vergangenheitsbewältigung': Ein deutscher Sonderweg?" in Hammerstein et al., *Aufarbeitung der Diktatur*, 21–36, and the discussions in the same volume under the title, "DIN-Norm oder neuer deutscher Sonderweg: Aufarbeitung made in Germany als Modell?" 297–311; Annette Weinke, "La rielaborazione guiridica del passato della DDR: Un 'Sonderweg' tedesco?" in *Annali dell'Instituto storico italo-germanico in Trento: Quaderni, 82: Riflessioni sulla DDR—Prospettive internazionali e interdisciplinari vent'anni dopo*, ed. Magda Martini and Thomas Schaarschmidt (Bologna, 2011), 347–375.
103. A few statistics are given in Horst Dreier, "Verfassungsstaatliche Vergangenheitsbewältigung," in *Festschrift 50 Jahre Bundesverfassungsgericht, Bd. 1: Verfassungsgerichtsbarkeit—Verfassungsprozess*, ed. Peter Badura and Horst Dreier (Tübingen, 2001), 174; Hans-Ulrich Derlien, "Elitenzirkulation in Ostdeutschland 1989–1995," *Aus Politik und Zeitgeschichte* 48, no. B5 (1998): 3–17; Heike Solga, "The Fate of the East German Upper Service Class after 1989: Types of System Transformation and Changes in Elite Recruitment," in Srubar, *Eliten, politische Kultur und Privatisierung*, 97–117.v
104. See Jon Elster, *Die Akten schließen: Recht und Gerechtigkeit nach dem Ende von Diktaturen* (Bonn, 2005).
105. Offe, *Der Tunnel am Ende des Lichts*, 194.
106. On this, see the discussion in Christian Meier, *Das Gebot zu vergessen und die Unabweisbarkeit des Erinnerns* (Munich, 2010), 90–97.

107. Heiko Wingenfeld's communications studies work leaves out this dimension. Heiko Wingenfeld, *Die öffentliche Debatte über die Strafverfahren wegen SED-Unrecht Vergangenheitsaufarbeitung in der bundesdeutschen Öffentlichkeit der 90er Jahre* (Berlin, 2006).
108. That this did not apply to the same extent among exponents of legal scholarship is shown in the discussions at the Giessen conference of criminal law teachers in October 1991 as sketched by Stolleis, *Geschichte des öffentlichen Rechts*, vol. 4, 644–645.
109. Mouralis, *Une épuration allemande*, 284–285; Guillaume Mouralis, "Jenseits der indigenen Diskurse über die Vergangenheit: Der Umgang der Justiz-Juristen mit DDR-Systemverbrechen im vereinigten Deutschland zwischen 'Geschichts-' und 'Vergangenheitspolitik,'" Vortrag im Rahmen des Colloquiums "La recherche française sur la RDA et la transition," Humboldt University, Berlin, 19 March 2005.
110. Figures as given in Klaus Marxen, Gerhard Werle, and Petra Schäfter, *Die Strafverfolgung von DDR-Unrecht: Fakten und Zahlen* (Berlin, 2007), 25, 54. An overview of the investigations is supplied in Joachim Riedel, "Zwei deutsche Diktaturen und ihre strafrechtliche Aufarbeitung im Vergleich," in *Die Ermittler von Ludwigsburg: Deutschland und die Aufklärung nationalsozialistischer Verbrechen*, ed. Hans H. Pöschko (Berlin, 2008), 153–161.
111. Stolleis, *Geschichte des öffentlichen Rechts*, vol. 4, 644.
112. In his lecture at the gathering of TJ experts in Salzburg, the Christian Democratic premier of Saxony identified this as an especially problematic aspect: "Also, because so many judges and lawyers have been 'imported' into eastern Germany from the western part of the country, many eastern Germans perceive themselves to be subject to judgement by foreigners who do not understand the experience of life under dictatorship." Quoted in Albon, "Project on Justice in Times of Transition," 49.
113. Figures as in Eckart Conze, *Die Suche nach Sicherheit: Eine Geschichte der Bundesrepublik Deutschland von 1949 bis in die Gegenwart* (Munich, 2009), 781.
114. On the legal and mental aspects of German-German "reunification," see Stolleis, *Geschichte des öffentlichen Rechts*, vol. 4, 639–645; Michael Stolleis, "Angst (West)," *Frankfurter Allgemeine Zeitung*, 26 May 1992.
115. See Peter Quint, *The Imperfect Union: Constitutional Structures of German Unification*. Princeton, NJ, 1997.
116. Critically, see Bernhard Schlink, "Rechtsstaat und revolutionäre Gerechtigkeit," *Vergangenheitsschuld und gegenwärtiges Recht*, ed. Bernhard Schlink (Frankfurt, 2002), 38–60.
117. See Klaus Marxen and Gerhard Werle, *Die strafrechtliche Aufarbeitung von DDR-Unrecht: Eine Bilanz* (Berlin, 1999), 244–245.
118. See Mouralis, *Une épuration allemande*, 39–71.
119. See Jens-Uwe Heuer, *Im Streit: Ein Jurist zwischen zwei deutschen Staaten* (Baden-Baden, 2002); Daniela Dahn, *Wehe dem Sieger! Ohne Osten kein Westen* (Reinbek, 2009).
120. Dirk van Laak, "Widerstand gegen die Geschichtsgewalt: Zur Kritik an der 'Vergangenheitsbewältigung,'" in Frei et al., *Geschichte vor Gericht*, 13.
121. Klaus Kinkel, "Begrüßungsansprache auf dem 15. Deutschen Richtertag am 23. September 1991 in Köln," *Deutsche Richterzeitung* 1 (1992): 4–5.
122. See Wolfgang Naucke, "NS-Strafrecht: Perversion oder Anwendungsfall moderner Kriminalpolitik." *Rechtshistorisches Journal* 11 (1992): 279–292.
123. See Quint, *The Imperfect Union*, 205; Stefan König, "Bülowplatz-Prozess gegen Erich Mielke Vom Umgang der Justiz mit (ihrer) Geschichte," in *Die Normalität*

des Verbrechens: Bilanz und Perspektiven der Forschung zu den nationalsozialistischen Gewaltverbrechen, ed. Helge Gabitz, Klaus Bästlein, and Johannes Tuchel (Berlin, 1994), 503–519.
124. See Dreier, "Verfassungsstaatliche Vergangenheitsbewältigung," 203–220; Ingo Müller, "NS-Justiz und DDR-Justiz vor deutschen Gerichten,"in *Kontinuitäten und Zäsuren: Rechtswissenschaft und Justiz im "Dritten Reich" und in der Nachkriegszeit*, ed. Eva Schumann (Göttingen, 2008), 233–245.
125. A summary of the most important legal questions is found in Klaus Lüderssen, *Der Staat geht unter Das Unrecht bleibt? Regierungskriminalität in der ehemaligen DDR* (Frankfurt, 1992).
126. Kinkel, "Begrüßungsansprache," 4n121; Klaus Kinkel, "Gerichtsverfahren straffen," *Frankfurter Allgemeine Zeitung*, 24 September 1991. The speech was criticized by numerous legal scholars. According to Waldemar Hummer and Jelka Mayr-Singer, Kinkel's speech showed that "desire fathers the thought." This was an attempt to "overcome the past not through the executive (by unification) or through the legislature (by law) but through the judiciary (by criminal justice)." Waldemar Hummer and Jelka Mayr-Singer, "Der 'deutsche Sonderweg' bei der Aufarbeitung von SED-Unrecht: Vergangenheitsbewältigung durch Strafjustiz," *Neue Justiz* 54, no. 11 (2000): 566.
127. On the partisan implications of the statute of limitations issue, see Miquel, *Ahnden oder Amnestieren?* 285–319.
128. Lüderssen, *Der Staat geht unter*, 115–120.
129. In the same vein, see also, Schlink, "Rechtsstaat und revolutionäre Gerechtigkeit."
130. On the legal-policy discussion of the Law to Suspend the Statute of Limitations for SED Acts of Injustice of 27 September 1993, see Mouralis, *Une épuration allemande*, 191–211.
131. Petra Bock approaches this from the perspective of democracy theory, although he mildly mystifies the role of the civil rights activists. Petra Bock, "Von der Tribunal-Idee zur Enquete-Kommission: Zur Vorgeschichte der Enquete-Kommission des Bundestages 'Aufarbeitung von Geschichte und Folgen der SED-Diktatur in Deutschland,'" *Deutschland Archiv* 28, no. 1 (1995): 1171–1183.
132. The journal *Kritische Justiz* initiated a discussion on a possible amnesty law in 1990, in which the Munich journalist Andreas Zielcke proposed holding public hearings on the Ugandan model. Andreas Zielcke, "Gnade vor Recht?" *Kritische Justiz* 4 (1990): 467.
133. Friedrich Schorlemmer, "Die frühere Stasi darf nicht späte Siege über ihre Opfer feiern," *Frankfurter Rundschau*, 28 August 1991.
134. Wolfgang Thierse, "Schuld sind immer die anderen: Ein Plädoyer für die selbstkritische Bewältigung der eigenen Geschichte," *Die Zeit*, 6 September 1991.
135. See Matthias Middell, "Marxistische Geschichtswissenschaft," in *Kompass der Geschichtswissenschaft*, 2nd ed., ed. Joachim Eibach and Günther Lottes (Göttingen, 2006), 69–85.
136. Thierse, "Schuld sind immer die anderen."
137. Wolfgang Ullmann, "Königsprozess oder Nürnberger Tribunal? Die DDR ist nur als 'Staatskriminalität' juristisch zu fassen," in *Ein Volk am Pranger? Die Deutschen auf der Suche nach einer neuen politischen Kultur*, ed. Albrecht Schönherr (Berlin ,1992), 31–41.
138. Ibid., 39.
139. On following passage, see Ronen Steinke, *The Politics of International Criminal Justice: German Perspectives from Nuremberg to The Hague* (Oxford, 2012), 57.

140. Thilo Marauhn, "Völkerrechtliche Praxis der Bundesrepublik Deutschland im Jahre 1991," *Zeitschrift für ausländisches öffentliches Recht und Völkerrecht* 53 (1993): 957, 963–964.
141. Klaus Kinkel, "Wiedervereinigung und Strafrecht," *Juristenzeitung* 47, no. 10 (1992): 487.
142. Wolfgang Hoffmann, "Tödliche Geschäfte," *Die Zeit*, 10 August 1990; "Ruhig schlafen," *Der Spiegel*, 3 October 1988. Accusations of "checkbook diplomacy" were raised from the American side; Manfred Görtemaker *Die Berliner Republik: Wiedervereinigung und Neuorientierung* (Bonn, 2009), 66–70.
143. Otto Trifterer, "Was kann das Völkerstrafrecht zur Bewältigung der Regierungskriminalität der DDR beitragen?" in *Deutsche Wiedervereinigung: Die Rechtseinheit—Arbeitskreis Strafrecht, Bd. II: Die Verfolgung von Regierungskriminalität der DDR nach der Wiedervereinigung*, ed. Ernst-Joachim Lampe (Cologne, 1993), 156; see also Silke Buchner, *Die Rechtswidrigkeit der Taten von "Mauerschützen" im Lichte von Art. 103 II GG unter besonderer Berücksichtigung des Völkerrechts* (Frankfurt, 1996); Eckart Klein, "Die Bedeutung der Nürnberger Prozesse für die Bewältigung des SED-Unrechts," *Zeitschrift für Rechtspolitik* 6 (1992): 208–213.
144. Forn an overview of the various reactions, Schönherr, *Ein Volk am Pranger?*
145. Robert Leicht, "Am Pranger der Gerechtigkeit," *Die Zeit*, 11 October 1991.
146. Richard von Weizsäcker, "Arbeit an der Vergangenheit als wesentlicher Beitrag zur deutschen Einigung: Ansprache des Bundespräsidenten bei der Verleihung des Heinrich-Heine-Preises in Dsseldorf am 13.12.1991," *Bulletin der Bundesregierung Nr. 143*, 17 December 1991, reprinted in Schönherr, *Volk am Pranger?* 175–190, here 183.
147. See Conze et al., *Das Amt*, 401–435.
148. See Philipp Gassert, "Das Russell-Tribunal von 1966/67: 'Blaming and Shaming' und die Nürnberger Prinzipien," in Frei and Weinke, *Toward a New Moral World Order?* 92–103.
149. See Annette Weinke, "Der Umgang mit der Stasi und ihren Mitarbeitern," *Vergangenheitsbewältigung am Ende des zwanzigsten Jahrhunderts*, ed. Helmut König, Michael Kohlstruck, and Andreas Wöll (Opladen, 1998), 167–191.
150. Quoted in Bock, "Von der Tribunal-Idee zur Enquete-Kommission," 1176; a thorough treatment in Andrew H. Beattie, *Playing Politics with History: The Bundestag Inquiries into East Germany* (New York, 2008), 26–27.
151. Quoted in ibid., 28.
152. Quoted in Bock, "Von der Tribunal-Idee zur Enquete-Kommission," 1177.
153. This and the following quoted passages are from Joachim Gauck, Friedrich Schorlemmer, Wolfgang Thierse, Wolfgang Ullmann, and Reinhard Höppner, "Begreifen, was gewesen ist: Plädoyer für ein Tribunal," *Frankfurter Allgemeine Zeitung*, 23 January 1992. (Among the signatories were Gerd and Ulrike Poppe, Hans Misselwitz, Marianne Birthler, and Burghard Brinksmeier.) Also in *Blätter für deutsche und internationale Politik* 3 (1992): 379–382.
154. Conze, *Die Suche nach Sicherheit*, 745, comments that the period since 1990 has seen a "consensual and almost normative cementing of all the major lines of development in the Federal Republic since 1949."
155. Quoted in Bock, "Von der Tribunal-Idee," 1180. In 1982, at the height of the Western movement against new deployments of nuclear missiles, Eppelmann had joined the scientist and GDR dissident Robert Havemann in issuing the "Berlin Appeal" against nuclear weapons and militarism. Eppelmann's intellectual development is outlined by Fehr, "Öffentlicher Sprachwandel und Eliten-Konkurrenz," 82.

156. See James A. McAdams, *Judging the Past in Unified Germany* (Cambridge, 2001); Helga A. Welsh, "When Discourse Trumps Policy: Transitional Justice in Unified Germany," *German Politics* 15, no. 2 (2006): 137–152; Jennifer A. Yoder, "Truth without Reconciliation: An Appraisal of the Enquete Commission on the SED Dictatorship in Germany," *German Politics* 8, no. 3 (1999): 59–80.
157. This is the tendency in Anne K. Krüger, "'Keine Aussöhnung ohne Wahrheit': Die Enquete-Kommissionen zur 'Aufarbeitung' und 'Überwindung der SED-Diktatur,'" in Buckley-Zistel and Kater, *Nach Krieg, Gewalt und Repression*, 131–149.
158. Beattie, *Playing Politics with History*, 9.
159. Ibid., 6.
160. A different position is held by Hartmut Fehr, who sees fundamental semantic shifts in the postsocialist phase of power consolidation. He argues, for example, that the term "antitotalitarianism" had represented a general critique of power and rule, but that after 1989 it came to be deployed only instrumentally as a means of defining enemy images. The "1968" movement of the West became a common enemy image for both the old Western liberal-conservative forces and for the former counter-elites under real-existing socialism. Fehr, "Öffentlicher Sprachwandel und Eliten-Konkurrenz," 92.
161. Beattie, *Playing Politics with History*, 62.
162. Ibid., 238.
163. Ibid., 205.
164. In an event-driven interpretation of the twentieth century, Möller not only saw both systems as equivalent, but also assessed the fall of National Socialism as a first victory in a struggle against totalitarianism that was completed only with the dissolution of the Soviet imperium in 1989–1991. Manfred Hettling, "Umschreiben notwendig? Die Historiker und das Jahr 1989," in Bauerkämper et al., *Doppelte Zeitgeschichte*, 394–395.
165. Beattie, *Playing Politics with History,* 206–207; a similar critique is found in Berger, *The Search for Normality National Identity and Historical Consciousness in Germany since 1800* (Providence, RI, 1997), 157.
166. In listing the institutions of German "memory governance," Thomas Lindenberger includes the Federal Adviser for Culture and Media, the Federal Archives (Bundesarchiv), the agency overseeing the Stasi files (BStU), the Foundation Memorial to the Murdered Jews of Europe, the Federal Foundation for the Reappraisal of the SED Dictatorship, and several monuments of national relevance. Thomas Lindenberger, "Governing Conflicted Memories: Some Remarks about the Regulation of History Politics in Unified Germany," in Blaive et al., *Clashes in European Memory*, 73–84.
167. Frei, "1989 und wir? Eine Vergangenheit zwischen 'Erinnerungskultur' und Geschichtsbewusstsein," in Frei, *1945 und wir*, 19.
168. Fehr, "Öffentlicher Sprachwandel und Eliten-Konkurrenz," 90.
169. E.g., Rousso, "Égo-Histoire," 131.
170. Excerpts from the final report are also reproduced in Rainer Eppelmann, "Die Enquete-Kommissionen," in *Bilanz und Perspektiven der DDR-Forschung*, ed. Rainer Eppelmann, Bernd Faulenbach, and Ulrich Mählert (Paderborn, 2003), 401–406.
171. Lüderssen, *Der Staat geht unter*, 15.
172. Like many other aspects of the German-German transformation, the amnesty debate has yet to be historically researched; a first approach is offered in Mouralis, *Une épuration allemande*, 152–166.
173. Herwig Roggemann, "Amnestie in beiden deutschen Staaten: Rechtsvergleichende Anmerkungen zum Staatsratsbeschluss von 1987," *Recht in Ost und West* 31 (1987): 281–291.

174. See Meier, *Das Gebot zu vergessen und die Unabweisbarkeit des Erinnerns*.
175. As debates about the law and historical justice have been a fixture after each of the systemic ruptures in twentieth century German history, it is surprising that a systematic longitudinal treatment of the amnesty issue has yet to be published; the theme is handled in essay form by Otto Kirchheimer, *Politische Justiz: Verwendung juristischer Verfahrensmöglichkeiten zu politischen Zwecken* (Frankfurt, 1985), 566–605.
176. Regarding the impunity laws of 1949 and 1954, see Frei, *Vergangenheitspolitik*; Norbert Frei, "Amnestiepolitik in den Anfangsjahren der Bundesrepublik," in *Amnestie oder die Politik der Erinnerung in der Demokratie*, ed. Gary Smith and Avishai Margalit (Frankfurt, 1997), 129.
177. The most thorough treatment is still in Reinhard Schiffers, *Zwischen Bürgerfreiheit und Staatsschutz: Wiederherstellung und Neufassung des politischen Strafrechts in der Bundesrepublik Deutschland 1949–1951* (Düsseldorf, 1989); Alexander von Brünneck, *Politische Justiz gegen Kommunisten in der Bundesrepublik Deutschland 1949–1968* (Frankfurt, 1978).
178. In this vein, see Kirchheimer, *Politische Justiz*, 592.
179. Johann-Georg Schätzler, *Handbuch des Gnadenrechts* (Munich, 1976), 130–131.
180. Detleft Marten, *Rechtsstaatlichkeit und Gnade* (Berlin, 1978), 27.
181. Norbret Frei, Ralf Ahrens, Jörg Osterloh, and Tim Schanetzky, eds., *Flick: Der Konzern, die Familie, die Macht* (Munich, 2009), 746.
182. Dieter Lutz, "Amnestie: Eine Einführung," *Vierteljahresschrift für Sicherheit und Frieden*, Sonderheft Amnestie 4 (1993): 192.
183. Falco Werkentin, *Politische Strafjustiz in der Ära Ulbricht* (Berlin, 1995), 384.
184. Quoted in Johannes Raschka, *Justizpolitik im SED-Staat: Anpassung und Wandel des Strafrechts während der Amtszeit Honeckers* (Cologne, 2000), 59.
185. See Werkentin, *Politische Strafjustiz in der Ära Ulbricht*, 388.
186. Raschka, *Justizpolitik im SED-Staat*, 235.
187. Lutz, "Amnestie," 190; Klaus Bästlein, "Der letzte 'Tag der Republik': Aus den staatsanwaltschaftlichen Ermittlungen zum 7./8. Oktober 1989 in Berlin," *Deutschland Archiv* 42, no. 5 (2009): 821–831.
188. See Thomas Blanke, "Der 'Rechtshistorikerstreit' um Amnestie: Politische Klugheit, moralische Richtigkeit und Gerechtigkeit bei der Aufarbeitung deutscher Vergangenheiten," in *Justiz, Die juristische Aufarbeitung des Unrechts-Staats*, 727–752; Mouralis, *Une épuration allemande*, 153.
189. The SPD parliamentary deputy Hertha Däubler-Gmelin, Otto Graf Lambsdorff of the FDP, and his party colleague Burkhard Hirsch even spoke out for a "grand amnesty" in the Bundestag debate of 5 September 1990; Bundestag Record II/222, 17499–17500, 17537.
190. See Anne Sa'adah, *Germany's Second Chance: Trust, Justice, and Democratization* (Cambridge, 1998), 59–68.
191. See Geoff Eley, *Forging Democracy The History of the Left in Europe, 1850–2000* (Oxford, 2002), 446–449; Václav Havel, *Living in Truth* (London, 1986).
192. This factor is underestimated in Meier, *Das Gebot zu vergessen und die Unabweisbarkeit des Erinnerns*, 91.
193. See Ehrhart Neubert, *Unsere Revolution: Die Geschichte der Jahre 1989/90* (Munich, 2008), 414–415.
194. Regarding the ban on individual amnesty, see Marxen, *Rechtliche Grenzen der Amnestie* (Heidelberg, 1984), 29–38.
195. See Blanke, "Der 'Rechtshistorikerstreit' um Amnestie," 732.

196. Figures according to Deutscher Bundestag, "Bundestagswahlergebnisse seit 1914," https://www.bundestag.de/parlament/wahlen/ergebnisse_seit1949/244692.
197. Quoted in Blanke, "Der 'Rechtshistorikerstreit' um Amnestie," 727.
198. Egon Bahr, "'Ich will unser Blut zurücks'" interview, *Der Spiegel*, 24 October 1994.
199. Egon Bahr, "Drei Jahre nach der Einheit: Für eine Amnestie," *Vierteljahresschrift für Sicherheit und Frieden, Sonderheft Amnestie* 4 (1993): 209–211, 209.
200. Bahr, "'Ich will unser Blut zurück.'"
201. See Kirchheimer, *Politische Justiz*, 597.
202. Hermann Lübbe, "Der Nationalsozialismus im deutschen Nachkriegsbewußtsein," *Historische Zeitschrift* 236 (1983): 579–59.
203. For a critical view on the marginalization of the GDR civil rights activists in the conservative history discourses of the "Berlin Republic," see Dieter Segert, *Das 41. Jahr: Eine andere Geschichte der DDR* (Cologne, 2008), 272–279.
204. Bahr's comment on the holdouts: "I have the highest regard for Bärbel Bohley, but it cannot be that a handful of people should have the power to torpedo or veto an overwhelming majority in the German Bundestag who favor the goal of reconciliation. I know this is hard to bear for the civil rights activists. I treasure people like Stephan Hilsberg for their moral integrity. But after four years it's time to take stock and ask: How successful have you been? Is it the unavoidable destiny of the SPD to remain in this weak position?" Bahr, "'Ich will unser Blut zurück,'" n98.
205. On the phenomenon of the "jubilee amnesty," see Marxen, *Rechtliche Grenzen der Amnestie*, 11–27.
206. Hans Hubertus von Roenne, *"Politisch untragbar . . .?" Die Überprüfung von Richtern und Staatsanwälten der DDR im Zuge der Vereinigung Deutschlands* (Berlin, 1997), 317; see also Annette Weinke, "Die DDR-Justiz im Umbruch 1989/90," in *Justiz im Dienste der Parteiherrschaft: Rechtspraxis und Staatssicherheit in der DDR*, 2nd ed., ed. Roger Engelmann and Clemens Vollnhals (Berlin, 2000), 411–431.
207. "'Ein grotesker Zustand,'" interview with Hans Otto Bräutigam, *Der Spiegel*, 18 March 1991.
208. Quoted in *die tageszeitung*, 12 December 1994.
209. "'Sozis gegen Schlussstrich,'" *die tageszeitung*, 21 December 1994.
210. The "131 Law" refers to the Implementation Law for Article 131 of the Basic Law (GG), which foresaw a guarantee to rehire displaced civil servants. Frei, *Vergangenheitspolitik*.
211. Uwe Wesel, "'Plädoyer für ein Schlußgesetz,'" *Die Zeit*, 6 June 1995. Various exception rules enacted in the "131 Law" allowed (especially younger) SS and Gestapo men to join West German federal and state law enforcement agencies; see esp. Frei, *Vergangenheitspolitik*, 79–85.
212. Wesel, "'Plädoyer für ein Schlußgesetz.'"
213. Marion Gräfin Dönhoff, "'Gerechtigkeit ist nicht Vergeltung,'" *Die Zeit*, 13 January 1995.
214. Ibid.
215. Konrad H. Jarausch, "Von der Geschichte belehrt: Die Schwierigkeiten der ZEIT mit der Vereinigung," in *DIE ZEIT und die Bonner Republik: Eine meinungsbildende Wochenzeitung zwischen Wiederbewaffnung und Wiedervereinigung*, ed. Christian Haase and Axel Schildt (Göttingen, 2008), 292.
216. Marion Gräfin von Dönhoff, "Die Nürnberger Prozesse: Ein abschreckendes Beispiel," in *Ein Manifest II: Weil das Land Versöhnung braucht*, ed. Marion Gräfin von Dönhoff (Reinbek, 1993), 87.
217. Ibid., 88.

218. Ibid., 89.
219. See Conze et al., *Das Amt*, 407; Axel Schildt, "Immer mit der Zeit: Der Weg der Wochenzeitung DIE ZEIT durch die Bonner Republik—eine Skizze," in Haase and Schildt, *DIE ZEIT und die Bonner Republik*, 17–18.
220. On the tension between the historicist objectivity ideal and dynamic history interpretation, see Schulze Wessel, "Geschichte vor Gericht."
221. See Annette Leo, "Antifaschismus," in *Erinnerungsorte der DDR*, ed. Martin Sabrow (Bonn, 2010), 28–40.
222. Bernhard Brunner, *Der Frankreich-Komplex: Die nationalsozialistischen Verbrechen in Frankreich und die Justiz der Bundesrepublik Deutschland* (Göttingen, 2004), 380; on Schätzler, see also Claudia Moisel, *Frankreich und die deutschen Kriegsverbrecher: Politik und Praxis der Strafverfolgung nach dem Zweiten Weltkrieg* (Göttingen, 2004).
223. Ibid., 263–264.
224. Schätzler, *Hanbuch des Gnadenrecht*, 126.
225. Johann-Georg Schätzler "Staatenfusion und Abrechnungsmentalität," in Schätzler, *Hanbuch des Gnadenrecht*, 112.
226. Ibid., 106.
227. Johann-Georg Schätzler, "Innerer Frieden und Amnestie am Beispiel der deutschen Einheit," in Schätzler *Hanbuch des Gnadenrecht*, 199.
228. Ibid., 197.
229. Schätzler, "Staatenfusion und Abrechnungsmentalität," 113.
230. Ibid., 114.
231. Schätzler, "Innerer Frieden und Amnestie," 195.
232. On the idea of primary experience, see Hans Günter Hockerts, "Zugänge zur Zeitgeschichte: Primärerfahrung, Erinnerungskultur, Geschichtswissenschaft," *Aus Politik und Zeitgeschichte*, no. B28 (2001): 15–30.
233. This formulation from Hans-Ulrich Wehler, *Deutsche Gesellschaftsgeschichte, Bd. 5: Bundesrepublik und DDR, 1949–1990* (Munich, 2008), 311.
234. On the West German practice of professional blacklisting, see Dominik Rigoll, *Staatsschutz in Westdeutschland: Von der Entnazifizierung zur Extremistenabwehr* (Göttingen, 2013).
235. Falco Werkentin, "'68er im Dienste der Diktatoren,'" *die tageszeitung*, 20 October 1995. In a similar tenor, Norbert Frei, "'Wider die falschen Analogien'" *Süddeutsche Zeitung*, 10 March 1995.
236. Mouralis, *Une épuration allemande*, 155.
237. Quoted in "'Unrecht muss Unrecht bleiben,'" *die tageszeitung*, 9 January 1995.
238. "'Kohl gegen Amnestie für SED-Täter,'" *die tageszeitung*, 9 January 1995.
239. Joachim Gauck, "'Wut und Schmerz der Opfer,'" *Die Zeit*, 20.1.1995.
240. Frédéric Mégret, "The Politics of International Criminal Justice," *European Journal of International Law* 13, no. 5 (2002): 1261–1284.

Final Reflections

1. There are parallels here to the problematics of the West German restitutions policy or "making good again" (*Wiedergutmachung*). Constantin Goschler presents a thorough discussion of its potentials as a universalist model on the basis of empirical findings. Goschler, *Schuld und Schulden*, 488–494.
2. See Mégret, "The Politics of International Criminal Justice."

3. Steiger, "Art. Völkerrecht," 130–131, is instructive on the argumentative tropes advanced by "old" and "new" international law rejectionists.
4. See Franzki, "Mit Recht Erinnern," 455.
5. See Pendas, "Auf dem Weg zu einem globalen Rechtssystem?"
6. According to Ronen Steinke, the proposal by Germany and "like-minded states" that the ICC be institutionally independent of the Security Council was one of the main reasons for the United States' withdrawal from the project. Steinke, *The Politics of International Criminal Justice*, 87–130.
7. Quoted in ibid., 3.
8. See ibid., 116. In a recent article based on Foreign Office files, Markus Eikel rejects Steinke's findings that the West German delegation adopted a restrictive line in order to soothe the concerns of the FRG Defense Ministry; Markus Eikel, "'Die Herrschaft des Rechts und nicht das Recht des Stärkeren': Die Bundesrepublik Deutschland und die Entstehungsgeschichte des Internationalen Strafgerichtshofs," in VfZ 66, no. 1 (2018): 9–41, 26.
9. See Weinke, "'Von Nürnberg nach Den Haag'?" 21.

BIBLIOGRAPHY

I. Archival Sources

1. Politisches Archiv des Auswärtigen Amtes (PAAA), Berlin
   Nachlass Hellmut Becker
   B80, B83
2. Zentrale Stelle der Landesjustizverwaltungen (ZSL), Ludwigsburg
   Generalakten
3. Bundesarchiv (BArch), Koblenz
   Nachlass Hermann Jahrreiß, N 1420
   B136, B141
4. Hauptstaatsarchiv Stuttgart (HStA)
   EA 4/106
5. New York Public Library (NYPL)
   Raphael Lemkin Papers
6. Institut für Zeitgeschichte (IfZ)
   IfZ Hausarchiv
   Gründungsunterlagen, ID 1/1
   Kuratorium, Sitzungen, ID 4/2
   Wissenschaftlicher Beirat, Ergebnisprotokolle, ID 7/1
   Wissenschaftlicher Beirat, Sitzungen, ID 8/1
   Korrespondenz Hermann Mau, ID 101/1-8
   Staatliches Archivlager Göttingen ("Nürnberger Akten") ID 200

II. Periodicals

Berliner Monatshefte
Bundesgesetzblatt
The Christian Century
Frankfurter Allgemeine Zeitung (FAZ)
Frankfurter Zeitung (FZ)
Norddeutsche Allgemeine Zeitung
Der Spiegel
Süddeutsche Zeitung
Tagesspiegel
Die Tageszeitung

Volkszeitung-Tribüne
Die Zeit

III. Printed Matter and Secondary Literature

Ahlbrecht, Heiko. *Geschichte der völkerrechtlichen Strafgerichtsbarkeit im 20. Jahrhundert.* Baden-Baden, 1999.

Ahrens, Ralf. "Kartelle und Verschwörungen: Franz Neumanns 'Behemoth' und die Nürnberger Prozesse." In *Unternehmen im Nationalsozialismus: Zur Historisierung einer Forschungskonjunktur*, edited by Norbert Frei and Tim Schanetzky, 26–35. Göttingen, 2010.

Albertin, Lothar. *Liberalismus und Demokratie am Anfang der Weimarer Republik.* Düsseldorf, 1972.

Albon, Mary. "Project on Justice in Times of Transition: Report of the Project's Inaugural Meeting." In Kritz, *Transitional Justice*, 42–54.

Alvarez, Al. "Es geschah nicht überall." In Krummacher, *Die Kontroverse*, 176–181.

Anders, Freia. "Kontinuität oder Diskontinuität? Plädoyer für eine rechtshistorische Perspektive bei der Nutzung von Strafakten als Quellen." In *Vom Recht zur Geschichte: Akten aus NS-Prozessen als Quellen der Zeitgeschichte*, edited by Jürgen Finger, Sven Keller, and Andreas Wirsching, 27–37. Göttingen, 2009.

Anghie, Antony. "Finding the Peripheries: Sovereignty and Colonialism in Nineteenth Century International Law." *Harvard International Law Journal* 40, no. 1 (1999): 1–80.

Arendt, Hannah. "Adolf Eichmann: Von der Banalität des Bösen." *Merkur* 186, no. 8 (1963): 759–776.

———. *Eichmann in Jerusalem: A Report on the Banality of Evil.* New York, 1963.

———. *Eichmann in Jerusalem: Ein Bericht von der Banalität des Bösen.* 2nd ed. Munich, 2007.

———. *Elemente und Ursprünge totaler Herrschaft.* 2nd ed. Munich, 1986.

———. *The Origins of Totalitarianism.* New York, 1951.

Arendt, Hannah, and Karl Jaspers. *Briefwechsel 1926–1969.* Frankfurt, 1991.

Arenhövel, Mark. *Demokratie und Erinnerung: Der Blick zurück auf Diktatur und Menschenrechtsverbrechen.* Frankfurt, 2000.

Arndt, Adolf. "Das Verbrechen der Euthanasie (Probleme der Frankfurter Euthanasie-Prozesse)." In *Der Konstanzer Juristentag*, 184–200. Tübingen, 1947.

Aronson, Shlomo. "Preparations for the Nuremberg Trial: The OSS, Charles Dwork, and the Holocaust." *Holocaust and Genocide Studies* 12, no. 2 (1998): 257–281.

Arthur, Paige. "How 'Transitions' Reshaped Human Rights: A Conceptual History of Transitional Justice." *Human Rights Quarterly* 31, no. 2 (2009): 321–367.

Ash, Mitchell G. "Learning from Persecution: Emigré Jewish Social Scientists' Studies of Authoritarianism and Anti-Semitism after 1933." In *Jüdische Welten: Juden in Deutschland vom 18. Jahrhundert bis in die Gegenwart*, edited by Marion Kaplan and Beate Meyer, 271–294. Göttingen, 2005.

Auswärtiges Amt. *Die völkerrechtswidrige Führung des belgischen Volkskrieges: Denkschrift.* Berlin, 1915.

Baden, Prinz Max von. *Völkerbund und Rechtsfriede.* Berlin, 1919.

Bahr, Egon. "Drei Jahre nach der Einheit: Für eine Amnestie." *Vierteljahresschrift für Sicherheit und Frieden, Sonderheft Amnestie* 4 (1993): 209–211.

Barkan, Elazar. *The Guilt of Nations: Restitution and Negotiating Historical Injustices.* New York, 2000.
———. "Introduction: Truth and Reconciliation in History." *American Historical Review* 114, no. 4 (2009): 899–913.
Bast, Jürgen. *Totalitärer Pluralismus: Zu Franz L. Neumanns Analyse der politischen und rechtlichen Struktur der NS-Herrschaft.* Tübingen, 1999.
Bästlein, Klaus. "Der letzte 'Tag der Republik': Aus den staatsanwaltschaftlichen Ermittlungen zum 7./8. Oktober 1989 in Berlin." *Deutschland Archiv* 42, no. 5 (2009): 821–831.
Bauerkämper, Arnd, Martin Sabrow, and Bernd Stöver, eds. *Doppelte Zeitgeschichte: Deutsch-deutsche Beziehungen 1945–1990.* Bonn, 1999.
Baumann, Immanuel. *Dem Verbrechen auf der Spur: Eine Geschichte der Kriminologie und Kriminalpolitik in Deutschland 1880 bis 1980.* Göttingen, 2006.
Beattie, Andrew H. *Playing Politics with History: The Bundestag Inquiries into East Germany.* New York, 2008.
Beck, Ulrich. *Der kosmopolitische Blick oder: Krieg ist Frieden.* Frankfurt, 2004.
Becker, Frank, and Elke Reinhardt-Becker. *Systemtheorie: Eine Einführung für die Geschichts- und Kulturwissenschaften.* Frankfurt, 2001.
Becker, Hellmut. "Das Arbeitsprogramm vor 25 Jahren." In *25 Jahre Institut für Zeitgeschichte: Statt einer Festschrift*, 25–29. Stuttgart, 1975.
Belgium and Official Commission of the Belgian Government. *Reports on the Violation of the Rights of Nations and of the Laws and Customs of War in Belgium.* London, 1914.
Berg, Nicolas. *Der Holocaust und die westdeutschen Historiker: Erforschung und Erinnerung.* 3rd rev. ed. Göttingen, 2004.
———. "Lesarten des Judenmords." In *Wandlungsprozesse in Westdeutschland: Belastung, Integration, Liberalisierung 1945–1980*, edited by Ulrich Herbert, 91–139. Göttingen, 2002.
———. "'Phantasie der Bürokratie': Raul Hilbergs Pionierstudie zur Vernichtung der europäischen Juden." In Danyel et al., *50 Klassiker der Zeitgeschichte*, 71–83.
———. "Jean Améry und Hans Egon Holthusen: Eine Merkur-Debatte in den 1960er Jahren." In *Mittelweg 36, Zeitschrift des Hamburger Instituts für Sozialforschung*, 2012 no. 2: 28–48.
Berger, Stefan. *The Search for Normality: National Identity and Historical Consciousness in Germany since 1800.* Providence, RI, 1997.
Berghahn, Volker H. *Europa im Zeitalter der Weltkriege: Die Entgrenzung und Entfesselung der Gewalt.* Frankfurt, 2002.
Bethke, Hannah. "Theodor Eschenburg in der NS-Zeit." Expert report on behalf of the DVPW, 3 September 2012. In *Die Versprechen der Demokratie: 25. wissenschaftlicher Kongress der Deutschen Vereinigung für politische Wissenschaft*, edited by Hubertus Buchstein, 527–567. Baden-Baden, 2013.
Bettelheim, Bruno. "Eichmann—das System—die Opfer." In Krummacher, *Die Kontroverse*, 91–113.
Betts, Paul. "Germany, International Justice and the Twentieth Century." *History and Memory* 17, nos. 1–2 (2005): 45–86.
Bevernage, Berber. "Writing the Past Out of the Present: History and Politics of Time in Transitional Justice." *History Workshop Journal* 69, no. 1 (2010): 111–131.
Bialas, Wolfgang, and Anson Rabinbach. "Introduction: The Humanities in Nazi Germany." In *Nazi Germany and the Humanities*, edited by Wolfgang Bialas and Anson Rabinbach, viii–lii. Oxford, 2007.

Bilsky, Leora, David Bloxham, Lawrence Douglas, and Annette Weinke. "Forum: The Eichmann Trial Fifty Years On." *German History* 29, no. 2 (2011): 265–282.

Birn, Ruth Bettina. "Staatsanwalt Zeug in Jerusalem: Zum Kenntnisstand der Anklagebehörde im Eichmann-Prozess und der Strafverfolgungsbehörden der Bundesrepublik." *Einsicht* 5 (2011): 26–32.

Blaive, Muriel. "The Memory of the Holocaust and of Communist Repression in a Comparative Perspective: The Cases of Hungary, Poland and Czechoslovakia/the Czech Republic." In Blaive et al., *Clashes in European Memory*, 154–172.

Blaive, Muriel, Christian Gerbel, and Thomas Lindenberger, eds. *Clashes in European Memory: The Case of Communist Repression and the Holocaust*. Innsbruck, 2011.

Blanke, Thomas. "Der 'Rechtshistorikerstreit' um Amnestie: Politische Klugheit, moralische Richtigkeit und Gerechtigkeit bei der Aufarbeitung deutscher Vergangenheiten." In Justiz, *Die juristische Aufarbeitung des Unrechts-Staats*, 727–752.

Bloxham, Donald. "From Streicher to Sawoniuk: The Holocaust in the Courtroom." In Stone, *The Historiography of the Holocaust*, 397–419.

———. *Genocide on Trial: War Crimes Trials and the Formation of Holocaust History and Memory*. Oxford, 2001.

———. *Genocide, the World Wars, and the Unweaving of Europe*. London, 2008.

———. "Milestones and Mythologies: The Impact of Nuremberg." In Heberer and Matthäus, *Atrocities on Trial*, 263–282.

Bloxham, Donald, and Robert Gerwarth. "Introduction." In Bloxham and Gerwarth, *Political Violence in Twentieth-Century Europe*, 1–10.

———, eds. *Political Violence in Twentieth-Century Europe*. Cambridge, 2011.

Bluntschli, Johannes Caspar. *Denkwürdiges aus meinem Leben, Teil III/2 ("Heidelberg 1861–1881")*. Nördlingen, 1884.

Boberach, Heinz. "Die strafrechtliche Verfolgung der Ermordung von Patienten in nassauischen Heil- und Pflegeanstalten nach 1945." In *Euthanasie in Hadamar: Die nationalsozialistische Vernichtungspolitik in hessischen Anstalten*, edited by Christina Vanja and Martin Vogt, 165–174. Kassel, 1991.

Bock, Michael. "Metamorphosen der Vergangenheitsbewältigung." In *Die intellektuelle Gründung der Bundesrepublik: Eine Wirkungsgeschichte der Frankfurter Schule*, edited by Clemens Albrecht, Günter C. Behrmann, Michael Bock, Harald Homann, and Friedrich H. Tenbruck, 530–566. Frankfurt, 1999.

Bock, Petra. "Von der Tribunal-Idee zur Enquete-Kommission: Zur Vorgeschichte der Enquete-Kommission des Bundestages 'Aufarbeitung von Geschichte und Folgen der SED-Diktatur in Deutschland.'" *Deutschland Archiv* 28, no. 1 (1995): 1171–1183.

Bock, Petra, and Edgar Wolfrum. "Einleitung." In *Umkämpfte Vergangenheit: Geschichtsbilder, Erinnerung und Vergangenheitspolitik im internationalen Vergleich*, edited by Petra Bock and Edgar Wolfrum, 7–14. Göttingen, 1999.

Böhme, Klaus, ed. *Aufrufe und Reden deutscher Professoren im Ersten Weltkrieg*. Stuttgart, 1975.

Bolton, Jonathan. *Worlds of Dissent: Charter 77, the Plastic People of the Universe, and Czech Culture under Communism*. Cambridge, MA, 2012.

Borgwardt, Elizabeth. *A New Deal for the World: America's Vision for Human Rights*. Cambridge, MA, 2005.

Borneman, John. *Settling Accounts: Violence, Justice, and Accountability in Postsocialist Europe*. Princeton, NJ, 1997.

Bösch, Frank, and Constantin Goschler. "Der Nationalsozialismus und die deutsche Public History." In *Public History: Öffentliche Darstellungen des Nationalsozialismus jenseits der*

Geschichtswissenschaft, edited by Frank Bösch and Constantin Goschler, 7–23. Frankfurt, 2009.

Botsch, Gideon. *"Politische Wissenschaft" im Zweiten Weltkrieg: Die "Deutschen Auslandswissenschaften" im Einsatz 1940–1945*. Paderborn, 2006.

Brochhagen, Ulrich. *Nach Nürnberg: Vergangenheitsbewältigung und Westintegration in der Ära Adenauer*. Hamburg, 1994.

Brocke, Bernhard vom. "Wissenschaft und Militarismus: Der Aufruf der 93 'An die Kulturwelt!' und der Zusammenbruch der internationalen Gelehrtenpolitik im Ersten Weltkrieg." In *Wilamowitz nach 50 Jahren*, edited by William L. Calder III, Helmut Flashar, and Theodor Lindken, 649–719. Darmstadt, 1985.

Broszat, Martin. "Hitler und die Genesis der 'Endlösung': Aus Anlass der Thesen von David Irving." *Vierteljahrshefte für Zeitgeschichte* 25, no. 4 (1977): 739–775.

———. "Siegerjustiz oder strafrechtliche 'Selbstreinigung': Aspekte der Vergangenheitsbewältigung der deutschen Justiz während der Besatzungszeit 1945–1949." *Vierteljahrshefte für Zeitgeschichte* 29, no. 4 (1981): 477–544.

Browning, Christopher R. *Die Entfesselung der "Endlösung": Nationalsozialistische Judenpolitik 1939–1942*. Munich, 2003.

———. "German Memory, Judicial Interrogation, and Historical Reconstruction: Writing Perpetrator History from Postwar Memory." In *Probing the Limits of Representation: Nazism and the "Final Solution,"* edited by Saul Friedländer, 22–36. Cambridge, MA, 1992.

———. "Zur Genesis der 'Endlösung': Eine Antwort an Martin Broszat." *Vierteljahrshefte für Zeitgeschichte* 29, no. 1 (1981): 97–109.

Brundage, W. Fitzhugh, and Konrad H. Jarausch. "Massen: Mobilisierung und Partizipation." In *Wettlauf um die Moderne: Die USA und Deutschland 1890 bis heute*, edited by Christof Mauch and Kiran Klaus Patel, 295–329. Bonn, 2008.

Brunkhorst, Hauke. "Kritik am Dualismus des internationalen Rechts: Hans Kelsen und die Völkerrechtsrevolution des 20. Jahrhunderts." In *Transnationale Verrechtlichung: Nationale Demokratien im Kontext globaler Politik*, edited by Regina Kreide and Andreas Niederberger, 30–62. Frankfurt, 2008.

Brünneck, Alexander von. *Politische Justiz gegen Kommunisten in der Bundesrepublik Deutschland 1949–1968*. Frankfurt, 1978.

Brunner, Bernhard. *Der Frankreich-Komplex: Die nationalsozialistischen Verbrechen in Frankreich und die Justiz der Bundesrepublik Deutschland*. Göttingen, 2004.

Buchheim, Hans. "Das Euthanasieprogramm." In *Gutachten des Instituts für Zeitgeschichte*, Munich, 1958: 60–77.

Buchheim, Hans, Martin Broszat, Hans-Adolf Jacobsen, and Helmut Krausnick. *Anatomie des SS-Staates*. Vol. 1. Olten, 1965.

Buchner, Silke. *Die Rechtswidrigkeit der Taten von "Mauerschützen" im Lichte von Art. 103 II GG unter besonderer Berücksichtigung des Völkerrechts*. Frankfurt, 1996.

Buchstab, Günther. "Die Nürnberger Prozesse und der 'Heidelberger Kreis' (1949–1955)." In *Macht und Zeitkritik: Festschrift für Hans-Peter Schwarz zum 65. Geburtstag*, edited by Peter Weilmann et al., 61–74. Paderborn, 1999.

Buckley-Zistel, Susanne. "Einleitung: Nach Krieg, Gewalt und Repression." In Buckley-Zistel and Kater, *Nach Krieg, Gewalt und Repression*, 7–20.

Buckley-Zistel, Susanne, and Anika Oettler. "Was bedeut: Transitional Justice?" In Buckley-Zistel and Kater, *Nach Krieg, Gewalt und Repression*, 21–37.

Buckley-Zistel, Susanne, and Thomas Kater, eds. *Nach Krieg, Gewalt und Repression: Vom schwierigen Umgang mit der Vergangenheit*. Baden-Baden, 2011.

Budde, Gunilla, Sebastian Conrad, and Oliver Janz, eds. *Transnationale Geschichte: Themen, Tendenzen und Theorien*. Göttingen, 2006.
Burchard, Christoph. "The Nuremberg Trial and Its Impact on Germany." *Journal of International Criminal Justice* 4, no. 4 (2006): 800–829.
Buscher, Frank M. "Bestrafen und Erziehen: 'Nürnberg' und das Kriegsverbrecherprogramm der USA." In Frei, *Transnationale Vergangenheitspolitik*, 94–139.
Canovan, Margaret. *The Political Thought of Hannah Arendt*. New York, 1974.
Carstens, Karl. "Hermann Jahrreiß." In *Festschrift für Hermann Jahrreiß zu seinem siebzigsten Geburtstag*, edited by Karl Carstens and Hans Peters, 1. Cologne, 1964.
Cohen, David. "Transitional Justice in Divided Germany after 1945." In *Retribution and Reparation in the Transition to Democracy*, edited by Jon Elster, 59–88. Cambridge, 2006.
Committee on Alleged German Outrages. *Report of the Committee on Alleged German Outrages Appointed by His Britannic Majesty's Government and Presided Over by the Right Hon. Viscount Bryce*. London, 1914.
Conrad, Sebastian. *Auf der Suche nach der verlorenen Nation: Geschichtsschreibung in Westdeutschland und Japan, 1945–1960*. Göttingen, 1999.
Conrad, Sebastian, and Andreas Eckert. "Globalgeschichte, Globalisierung, Multiple Modernen." In *Globalgeschichte: Theorien, Ansätze, Themen*, edited by Sebastian Conrad, Andreas Eckert, and Ulrike Freitag, 7–49. Frankfurt, 2007.
Conze, Eckart. "Abschied von Staat und Politik? Überlegungen zur Geschichte der internationalen Politik." In *Geschichte der internationalen Beziehungen: Erneuerung und Erweiterung einer historischen Disziplin*, edited by Eckart Conze, Ulrich Lappenküper, and Guido Müller, 15–43. Cologne, 2004.
———. *Die Suche nach Sicherheit: Eine Geschichte der Bundesrepublik Deutschland von 1949 bis in die Gegenwart*. Munich, 2009.
———. "Völkerstrafrecht und Völkerstrafrechtspolitik." In Dülffer and Loth, *Dimensionen internationaler Geschichte*, 189–209.
———. "Zwischen Staatenwelt und Gesellschaftswelt: Die gesellschaftliche Dimension der Internationalen Geschichte." In *Internationale Geschichte: Themen—Ergebnisse—Aussichten*, edited by Wilfried Loth and Jürgen Osterhammel, 117–140. Munich, 2009.
Conze, Eckart, Norbert Frei, Peter Hayes, and Moshe Zimmermann. *Das Amt und die Vergangenheit: Deutsche Diplomaten im Dritten Reich und in der Bundesrepublik*. Munich, 2010.
Cooper, John. *Raphael Lemkin and the Struggle for the Genocide Convention*. London, 2008.
Cornelißen, Christoph. "Erforschung und Erinnerung: Historiker und die zweite Geschichte." In *Der Nationalsozialismus—Die zweite Geschichte: Überwindung—Deutung—Erinnerung*, edited by Peter Reichel, Harald Schmid, and Peter Steinbach, 217–242. Bonn, 2009.
———. "Erinnerungskulturen, Version: 1.0." *Docupedia-Zeitgeschichte*, 11 February 2010. https://docupedia.de/zg/Erinnerungskulturen?oldid=75513.
———. "'Schuld am Weltfrieden': Politische Kommentare und Deutungsversuche deutscher Historiker zum Versailler Vertrag." In Krumeich, *Versailles 1919*, 237–258.
———. "'Vergangenheitsbewältigung': Ein deutscher Sonderweg?" In Hammerstein et al., *Aufarbeitung der Diktatur*, 21–36.
Crozier, Michael, Samuel P. Huntington, and Joji Watanuki. *The Crisis of Democracy: Report on the Governability of Democracies to the Trilateral Commission*. New York, 1975.
Dahn, Daniela. *Wehe dem Sieger! Ohne Osten kein Westen*. Reinbek, 2009.
Dam, Henrik G. van, and Ralph Giordano, eds. *KZ-Verbrechen vor deutschen Gerichten, Bd. II: Einsatzkommando Tilsit—Der Prozess zu Ulm*. Frankfurt, 1966.

Danyel, Jürgen, Jan-Holger Kirsch, and Martin Sabrow, eds. *50 Klassiker der Zeitgeschichte*. Göttingen, 2007.
Darcy, Shane, and William A. Schabas, eds. *Truth Commissions and Courts: The Tension Between Criminal Justice and the Search for Truth*. Dordrecht, 2004.
Delbrück, Hans. "Die deutsche Kriegserklärung 1914 und der Einmarsch in Belgien." *Preussische Jahrbücher* 175 (1919): 271–280.
Derlien, Hans-Ulrich. "Elitenzirkulation in Ostdeutschland 1989–1995." *Aus Politik und Zeitgeschichte* 48, no. B5 (1998): 3–17.
DB (Deutscher Bundestag). *Stenographische Berichte*. Bonn, 1949.
Dicke, Klaus, and Manuel Fröhlich. "Menschenrechte." In Woyke, *Handwörterbuch Internationale Politik*, 326–334.
Dickmann, Fritz. "Die Kriegsschuldfrage auf der Friedenskonferenz von 1919." *Historische Zeitschrift* 197 (1963): 1–101.
Dieckmann, Christoph. "Der Krieg und die Ermordung der litauischen Juden." In Herbert, *Nationalsozialistische Vernichtungspolitik*, 292–329.
Dietz, Bernhard, and Christopher Neumann. "Vom Nutzen der Sozialwissenschaften für die Zeitgeschichte: Werte und Wertewandel als Gegenstand historischer Forschung." *Vierteljahrshefte für Zeitgeschichte* 60, no. 2 (2012): 293–304.
Dillmann, Franz. "Beschweigen ist unverfänglicher als Aufdeckung: Die juristische Fakultät im Nationalsozialismus." In *Nachhilfe zur Erinnerung: 600 Jahre Universität zu Köln*, edited by Wolfgang Blaschke, 98–110. Cologne, 1988.
Diner, Dan. "Hannah Arendt Reconsidered: Über das Banale und das Böse in ihrer Holocaust-Erzählung." In Smith, *Hannah Arendt Revisited*, 120–135.
———. "Kaleidoskopisches Denken: Überschreibungen und autobiographische Codierungen in Hannah Arendts Hauptwerk." In Danyel et al., *50 Klassiker der Zeitgeschichte*, 37–41.
———. "Rassistisches Völkerrecht: Elemente einer nationalsozialistischen Weltordnung." *Vierteljahrshefte für Zeitgeschichte* 37, no. 1 (1989): 23–56.
Dipper, Christof. "Die Epoche der Moderne: Konzeption und Kerngehalt." In *Vergangenheit und Zukunft der Moderne*, edited by Ulrich Beck and Martin Muslow, 103–180. Frankfurt, 2014.
———. "Moderne, Version: 1.0." *Docupedia-Zeitgeschichte*, 25 August 2010. http://docupedia.de/zg/Moderne?oldid=106453.
Dirr, Pius, ed. *Bayerische Dokumente zum Kriegsausbruch und Versailler Schuldspruch*. 3rd ed. Munich, 1925.
DK (Deutsche Kriegsschuldforscher). *Berliner Monatshefte* 7 (1929): 552–590.
Doering-Manteuffel, Anselm, and Lutz Raphael. *Nach dem Boom: Perspektiven auf die Zeitgeschichte seit 1970*. Göttingen, 2008.
Donert, Celia. "Charta 77 und die Roma: Menschenrechte und Dissidenten in der sozialistischen Tschechoslowakei." In Hoffmann, *Moralpolitik*, 397–423.
Dönhoff, Marion Gräfin von. "Die Nürnberger Prozesse: Ein abschreckendes Beispiel." In *Ein Manifest II: Weil das Land Versöhnung braucht*, edited by Marion Gräfin von Dönhoff, 79–89. Reinbek, 1993.
Douglas, Lawrence. *The Memory of Judgment: Making Law and History in the Trials of the Holocaust*. New Haven, CT, 2001.
———. "Was damals Recht war ... Nulla Poena and the Prosecution of Crimes Against Humanity in Occupied Germany." In Priemel and Stiller, *NMT*, 719–754.
Dreier, Horst. "Verfassungsstaatliche Vergangenheitsbewältigung." In *Festschrift 50 Jahre Bundesverfassungsgericht, Bd. 1: Verfassungsgerichtsbarkeit—Verfassungsprozess*, edited by Peter Badura and Horst Dreier, 159–208. Tübingen, 2001.

Dressen, Willi. "NS-'Euthanasie'-Prozesse in der Bundesrepublik Deutschland im Wandel der Zeit." In *NS-"Euthanasie" vor Gericht: Fritz Bauer und die Grenzen juristischer Bewältigung*, edited by Hanno Loewy and Bettina Winter, 35–58. Frankfurt, 1996.
Dreyer, Michael, and Oliver Lembcke. *Die deutsche Diskussion um die Kriegsschuldfrage 1918/19*. Berlin, 1993.
Dülffer, Jost. "Regeln im Krieg? Kriegsverbrechen und die Haager Friedenskonferenzen." In *Frieden stiften: Deeskalations- und Friedenspolitik im 20. Jahrhundert*, edited by Jost Dülffer and Marc Frey, 77–88. Cologne, 2008.
Dülffer, Jost, and Wilfried Loth, eds. *Dimensionen internationaler Geschichte*. Munich, 2012.
Earl, Hilary. *The Nuremberg Einsatzgruppen Trial, 1945–1958: Atrocity, Law, and History*. Cambridge, 2009.
Eckel, Jan. *Die Ambivalenz des Guten: Menschenrechte in der internationalen Politik seit den 1940ern*. Göttingen, 2014.
———. *Hans Rothfels: Eine intellektuelle Biographie im 20. Jahrhundert*. Göttingen, 2005.
———. "Utopie der Moral, Kalkül der Macht: Menschenrechte in der globalen Politik seit 1945." *Archiv für Sozialgeschichte* 49 (2009): 437–484.
Eckel, Jan, and Claudia Moisel. "Nachgeschichte und Gegenwart des Nationalsozialismus in internationaler Perspektive." In *Das "Dritte Reich": Eine Einführung*, edited by Dietmar Süss and Winfried Süss, 333–353. Munich, 2008.
Eckel, Jan, and Samuel Moyn, eds. *Moral für die Welt? Menschenrechtspolitik in den 1970er Jahren*. Göttingen, 2012.
Eckert, Astrid. *Kampf um die Akten: Die Westalliierten und die Rückgabe von deutschem Archivgut nach dem Zweiten Weltkrieg*. Stuttgart, 2004.
Eichmüller, Andreas. *Keine Generalamnestie: Die Strafverfolgung von NS-Verbrechen in der frühen Bundesrepublik*. Munich, 2012.
Eisenbach, Artur. *Hitlerowska polityka zaglady Żydów*. Warsaw, 1961.
Eisfeld, Rainer. "Theodor Eschenburg: By the way, he forgot to mention. . ." *Zeitschrift für Geschichtswissenschaft* 59, no. 1 (2011): 27–44.
Elder, Tanya. "What You See Before Your Eyes: Documenting Raphael Lemkin's Life by Exploring His Archival Papers, 1900–1959." *Journal of Genocide Research* 7, no. 4 (2005): 469–499.
Eley, Geoff. *Forging Democracy: The History of the Left in Europe, 1850–2000*. Oxford, 2002.
Elster, Jon. *Die Akten schliessen: Recht und Gerechtigkeit nach dem Ende von Diktaturen*. Bonn, 2005.
Engel, David. *Historians of the Jews and the Holocaust*. Stanford, 2010.
Eppelmann, Rainer. "Die Enquete-Kommissionen." In *Bilanz und Perspektiven der DDR-Forschung*, edited by Rainer Eppelmann, Bernd Faulenbach, and Ulrich Mählert, 401–406. Paderborn, 2003
Erler, Hans, Arnold Paucker, and Ernst Ludwig Ehrlich, eds. *"Gegen alle Vergeblichkeit": Jüdischer Widerstand gegen den Nationalsozialismus*. Frankfurt, 2003.
Eser, Albin, Jörg Arnold, and Julie Trappe, eds. *Strafrechtsentwicklung in Osteuropa: Zwischen bewältigten und neuen Herausforderungen*. Berlin, 2005.
Evans, Richard J. "History, Memory and the Law: The Historian and Expert Witness." *History and Theory* 41, no. 3 (2002): 326–345.
———. *Rituale der Vergeltung: Die Todesstrafe in der deutschen Geschichte 1532–1987*. Berlin, 2001.
Feher, Michel. "Terms of Reconciliation." In Hesse and Post, *Human Rights in Political Transitions*, 325–338.

Fehr, Hartmut. "Öffentlicher Sprachwandel und Eliten-Konkurrenz: Zur Rolle politischer Semantik in den Dekommunisierungskampagnen post-kommunistischer Gesellschaften (Tschechische Republik, Polen und Ostdeutschland)." In Srubar, *Eliten, politische Kultur und Privatisierung*, 65–96.
Feidel, Frank. "Francis Lieber and the Codification of the International Law of War." In *Préludes et Pionniers: Les Précurseurs de la Croix-Rouge 1840–1860*, edited by Roger Durand and Jacques Meurant, 31–45. Geneva, 1991.
Fisch, Jörg. *Das Selbstbestimmungsrecht der Völker: Die Domestizierung einer Illusion*. Munich, 2010.
———. "Völkerrecht." In Dülffer and Loth, *Dimensionen internationaler Geschichte*, 151–168.
Fischer, Torben, and Matthias N. Lorenz, eds. *Lexikon der "Vergangenheitsbewältigung" in Deutschland*. Bielefeld, 2007.
Fischer-Lescano, Andreas, and Philipp Liste. "Völkerrechtspolitik: Zur Trennung und Verknüpfung von Politik und Recht der Weltgesellschaft." *Zeitschrift für internationale Beziehungen* 12, no. 2 (2005): 209–249.
Fischl, Viktor. "The Jews and the Conscience of the World." *Spirit of Czechoslovakia* 4 (1943): 11.
Flasch, Kurt. *Die geistige Mobilmachung: Die deutschen Intellektuellen und der Erste Weltkrieg—ein Versuch*. Berlin, 2000.
Fleck, Dieter, ed. *Handbuch des humanitären Völkerrechts in bewaffneten Konflikten*. Munich, 1994.
Forsthoff, Ernst. "Der Zeithistoriker als gerichtlicher Sachverständiger." *Neue Juristische Wochenschrift* 13 (1965): 574–575.
Foucault, Michel. "Nietzsche, die Genealogie, die Historie." In *Michel Foucault: Schriften in vier Bänden—Dits et Ecrits II*, edited by Daniel Defert, François Ewald, and Jacques Lagrange, 166–191. Frankfurt, 2002.
———. "Theorien und Institutionen des Strafvollzugs." In Defert et al., *Michel Foucault*, 486–490.
Fox, John. "The Final Solution: Intended or Contingent? The Stuttgart Conference of May 1984 and the Historical Debate." *Patterns of Prejudice* 18, no. 3 (1984): 27–39.
Fraenkel, Ernst. "Der Doppelstaat (1974)." In *Gesammelte Schriften, Bd. 2: Nationalsozialismus und Widerstand*, edited by Alexander von Brünneck, Hubertus Buchstein, and Gerhard Göhler. Baden-Baden, 1999.
———. *The Dual State*. New York, 1941.
Franzki, Hannah. "Mit Recht Erinnern: Völkerrechtliche Ahndung von Kriegsverbrechen zwischen Aufarbeitungsimperativ und selektiver Geschichtsschreibung." *Geschichte in Wissenschaft und Unterricht* 63, nos. 7–8 (2012): 448–464.
Freeman, Mark. *Truth Commissions and Procedural Fairness*. Cambridge, 2006.
Frei, Norbert, ed. *1945 und wir: Das Dritte Reich im Bewusstsein der Deutschen*. Munich, 2009.
———. "1989 und wir? Eine Vergangenheit zwischen 'Erinnerungskultur' und Geschichtsbewusstsein." In Frei, *1945 und wir*, 7–21.
———. "Abschied von der Zeitgenossenschaft: Der Nationalsozialismus und seine Erforschung auf dem Weg in die Geschichte." In Frei, *1945 und wir*, 41–62.
———. "Amnestiepolitik in den Anfangsjahren der Bundesrepublik." In *Amnestie oder die Politik der Erinnerung in der Demokratie*, edited by Gary Smith and Avishai Margalit, 120–137. Frankfurt, 1997.
———. "Amnestiepolitik in den Bonner Anfangsjahren: Die Westdeutschen und die NS-Vergangenheit." *Kritische Justiz* 29, no. 4 (1996): 484–494.

———. "Nach der Tat: Die Ahndung deutscher Kriegs- und NS-Verbrechen in Europa—eine Bilanz." In Frei, *Transnationale Vergangenheitspolitik*, 7–36.

———, ed. *Transnationale Vergangenheitspolitik: Der Umgang mit deutschen Kriegsverbrechern in Europa nach dem Zweiten Weltkrieg*. Göttingen, 2006.

———. *Vergangenheitspolitik: Die Anfänge der Bundesrepublik und die NS Vergangenheit*. Munich, 1996.

———. "Von deutscher Erfindungskraft oder: Die Kollektivschuldthese in der Nachkriegszeit." *Rechtshistorisches Journal*, no. 16 (1997): 621–634.

Frei, Norbert, and Annette Weinke, eds. *Toward a New Moral World Order? Menschenrechtspolitik und Völkerrecht seit 1945*. Göttingen, 2013.

Frei, Norbert, Dirk van Laak, and Michael Stolleis, eds. *Geschichte vor Gericht: Historiker, Richter und die Suche nach Gerechtigkeit*. Munich, 2000.

Frei, Norbert, Ralf Ahrens, Jörg Osterloh, and Tim Schanetzky. *Flick: Der Konzern, die Familie, die Macht*. Munich, 2009.

Freytagh-Loringhoven, Axel Freiherr von. *Völkerrechtliche Neubildungen im Kriege*. Hamburg, 1941.

Friedemann, Peter, and Lucian Hölscher. "Internationale, International, Internationalismus." In *Geschichtliche Grundbegriffe: Historisches Lexikon zur politisch-sozialen Sprache in Deutschland*, vol. 3, 1st reprinted ed., edited by Otto Brunner, Werner Conze, and Reinhart Koselleck, 367–397. Stuttgart, 1995.

Friedländer, Saul. "From Anti-Semitism to Extermination: A Historiographical Study of Nazi Policies toward the Jews and an Essay in Interpretation." *Yad Vashem Studies* 16, no. 1 (1984): 1–50.

Fukuyama, Francis. *The End of History and the Last Man*. London, 1992.

Gassert, Philipp. "Das Russell-Tribunal von 1966/67: 'Blaming and Shaming' und die Nürnberger Prinzipien." In Frei and Weinke, *Toward a New Moral World Order?* 92–103.

Geiss, Immanuel, ed. *Julikrise und Kriegsausbruch 1914*. Vol. 1. Hannover, 1963.

———. "Die manipulierte Kriegsschuldfrage: Deutsche Reichspolitik in der Julikrise 1914 und deutsche Kriegsziele im Spiegel des Schuldreferats des Auswärtigen Amtes, 1919–1931." *Militärgeschichtliche Mitteilungen* 34 (1983): 31–60.

Genschel, Helmut. *Die Verdrängung der Juden aus der Wirtschaft im Dritten Reich*. Göttingen, 1966.

Gerwarth, Robert, and Stephan Malinowski. "Der Holocaust als 'kolonialer Genozid'?" *Geschichte und Gesellschaft* 33, no. 3 (2007): 439–466.

Geulen, Christian. "Gouverneure, Gouvernementalität und Globalisierung: Zur Geschichte und Aktualität imperialer Gewalt." In Krasmann and Martschukat, *Rationalitäten der Gewalt*, 117–135.

Gimbel, John. "The Origins of the Institut für Zeitgeschichte: Scholarship, Politics, and the American Occupation, 1945–1949." *American Historical Review* 70, no. 3 (1965): 714–731.

Ginzburg, Carlo. *The Judge and the Historian: Marginal Notes on a Late-Twentieth-Century Miscarriage of Justice*. London, 1999.

Glueck, Sheldon. "Trial and Punishment of the Axis War Criminals." *Free World* 4 (1942): 138–146.

———. *War Criminals: Their Prosecution and Punishment*. New York, 1944.

Görtemaker, Manfred. *Die Berliner Republik: Wiedervereinigung und Neuorientierung*. Bonn, 2009.

Golczewski, Frank. *Kölner Universitätslehrer und der Nationalsozialismus: Personengeschichtliche Ansätze*. Cologne, 1988.

Golsan, Richard J. *Vichy's Afterlife: History and Counterhistory in Postwar France.* Lincoln, NE, 2000.
Gong, Gerrit W. *The "Standard of Civilization" in International Society.* Oxford, 1984.
Goschler, Constantin. *Schuld und Schulden: Die Politik der Wiedergutmachung für NS-Verfolgte seit 1945.* Göttingen, 2005.
Gosewinkel, Dieter. *Adolf Arndt: Die Wiederbegründung des Rechtsstaats aus dem Geist der Sozialdemokratie (1945–1961).* Bonn, 1991.
Gosewinkel, Dieter, Dieter Rucht, Wolfgang van den Daele, and Jürgen Kocka, eds. *Zivilgesellschaft: National und transnational.* Berlin, 2004.
Graf, Rüdiger, and Kim Christian Priemel. "Zeitgeschichte in der Welt der Sozialwissenschaften: Legitimität und Originalität einer Disziplin." *Vierteljahrshefte für Zeitgeschichte* 59, no. 4 (2011): 479–508.
Graml, Hermann. "Zur Frage der Demokratiebereitschaft des deutschen Bürgertums nach dem Ende der NS-Herrschaft: Hermann Maus Bericht über eine Reise nach Munich im März 1946." In *Miscellanea: Festschrift für Helmut Krausnick*, edited by Wolfgang Benz in collaboration with Ino Arndt, Hellmuth Auerbach, Martin Broszat, Hermann Graml, and Lothar Gruchmann. Stuttgart, 1980.
Gradvohl, Paul. "La maison de la terreur-musée ou Terror Háza Múzeum." In *Lieux de mémoire en Europe centrale*, edited by Antoine Marès, 109–122. Paris, 2009.
Gross, Raphael, ed. *Anständig geblieben: Nationalsozialistische Moral.* Frankfurt, 2010.
———. "Der Führer als Betrüger: Moral und Antipositivismus in Deutschland 1945/46 am Beispiel Fritz von Hippels." In Gross, *Anständig geblieben*, 124–142. Frankfurt, 2010.
———. "Mächtiger als die Gerichte? Geschichte und historische Gerechtigkeit." In Frei et al., *Geschichte vor Gericht*, 164–172.
———. "Moralität des Bösen: Adolf Eichmann und die deutsche Gesellschaft." In Gross, *Anständig geblieben*, 171–200.
Große Kracht, Klaus. "Kriegsschuldfrage und zeithistorische Forschung in Deutschland: Historiographische Nachwirkungen des Ersten Weltkriegs." *Zeitgeschichte Online*, May 2004. http://www.zeitgeschichte-online.de/thema/kriegsschuldfrage-und-zeithistorische-forschung-deutschland.
Guest, Iain. *Behind the Disappearances: Argentina's Dirty War Against Human Rights and the United Nations.* Philadelphia, 1990.
Guilhot, Nicolas. *The Democracy Makers: Human Rights and the Politics of Global Order.* New York, 2005.
———. "'The Transition to the Human World of Democracy': Notes for a History of a Concept of Transition, from Early Marxism to 1989." *European Journal of Social Theory* 5, no. 2 (2002): 219–243.
Gusy, Christoph. "Die Rezeption der EMRK in Deutschland." In *Menschenrechte in der Bewährung: Die Rezeption der Europäischen Menschenrechtskonvention in Frankreich und Deutschland im Vergleich*, edited by Constance Grewe and Christoph Gusy, 129–159. Baden-Baden, 2005.
Haase, Christian, and Axel Schildt, eds. *DIE ZEIT und die Bonner Republik: Eine meinungsbildende Wochenzeitung zwischen Wiederbewaffnung und Wiedervereinigung.* Göttingen, 2008.
Habermas, Jürgen. "Hat die Konstitutionalisierung des Völkerrechts noch eine Chance?" In *Der gespaltene Westen*, edited by Jürgen Habermas, 113–194. Frankfurt, 2004.
Hachtmann, Rüdiger. *Wissenschaftsmanagement im "Dritten Reich": Geschichte der Generalverwaltung der Kaiser-Wilhelm-Gesellschaft.* 2 vols. Göttingen, 2007.

Hahn, Erich J. C. "The German Foreign Ministry and the Question of War Guilt in 1918–1919." In *German Nationalism and the European Response, 1890–1945*, edited by Carole Fink, Isabel Hull, and MacGregor Knox, 43–70. Norman, OK, 1985.

Halliday, Fred. "Three Concepts of Internationalism." *International Affairs* 64 (1988): 187–198.

Hamel, Walter. *Reich und Staat im Mittelalter*. Hamburg, 1944.

Hammerstein, Katrin, Ulrich Mählert, and Edgar Wolfrum, eds. *Aufarbeitung der Diktatur— Diktat der Aufarbeitung? Normierungsprozesse beim Umgang mit diktatorischer Vergangenheit*. Göttingen, 2009.

Hankel, Gerd. "Auf verlorenem Posten: Friedenspolitik und Völkerrecht in der Weimarer Republik." In Kramer and Wette, *Recht ist, was den Waffen nützt*, 176–189.

———. *Die Leipziger Prozesse: Deutsche Kriegsverbrechen und ihre strafrechtliche Verfolgung nach dem Ersten Weltkrieg*. Hamburg, 2003.

Hankel, Gerd, and Gerhard Stuby, eds. *Strafgerichte gegen Menschheitsverbrechen: Zum Völkerstrafrecht 50 Jahre nach den Nürnberger Prozessen*. Hamburg, 1995.

Haupt, Heinz-Gerhard. "Historische Komparatistik in der internationalen Geschichtsschreibung." In Budde et al., *Transnationale Geschichte*, 137–149.

Haupts, Leo. *Die Universität zu Köln im Übergang vom Nationalsozialismus zur Bundesrepublik*. Cologne, 2007.

Hausmann, Frank-Rutger. *"Deutsche Geisteswissenschaft" im Zweiten Weltkrieg: Die "Aktion Ritterbusch" (1940–1945)*. Dresden, 1998.

Havel, Václav. *Living in Truth*. London, 1986.

Hayner, Priscilla. "Fifteen Truth Commissions—1974 to 1994: A Comparative Study." In Kritz, *Transitional Justice*, 225–261.

———. *Unspeakable Truths: Facing the Challenge of Truth Commissions*. New York, 2002.

———. *Unspeakable Truths: Transitional Justice and the Challenge of Truth Commissions*. New York, 2011.

Heberer, Patricia. "Early Postwar Justice in the American Zone: The 'Hadamar Murder Factory' Trial." In Heberer and Matthäus, *Atrocities on Trial*, 25–47.

Heberer, Patricia, and Jürgen Matthäus, eds. *Atrocities on Trial: Historical Perspectives on the Politics of Prosecuting War Crimes*. Lincoln, NE, 2008.

Heil, Johannes, and Rainer Erb, eds. *Geschichtswissenschaft und Öffentlichkeit: Der Streit um Daniel J. Goldhagen*. Frankfurt, 1998.

Heinemann, Ulrich. *Die verdrängte Niederlage: Politische Öffentlichkeit und Kriegsschuldfrage in der Weimarer Republik*. Göttingen, 1983.

Henke, Klaus-Dietmar, and Claudio Natoli, eds. *Mit dem Pathos der Nüchternheit: Martin Broszat, das Institut für Zeitgeschichte und die Erforschung des Nationalsozialismus*. Frankfurt, 1991.

Henne, Thomas. "Die neue Wertordnung im Zivilrecht: Speziell im Familien- und Arbeitsrecht." In *Das Bonner Grundgesetz: Altes Recht und neue Verfassung in den ersten Jahrzehnten der Bundesrepublik Deutschland (1949–1969)*, edited by Michael Stolleis, 13–37. Berlin, 2006.

Herbert, Ulrich. *Best: Biographische Studien über Radikalismus, Weltanschauung und Vernunft, 1903–1989*. Bonn, 1996.

———. "Europe in High Modernity: Reflections on a Theory of the 20th Century." *Journal of Modern European History* 5 (2007): 5–20.

———, ed. *Nationalsozialistische Vernichtungspolitik 1939–1945: Neue Forschungen und Kontroversen*. Frankfurt, 1998.

———. "Vernichtungspolitik: Neue Antworten und Fragen zur Geschichte des 'Holocaust.'" In Herbert, *Nationalsozialistische Vernichtungspolitik*, 9–66.

Herren, Madeleine. *Internationale Organisationen seit 1865: Eine Globalgeschichte der internationalen Ordnung*. Darmstadt, 2009.
Herwig, Holger. "Clio Deceived: Patriotic Self-Censorship in Germany after the Great War." In Wilson, *Forging the Collective Memory*, 87–127.
Herz, John H. *From Dictatorship to Democracy: Coping with the Legacies of Authoritarianism and Totalitarianism*. Westport, CT, 1982.
———. *Vom Überleben: Wie ein Weltbild entstand—Autobiographie*. Düsseldorf, 1984.
Hesse, Carla, and Robert Post, eds. *Human Rights in Political Transitions: Gettysburg to Bosnia*. New York, 1999.
Hettling, Manfred. "Umschreiben notwendig? Die Historiker und das Jahr 1989." In Bauerkämper et al., *Doppelte Zeitgeschichte*, 391–403.
———, ed. *Volksgeschichten im Europa der Zwischenkriegszeit*. Göttingen, 2003.
Heuer, Jens-Uwe. *Im Streit: Ein Jurist zwischen zwei deutschen Staaten*. Baden-Baden, 2002.
Hilberg, Raul. "Die bleibende Bedeutung des 'Behemoth.'" In Iser and Strecker, *Kritische Theorie der Politik*, 75–82.
———. *The Destruction of the European Jews*. New York, 1961.
———. *Unerbetene Erinnerung: Der Weg eines Holocaust-Forschers*. Frankfurt, 1994.
Hirsch, Francine. "The Soviets at Nuremberg: International Law, Propaganda, and the Making of Postwar Order." *American Historical Review* 113, no. 3 (2008): 701–730.
Hirschfeld, Gerhard, Gerd Krumeich, and Irina Renz, eds. *Enzyklopädie Erster Weltkrieg*. Paderborn, 2003.
Hobbes, Thomas. *Leviathan*. Edited by Richard Tuck. Cambridge, 2005.
Hobsbawm, Eric. *The Age of Empire, 1875–1975*. London, 1987.
———. *The Age of Extremes: The Short Twentieth Century, 1914–1991*. London, 1994.
Hockerts, Hans Günter. "Zugänge zur Zeitgeschichte: Primärerfahrung, Erinnerungskultur, Geschichtswissenschaft." *Aus Politik und Zeitgeschichte*, no. B28 (2001): 15–30.
Hoffmann, Stefan-Ludwig. "Einführung: Zur Genealogie der Menschenrechte." In Hoffmann, *Moralpolitik*, 7–37.
———, ed. *Moralpolitik: Geschichte der Menschenrechte im 20. Jahrhundert*. Göttingen, 2010.
Holthusen, Hans Egon. "Hannah Arendt, Eichmann und die Kritiker." *Vierteljahrshefte für Zeitgeschichte* 13, no. 2 (1965): 178–190.
———. *Der unbehauste Mensch*. Frankfurt, 1951.
Horn, Sabine. *Erinnerungsbilder: Auschwitz-Prozess und Majdanek-Prozess im westdeutschen Fernsehen*. Essen, 2009.
Horne, John, ed. *State, Society, and Mobilization in Europe during the First World War*. Cambridge, 1997.
Horne, John, and Alan Kramer. *Deutsche Kriegsgreuel 1914: Die umstrittene Wahrheit*. Hamburg, 2004.
Horstmann, Thomas, and Heike Litzinger. "Der Kreis von Königstein und die NS-Verbrechen: Eine Einführung." In *An den Grenzen des Rechts: Gespräche mit Juristen über die Verfolgung von NS-Verbrechen*, edited by Thomas Horstmann and Heike Litzinger, 9–31. Frankfurt, 2006.
Hueck, Ingo J. "Die deutsche Völkerrechtswissenschaft im Nationalsozialismus: Das Berliner Kaiser-Wilhelm-Institut für ausländisches öffentliches Recht und Völkerrecht, das Hamburger Institut für Auswärtige Politik und das Kieler Institut für Internationales Recht." In *Geschichte der Kaiser-Wilhelm-Gesellschaft im Nationalsozialismus: Bestandsaufnahme und Perspektiven der Forschung*, vol. 2, edited by Doris Kaufmann, 490–527. Göttingen, 2000.

———. "The Discipline of the History of International Law: New Trends and Methods on the History of International Law." *Journal of the History of International Law / Revue d'Histoire du Droit International* 3 (2001): 194–217.
Hull, Isabel V. *A Scrap of Paper: Breaking and Making International Law during the Great War*. Ithaca, NY, 2014.
Hummer, Waldemar, and Jelka Mayr-Singer. "Der 'deutsche Sonderweg' bei der Aufarbeitung von SED-Unrecht: Vergangenheitsbewältigung durch Strafjustiz." *Neue Justiz* 54, no. 11 (2000): 561–616.
———. "Internationale Strafgerichtsbarkeit." In Woyke, *Handwörterbuch Internationale Politik*, 216–228.
Huntington, Samuel P. *Kampf der Kulturen: Die Neugestaltung der Weltpolitik im 21. Jahrhundert*. Munich, 1996.
———. *The Third Wave: Democratization in the Late Twentieth Century*. Norman, OK, 1991.
———. "The Third Wave: Democratization in the Late Twentieth Century." In Kritz, *Transitional Justice*, 65–81.
Hürter, Johannes. *Hitlers Heerführer: Die deutschen Oberbefehlshaber im Krieg gegen die Sowjetunion 1941/42*. Munich, 2006.
Hyse, Luc. "Justice after Transition: On the Choices Successor Elites Make in Dealing with the Past." *Law and Social Inquiry* 20, no. 20 (1995): 51–78.
Ignatieff, Michael. "Human Rights." In Hesse and Post, *Human Rights in Political Transitions*, 313–324.
———. *Human Rights as Politics and Idolatry*. Princeton, NJ, 2001.
International Military Tribunal, Secretariat. *Der Prozess gegen die Hauptkriegsverbrecher vor dem Internationalen Militärgerichtshof: Nürnberg 14. November 1945–1. Oktober 1946—Amtlicher Text in deutscher Sprache*. 42 volumes. Vol. 17: *Verhandlungsniederschriften 25. Juni 1946 bis 8. Juli 1946*. Nuremberg, 1947.
———. *Trial of the Major War Criminals Before the International Military Tribunal: Nuremberg, 14 November 1945–October 1946, Trial Proceedings*. http://avalon.law.yale.edu/subject_menus/imt.asp.
Irye, Akira. "Nationale Geschichte, Internationale Geschichte, Globale Geschichte." In *Deutschland und die USA in der internationalen Geschichte des 20. Jahrhunderts: Festschrift für Detlef Junker*, edited by Manfred Berg and Philipp Gassert, 21–39. Stuttgart, 2004.
Iser, Mattias, and David Strecker, eds. *Kritische Theorie der Politik: Franz L. Neumann—eine Bilanz*. Baden-Baden, 2002.
Jackson, Robert H. *Report of Robert H. Jackson, United States Representative to the International Conference on Military Trials*. Washington, DC, 1949.
Jäger, Wolfgang. *Historische Forschung und politische Kultur in Deutschland: Die Debatte 1914–1980 über den Ausbruch des Ersten Weltkriegs*. Göttingen, 1984.
Jahrreiß, Hermann. *Das Problem der rechtlichen Liquidation des Weltkrieges für Deutschland*. Leipzig, 1924.
———. *Paris 1919 und Europa: Die Ordnungsversuche der atlantischen Weltmächte*. Hamburg, 1943.
———. "Sich mühen um Recht und Gesetz." In *Festschrift der Rechtswissenschaftlichen Fakultät zur 600-Jahr-Feier der Universität zu Köln*, 699–706. Cologne, 1988.
———. "Wandel der Weltordnung: Zugleich eine Auseinandersetzung mit der Völkerrechtslehre von Carl Schmitt." *Zeitschrift für öffentliches Recht* 21 (1941): 513–536.
Jansen, Christian. "Pazifismus in Deutschland: Entwicklung und innere Widersprüche (1800 bis 1940)." In Kramer and Wette, *Recht ist, was den Waffen nützt*, 59–78.

Jarausch, Konrad H. "Die Provokation des 'Anderen': Amerikanische Perspektiven auf die deutsche Vergangenheitsbewältigung." In Bauerkämper et al., *Doppelte Zeitgeschichte*, 432–447.

———. "Von der Geschichte belehrt: Die Schwierigkeiten der ZEIT mit der Vereinigung." In Haase and Schildt, *DIE ZEIT und die Bonner Republik*, 280–294.

———. "World Power or Tragic Fate? The Kriegsschuldfrage as Historical Neurosis." *Central European History* 5 (1972): 79–92.

Jay, Martin. "Die Antisemitismusanalyse der Kritischen Theorie." In *Die Frankfurter Schule und Frankfurt: Eine Rückkehr nach Deutschland*, edited by Monika Boll and Raphael Gross, 136–149. Göttingen, 2009.

Jeismann, Michael. "Propaganda." In Hirschfeld et al., *Enzyklopädie Erster Weltkrieg*, 198–209.

Jescheck, Hans Heinrich. "Die Todesstrafe im ausländischen Recht." In *Die Frage der Todesstrafe: Zwölf Antworten*, edited by Reinhart Maurach, Eberhard Schmidt, and Wolfgang Preiser, 49–54. Munich, 1992.

Joas, Hans. *Die Sakralität der Person: Eine neue Genealogie der Menschenrechte*. Berlin, 2011.

Jochnik, Chris af, and Roger Normand. "The Legitimation of Violence: A Critical History of the Laws of War." *Harvard International Law Journal* 35, no. 1 (1994): 49–95.

Jockusch, Laura. *Collect and Record! Jewish Holocaust Documentation in Early Postwar Europe*. Oxford, 2012.

Justiz, Redaktion Kritische, ed. *Die juristische Aufarbeitung des Unrechts-Staats*. Baden-Baden, 1998.

Jütte, Robert, Hans-Walter Schmuhl, and Winfried Süss, eds. *Medizin und Nationalsozialismus: Bilanz und Perspektiven der Forschung*, 2nd ed. Göttingen, 2011.

Kaelble, Hartmut. "Historischer Vergleich, Version: 1.0." *Docupedia-Zeitgeschichte*, 14 August 2012. http://docupedia.de/zg/Historischer_Vergleich?oldid=84623.

Kaesler, Dirk. *Max Weber: Preusse, Denker, Muttersohn—eine Biographie*. Munich, 2014.

Kampmark, Binoy. "'No Peace with the Hohenzollerns': American Attitudes on Political Legitimacy towards Hohenzollern Germany, 1917–1918." *Diplomatic History* 34, no. 5 (2010): 769–791.

———. "Sacred Sovereigns and Punishable War Crimes: The Ambivalence of the Wilson Administration towards a Trial of Kaiser Wilhelm II." *Australian Journal of Politics and History* 53, no. 4 (2007): 519–537.

Kansteiner, Wulf. "Losing the War, Winning the Memory Battle: The Legacy of Nazism, World War II, and the Holocaust in the Federal Republic of Germany." In *The Politics of Memory in Postwar Europe*, edited by Richard Ned Lebow, Wulf Kansteiner, and Claudio Fogu, 102–146. Durham, NC, 2006.

Kaplan-Feuereisen, Omry. "Geschichtserfahrung und Völkerrecht: Jacob Robinson und die Gründung des Institute of Jewish Affairs." *Leipziger Beiträge zur jüdischen Geschichte und Kultur* 2 (2004): 307–327.

———. "Im Dienste der jüdischen Nation: Jacob Robinson und das Völkerrecht." *Osteuropa: Impulse für Europa—Tradition und Moderne der Juden Osteuropas* 58, nos. 8–10 (2008): 279–293.

———. "Jacob Robinson." *The YIVO Encyclopedia of Jews in Eastern Europe*, 18 November 2010. http://www.yivoencyclopedia.org/article.aspx/Robinson_Jacob.

Karstedt, Susanne. "The Nuremberg Tribunal and German Society." In *The Legacy of Nuremberg: Civilizing Influence or Institutional Vengeance?* edited by David A. Blumenthal and Timothy L. H. McCormack, 13–35. Leiden, 2008.

Katz, Barry M. "The Criticism of Arms: The Frankfurt School Goes to War." *Journal of Modern History* 59, no. 3 (1987): 439–478.

———. *Foreign Intelligence: Research and Analysis in the Office of Strategic Services 1942–1945*. Cambridge, MA, 1989.

Kautsky, Karl. *Wie der Weltkrieg entstand: Dargestellt nach dem Aktenmaterial des Deutschen Auswärtigen f Amts*. Berlin, 1919.

Kelsen, Hans. "Collective and Individual Responsibility in International Law with Particular Regard to the Punishment of War Criminals." *California Law Review* 31, no. 5 (1943): 530–571.

———. *Peace Through Law*. Chapel Hill, NC, 1944.

———. "Will the Judgment in the Nuremberg Trial Constitute a Precedent in International Law?" *International Law Quarterly* 1, no. 2 (1947): 153–171.

Kempner, Robert M. W., and Jörg Friedrich: *Ankläger einer Epoche: Lebenserinnerungen*. Frankfurt, 1986.

Kershaw, Ian. *Der NS-Staat: Geschichtsinterpretationen und Kontroversen im Überblick*. Rev. ed. Reinbek, 1999.

———. "War and Political Violence in Twentieth Century Europe." *Contemporary European History* 14, no. 1 (2005): 107–123.

Kersting, Franz-Werner, Karl Teppe, and Bernd Walter, eds. *Nach Hadamar: Zum Verhältnis von Psychiatrie und Gesellschaft im 20. Jahrhundert*. Paderborn, 1993.

Kießling, Friedrich. "(Welt-)Öffentlichkeit." In Dülffer and Loth, *Dimensionen internationaler Geschichte*, 85–105.

King, Richard H., and Dan Stone. *Hannah Arendt and the Uses of History: Imperialism, Race, Nation and Genocide*. New York, 2007.

———. "Introduction." In King and Stone, *Hannah Arendt and the Uses of History*, 1–17.

Kinkel, Klaus. "Begrüssungsansprache auf dem 15. Deutschen Richtertag am 23. September 1991 in Köln." *Deutsche Richterzeitung* 1 (1992): 4–5.

———. "Wiedervereinigung und Strafrecht." *Juristenzeitung* 47, no. 10 (1992): 485–489.

Kirchheimer, Otto. *Political Justice: The Use of Legal Procedure for Political Ends*. Princeton, NJ, 1961.

———. *Politische Justiz: Verwendung juristischer Verfahrensmöglichkeiten zu politischen Zwecken*. Frankfurt, 1985.

Klee, Ernst. *Das Kulturlexikon zum Dritten Reich: Wer war was vor und nach 1945*. Frankfurt, 2007.

———. *Das Personenlexikon zum Dritten Reich: Wer war was vor und nach 1945*. Frankfurt, 2003.

Klein, Eckart. "Die Bedeutung der Nürnberger Prozesse für die Bewältigung des SEDUnrechts." *Zeitschrift für Rechtspolitik* 6 (1992): 208–213.

Klein, Fritz. *Deutschland im Ersten Weltkrieg*. 3 vols. Berlin, 1968.

Knigge, Volkhard. "Gesellschaftsverbrechen erinnern: Zur Entstehung und Entwicklung des Konzepts seit 1945." In *Der Kommunismus im Museum: Formen der Auseinandersetzung in Deutschand und Ostmitteleuropa*, edited by Volkhard Knigge and Ulrich Mählert, 19–30. Weimar, 2005.

Knoch, Habbo. "Verschobene Schuld: Täterbilder und historische Fotografien in einem Illustriertenbericht zum Eichmann-Prozess." In *History: Ein Studienbuch*, edited by Gerhard Paul, 302–316. Göttingen, 2006.

Klose, Fabian. *Menschenrechte im Schatten kolonialer Gewalt: Die Dekolonisierungskriege in Kenia und Algerien 1945–1962*. Munich, 2009.

Kochavi, Arieh J. *Prelude to Nuremberg: Allied War Crimes Policy and the Question of Punishment*. Chapel Hill, NC, 1998.

Kohler, Josef. "Das neue Völkerrecht." *Zeitschrift für Völkerrecht* 9 (1916), 6–7.

Kolb, Eberhard. *Deutschland 1918–1933: Eine Geschichte der Weimarer Republik*. Munich, 2010.

König, Helmut. "Kein Neubeginn: Hannah Arendt, die NS-Vergangenheit und die Bundesrepublik." In *Streit um den Staat: Intellektuelle Debatten in der Bundesrepublik 1960–1980*, edited by Dominik Geppert and Jens Hacke, 113–134. Göttingen, 2011.

König, Stefan. "Bülowplatz-Prozess gegen Erich Mielke: Vom Umgang der Justiz mit (ihrer) Geschichte." In *Die Normalität des Verbrechens: Bilanz und Perspektiven der Forschung zu den nationalsozialistischen Gewaltverbrechen*, edited by Helge Gabitz, Klaus Bästlein, and Johannes Tuchel, 503–519. Berlin, 1994.

Kopeček, Michal. "Human Rights Facing a National Past: Dissident 'Civic Patriotism' and the Return of History in East Central Europe, 1968–1989." *Geschichte und Gesellschaft* 38 (2012): 573–602.

———. "The Rise and Fall of Czech Post-dissident Liberalism after 1989." *East European Politics and Societies* 25, no. 2 (2011): 244–271.

Koselleck, Reinhart. "Geschichte, Recht und Gerechtigkeit." In *Zeitschichten: Studien zur Historik*, edited by Reinhart Koselleck, 336–358. Frankfurt, 2000.

Koskenniemi, Martti. "Between Impunity and Show Trials." *Max Planck Yearbook of United Nations Law* 6 (2002): 1–35.

———. *The Gentle Civilizer of Nations: The Rise and Fall of International Law 1870–1960*. Cambridge, 2002.

Krach, Tillmann. *Jüdische Rechtsanwälte in Preussen: Über die Bedeutung der freien Advokatur und ihre Zerstörung durch den Nationalsozialismus*. Munich, 1991.

Kraft, Claudia. "Pacto de silencio und gruba kreska: Vom Umgang mit Vergangenheit in Transformationsprozessen." In Hammerstein et al., *Aufarbeitung der Diktatur*, 97–107.

———. "Völkermord als delictum iuris gentium: Raphael Lemkins Vorarbeiten für eine Genozidkonvention." *Jahrbuch des Simon-Dubnow-Instituts* 4 (2005): 79–98.

Kramer, Helmut, and Wolfram Wette, eds. *Recht ist, was den Waffen nützt: Justiz und Pazifismus im 20. Jahrhundert*. Berlin, 2004.

Krasmann, Susanne, and Jürgen Martschukat, eds. *Rationalitäten der Gewalt: Staatliche Ordnungen vom 19. bis zum 21. Jahrhundert*. Bielefeld, 2007.

Krause, Peter. "'Eichmann und wir': Die bundesdeutsche Öffentlichkeit und der Jerusalemer Eichmann-Prozess 1961." In *NS-Prozesse und die Öffentlichkeit in Deutschland 1945–1969*, edited by Jörg Osterloh and Clemens Vollnhals, 283–306. Göttingen, 2011.

Krausnick, Helmut. "Correspondence." *Simon Wiesenthal Center Annual* 6 (1989): 311–329.

———. *Hitlers Einsatzgruppen: Die Truppen des Weltanschauungskrieges 1938–1942*. Frankfurt, 1985.

———. "Judenverfolgung: Schriftliches Sachverständigengutachten für den Auschwitz-Prozess." In Buchheim et al., *Anatomie des SS-Staates*, 283–448.

Kritz, Neil J. "The Dilemmas of Transitional Justice." In Kritz, *Transitional Justice*, xix–xxx.

———, ed. *Transitional Justice: How Emerging Democracies Reckon with Former Regimes*. Vol. 1. Washington, DC, 1995.

Krivec, Boris. "Von Versailles nach Rom: Der lange Weg vom nullum crimen, nulla poena sine lege: Bedeutung und Entwicklung des strafrechtlichen Gesetzesvorbehalts im völkerrechtlichen Strafrecht." PhD diss. Hamburg, 2004.

Krösche, Heike. "Abseits der Vergangenheit: Das Interesse der deutschen Nachkriegsöffentlichkeit am Nürnberger Prozess gegen die Hauptkriegsverbrecher." In Osterloh and Vollnhals, *NS-Prozesse und deutsche Öffentlichkeit*, 93–105.

Kroeschell, Karl. *Rechtsgeschichte Deutschlands im 20. Jahrhundert*. Göttingen, 1992.

Krüger, Anne K. "'Keine Aussöhnung ohne Wahrheit': Die Enquete-Kommissionen zur 'Aufarbeitung' und 'Überwindung der SED-Diktatur.'" In Buckley-Zistel and Kater, *Nach Krieg, Gewalt und Repression*, 131–149.

———. "Transitional Justice, Version: 1.0." *Docupedia-Zeitgeschichte*, 25 January 2013. http://docupedia.de/zg/Transitional_Justice?oldid=85576.

Krumeich, Gerd. "Die Dolchstoß-Legende." In *Deutsche Erinnerungsorte*, vol. 1, edited by Etienne François Hagen Schulze, 585–599. Munich, 2001.

———, ed. *Versailles 1919: Ziele—Wirkung—Wahrnehmung*. Essen, 2001.

Krumeich, Gerd, and Gerhard Hirschfeld. "Die Geschichtsschreibung zum Ersten Weltkrieg." In Hirschfeld et al., *Enzyklopädie Erster Weltkrieg*, 304–313.

Krummacher, Friedrich A., ed. *Die Kontroverse: Hannah Arendt, Eichmann und die Juden*. Munich, 1964.

Kühl, Stefan. *Die Internationale der Rassisten: Aufstieg und Niedergang der internationalen Bewegung für Eugenik und Rassenhygiene im 20. Jahrhundert*. Frankfurt, 1997.

Kundrus, Birthe. "Kolonialismus: Imperialismus, Nationalsozialismus? Chancen und Grenzen eines neuen Paradigmas." In *Kolonialgeschichten: Regionale Perspektiven auf ein globales Phänomen*, edited by Claudia Kraft, Alf Lüdtke, and Jürgen Martschukat, 187–210. Frankfurt, 2010.

Kwiet, Konrad. "Rehearsing for Murder: The Beginning of the Final Solution in Lithuania in June 1941." *Holocaust and Genocide Studies* 12, no. 1 (1998): 3–26.

Laak, Dirk van. "Widerstand gegen die Geschichtsgewalt: Zur Kritik an der 'Vergangenheitsbewältigung.'" In Frei et al., *Geschichte vor Gericht*, 11–28.

Lamberti, Marjorie. "German Antifascist Refugees in America and the Public Debate on 'What Should Be Done with Germany after Hitler, 1941–1945.'" *Central European History* 40, no. 2 (2007): 279–305.

Landwehr, Achim. *Historische Diskursanalyse*. Frankfurt, 2008.

Lappenküper, Ulrich, and Reiner Marcowitz, eds. *Macht und Recht: Völkerrecht in den internationalen Beziehungen*. Paderborn, 2010.

Lemkin, Raphael. *Axis Rule in Occupied Europe: Laws of Occupation, Analysis of Government, Proposals for Redress*. New York, 1944.

Leo, Annette. "Antifaschismus." In *Erinnerungsorte der DDR*, edited by Martin Sabrow, 28–40. Bonn, 2010.

Levy, Daniel, and Natan Sznaider. *Erinnerung im globalen Zeitalter: Der Holocaust*. Frankfurt, 2001.

Lewis, Mark. *The Birth of the New Justice: The Internationalization of Crime and Punishment, 1919–1950*. Oxford, 2014.

———. "The World Jewish Congress and the Institute of Jewish Affairs at Nuremberg: Ideas, Strategies, and Political Goals, 1942–1946." *Yad Vashem Studies* 36, no. 1 (2008): 181–210.

Lindenberger, Thomas. "Governing Conflicted Memories: Some Remarks about the Regulation of History Politics in Unified Germany." In Blaive et al., *Clashes in European Memory*, 73–84.

Lingen, Kerstin von. *Kesselrings letzte Schlacht: Kriegsverbrecherprozesse, Vergangenheitspolitik und Wiederbewaffnung—Der Fall Kesselring*. Paderborn, 2004.

———. "'Crimes against Humanity': Eine umstrittene Universalie im Völkerrecht des 20. Jahrhunderts." *Zeithistorische Forschungen / Studies in Contemporary History* 8, no. 3 (2011) .http://www.zeithistorische-forschungen.de/16126041-vonLingen-3-2011.

Longerich, Peter. *"Davon haben wir nichts gewusst!" Die Deutschen und die Judenverfolgung*. Munich, 2006.

———. *Politik der Vernichtung: Eine Gesamtdarstellung der nationalsozialistischen Judenverfolgung 1933–1945*. Munich, 1998.
Lösch, Anna Maria Gräfin von. *Der nackte Geist: Die Juristische Fakultät der Berliner Universität im Umbruch von 1933*. Tübingen, 1999.
Lower, Wendy. "Hitler's 'Garden of Eden': Nazi Colonialism, Volksdeutsche and the Holocaust 1941–1944." In *Gray Zones: Ambiguity and Compromise in the Holocaust and Its Aftermath*, edited by Jonathan Petropoulos and John Roth, 185–204. New York, 2005.
Lübbe, Hermann. "Der Nationalsozialismus im deutschen Nachkriegsbewusstsein." *Historische Zeitschrift* 236 (1983): 579–599.
Luckau, Alma. *The German Peace Delegation at the Paris Peace Conference*. New York, 1971. Originally published in 1941.
Lüderssen, Klaus. *Der Staat geht unter: Das Unrecht bleibt? Regierungskriminalität in der ehemaligen DDR*. Frankfurt, 1992.
Lutz, Dieter S. "Amnestie: Eine Einführung." *Vierteljahresschrift für Sicherheit und Frieden, Sonderheft Amnestie* 4 (1993): 188–193.
Maguire, Peter. *Law and War: An American Story*. New York, 2001.
Maier, Charles S. "Consigning the Twentieth Century to History: Alternative Narratives for the Modern Era." *American Historical Review* 105, no. 3 (2000): 807–831.
Majer, Dietmut. "Das besetzte Osteuropa als deutsche Kolonie (1939–1944): Die Pläne der NS-Führung zur Beherrschung Osteuropas." In *Gesetzliches Unrecht: Rassistisches Recht im 20. Jahrhundert*, edited by Fritz Bauer Institut, 111–134. Frankfurt, 2005.
Mallmann, Klaus-Michael. "Die Türöffner der 'Endlösung': Zur Genesis des Genozids." In *Gestapo im Zweiten Weltkrieg: "Heimatfront" und besetztes Europa*, edited by Gerhard Paul and Klaus-Michael Mallmann, 437–463. Darmstadt, 2000.
Mallmann, Klaus-Michael, and Andrej Angrick, eds. *Die Gestapo nach 1945: Karrieren, Konflikte, Konstruktionen*. Darmstadt, 2009.
———. "Die Mörder sind unter uns: Gestapo-Bedienstete in den Nachfolgegesellschaften des Dritten Reichs." In Mallmann and Angrick, *Die Gestapo nach 1945*, 7–54.
Mann, Golo. "Der verdrehte Eichmann." In *f.*
Marauhn, Thilo. "Völkerrechtliche Praxis der Bundesrepublik Deutschland im Jahre 1991." *Zeitschrift für ausländisches öffentliches Recht und Völkerrecht* 53 (1993): 963–1098.
Marcuse, Herbert. "Some Social Implications of Modern Technology." *Studies in Philosophy and Social Science* 9 (1941): 414–439.
Marquardt-Bigman, Petra. *Amerikanische Geheimdienstanalysen über Deutschland 1942–1949*. Munich, 1995.
Marrus, Michael. "History and the Holocaust in the Courtroom." In *Lessons and Legacies: The Holocaust and Justice*, vol. 5, edited by Ronald Smelser, 215–239. Evanston, IL, 2002.
———. "A Jewish Lobby at Nuremberg: Jacob Robinson and the Institute of Jewish Affairs, 1945–46." In *The Nuremberg Trials: International Criminal Law Since 1945*, edited by Herbert R. Reginbogin and Christoph Safferling, 63–71. Munich, 2006.
———. "The Nuremberg Doctors' Trial and the Limitations of Context." In Heberer and Matthäus, *Atrocities on Trial*, 103–122.
Marten, Detlef. *Rechtsstaatlichkeit und Gnade*. Berlin, 1978.
Marxen, Klaus. *Rechtliche Grenzen der Amnestie*. Heidelberg, 1984.
Marxen, Klaus, and Gerhard Werle. *Die strafrechtliche Aufarbeitung von DDR-Unrecht: Eine Bilanz*. Berlin, 1999.
Marxen, Klaus, Gerhard Werle, and Petra Schäfter. *Die Strafverfolgung von DDR-Unrecht: Fakten und Zahlen*. Berlin, 2007.

Matthäus, Jürgen. "Der Eichmann-Prozess und seine Folgen: Strafverfolgung von NS-Verbrechen und Geschichtsschreibung." In Renz, *Interessen um Eichmann*, 217–240.

———. "Jenseits der Grenze: Die ersten Massenerschiessungen von Juden in Litauen (Juni–August 1941)." *Zeitschrift für Geschichtswissenschaft* 44, no. 2 (1996): 101–117.

———. "The Lessons of Leipzig: Punishing German War Criminals after the First World War." In Heberer and Matthäus, *Atrocities on Trial*, 3–23.

Maunz, Theodor. *Das Reich der spanischen Grossmachtzeit*. Hamburg, 1944.

Mazower, Mark. *Dark Continent: Europe's Twentieth Century*. London, 1998.

———. "Ende der Zivilisation und Aufstieg der Menschenrechte: Die konzeptionelle Trennung Mitte des 20. Jahrhunderts." In Hoffmann, *Moralpolitik*, 41–62.

———. *Governing the World: The History of an Idea*. London, 2012.

———. *No Enchanted Palace: The End of Empire and the Ideological Origins of the United Nations*. Princeton, NJ, 2009.

———. "The Strange Triumph of Human Rights, 1933–1950." *Historical Journal* 47, no. 2 (2004): 379–398.

McAdams, A. James. *Judging the Past in Unified Germany*. Cambridge, 2001.

———. "Vergangenheitsaufarbeitung nach 1989: Ein deutscher Sonderweg?" *Deutschland Archiv* 36, no. 5 (2003): 851–860.

McDonnell, Michael A., and A. Dirk Moses. "Raphael Lemkin as Historian of Genocide in the Americas." *Journal of Genocide Research* 7, no. 4 (2005): 501–529.

McMillan, James. "War." In Bloxham and Gerwarth, *Political Violence in Twentieth-Century Europe*, 40–86.

Mégret, Frédéric. "The Politics of International Criminal Justice." *European Journal of International Law* 13, no. 5 (2002): 1261–1284.

Meier, Christian. *Das Gebot zu vergessen und die Unabweisbarkeit des Erinnerns*. Munich, 2010.

Mergel, Thomas. "Kulturgeschichte der Politik, Version: 1.0." *Docupedia-Zeitgeschichte*, 11 Feburary 2010. https://docupedia.de/zg/Kulturgeschichte_der_Politik_Version_1.0_Thomas_Mergel/Text.

Merrit, A. J., and R. L. Merrit. *Public Opinion in Occupied Germany: The OMGUS Surveys 1945–1949*. Urbana, IL, 1970.

———. *Public Opinion in Semisovereign Germany: The HICOG Surveys 1949–1955*. Urbana, IL, 1980.

Messerschmidt, Manfred. "Vorwärtsverteidigung: Die 'Denkschrift der Generäle' für den Nürnberger Gerichtshof." In *Vernichtungskrieg: Die Verbrechen der Wehrmacht 1941–1944*, edited by Hannes Heer and Klaus Naumann, 531–550. Hamburg, 1995.

Messinger, Gary S. *British Propaganda and the State in the First World War*. Manchester, 1992.

Metzler, Gabriele. "Staatsversagen und Unregierbarkeit in den siebziger Jahren?" In *Das Ende der Zuversicht? Die siebziger Jahre als Geschichte*, edited by Konrad H. Jarausch, 243–260. Göttingen, 2008.

Meusch, Matthias. "Die strafrechtliche Verfolgung der Hadamarer 'Euthanasie'-Morde." In *Hadamar: Heilstätte—Tötungsanstalt—Therapiezentrum*, edited by Uta George, 305–326. Marburg, 2006.

Meyer, Kristina. *Die SPD und die NS-Vergangenheit 1945–1990*. Göttingen, 2015.

Meyer-Seitz, Christian. *Die Verfolgung von NS-Straftaten in der Sowjetischen Besatzungszone*. Berlin, 1998.

Middell, Matthias. "Marxistische Geschichtswissenschaft." In *Kompass der Geschichtswissenschaft*, 2nd ed., edited by Joachim Eibach and Günther Lottes, 69–85. Göttingen, 2006.

Ministère des affaires étrangères. *Les violations des lois de la guerre par l'Allemagne*. Paris, 1915.

Minow, Martha. *Between Vengeance and Forgiveness: Facing History after Genocide and Mass Violence*. Boston, 1998.
Miquel, Marc von. *Ahnden oder amnestieren? Westdeutsche Justiz und Vergangenheitspolitik in den sechziger Jahren*. Göttingen, 2004.
Mitchell, Allan. *Revolution in Bavaria 1918–1919: The Eisner Regime and the Soviet Republic*. Princeton, NJ, 1965.
Moisel, Claudia. *Frankreich und die deutschen Kriegsverbrecher: Politik und Praxis der Strafverfolgung nach dem Zweiten Weltkrieg*. Göttingen, 2004.
Mommsen, Hans. "Hannah Arendt und der Prozess gegen Adolf Eichmann." In Arendt, *Eichmann in Jerusalem: Ein Bericht*, 9–48.
Mommsen, Wolfgang J. "Die kulturellen Eliten im Ersten Weltkrieg." In *Bürgerliche Kultur und politische Ordnung: Künstler, Schriftsteller und Intellektuelle in der deutschen Geschichte 1830–1933*, 2nd ed., edited by Wolfgang J. Mommsen, 178–195. Frankfurt, 2002.
———. *Max Weber und die deutsche Politik 1890–1920*. Tübingen, 1974.
———. *Max Weber und die deutsche Revolution 1918/19*. Heidelberg, 1994.
Montgelas, Graf Max, and Walther Schücking, eds. *Die deutschen Dokumente zum Kriegsausbruch 1914: Vollständige Sammlung der von Karl Kautsky zusammengestellten Aktenstücke mit einigen Ergänzungen im Auftrage des Auswärtigen Amtes nach gemeinsamer Durchsicht mit Karl Kautsky*. 4 vols. Charlottenburg, 1919.
Moran, Mayo. "'In the Glass Darkly': Legacies of Nazi and Fascist Law in Europe." *University of Toronto Law Journal* 54, no. 4 (2004): 449–463.
Moses, Dirk A. "Besatzung, Kolonialherrschaft und Widerstand: Das Völkerrecht und die Legitimierung von Terror." *Peripherie: Zeitschrift für Politik und Ökonomie in der Dritten Welt* 29, no. 116 (2009): 399–424.
———. "The Holocaust and Genocide." In Stone, *The Historiography of the Holocaust*, 533–551.
Mouralis, Guillaume. *Une épuration allemande: La RDA en procès 1949–2004*. Paris, 2008.
———. "Jenseits der indigenen Diskurse über die Vergangenheit: Der Umgang der Justiz-Juristen mit DDR-Systemverbrechen im vereinigten Deutschland zwischen 'Geschichts-' und 'Vergangenheitspolitik.'" Vortrag im Rahmen des Colloquiums "La recherche française sur la RDA et la transition." Humboldt University, Berlin, 19 March 2005.
Moyn, Samuel. "The First Historian of Human Rights." *American Historical Review* 116, no. 1 (2011): 58–79.
———. *The Last Utopia: Human Rights in History*. Cambridge, MA, 2010.
———. "Personalismus, Gemeinschaft und die Ursprünge der Menschenrechte." In Hoffmann, *Moralpolitik*, 63–91.
Müller, Ingo. "NS-Justiz und DDR-Justiz vor deutschen Gerichten." In *Kontinuitäten und Zäsuren: Rechtswissenschaft und Justiz im "Dritten Reich" und in der Nachkriegszeit*, edited by Eva Schumann, 233–245. Göttingen, 2008.
Müller, Tim B. "Bearing Witness to the Liquidation of Western Dasein: Herbert Marcuse and the Holocaust 1941–1948." Special issue on "Intellectuals," *New German Critique* 85 (2002): 133–164.
———. "Die epistemischen Bedingungen der Macht: Wissenschaft, Staatsapparate und Stiftungen im frühen Kalten Krieg—Der institutionelle Kontext Otto Kirchheimers, Herbert Marcuses und Franz Neumanns in Amerika." In *Kritische Verfassungspolitologie: Das Staatsverständnis von Otto Kirchheimer*, edited by Robert Christian van Ooyen and Frank Schale, 35–66. Baden-Baden, 2011.
———. *Krieger und Gelehrte: Herbert Marcuse und die Denksysteme im Kalten Krieg*. Hamburg, 2010.

Muller, Jan-Werner. *Contesting Democracy: Political Ideas in Twentieth-Century Europe*. New Haven, CT, 2011.
Nagornaja, Oksana. "Einführung." *Erklärung des Generalfeldmarschalls von Hindenburg vor dem Parlamentarischen Untersuchungsausschuß ["Dolchstoßlegende"], 18. November 1919*. 1000 deutsche Schlüsseldokumente. www.1000dokumente.de/index.html?c=dokument_de&dokument=0026_dol& object=context&st=&l=de. Accessed 5 June 2018.
Naucke, Wolfgang. "NS-Strafrecht: Perversion oder Anwendungsfall moderner Kriminalpolitik." *Rechtshistorisches Journal* 11 (1992): 279–292.
Neal, Andrew W. "Foucault in Guantánamo: Eine Archäologie des Ausnahmezustands." In Krasmann and Martschukat, *Rationalitäten der Gewalt*, 47–74.
Nehring, Holger. "Transnationale soziale Bewegungen." In Dülffer and Loth, *Dimensionen internationaler Geschichte*, 129–149.
Neubert, Ehrhart. *Unsere Revolution: Die Geschichte der Jahre 1989/90*. Munich, 2008.
Neumann, Franz Leopold. *Behemoth: Struktur und Praxis des Nationalsozialismus 1933–1944*. 5th ed. Frankfurt, 2004.
———. *Behemoth: The Structure and Practice of National Socialism*. London, 1942.
———. *Behemoth: The Structure and Practice of National Socialism, 1933–1944*. Introduction by Peter Hayes. Chicago, 2009.
———. "The War Crimes Trials." *World Politics* 2, no. 1 (1949): 135–147.
Nolan, Mary. "Human Rights and Market Fundamentalism in the Long 1970s." In Frei and Weinke, *Toward a New Moral World Order?* 172–181.
Nolte, Paul. "Soziologie als kulturelle Selbstvergewisserung: Die Demokratisierung der deutschen Gesellschaft nach 1945." In *Soziale Konstellation und historische Perspektive: Festschrift für M. Rainer Lepsius*, edited by Steffen Sigmund, 18–40. Wiesbaden, 2008.
Nolzen, Armin. "Franz Leopold Neumanns 'Behemoth': Ein vergessener Klassiker der NSForschung, Version: 1.0." *Docupedia-Zeitgeschichte*, 30 May 2011. https://docupedia.de/zg/Nolzen_-_Neumann.2C_Behemoth?oldid=79047.
O'Donnell, Guillermo, and Philippe C. Schmitter. *Transitions from Authoritarian Rule: Tentative Conclusions about Uncertain Democracies*. Baltimore, 2013.
Offe, Claus. *Der Tunnel am Ende des Lichts: Erkundungen der politischen Transformation im Neuen Osten*. Frankfurt, 1994.
Ogorreck, Ralf. *Die Einsatzgruppen und die "Genesis der Endlösung."* Berlin, 1996.
Olick, Jeffrey K. *In the House of the Hangman: The Agonies of German Defeat*. Chicago, 2005.
Olick, Jeffrey K., and Brenda Coughlin. "The Politics of Regret: Analytical Frames." In Torpey, *Politics and the Past*, 37–62.
Opitz, Peter J. *Menschenrechte und Internationaler Menschenrechtsschutz im 20. Jahrhundert: Geschichte und Dokumente*. Munich, 2002.
Oppenheim, Lassa. *International Law: A Treatise*. 2 vols. London, 1906.
Osiel, Mark. *Mass Atrocity, Collective Memory, and the Law*. New Brunswick, NJ, 1997.
Osterhammel, Jürgen. *Die Entzauberung Asiens: Europa und die asiatischen Reiche im 18. Jahrhundert*. Munich, 1998.
Osterloh, Jörg, and Clemens Vollnhals. *NS-Prozesse und deutsche Öffentlichkeit: Besatzungszeit, frühe Bundesrepublik und DDR*. Göttingen, 2011.
Ott, Walter, and Franziska Buob. "Did Legal Positivism Render German Jurists Defenseless during the Third Reich?" *Social and Legal Studies* 2 (1993): 91–104.
Park, Gloria. "Truth as Justice." *Harvard International Review* 31, no. 4 (2010). http://hir.harvard.edu/big-ideas/truth-as-justice.
Pauer, Jan. "Die Aufarbeitung der Diktaturen in Tschechien und der Slowakei." *Aus Politik und Zeitgeschichte* 56, no. B42 (2006): 25–32.

Paul, Gerhard. "Täterbilder—Täterprofile—Taten: Ergebnisse der neueren Forschung zu den Tätern des Holocaust." In Erler et al., *"Gegen alle Vergeblichkeit,"* 142–164.
Pendas, Devin O. "Auf dem Weg zu einem globalen Rechtssystem? Die Menschenrechte und das Scheitern des legalistischen Paradigmas des Krieges." In Hoffmann, *Moralpolitik*, 226–255.
———. "'Law, Not Vengeance': Human Rights, the Rule of Law, and the Claims of Memory in German Holocaust Trials." In *Truth Claims: Representation and Human Rights*, edited by Mark Philip Bradley and Patrice Petro, 23–41. New Brunswick, NJ, 2002.
———. "Retroactive Law and Proactive Justice." *Central European History* 43, no. 3 (2010): 428–463.
Perels, Joachim. "Franz L. Neumanns Beitrag zur Konzipierung der Nürnberger Prozesse." In Iser and Strecker, *Kritische Theorie der Politik*, 83–94.
———. "Pläne der US-Administration für ein anderes Deutschland: Die Arbeiten der Neumann-Gruppe." In *Das juristische Erbe des "Dritten Reiches": Beschädigungen der demokratischen Rechtsordnung*, edited by Joachim Perels, 39–46. Frankfurt, 1999.
Peters, Edward M. *Folter: Geschichte der Peinlichen Befragung*. Hamburg, 2003.
Phillips, Timothy. "The Project on Justice in Times of Transition." In *The New Humanitarians*, edited by Chris E. Stout. Westport, CT, 2008.
Pieroth, Bodo. "Der Rechtsstaat und die Aufarbeitung der vorrechtsstaatlichen Vergangenheit." *Veröffentlichungen der Vereinigung der Deutschen Staatsrechtslehrer* 51 (1992): 91–115.
Pingel, Falk. "Die NS-Psychiatrie im Spiegel des historischen Bewusstseins und sozialpolitischen Denkens in der Bundesrepublik." In Kersting et al., *Nach Hadamar*, 174–201.
Pöhlmann, Markus. *Kriegsgeschichte und Geschichtspolitik: Der Erste Weltkrieg—Die amtliche deutsche Militärgeschichtsschreibung 1914–1956*. Paderborn, 2002.
Pohl, Dieter. *Holocaust: Die Ursachen—das Geschehen—die Folgen*. Freiburg, 2000.
———. "Prosecutors and Historians: Holocaust Investigations and Historiography in the Federal Republic 1955–1975." In *Holocaust and Justice: Representation and Historiography of the Holocaust in Post-war Trials*, edited by David Bankier and Dan Michman, 117–129. Jerusalem, 2010.
Poliakov, Léon. *Bréviaire de la Haine: Le Troisième Reich et les Juifs*. Paris, 1951.
Poliakov, Léon, and Joseph Wulf. *Das Dritte Reich und die Juden: Dokumente und Aufsätze*. Berlin, 1955.
Priemel, Kim Christian. "Der Sonderweg vor Gericht: Angewandte Geschichte im Nürnberger Krupp-Prozess." *Historische Zeitschrift* 294, no. 2 (2012): 391–426.
Priemel, Kim Christian, and Alexa Stiller, eds. *NMT: Die Nürnberger Militärtribunale zwischen Geschichte, Gerechtigkeit und Rechtsschöpfung*. Hamburg, 2013.
———, eds. *Reassessing the Nuremberg Military Tribunals: Transitional Justice, Trial Narratives, and Historiography*. New York, 2012.
Puttkamer, Ellinor von. "Die Haftung der politischen und militärischen Führung des Ersten Weltkriegs für Kriegsurheberschaft und Kriegsverbrechen." *Archiv des Völkerrechts* 1 (1948/1949): 424–449.
Pyta, Wolfram. *Hindenburg: Herrschaft zwischen Hohenzollern und Hitler*. Munich, 2007.
Quataert, Jean H. *Advocating Dignity: Human Rights Mobilizations in Global Politics*. Philadelphia, 2009.
Quint, Peter. *The Imperfect Union: Constitutional Structures of German Unification*. Princeton, NJ, 1997.
Rabinbach, Anson, ed. *Begriffe aus dem Kalten Krieg: Totalitarismus, Antifaschismus, Genozid*. Göttingen, 2009.

———. "Genozid: Genese eines Konzepts." In Rabinbach, *Begriffe aus dem Kalten Krieg*, 43–72.

———. "Totalitarismus: Konjunkturen eines Begriffs." In Rabinbach, *Begriffe aus dem Kalten Krieg*, 7–27.

Radbruch, Gustav. "Gesetzliches Unrecht und übergesetzliches Recht." In *Süddeutsche Juristen-Zeitung* 1 (1946): 105–108.

Radkau, Joachim. *Max Weber: Die Leidenschaft des Denkens*. Munich, 2005.

Raim, Edith. "NS-Prozesse und Öffentlichkeit: Die Strafverfolgung von NS-Verbrechen durch die deutsche Justiz in den westlichen Besatzungszonen 1945–1949." In Osterloh and Vollnhals, *NS-Prozesse und deutsche Öffentlichkeit*, 33–51.

Raphael, Lutz. *Geschichtswissenschaft im Zeitalter der Extreme: Theorien, Methoden, Tendenzen von 1900 bis zur Gegenwart*. Munich, 2003.

———. "Ordnungsmuster der 'Hochmoderne'? Die Theorie der Moderne und die Geschichte der europäischen Gesellschaften im 20. Jahrhundert." In *Dimensionen der Moderne: Festschrift für Christof Dipper*, edited by Lutz Raphael and Ute Schneider, 73–91. Frankfurt, 2008.

———. "Die Verwissenschaftlichung des Sozialen als methodische und konzeptionelle Herausforderung für eine Sozialgeschichte des 20. Jahrhunderts." *Geschichte und Gesellschaft* 22 (1996): 165–193.

Raschka, Johannes. *Justizpolitik im SED-Staat: Anpassung und Wandel des Strafrechts während der Amtszeit Honeckers*. Cologne, 2000.

Rathkolb, Oliver. "Historical Perceptions of the Repression of the Holocaust in Czech, Polish and Hungarian Public Opinion and the Austrian 'Special Case.'" In Blaive et al., *Clashes in European Memory*, 173–191.

Reichel, Peter. "Vergangenheitsbewältigung." In *Deutsche Geschichte im 20. Jahrhundert: Ein Lexikon*, edited by Axel Schildt, 375–378. Munich, 2005.

———. *Vergangenheitsbewältigung in Deutschland: Die Auseinandersetzung mit der NS-Diktatur von 1945 bis heute*. Munich, 2001.

Reichtagsprotokolle. *Reichstagsdrucksachen, 13. Legislaturperiode, II. Session, Nr. 19*. Berlin, 1914.

Reitlinger, Gerald. *Die Endlösung: Hitlers Versuch der Ausrottung der Juden Europas 1939–1945*. 5th ed. Berlin, 1970.

———. *The Final Solution: The Attempt to Exterminate the Jews of Europe, 1939–1945*. London, 1953.

Renz, Werner. *Interessen um Eichmann: Israelische Justiz, deutsche Strafverfolgung und alte Kameradschaften*. Frankfurt, 2012.

Requate, Jörg, and Martin Schulze Wessel, eds. *Europäische Öffentlichkeit: Transnationale Kommunikation seit dem 18. Jahrhundert*. Frankfurt, 2002.

Riedel, Joachim. "Zwei deutsche Diktaturen und ihre strafrechtliche Aufarbeitung im Vergleich." In *Die Ermittler von Ludwigsburg: Deutschland und die Aufklärung nationalsozialistischer Verbrechen*, edited by Hans H. Pöschko, 153–161. Berlin, 2008.

Ringer, Fritz. *Max Weber: An Intellectual Biography*. Chicago, 2004.

Ricœur, Paul. *History, Memory, Forgetting*. London, 2004.

Riesenberger, Dieter. *Geschichte der Friedensbewegung in Deutschland: Von den Anfängen bis 1933*. Göttingen, 1985.

Rigoll, Dominik. *Staatsschutz in Westdeutschland: Von der Entnazifizierung zur Extremistenabwehr*. Göttingen, 2013.

Roenne, Hans Hubertus von. *"Politisch untragbar . . . ?" Die Überprüfung von Richtern und Staatsanwälten der DDR im Zuge der Vereinigung Deutschlands*. Berlin, 1997.

Roggemann, Herwig. "Amnestie in beiden deutschen Staaten: Rechtsvergleichende Anmerkungen zum Staatsratsbeschluss von 1987." *Recht in Ost und West* 31 (1987): 281–291.
Röhl, John C. G. *Wilhelm II: Der Weg in den Abgrund 1900–1941*. Munich, 2008.
Rohstock, Anne. "Kein Vollzeitrepublikaner: Die Findung des Demokraten Theodor Eschenburg." In *Gesichter der Demokratie: Porträts zur deutschen Zeitgeschichte*, edited by Bastian Hein, Manfred Kittel and Horst Möller, 193–210. Munich, 2012.
Römer, Felix. "Richtlinien für die Behandlung politischer Kommissare [Kommissarbefehl], 6. Juni 1941." *100(0) Schlüsseldokumente zur deutschen Geschichte*. http://www.1000dokumente.de/index.html?c=dokument_de&dokument=0088_kbe&object=context&st=&l=de.
Rotberg, Robert I., and Dennis Thompson, eds. *Truth V. Justice: The Morality of Truth Commissions*. Princeton, NJ, 2000.
Rottleuthner, Hubert. "Das Nürnberger Juristenurteil und seine Rezeption: In Ost und West." *Neue Justiz* 12 (1997): 617–624.
Rousso, Henry. "Das Dilemma eines europäischen Gedächtnisses." *Studies in Contemporary History* 1, no. 3 (2004). http://www.zeithistorische-forschungen.de/16126041-Rousso-3-2004.
———. "Égo-Histoire: Vichy in Geschichte, Erinnerung und Recht." In *Frankreich und die "dunklen Jahre": Das Regime von Vichy in Geschichte und Gegenwart*, edited by Henry Rousso, 82–178. Göttingen, 2010.
———. *The Haunting Past: History, Memory, and Justice in Contemporary France*. Philadelphia, 1998.
———. "History of Memory, Policies of the Past: What For?" In *Conflicted Memories: Europeanizing Contemporary Histories*, edited by Konrad H. Jarausch and Thomas Lindenberger, 23–37. Oxford, 2007.
———. "Justiz, Geschichte und Erinnerung in Frankreich: Überlegungen zum Papon-Prozess." In Frei et al., *Geschichte vor Gericht*, 141–163.
Rückerl, Adalbert. *NS-Verbrechen vor Gericht: Versuch einer Vergangenheitsbewältigung*. 2nd ed. Heidelberg, 1984.
Sa'adah, Anne. *Germany's Second Chance: Trust, Justice, and Democratization*. Cambridge, 1998.
Safferling, Christoph, and Philipp Graebke. "Strafverteidigung im Nürnberger Hauptkriegsverbrecherprozess: Strategien und Wirkung." *Zeitschrift für die Gesamte Strafrechtswissenschaft* 123 (2011): 47–81.
Salewski, Michael. "Das Weimarer Revisionssyndrom." *Aus Politik und Zeitgeschichte* 30, no. 2 (1980): 14–25.
Salter, Michael. *Nazi War Crimes, US Intelligence, and Selective Prosecution at Nuremberg: Controversies Regarding the Role of the Office of Strategic Services*. London, 2007.
———. "Neo-Fascist Legal Theory on Trial: An Interpretation of Carl Schmitt's Defence at Nuremberg from the Perspective of Franz Neumann's Critical Theory of Law." *Res Publica* 5 (1999): 161–194.
Salzborn, Samuel. "Leviathan und Behemoth: Staat und Mythos bei Thomas Hobbes und Carl Schmitt." In *Der Hobbes-Kristall: Carl Schmitts Hobbes-Interpretation in der Diskussion*, edited by Rüdiger Vogt, 143–164. Stuttgart, 2009.
Sargent, Daniel. "Eine Oase in der Wüste? Amerikas Wiederentdeckung der Menschenrechte." In Eckel and Moyn, *Moral für die Welt?* 259–289.
Sarrazin, Philipp. "Diskursanalyse." In *Geschichte: Ein Grundkurs*, edited by Hans-Jürgen Goertz, 199–217. Reinbek, 2007.

Schäfer, Rita. "Gender in der südafrikanischen Wahrheits- und Versöhnungskommission." In Buckley-Zistel and Kater, *Nach Krieg, Gewalt und Repression*, 151–166.

Schätzler, Johann-Georg. *Handbuch des Gnadenrechts*. Munich, 1976.

———. "Innerer Frieden und Amnestie am Beispiel der deutschen Einheit." *Vierteljahresschrift für Sicherheit und Frieden, Sonderheft Amnestie* 4 (1993): 194–200.

———. "Staatenfusion und Abrechnungsmentalität." *Deutschland Archiv* 30, no. 1 (1997): 105–115.

Schaller, Dominik. "Raphael Lemkin's View of European Colonial Rule in Africa: Between Condemnation and Admiration." *Journal of Genocide Research* 7, no. 4 (2005): 532–538.

Scheffler, Wolfgang. *Judenverfolgung im Dritten Reich*. Berlin, 1960.

———. *Die nationalsozialistische Judenpolitik*. Berlin, 1960.

Scheuner, Ulrich. *Das europäische Gleichgewicht und die britische Seeherrschaft*. Hamburg, 1944.

Schiffers, Reinhard. *Zwischen Bürgerfreiheit und Staatsschutz: Wiederherstellung und Neufassung des politischen Strafrechts in der Bundesrepublik Deutschland 1949–1951*. Düsseldorf, 1989.

Schildt, Axel. "Immer mit der Zeit: Der Weg der Wochenzeitung DIE ZEIT durch die Bonner Republik—eine Skizze." In Haase and Schildt, *DIE ZEIT und die Bonner Republik*, 9–27.

———. "Modernisierung, Version: 1.0." *Docupedia-Zeitgeschichte*, 11 February 2010. http://docupedia.de/zg/Modernisierung?oldid=84640.

Schlichte, Klaus. "Das formierende Säkulum: Macht und Recht in der internationalen Politik des 19. Jahrhunderts." In Lappenküper and Marcowitz, *Macht und Recht*, 161–177.

Schlink, Bernhard. "Rechtsstaat und revolutionäre Gerechtigkeit." In *Vergangenheitsschuld und gegenwärtiges Recht*, edited by Bernhard Schlink, 38–60. Frankfurt, 2002.

Schmitt, Carl. *Völkerrechtliche Grossraumordnung mit Interventionsverbot für raumfremde Mächte: Ein Beitrag zum Reichsbegriff im Völkerrecht*. Berlin, 1939.

Schmoeckel, Mathias. *Die Grossraumtheorie: Ein Beitrag zur Geschichte der Völkerrechtswissenschaft im Dritten Reich, insbesondere der Kriegszeit*. Berlin, 1994.

Schmuhl, Hans-Walter. "'Euthanasie' und Krankenmord." In Jütte et al., *Medizin und Nationalsozialismus*, 214–255.

———. "Nürnberger Ärzteprozess und 'Euthanasie'-Prozesse." In Jütte et al., *Medizin und Nationalsozialismus*, 267–282.

Schöller, Peter. *Der Fall Löwen und das Weißbuch: Eine kritische Untersuchung der deutschen Dokumentation über die Vorgänge in Löwen vom 25. bis 28. August 1914*. Cologne, 1958.

Schoenberner, Gerhard. *Der gelbe Stern: Die Judenverfolgung in Europa 1933 bis 1945*. Hamburg, 1960.

Schönherr, Albrecht, ed. *Ein Volk am Pranger? Die Deutschen auf der Suche nach einer neuen politischen Kultur*. Berlin, 1992.

Schröder, Friedrich-Christian, and Herbert Küpper, eds. *Die rechtliche Aufarbeitung der kommunistischen Vergangenheit in Osteuropa*. Frankfurt, 2010.

Schroers, Rolf. "Der banale Eichmann und seine Opfer." In Krummacher, *Die Kontroverse*, 199–206.

Schüle, Erwin. "Die strafrechtliche Aufarbeitung des Verhaltens in totalitären Systemen: Der Eichmann-Prozess aus deutscher Sicht." In *Möglichkeiten und Grenzen für die Bewältigung historischer und politischer Schuld in Strafprozessen*, edited by Karl Forster, 65–86. Würzburg, 1962.

Schulz, Matthias. "Macht, internationale Politik und Normenwandel." In Lappenküper and Marcowitz, *Macht und Recht*, 113–134.

Schulze, Winfried. *Deutsche Geschichtswissenschaft nach 1945*. Munich, 1993.

Schulze Wessel, Martin. "Geschichte vor Gericht: Zum juristischen und geschichtswissenschaftlichen Umgang mit dem Unrecht untergegangener Staatsordnungen in Deutschland und im östlichen Europa." In *Bewusstes Erinnern und bewusstes Vergessen*, edited by Angelika Nussberger and Caroline von Gall, 9–26. Tübingen, 2011.
Schwabe, Klaus. "'Gerechtigkeit für die Grossmacht Deutschland': Die deutsche Friedensstrategie in Versailles." In Krumeich, *Versailles 1919*, 71–86.
Schwarz, Gotthart. *Theodor Wolff und das "Berliner Tageblatt": Eine liberale Stimme in der deutschen Politik 1906–1933.* Tübingen, 1968.
Schwengler, Walter. *Völkerrecht, Versailler Vertrag und Auslieferungsfrage: Die Strafverfolgung wegen Kriegsverbrechen als Problem des Friedensschlusses 1919/20.* Stuttgart, 1982.
Schwingel, Markus. *Pierre Bourdieu zur Einführung.* Hamburg, 2003.
Segert, Dieter. *Das 41. Jahr: Eine andere Geschichte der DDR.* Cologne, 2008.
Segesser, Daniel Marc. *Recht statt Rache oder Rache durch Recht? Die Ahndung von Kriegsverbrechen in der internationalen wissenschaftlichen Debatte 1872–1945.* Paderborn, 2010.
Segesser, Daniel Marc, and Myriam Gessler. "Raphael Lemkin and the International Debate on the Punishment of War Crimes (1919–1948)." In "The 'Founder of the United Nations' Genocide Convention' as a Historian of Mass Violence." Special issue, *Journal of Genocide Research* 7, no. 4 (2005): 453–468.
Sheehan, James J. *Kontinent der Gewalt: Europas langer Weg zum Frieden.* Bonn, 2008.
Shklar, Judith N. *Legalism: Law, Morals, and Political Trials.* Cambridge, 1986.
Sikkink, Kathryn. *The Justice Cascade: How Human Rights Prosecutions Are Changing World Politics.* New York, 2011.
Slaughter, Anne-Marie. "Defining the Limits: Universal Jurisdiction and National Courts." In *Universal Jurisdiction and the Prosecution of Serious Crimes Under International Law*, edited by Stephen Macedo, 170–190. Philadelphia, 2004.
Smith, Bradley F. *The American Road to Nuremberg: The Documentary Record 1944–1945.* Stanford, CA, 1982.
Smith, Gary, ed. *Hannah Arendt Revisited: "Eichmann in Jerusalem" und die Folgen.* Frankfurt, 2000.
Söllner, Alfons. "Wissenschaftliche Kompetenz und politische Ohnmacht: Deutsche Emigranten im amerikanischen Staatsdienst 1942–1949." In *Deutsche Politikwissenschaftler in der Emigration: Studien zu ihrer Akkulturation und Wirkungsgeschichte*, edited by Alfons Söllner, 118–132. Opladen, 1996.
———. "Jüdische Emigranten in den USA: Ihr Einfluss auf die amerikanische Deutschlandpolitik 1933–1949." In Erler et al., *"Gegen alle Vergeblichkeit,"* 365–387.
———, ed. *Zur Archäologie der Demokratie in Deutschland: Analysen politischer Emigranten im amerikanischen Geheimdienst, Bd. 1: 1943–1945.* Frankfurt, 1982.
Solga, Heike. "The Fate of the East German Upper Service Class after 1989: Types of System Transformation and Changes in Elite Recruitment." In Srubar, *Eliten, politische Kultur und Privatisierung*, 97–117.
Spaight, James M. *Bombing Vindicating.* London, 1944.
Srubar, Ilja, ed. *Eliten, politische Kultur und Privatisierung in Ostdeutschland, Tschechien und Mittelosteuropa.* Konstanz, 1998.
Stahl, Daniel. *Nazi-Jagd: Südamerikas Diktaturen und die Ahndung von NS-Verbrechen.* Göttingen, 2013.
Steiger, Heinhard. "Art. Völkerrecht." In *Geschichtliche Grundbegriffe: Historisches Lexikon zur politisch-sozialen Sprache in Deutschland*, vol. 7, edited by Otto Brunner, Werner Conze, and Reinhart Koselleck, 97–140. Stuttgart, 1992.

Steinbacher, Sybille. "Martin Broszat und die Erforschung der nationalsozialistischen Judenpolitik." In *Martin Broszat, der "Staat Hitlers" und die Historisierung des Nationalsozialismus*, edited by Norbert Frei, 130–145. Göttingen, 2007.

Steinke, Ronen. *The Politics of International Criminal Justice: German Perspectives from Nuremberg to The Hague*. Oxford, 2012.

Steiniger, P. A., and Kazimierz Leszczynski, eds. *Fall 3: Das Urteil im Juristenprozess vom 4.12.1947*. East Berlin, 1969.

Stiller, Alexa. "Semantics of Extermination: The Use of the New Term of Genocide in the Nuremberg Trials and the Genesis of a Master Narrative." In Priemel and Stiller, *Reassessing the Nuremberg Military Tribunals*, 104–133.

Stollberg-Rilinger, Barbara, ed. *Was heisst Kulturgeschichte des Politischen?* Berlin, 2005.

Stolleis, Michael. *Geschichte des öffentlichen Rechts in Deutschland, Bd. 3: Staats- und Verwaltungsrechtswissenschaft in Republik und Diktatur 1914–1945*. Munich, 1999.

———. *Geschichte des öffentlichen Rechts in Deutschland, Bd. 4: Staats- und Verwaltungsrechtswissenschaft in West und Ost 1945–1990*. Munich, 2012.

———. "Der Historiker als Richter: Der Richter als Historiker." In Frei et al., *Geschichte vor Gericht*, 173–182.

———. "International Law under German National Socialism: Some Contributions to the History of Jurisprudence." In *East Asian and European Perspectives on International Law*, edited by Michael Stolleis and Masaharu Yanagihara, 203–213. Baden-Baden, 2004.

———. *Juristen: Ein biographisches Lexikon: Von der Antike bis zum 20. Jahrhundert*. Munich, 2001.

Stone, Dan, ed. *The Historiography of the Holocaust*. London, 2004.

———. "Raphael Lemkin on the Holocaust." *Journal of Genocide Research* 7, no. 4 (2005): 539–550.

Streim, Alfred. *Die Behandlung sowjetischer Kriegsgefangener im "Fall Barbarossa": Eine Dokumentation*. Heidelberg, 1981.

———. "Correspondence." *Simon Wiesenthal Center Annual* 6 (1988): 311–347.

———. "The Task of the SS Einsatzgruppen." *Simon Wiesenthal Center Annual* 4 (1987): 309–328.

———. "Zur Eröffnung des allgemeinen Judenvernichtungsbefehls gegenüber den Einsatzgruppen." In *Der Mord an den Juden im Zweiten Weltkrieg: Entschlussbildung und Verwirklichung*, edited by Eberhard Jäckel and Jürgen Rohwer, 107–119. Stuttgart, 1985.

Sznaider, Natan. "Suffering as a Universal Frame for Understanding Memory Politics." In Blaive et al., *Clashes in European Memory*, 239–254.

Szöllösi-Janze, Margit. *Fritz Haber: 1868–1934—Eine Biographie*. Munich, 1998.

Teitel, Ruti G. *Transitional Justice*, Oxford, 2000.

———. "Transitional Justice Genealogy." *Harvard Human Rights Journal* 16 (2003): 69–94.

Teppe, Karl. "Bewältigung von Vergangenheit? Der westfälische 'Euthanasie'-Prozess." In Kersting et al., *Nach Hadamar*, 202–252.

Thiessen, Hillard von, and Christian Windler, eds. *Akteure der Aussenbeziehungen: Netzwerke und Interkulturalität im historischen Wandel*. Cologne, 2010.

Todorov, Tzvetan. "The Touvier Affair." In *Memory, the Holocaust and French Justice: The Bousquet and Touvier Affairs*, edited by Richard J. Golsan, 114–121. Hanover, 1996.

Toppe, Andreas. *Militär und Kriegsvölkerrecht: Rechtsnorm, Fachdiskurs und Kriegspraxis in Deutschland 1899–1940*. Munich, 2007.

Torpey, John. "Introduction: Politics and the Past." In Torpey, *Politics and the Past*, 1–34.

———, ed. *Politics and the Past: On Repairing Historical Injustices*. Lanham, MD, 2003.

Trappe, Julie. "Verjährung, Rückwirkungsverbot und Menschenrechtsschutz." In Hammerstein et al., *Aufarbeitung der Diktatur*, 123–134.
Triferer, Otto. "Was kann das Völkerstrafrecht zur Bewältigung der Regierungskriminalität der DDR beitragen?" In *Deutsche Wiedervereinigung: Die Rechtseinheit—Arbeitskreis Strafrecht, Bd. II: Die Verfolgung von Regierungskriminalität der DDR nach der Wiedervereinigung*, edited by Ernst-Joachim Lampe, 131–160. Cologne, 1993.
Troebst, Stephan. "Rettung, Überleben oder Vernichtung? Geschichtspolitische Kontroversen über Bulgarien und den Holocaust." *Südosteuropa* 59, no. 1 (2011) 97–127.
Tuchel, Johannes. "Die NS-Prozesse als Materialgrundlage für die historische Forschung: Thesen zu Möglichkeiten und Grenzen interdisziplinärer Zusammenarbeit." In *Vergangenheitsbewältigung durch Strafverfahren? NSProzesse in der Bundesrepublik Deutschland*, edited by Jürgen Weber and Peter Steinbach, 134–144. Munich, 1984.
Ullmann, Wolfgang. "Königsprozess oder Nürnberger Tribunal? Die DDR ist nur als 'Staatskriminalität' juristisch zu fassen." In Schönherr, *Ein Volk am Pranger?* 31–41.
Ungern-Sternberg, Jürgen von, and Wolfgang von Ungern-Sternberg. *Der Aufruf "An die Kulturwelt!" Das Manifest der 93 und die Anfänge der Kriegspropaganda im Ersten Weltkrieg*. Stuttgart, 1996.
Vagts, Detlef F. "International Law in the Third Reich." *American Journal of International Law* 84, no. 3 (1990): 661–704.
Varwick, Johannes. "Völkerrecht/Internationales Recht." In Woyke, *Handwörterbuch Internationale Politik*, 557–564.
Vec, Milos. "Universalization, Particularization, and Discrimination: European Perspectives on a Cultural History of 19th Century International Law." *InterDisciplines* 3, no. 1 (2012): 79–102.
Volkskammer der Deutschen Demokratischen Republik. Stenografische Protokolle. Berlin, 1990.
Vormbaum, Thomas. "Juristische Zeitgeschichte, Version: 1.0." *Docupedia-Zeitgeschichte*, 22 March 2010. http://docupedia.de/zg/Juristische_Zeitgeschichte?oldid=75524.
Vowinckel, Annette. *Geschichtsbegriff und historisches Denken bei Hannah Arendt*. Cologne, 2001.
Walther, Manfred. "Hat der juristische Positivismus die deutschen Juristen wehrlos gemacht?" In Justiz, *Die juristische Aufarbeitung des Unrechts-Staats*, 299–322.
Weber, Max. *Max-Weber-Gesamtausgabe, Bd. I/16: Zur Neuordnung Deutschlands—Schriften und Reden 1918–1920*, edited by Wolfgang J. Mommsen and Wolfgang Schwentker. Tübingen, 1988.
———. "Parlament und Regierung im neugeordneten Deutschland: Zur politischen Kritik des Beamtentums und Parteiwesens." In *Max Weber: Gesammelte Politische Schriften*, 5th ed., edited by Johannes Winckelmann, 306–443. Tübingen, 1988.
Wehberg, Hans. "Offener Brief an Joseph Kohler." *American Journal of International Law* 9 (1915): 924–927.
Wehler, Hans-Ulrich. *Deutsche Gesellschaftsgeschichte, Bd. 5: Bundesrepublik und DDR, 1949–1990*. Munich, 2008.
Weindling, Paul Julian. *Nazi Medicine and the Nuremberg Trials: From Medical War Crimes to Informed Consent*. London, 2004.
Weiner, Myron, Samuel Phillips Huntington, and Gabriel Abraham Almond, eds. *Understanding Political Development: An Analytic Study*. Glenview, IL, 1987.
Weinke, Annette. "'Alliierter Angriff auf die nationale Souveränität'? Die Strafverfolgung von Kriegs- und NS-Verbrechen in der Bundesrepublik, der DDR und Österreich." In Frei, *Transnationale Vergangenheitspolitik*, 37–93.

———. "Amnestie für Schreibtischtäter: Das verhinderte Verfahren gegen die Bediensteten des Reichssicherheitshauptamtes." In Mallmann and Angrick, *Die Gestapo nach 1945*, 200–220.

———. "'Bleiben die Mörder unter uns?' Öffentliche Reaktionen auf die Gründung und Tätigkeit der Zentralen Stelle Ludwigsburg." In Osterloh and Vollnhals, *NS-Prozesse und deutsche Öffentlichkeit*, 263–282.

———. "Die DDR-Justiz im Jahr der 'Wende': Zur Transformation der DDR-Juristen von 'Tätern' zu 'Opfern.'" *Deutschland-Archiv* 30, no. 1 (1997): 41–62.

———. "Die DDR-Justiz im Umbruch 1989/90." In *Justiz im Dienste der Parteiherrschaft: Rechtspraxis und Staatssicherheit in der DDR*, 2nd ed., edited by Roger Engelmann and Clemens Vollnhals, 411–431. Berlin, 2000.

———. *Eine Gesellschaft ermittelt gegen sich selbst: Die Geschichte der Zentralen Stelle Ludwigsburg 1958–2008.* Darmstadt, 2008.

———. "Gesetz Nr. 10 des Alliierten Kontrollrats vom 20. Dezember 1945." *100(0) Schlüsseldokumente zur deutschen Geschichte im 20. Jahrhundert*, 17 August 2011. http://www.1000dokumente.de/index.html?c=dokument_de&dokument=0229_kri&object=context&st=&l=de.

———. "Hintergründe der justiziellen 'Aufarbeitung' des KZ Buna/Monowitz: Möglichkeiten, Probleme und Grenzen—Informationstext im Rahmen des Projektes 'Ort des Gedenkens und der Information Norbert Wollheim.'" http://docplayer.org/11729999-Annette-weinke-hintergruende-der-justiziellen-aufarbeitung-des-kz-buna-monowitz-moeglichkeiten-probleme-und-grenzen-alliierte-strafverfolgung.html.

———. *Die Nürnberger Prozesse.* Munich, 2006.

———. "La rielaborazione guiridica del passato della DDR: Un 'Sonderweg' tedesco?" In *Annali dell'Instituto storico italo-germanico in Trento: Quaderni, 82: Riflessioni sulla DDR—Prospettive internazionali e interdisciplinari vent'anni dopo*, edited by Magda Martini and Thomas Schaarschmidt, 347–375. Bologna, 2011.

———. "Der Umgang mit der Stasi und ihren Mitarbeitern." In *Vergangenheitsbewältigung am Ende des zwanzigsten Jahrhunderts*, edited by Helmut König, Michael Kohlstruck, and Andreas Wöll, 167–191. Opladen, 1998.

———. *Die Verfolgung von NS-Tätern im geteilten Deutschland: Vergangenheitsbewältigungen 1949–1969 oder—eine deutsch-deutsche Beziehungsgeschichte im Kalten Krieg.* Paderborn, 2002.

———. "'Von Nürnberg nach Den Haag'? Das Internationale Militärtribunal in historischer Perspektive." In *Vom Tribunal zum Weltgericht: Neue Fragestellungen zum Verhältnis von Menschenrechtsverbrechen und Völkerstrafrecht 60 Jahre nach dem Nürnberger Hauptkriegsverbrecherprozess*, edited by the Justice Department of Nordrhein-Westfalen and Villa ten Hompel, 20–33. Geldern, 2008.

———. "'Waning Confidence in Germany's Rehabilitation': Das gespaltene Krisenmanagement der bundesdeutschen Aussenpolitik zum Eichmann-Prozess." In Renz, *Interessen um Eichmann*, 201–215.

Weitz, Eric D. "From Vienna to the Paris System: International Politics and the Entangled Histories of Human Rights, Forced Deportation and Civilizing Missions." *American Historical Review* 113 (2008): 1313–1343.

Weizsäcker, Richard von. "Arbeit an der Vergangenheit als wesentlicher Beitrag zur deutschen Einigung: Ansprache des Bundespräsidenten bei der Verleihung des Heinrich-Heine-Preises in Düsseldorf am 13.12.1991." In *Bulletin der Bundesregierung, Nr. 143 vom 17. Dezember 1991*, edited by Press and Information Office of the Federal Government of Germany. Reprinted in Schönherr, *Ein Volk am Pranger?* 175–190.

Welsh, Helga A. "Entnazifizierung in der DDR und die 'Wende.'" In *Wendezeiten—Zeitenwände: Zur "Entnazifizierung" und "Entstalinisierung,"* edited by Rainer Eckert, Alexander von Plato, and Jörn Schütrumpf, 65–71. Hamburg, 1991.
———. "When Discourse Trumps Policy: Transitional Justice in Unified Germany." *German Politics* 15, no. 2 (2006): 137–152.
Wendt, Bernd-Jürgen. "Über den geschichtswissenschaftlichen Umgang mit der Kriegsschuldfrage." In *Wissenschaftliche Verantwortung und politische Macht*, edited by Klaus Jürgen Gantzel, 1–63. Berlin, 1986.
Wengst, Udo. *Graf Brockdorff-Rantzau und die aussenpolitischen Anfänge der Weimarer Republik*. Frankfurt, 1973.
Werkentin, Falco. *Politische Strafjustiz in der Ära Ulbricht*. Berlin, 1995.
Werle, Gerhard. "Die Entwicklung des Völkerstrafrechts aus deutscher Perspektive." In *Die Macht und das Recht: Beiträge zum Völkerrecht und Völkerstrafrecht am Beginn des 21. Jahrhunderts*, edited by Gerd Hankel, 97–126. Hamburg, 2008.
Wheeler, Robert A. "The Failure of 'Truth and Clarity' at Berne: Kurt Eisner, the Opposition, and the Reconstruction of the International." *International Review of Social History* 18 (1973): 173–201.
Wieviorka, Annette. "Die Entstehung des Zeugen." In Smith, *Hannah Arendt Revisited*, 136–159.
Wiggenhorn, Harald. *Verliererjustiz: Die Leipziger Kriegsverbrecherprozesse nach dem Ersten Weltkrieg*. Baden-Baden, 2005.
Wigger, Iris. "'Gegen die Kultur und Zivilisation aller Weissen': Die internationale rassistische Kampagne gegen die 'Schwarze Schmach.'" In *Grenzenlose Vorurteile: Antisemitismus, Nationalismus und ethnische Konflikte in verschiedenen Kulturen*, edited by the Fritz Bauer Institute, 101–128. Frankfurt, 2002.
Wildenthal, Lora. *The Language of Human Rights in West Germany*. Philadelphia, 2013.
———. "Rudolf Laun und die Menschenrechte der Deutschen im besetzten Deutschland und in der frühen Bundesrepublik." In Hoffmann, *Moralpolitik*, 115–141.
Wildt, Michael. "Differierende Wahrheiten: Historiker und Staatsanwälte als Ermittler von NS-Verbrechen." In Frei et al., *Geschichte vor Gericht*, 46–59.
———. *Generation des Unbedingten: Das Führungskorps des Reichssicherheitshauptamtes*. 2nd ed. Hamburg, 2003.
———. "The Political Order of the Volksgemeinschaft: Ernst Fraenkel's Dual State Revisited." In *On Germans and Jews under the Nazi Regime: Essays by Three Generations of Historians—A Festschrift in Honor of Otto Dov Kulka*, edited by Moshe Zimmermann, 143–160. Jerusalem, 2006.
Willis, James F. *Prologue to Nuremberg: The Politics and Diplomacy of Punishing War Criminals of the First World War*. Westport, CT, 1982.
Wilson, Keith. "Introduction: Governments, Historians and 'Historical Engineering.'" In Wilson, *Forging the Collective Memory*, 1–27..
———, ed. *Forging the Collective Memory: Government and International Historians through Two World Wars*. Providence, RI, 1996.
Wilson, Richard Ashby. *Writing History in International Criminal Trials*. Cambridge, 2011.
Wilson, Trevor. "Lord Bryce's Investigation into Alleged German Atrocities in Belgium, 1914–1915." *Journal of Contemporary History* 14 (1979): 369–383.
Wingenfeld, Heiko. *Die öffentliche Debatte über die Strafverfahren wegen SED-Unrecht: Vergangenheitsaufarbeitung in der bundesdeutschen Öffentlichkeit der 90er Jahre*. Berlin, 2006.

Winkler, Heinrich August. *Auf ewig in Hitlers Schatten? Anmerkungen zur deutschen Geschichte.* Munich, 2007.
———. "Die verdrängte Schuld." In *Auf ewig in Hitlers Schatten? Über die Deutschen und ihre Geschichte*, 2nd ed., edited by Heinrich August Winkler, 58–71. Munich, 2007.
———. *Weimar, 1918–1933: Die Geschichte der ersten deutschen Demokratie.* Munich, 1993.
Winter, Jay. "Some Paradoxes of the First World War." In *The Upheaval of War: Family, Work and Welfare in Europe, 1914–1918*, edited by Jay Winter and Richard Wall, 9–42. Cambridge, 1988.
Wirsching, Andreas. *Der Preis der Freiheit: Geschichte Europas in unserer Zeit.* Munich, 2012.
Woyke, Wichard. *Handwörterbuch Internationale Politik.* Bonn, 2008.
Würtenberger, Thomas, and Gernot Sydow. "Versailles und das Völkerrecht." In Krumeich, *Versailles 1919*, 35–52.
Yoder, Jennifer A. "Truth Without Reconciliation: An Appraisal of the Enquete Commission on the SED Dictatorship in Germany." *German Politics* 8, no. 3 (1999): 59–80.
Zala, Sacha. "Geltung und Grenzen schweizerischen Geschichtsmanagements." In *Zeitgeschichte als Streitgeschichte: Grosse Kontroversen seit 1945*, edited by Martin Sabrow, Ralph Jessen, and Klaus Große Kracht, 306–325. Munich, 2003.
———. *Geschichte unter der Schere politischer Zensur: Amtliche Aktensammlungen im internationalen Vergleich.* Munich, 2001.
Zarah, Tara. "'The Psychological Marshall Plan': Displacement, Gender, and Human Rights after World War II." *Central European History* 44 (2011): 37–62.
Zielcke, Andreas. "Gnade vor Recht?" *Kritische Justiz* 4 (1990): 460–467.
Ziemann, Benjamin. "Germany after the First World War: A Violent Society? Result and Implications of Recent Research on Weimar Germany." *Journal of Modern European History* 1, no. 1 (2003): 80–95.
Zimmerer, Jürgen. "Nationalsozialismus postkolonial: Plädoyer zur Globalisierung der deutschen Gewaltgeschichte." *Zeitschrift für Geschichtswissenschaft* 57, no. 6 (2009): 529–548.
Zimmermann, Moshe. "Die transnationale Holocaust-Erinnerung." In Budde et al., *Transnationale Geschichte*, 202–216.
Zimmermann, Susan. "International—Transnational: Forschungsfelder und Forschungsperspektiven." In *Transnationale Netzwerke im 20. Jahrhundert. Historische Erkundungen zu Ideen und Praktiken, Individuen und Organisationen*, edited by Berthold Unfried, Jürgen Mittag, and Marcel van der Linden, 27–46. Leipzig, 2008.
Zolo, Danilo. "Hans Kelsen: International Peace Through International Law." *Jura Gentium* 3, no. 1 (2007). http://www.juragentium.org/topics/thil/en/kelsen.htm.

Index

abolitionism, 22
absolute ethics, 58
Achenbach, Ernst, 202
Adenauer, Konrad, 105, 107–8, 117, 196–97
ad hoc tribunals, 169, 175
administrative mass murder, 146–47
African National Congress (ANC), 171–72
aggressive war, 38, 70, 73–74, 83, 92, 114, 210
AJC. *See* American Jewish Committee
Aktion Reinhard, 144
Altmaier, Jacob, 109
Altstoetter, 101
American Civil War, 19, 23
American Jewish Committee (AJC), 81
amnesty, 191–207, 218
    jubilee, 199
Amnesty International, 164
ANC. *See* African National Congress
Anderson, Eugene M., 87
Anghie, Antony, 20
Anschütz, Gerhard, 101
anticolonial liberation struggles, 13
anti-Communism, 106–7, 115, 163, 168, 179, 206
anti-fascism, GDR, 189, 194, 201, 206
anti-Semitism, 91, 102, 147
antislavery movement, 2
appeasement policy, 89
arbitration, 39
Arendt, Hannah, 4, 79, 140–53, 269n138, 270n148, 270n155, 271n170
Argentina, 170
Army Council, 240n100

Arndt, Adolf, 121–24
Aronson, Shlomo, 83, 141
Aschenauer, Rudolf, 128, 138
as-if law, 192
Asquith, Herbert, 33, 38
Association for International Understanding, 22
Atlantic Charter, 72
Auschwitz, 147
Ausrottung, 108
Austro-Hungarian Empire, 29
Axis criminality, 89
Axis Rule in Occupied Europe: Laws of Occupation, Analysis of Government, Proposals for Redress (Lemkin), 76–79, 112

Baden, Maximilian von, 42, 55
Bahr, Egon, 196–99, 285n204
Balkan Wars, 2
barbarism, 80
Barbie, Klaus, 166
Barkan, Elazar, 173
Basic Law, 118
    Article 23, 178
    Article 131, 200
    Article 146, 178
Bauer, Fritz, 143–45
Bauer, Yehuda, 139
Beattie, Andrew H., 188, 190
Becker, Hellmut, 132
Bédier, Joseph, 30
Behemoth (Neumann), 8, 85, 88, 113
Belgium, 25, 30, 33, 34–35, 66
Bence, Georgy, 209

Ben-Gurion, David, 140
Berber, Friedrich, 70
Berg, Nicolas, 129
Berlin Republic, 179, 188, 198, 218
Berlin Wall, 177, 184
Bernays, Murray C., 83, 91
Bernheim Petition, 81
Best, Werner, 90
Bethmann-Hollweg, Theobald von, 21, 25, 32, 35, 44
Bettelheim, Bruno, 149
Bevernage, Berger, 173
Biedenkopf, Kurt, 178, 208
Bloxham, Donald, 84
Bluntschli, Johann Caspar, 19, 34
Bohley, Bärbel, 205–6, 285n204
Bolsheviks, 39
boomerang thesis, 147
Boraine, Alex, 172
Borgwardt, Elizabeth, 71
Borussian school of historiography, 29
Bosch, Robert, 55
Bottomley, Horatio William, 28
Brandt, Karl, 127
Brandt, Willy, 196–98
Bräutigam, Hans Otto, 199
Brentano, Lujo, 34
Brockdorff-Rantzau, Ulrich Graf von, 54–55, 61
Broszat, Martin, 181–82
Brown Scott, James, 41
Bryce, James, 30, 31
Bryce Commission, 30
Bucher, Ewald, 180
Buchheim, Hans, 127
Bund Neues Vaterland, 22

Caetano, Marcelo, 274n21
Carter, Jimmy, 14, 163
Catholic Church, 29
Cavell, Edith, 35, 73–74
CCL. *See* Control Council Law
CDU-CSU. *See* Christian Democratic Union and Christian Social Union
Ceaușescu, Elena, 166
Ceaușescu, Nicolae, 166
Central Council, 44

Central Europe Division, 113
Christian Democratic Union and Christian Social Union (CDU-CSU), 108–9, 115, 117–18, 120, 140, 178, 180, 183, 185, 192, 195–96
Christianity, 19
Churchill, Winston, 88
citizenship, 19
civilization/civilizing missions (European), 20, 65, 71, 80
The Clash of Civilizations (Huntington), 167
clausula rebus sic stantibus, 36
Clemenceau, Georges, 39, 45, 61
Code of International Offenses, 107
Cold War, 2, 9–10, 43, 72, 157, 161, 204
collective guilt, 100
color books, 31, 40, 44, 51, 57, 61, 67
command emergency, 90, 99, 114
Commissar order, 97
Communism, 13, 159, 204, 276n66
Communist Party of Germany (KPD), 44
compensation (Wiedergutmachung), 24, 207, 237n40
conscience public, 40
Contemporary History, 154, 216
Control Council Law (CCL), 100, 120, 121, 154
core state theory, 178
Coughlin, Brenda, 158
Council of Europe, 14–15
Council of People's Deputies, 50, 53
Crimean War, 19, 65
crimes against humanity, 55, 83, 97, 119, 184, 193, 203
crimes against peace, 97, 100
Les Crimes Allemands d'après des Témoignages Allemands (Bédier), 30–31
crimes of conspiracy, 80, 83, 85, 91–92, 97
criminal biology, 93
The Crisis of Democracy: On the Governability of Democracies (Huntington), 160
crisis of unification, 195–96
Critical Theory, 142
culture of war, 1, 229n3
Curtius, Friedrich, 56
Czechoslovakia, 168, 174–75

David, Eduard, 59
Davis, Jefferson, 23
DDP. *See* German Democratic Party
decolonization, 13
Dehler, Thomas, 109
Delbrück, Hans, 48, 51, 56, 61
democratization, 11, 13, 39, 154, 160, 162, 165, 167–68, 194, 211
de-Nazification, 130, 191–92
deskbound perpetrator, 143, 146
destruction, 109
The Destruction of the European Jews (Hilberg), 141
détente, 201
Deutsche Partei (DP), 107–8, 115
dignity, 57–58
Diner, Dan, 85
disappearances, 161, 164
discourses, 232n28
DNVP. *See* German National People's Party
Dönhoff, Marion Gräfin, 200–201
Donovan, William J., 87, 89, 92, 113
Douglas, Lawrence, 119
Doyle, Arthur Conan, 38
DP. *See* Deutsche Partei
Draft Code, 183
Das Dritte Reich und die Juden (Poliakov and Wulf), 141
dual state, 69
Dunant, Henry, 17, 23

Eastern Bloc, 167, 168
Ebermayer, Ludwig, 64
Ebert, Friedrich, 45, 59
Eichmann, Adolf, 4, 9, 134, 140–53
Eichmann in Jerusalem (Arendt), 147–48
Einsatzgruppen Trial, 128
Eisenhower, Dwight D., 106
Eisner, Kurt, 43–44, 50, 66
Elements of Shame (Arendt), 146
Ems Dispatch, 52
Enlightenment ideals, 7, 55
Enquete Commissions, 187–88, 190
Entente Powers, 18, 27, 42–43, 51, 60, 67
Eppelmann, Rainer, 187, 189
Epstein, Julius, 109
Erzberger, Matthias, 43, 50

Eschenburg, Theodor, 150
ethics, absolute, 58
European Convention of Human Rights, 106, 110, 216
euthanasia trials, 9, 122, 126
exceptionalism, German legal, 36
Exner, Franz, 93, 94, 96
expellee association (Sudeten German), 107, 110, 115
expulsion crimes, 110
extermination order, 128–29, 136

FDP. *See* Free Democratic Party
Federal Bureau of Investigation, 113
Federal Republic of Germany (FRG), 70, 104, 105, 110, 116–17, 118, 154, 175, 178–79, 187
Fehrenbach, Constantin, 55
Fehrenbach, Felix, 241n127
Felddienstordnung (field service regulations), 25
Fest, Joachim C., 146
Final Solution, 129, 138
Fiore, Pasquale, 19
Fischer, Alexander, 189
Fischer, Fritz, 155–56
Fischer-Lescano, Andreas, 13
Fischl, Viktor, 73–74
Foerster, Friedrich Wilhelm, 43
Fordism, 142
Four Freedoms speech (Roosevelt, F.), 71, 111, 226
Fourteen Points (Wilson, W.), 55
Fraenkel, Ernst, 69, 80
Franco-Prussian War of 1870-1871, 2, 21, 23–24, 33
franc-tireur/guerilla, 30, 33, 45
Frank, Hans, 90
Frankfurter Zeitung, 56, 59, 62
Frankfurt School, 85–92
Fraser, Donald M., 163
Free Democratic Party (FDP), 117
Free State of Bavaria, 43
Frei, Norbert, 190
Freytagh-Loringhoven, Axel Freiherr von, 70
FRG. *See* Federal Republic of Germany
Fried, Alfred Hermann, 22

Fröschmann, Georg, 93
Fryatt, Charles, 35, 54
Führer order/principle, 9, 99–100, 114, 127–40, 146, 215
Fukuyama, Francis, 162
Funk, Walther, 93

Gauck, Joachim, 206, 208
Gawlik, Hans, 140–41, 202
Geneva/Hague Conventions, 23–28, 33–37, 54, 66, 79, 80, 83, 211, 220, 226
   Article 3 Hague Convention, 24, 42
   codification of, 17–18
genocide, 9, 76–77, 79–80, 91, 102–11, 122, 128–29, 147, 158, 181, 183, 203, 212, 216, 227
Genocide Convention, 9, 216
   member states, 105
   West Germany in, 102–15
Genscher, Hans-Dietrich, 183, 208
geopolitics, 46, 94, 102
George V (King), 28
Gerlach, Manfred, 193–94
German Democratic Party (DDP), 48
German Democratic Republic, 10
Germanization, 78
German National People's Party (DNVP), 60
German Research Foundation, 95
Germany. *See also* West Germany
   state violence of, 3–4, 6–7
   war crimes of, 33
   war guilt of, 8, 33
Gerstenmaier, Eugen, 109
Geschichtsbarkeit (historability), 7, 85
Geyer, Michael, 91
Gilbert, Felix, 88, 142
Globke, Hans, 143–44, 196
Glueck, Sheldon, 74
Goldhagen controversy, 140
Gollancz, Victor, 85
Gorbachev, Mikhail, 193
Göring, Hermann, 195
government criminality, 182–83
grand area order, 95–96, 102
Great War of 1914, 2, 18

Griff nach der Weltmacht (Fischer, F.), 155–56
Gross, Raphael, 7–8
Große Kracht, Klaus, 42
Grossraum theory, 95
Guilhot, Nicolas, 162, 168
Gutzeit, Martin, 185

Haas, Ludwig, 55
Haber, Fritz, 28
Hadamar, 122–23
Hague Convention. *See* Geneva/Hague Conventions
Hahn, Erich J. C., 8
Hahn, Kurt, 56
Harmsworth, Albert C., 38
Harris, Whitney H., 84
Harrison, Austin, 35
Harrison, Frederic, 38
Hausner, Gideon, 145
Haußmann, Konrad, 55
Havel, Václav, 194
Hegelian school of thought, 19, 160–61
Heidelberg Association, 47, 49–65, 119–20, 245n177
   founding, 51, 67–68
   meetings of, 55
Heimpel, Hermann, 132
Heinemann, Ulrich, 44, 60
Heitmann, Steffen, 196
Helsinki process, 195
Herf, Jeffrey, 92
Hersmann, Werner, 137
Herz, John H., 87, 208, 274n27
Heß, Rudolf, 202
Hesse trials, 121
Heuss, Theodor, 130–31
Heydrich, Reinhard, 135
Hilberg, Raul, 141
Hilsberg, Stephan, 198
Himmler, Heinrich, 134
Hindenburg, Paul von, 44
historability (*Geschichtsbarkeit*), 7, 85
Historians' Controversy (*Historikerstreit*), 9, 188
historicism, 219
Historikerstreit (Historian's Controversy), 9, 188

Hitler, Adolf, 111, 226
Hobbes, Thomas, 85
Hodenberg, Hodo von, 119–20
Hoffmann, Stefan-Ludwig, 12
Hohenlohe-Langenburg, Gottfried zu, 55
Höhn, Reinhard, 95
Höhne, Heinz, 141
Holocaust research/remembrance/trials, 9, 76, 135, 138, 139, 141, 156, 157–58, 211, 216, 279n97
Holthusen, Hans Egon, 150–53
Honecker, Erich, 178, 180, 193
Höppner, Reinhard, 196
Horne, John, 28–29, 45, 237n50, 238n65
Höss, Rudolf, 134
HRV. *See* Human Rights Violations
Huber, Ernst Rudolf, 90, 132
Hull, Isabel V., 26, 36, 239n77
humanitarianism, 2, 13
humanitarian law, 3, 17, 18
Humanities War Mission, 95–96
Humanity, 3
human rights
  defining, 73
  history of, 12, 234n47, 234n50
  in international law, 4, 70–74
  language of, 7
  scholarship on, 11
  TJ and, 5–6
Human Rights Violations (HRV), 172
Huntington, Samuel P., 9, 159–75
Hussein, Saddam, 183

IACHR. *See* Inter-American Commission on Human Rights
ICC. *See* International Criminal Court
ICRC. *See* International Committee of the Red Cross
IFZ. *See* Institut für Zeitgeschichte
IJA. *See* Institute of Jewish Affairs
ILC. *See* International Law Commission
IMT. *See* International Military Tribunal
Independent Social Democratic Party of Germany (USPD), 43, 67
Institut de Droit International, 20, 36, 65
Institute of Jewish Affairs (IJA), 81–84

Institut für Zeitgeschichte (IFZ), 127, 133, 135–36, 149–50, 154
Inter-American Commission on Human Rights (IACHR), 158, 169
International Commission for Penal Reconstruction and Development (Cambridge Commission), 73
International Committee for Relief to the Wounded, 23
International Committee of the Red Cross (ICRC), 23
International Court of Arbitration, 25
International Criminal Court (ICC), 2, 103, 149, 183, 184, 186, 188, 208, 219
international criminal law, 1, 18–27, 230n5
internationalism, 2, 4, 65
international law
  history of, 12
  human rights turn in, 4, 70–74
  League of Nations and, 102
  modernization of, 15
International Law Commission (ILC), 107, 183
International Military Tribunal (IMT), 8, 15, 70, 84, 88, 96, 100, 102, 119, 128, 211
international public, 3
International Red Cross Movement, 17, 23
International Socialist Conference, 50
international society, 3

Jäckel, Eberhard, 139
Jackson, Robert, 8, 83, 86, 89, 129
Jäger, Herbert, 149
Jäger, Richard, 118
Jagow, Gottlieb von, 32
Jahrreiß, Hermann, 9, 92–102, 114, 215
Jaspers, Karl, 149, 208
Jodl, Alfred, 94, 96–97, 114
jubilee amnesty, 199
Judeo-Christian idea, 146
judges' privilege, 180
judiciability, 7–8
judicial interventionism, 8
July Crisis, 32, 44, 50–53, 60, 67, 213
juridification of history, 5
jurists, as lobbyists and historians, 74–85

jus in bello, 23
just war theory, 86

Kaléko, Mascha, 150
Kant, Immanuel, 151, 272n176
Katz, Barry, 90, 268n116
Kaul, Hans-Peter, 219–20
Kautsky, Karl, 48–49, 50, 56, 59, 60, 66
Kellogg-Briand Pact, 73, 81, 86, 97, 226
Kelsen, Hans, 98
Kempner, Robert M. W., 92
Kinkel, Klaus, 179–80, 183
Kirchheimer, Otto, 87, 90, 119
Klein, Alfons, 122
Koch, Erich, 47
Koellreuter, Otto, 90
Koester, Adolph, 29–30
Koestler, Arthur, 151
Kogon, Eugen, 151
Kohl, Helmut, 183, 194, 206
Koogan, John, 37
KPD. *See* Communist Party of Germany
Kramer, Alan, 28, 45–46
Kranzbühler, Otto, 93
Kraus, Herbert, 93
Krausnick, Helmut, 137
Krawinkel, Hermann, 94
Krenz, Egon, 192–93
Kriegsbrauch im Landkriege (manual of land warfare), 26
Kritz, Neil J., 168
Kroll, Gerhard, 131
Krüger, Hans, 149

Laak, Dirk van, 179
La Follette, Charles M., 124
Lafontaine, Oskar, 195
Langwerth von Simmern, Ernst Freiherr, 62
Lansing, Robert, 41
Lapradelle, Albert de, 40
Larnaude, Ferdinand, 40
Lasch, Karl, 70
Laternser, Hans, 93
Latin America, 164, 165, 173–74
Laun, Rudolf, 104
law of war, 4

League of Nations, 39, 63, 70–71, 75–76, 85, 97, 102, 112, 247n214
Lebensraum, 79
Left Hegelianism, 85, 87
legal historiography, trends in, 10–15
legalist paradigm, 100–101
legal think tanks, 112
Legien, Carl, 48, 51
Leicht, Robert, 184
Leipzig trials, 65
Lemkin, Raphael, 75–80, 105–9, 112, 115, 214, 259n172
Lepsius, Johannes, 49
Leviathan (Hobbes), 85
Levy, Daniel, 217
Lewis, Mark, 237n35
liberal internationalism, 2–3
Lie, Trygve, 105
Lieber Code, 23
Limbach, Jutta, 177
Lincoln, Abraham, 23
Lippmann, Walter, 41, 245n174
Liszt, Franz von, 34
Lithuania, 81
Lloyd George, David, 38–39, 64
London International Assembly, 73, 74
Long Nineteenth Century, 225, 229n2
Long Twentieth Century, 225
Ludendorff, Erich, 54, 64
Lueder, Carl, 34
Lusitania, 30, 35, 41
Luther, Martin, 105
Luxembourg, 25, 30, 34–35, 66

Magdeburg model, 196
Mandela, Nelson, 171–72
Manifesto of the Ninety-Three, 35–36, 43
Mann, Golo, 149
manual of land warfare (*Kriegsbrauch im Landkriege*), 26
Marcuse, Herbert, 88, 142, 268n116
Marxen, Klaus, 192
Marxism, 44, 87, 91, 160, 182
mass media, 2–3
Mau, Hermann, 131–34, 264n69
Mégret, Frédéric, 10
Meinecke, Friedrich, 56

memory governance, 283n166
Mende, Erich, 109
Mendelssohn Bartholdy, Albrecht, 34, 48–49, 61, 63, 67
Men of 20 July 1944 (German national-conservative resistance), 152, 156
Men of 1873, 65
Middleton, Lord, 38
Mielke, Erich, 180
military necessity. *See* necessities of war/military necessity
Ministries Trial, 102
minority rights, 72, 81, 86
modernity, 1, 229n1, 230n6
modernization theory, 162, 274n30
Möller, Horst, 189
Moltke, Helmuth Graf von, 21
Monday demonstrations, 193
Montgelas, Max Graf von, 48, 55, 60
Morgan, John Hartman, 30
Morgenthau, Henry, Jr., 80, 83
Moscow declaration, 77
Mouralis, Guillaume, 177
Moyn, Samuel, 21, 37
Moynier, Gustave, 23–24
Müller, Tim B., 88
Musmanno, Michael, 217

Napoleon III, 52
National Assembly, 50, 59
nationalism, 1, 23, 27, 104
National Socialism, 2, 5, 12–13, 14, 69, 75, 79, 82, 90, 111, 118, 130–31
Naumann, Friedrich, 48, 51
Nebenklage, 82
necessities of war/military necessity, 20–21, 26, 36
Neumann, Franz L., 8, 85–89, 91–92, 103, 113, 142
neutrality (agreements), 35, 40, 113
neutrals, 29
New Deal, 72, 86, 92, 113–14
New Order (of Hitler), 111
NGOs. *See* nongovernmental organizations
Niedhart, Gottfried, 20
Nipperdey, Hans Carl, 94
non-aggression treaty (Germany-Poland), 97

non-aggression treaty (Germany-Soviet Union), 97
nongovernmental organizations (NGOs), 2, 159
Northcliffe, Albert C., 38
Noske, Gustav, 30, 64
Nuremberg charter, 96
Nuremberg Defense Strategy, 92–102
Nuremberg historiography, 9
Nuremberg interregnum, 92
Nuremberg law, 106, 109
Nuremberg principles, 182
Nuremberg race laws, 144

OAS. *See* Organization of American States
OCCWC. *See* Office of the Chief Counsel for War Crimes
O'Donnell, Guillermo, 168
Office of Strategic Services (OSS), 8, 83–84, 87
Office of the Chief Counsel for War Crimes (OCCWC), 122
Ohlendorf, Otto, 128, 134–35
Olick, Jeffrey K., 158
Oncken, Hermann, 34
Operation Desert Storm, 183–84
Oppenheim, Lassa, 25
opposition movement, GDR, 198, 204
oral history, 31, 190
Orange Free State, 20
Organization of American States (OAS), 14–15
organized pacifism, 22
The Origins of Totalitarianism (Arendt), 146–47
Orwell, George, 151
OSS. *See* Office of Strategic Services
Ostpolitik, 196
Ottoman Empire, 1, 2
overcoming the past. *See Vergangenheitsbewältigung*
Oxford Manual, 20–21

pacifism (organized), 22, 65, 67, 213
Papon, Maurice, 166
Paris Peace Conference, 52
peace movement, 22

Peace of Westphalia, 58
Peace Society, 22
Peace Treaty, 37–49
Pendas, Devin, 121, 262n33
people's community (*Volksgemeinschaft*), 82, 99, 104, 115, 125, 142, 216
Pérez de Cuéllar, Javier, 183
The Persecution of Jews in the Third Reich (Scheffler), 141
Pingel, Falk, 126–27
Piper, Klaus, 146
Poliakov, Leon, 141
politics of the past, 3, 43, 101, 104, 106, 117, 123, 140, 175, 177, 179, 181, 183, 185, 187–89, 207
polycratic state, 146
positivist corruption, 101
preemptive historiography, 18
Preliminary Memorandum on the Outbreak of War, 32
Preuß, Hugo, 60
Priebke, Erich, 166
processing the past. *See Vergangenheitsbewältigung*
Professors' Memorandum, 48, 61–62
Protestantism, 20, 29
public history, 4

Quarck, Max, 51

Rabinbach, Anson, 77
Radbruch, Gustav, 101, 120, 123, 261n15
Raphael, Lutz, 161
Raschka, Johannes, 193
Rassow, Peter, 48, 243n138
reconciliation, 200–201
Red Army Faction, 205
Reich Main Security Office, 128
Reichstag fire, 47, 118, 184
Reitlinger, Gerald, 128–29
Report of the Committee on Alleged German Outrages, 30
restorative justice, 170
Ribbentrop, Joachim von, 93
Riegner telegram, 82
Riezler, Kurt, 32
Right Hegelianism, 19

Ritter, Gerhard, 130
Robinson, Jacob, 8, 80–82, 151, 214
Rolin-Jaequemyns, Gustave, 24
Rombach, Konrad-Gisbert Freiherr von, 55
Romen, Antonius Maria, 34
Roosevelt, Eleanor, 107
Roosevelt, Franklin D., 71–72, 86, 111, 214, 226
Root, Elihu, 36
Rössner, Hans, 149
Die Rote Fahne, 44
Rothfels, Hans, 242n137
Rousseau, Jean-Jacques, 79
rule of law, 20
Russell-Sartre Tribunal, 184, 199
Russo-Japanese War, 66
Russo-Ottoman War, 19
Rüttgers, Jürgen, 185

Saevecke, Theodor, 149
Salewski, Michael, 68
Sauter, Fritz, 93
Saxon Memorial Foundation, 189
Schaefgen, Christoph, 200
Scharping, Rudolf, 195
Schätzler, Johann-Georg, 202–4
Schäuble, Wolfgang, 185
Scheffler, Wolfgang, 141, 149
Scheidemann, Philipp, 30, 45, 54, 60
Schiffer, Eugen, 59
Schiller, Friedrich, 55
Schirach, Baldur von, 93
Schlieffen, Alfred von, 37
Schmid, Carlo, 109
Schmidt, Helmut, 194
Schmidt, Richard, 94
Schmitt, Carl, 70, 85, 95, 101
Schmitter, Philippe C., 168
Schoenberner, Gerhard, 141
Schorlemmer, Friedrich, 181
Schröder, Gerhard, 196
Schroers, Rolf, 149
Schücking, Walter, 53, 56, 60, 61
Schüle, Erwin, 140, 143, 145–46, 148
Schwanitz, Rolf, 185
Schwengler, Walter, 40
Scott, James Brown, 41

Index • 329

Second Italian War of Independence, 17
SED. *See* Socialist Unity Party of Germany
Seddon, James A., 23
SED injustice, 181
Seelos, Gebhard, 118
Segesser, Daniel, 36, 73
Seidl, Alfred, 93, 202
Seidl, Franz, 108–9
self-determination, 19, 71, 95, 119, 194
September Program, 32
Servatius, Robert, 147
Shinnar, Felix, 143
Short Twentieth Century, 225
show trials (Communist), 184
Sikkink, Kathryn, 158
Simons, Walter, 48, 56
Smith, Bradley F., 90
Social Democratic Party of Germany (SPD), 29–30, 124, 185, 198, 205
Socialist Unity Party of Germany (SED), 10
social movements, 21–22
Solf, Wilhelm, 43, 51
Sonderweg (special path), 147, 175–76, 219
South African Truth and Reconciliation Commission (TRC), 167, 171–72
Spaight, James Molony, 26
SPD. *See* Social Democratic Party of Germany
spearhead theory, 88, 91
stabbed in the back legend, 60
Stalin, Josef, 72
Stalinism, 14, 189
Stalinist crimes, 109
Stasi informants, 194
state criminality, 182–83
state immunity, 28
state injustice, 3
state of emergency, 218
state of injustice, GDR, 189
state of urgency, 36
state power, critiques of, 5–6
states of exception, 198
state sovereignty, 28
state violence, 231n17
    of Germany, 3–4, 6–7
statutes of limitations, 180–81, 195, 198, 201

Statutes of the Institute for International Law, 235n4
Stenger, Karl, 31
St. James Declaration, 70, 81, 111
Stolpe, Manfred, 199
St. Petersburg Declaration, 20, 81
Streckenbach, Bruno, 136, 137
Streim, Alfred, 138–40, 266n97
Strupp, Karl, 34
success story, 187, 189, 204, 209
system change, 11, 162, 165–66, 170, 208
Sznaider, Natan, 217

Taylor, Telford, 119
Teppe, Karl, 126
Thierse, Wolfgang, 181
Thimme, Friedrich, 49
Third Wave, 159–75
The Third Wave (Huntington), 9
Thirty Years' War, 33
Thoma, Richard, 64
Tilsit Special Commando, 136
TJ. *See* Transitional Justice
Torpey, John, 171, 210
totalitarianism and anti-totalitarianism, 72, 85, 146–47, 151, 157, 160, 174, 187–89, 192, 200, 215, 276n66
total war, 27
Touvier, Paul, 166
Transitional Justice (TJ), 3, 11–12, 170–71, 208
    defining, 10
    human rights and, 5–6
transitology, 159–75, 208, 212
transnational justice, 15, 233n38
Transvaal, 20
TRC. *See* South African Truth and Reconciliation Commission
Treaty of Versailles, 8, 18, 22, 37, 40, 45–46, 63, 94, 102, 121, 242n137
    Article 227, 240n111
    guilt clauses, 67, 213
Treitschke, Heinrich von, 29
Trifterer, Otto, 184
Triple Entente, 18
Troeltsch, Ernst, 34

truth commissions, 171–74, 176, 188, 190, 208–9, 218, 275n50
tu quoque, 43
Tutu, Desmond, 172
Tyranny on Trial, 84

Ulbricht, Walter, 192–93
Ullmann, Wolfgang, 182–83
unconditional surrender, 88
unification (treaty), German-German, 176, 178, 180, 187, 194, 202–3
United Nations, 14–15
United Nations Commission for the Investigation of War Crimes (UNWCC), 77
United Nations General Assembly, 103
Universal Declaration of Human Rights, 103
universalism, 19–20
unrestricted submarine warfare, 34
UNWCC. *See* United Nations Commission for the Investigation of War Crimes
US occupation rule, 274n27
USPD. *See* Independent Social Democratic Party of Germany

Vatican, 29
Velvet Revolutions of 1989, 159
Vergangenheitsbewältigung (overcoming the past/processing of the past), 10–11, 15, 66, 116–17, 125, 130, 145–46, 148, 158, 164–66, 168–70, 172–73, 175–90, 208–9, 216–17
Vernichtung, 108
Victims' Community, 117–27
Victoria (Queen), 28
victor's justice, 102
Videla, Jorge, 158
Vietnam War, 14
violence
 debates about, 6
 legitimation of, 14
 socialization of, 91
 state, 3–4, 6–7, 231n17
Volksgemeinschaft (people's community), 82, 99, 104, 115, 125, 142, 216
von Bülow, Bernhard Wilhelm, 42, 61–62

Wahl, Eduard, 109
Wahlmann, Adolf, 122–23
Walsh, William F., 84
Walzer, Michael, 100
Wannsee Protocol, 143
war crimes, 25, 39, 66, 97
 German, 33
war crimes trials, 38, 41
war criminal problem, 104
war guilt, 32, 213
 of Germany, 8, 33
 research, 45–46
 Weber, M., on, 52
War Guilt Department, 49, 68
War Guilt Intervention, 49–65
war of encirclement, 50
war positivism, 33–34, 37
War Rights on Land (Spaight), 26
war treason, 35
Weber, Alfred, 34, 64, 247n203
Weber, Max, 47, 49–65, 244n170, 245n180
 on dignity, 57–58
 on war guilt, 52
Wehberg, Hans, 34, 56
Weimar Republic, 13, 45, 213
Weinkauff, Hermann, 117–18
Weitz, Eric, 230n6
Weizsäcker, Ernst von, 130
Weizsäcker, Richard von, 184
Werkentin, Falco, 205
Wesel, Uwe, 199–200
West Germany
 in Genocide Convention, 102–15
 historians of, 127–40
Westlake, John, 36
whiggish history, 6
white book, 107
Wiedergutmachung (compensation), 24, 207, 237n40
Wieviorka, Annette, 100
Wildenthal, Lora, 104
Wilhelm II (Kaiser), 21, 28, 35, 39
Wilhelmine Reich, 18, 35, 53, 74
Wilhelmstrasse trial, 130
Willis, James F., 29
Wilson, Trevor, 31, 41–42

Wilson, Woodrow, 23
Wilsonian idealism, 13–14
Winkler, Heinrich August, 50, 243n152
Wirz, Henry, 23
Wolgast, Ernst, 93
World War I, 4, 8, 12, 46, 66, 73–74, 121
　international criminal law before, 18–27
World War II, 5, 69, 176, 211, 214
Wrenbury, Lord, 38
Wulf, Joseph, 141
Wurm, Theophil, 123

Yad Vashem, 144
The Yellow Star (Schoenberner), 141

Zentrale Rechtschutzstelle (ZRS), 144
Zero Hour, 170
Zeug, Dietrich, 144–45, 148–49, 155
Zimmerer, Jürgen, 250n47
Zimmerman, Alfred, 32
Zinn, Georg August, 122
Zorn, Philipp, 34
ZRS. *See* Zentrale Rechtschutzstelle

www.ingramcontent.com/pod-product-compliance
Lightning Source LLC
Chambersburg PA
CBHW051526020426
42333CB00016B/1792